S0-ADJ-653

PUBLIC MONEY AND PAROCHIAL EDUCATION

PUBLIC MONEY AND PAROCHIAL EDUCATION

Bishop Hughes, Governor Seward, and
the New York School Controversy

VINCENT P. LANNIE

Cleveland
The Press of Case Western Reserve University
1968

CARL A. RUDISILL LIBRARY
LENOIR RHYNE COLLEGE

311.8
L 28 p
67145
august, 1969

Copyright © 1968 by The Press of Case Western Reserve University,
Cleveland, Ohio 44106. All rights reserved.
Printed in the United States of America.
Library of Congress Catalogue Card Number 67–11480.

To
Lawrence Cremin
David Austin
Gordon Lee

⚉ Preface ⚉

Many Protestants of antebellum America feared the growing influence of the Roman Catholic Church in the United States. Samuel F. B. Morse, the Reverend William Brownlee, and countless others warned repeatedly of a papist alliance with European Catholic monarchies to conquer the country and subjugate it to monarchic and ecclesiastic rule. In his *Foreign Conspiracy Against the Liberties of the United States,* Morse insisted "that there is good reason for believing that the despots of Europe are attempting, by the spread of Popery in this country, to subvert its free institutions. . . ."[1] Such apprehensions were very real to thousands of Protestants and especially to the militant nativists. As increasing numbers of Catholic immigrants settled in America, the possibility of an eventual take-over began to look more and more plausible to Protestants. Whole sections of major cities were becoming overwhelmingly Catholic, Catholic churches appeared to be springing up everywhere, and bishops and priests were beginning to enter into public debate with Protestant ministers over their respective creeds. This numerical increase helped to develop, for good or ill, a more confident and militant Catholicism, which then came headlong into conflict with a suspicious and ever vigilant Protestantism. Catholic churchmen began to demand those rights which they believed were inalienable and to use every legitimate means to obtain them for their predominantly immigrant flocks. But this new breed of immigrant clergyman failed to understand the psychological dimensions of a deeply entrenched Protestant culture. Thus, Bishop John Hughes of New York could shock Protestants by forming a political party and could be insensitive enough to predict the decline of Protes-

1 Samuel F. B. Morse, *Foreign Conspiracy Against the Liberties of the United States* (New York: Leavitt, Lord and Company, 1835), p. 51.

tantism and an eventual Catholic ascendancy in the United States. Hughes as well as others simply could not penetrate the American mind and the country's Protestant heritage.

From the time of the Jamestown settlement and the Mayflower Compact, Catholics had been a persecuted sect and at best a suffered and impotent minority. Abhorrence and distrust of Romanism had come to the new world from old-world conflict and had developed into an essential part of the colonial mind and, later, the national temper. Sin, Satan, and popery were an unholy trinity to be shunned and cast into the everlasting abyss. "Hatred and fear of 'Popery' or 'Romanism' were imbibed with the milk a God-fearing Protestant child drew from its mother's breast."[2] Moreover, within the historical context of religious liabilities in Ireland, these Catholic ecclesiastics almost expected a certain amount of Protestant harassment to hamper their work. But one thing was certain. Protestants were the religious enemy and they who possessed the "truth" were not about to capitulate to heresy. "The oldest institution in Western civilization," remarks Marcus Hansen, "was not going to revise its program because a few Yankees looked upon it with disfavor."[3] Nor did the American Catholic Church intend to revise its mission and program.

No area of disagreement between Protestants and Catholics caused more friction than their different views concerning religion in the common schools. This disagreement centered around the type of religion to be taught in the schools, including the matter of the use of the Bible. Although the effort for free, publicly supported, and publicly-controlled schools was a long and often bitter struggle, the common school "design" began to take root as the Civil War holocaust appeared on the American horizon. Under the impetus of such educational reformers as Horace Mann, Henry Barnard, Calvin Stowe, Samuel Lewis, Calvin Wiley, and Caleb Mills, many states established public school systems and a majority of children received at least some elementary education. In *The Transformation of the School*, Lawrence Cremin concludes that by 1860, "universal education had won clear—if sometimes grudging—acceptance from the society at large."[4]

2 Neil McCluskey, *Public Schools and Moral Education* (New York: Columbia University, 1958), p. 48.
3 Marcus Lee Hansen, *The Immigrant in American History* (Cambridge, Mass.: Harvard University, 1948), p. 122.
4 Lawrence A. Cremin, *The Transformation of the School* (New York: Alfred A. Knopf, 1961), p. 13.

But this "society at large" did not include the majority of American Catholics, who rejected the reformers' nondenominational compromise as the only religious alternative to the teaching of sectarian doctrines in the public schools. Horace Mann became the leading proponent of this nondenominational approach to religion in the public schools. Although he excluded specific sectarian creeds from the classroom, the Massachusetts educator encouraged and even championed the inculcation of commonly accepted moral and religious beliefs in the public schools: "The Religion of Heaven should be taught to children, while the creeds of men should be postponed until their minds were sufficiently matured to weigh evidence and arguments."[5] Since this "Religion of Heaven" was embodied most perfectly in the Scriptures, Mann, Lewis, and other educators welcomed the Bible into the schools as long as it spoke "for itself" without note or comment.

Not only did Catholics agree with many Protestants that a moral education could never be divorced from specific doctrinal tenets, but they particularly denounced the nondenominational religious formula as essentially a Protestant basis for public school education. Catholic bishops and priests charged the public schools with being centers of Protestant sectarianism intent on subverting the religious faith of Catholic children. These schools adopted "as a regulation the reading of the Protestant Bible, and the reciting of Protestant hymns & sometimes of Protestant prayers." In addition, anti-Catholic schoolbooks and bigoted teachers exposed Catholic children to "insidious, if not open attacks on their religious principles & practices" so that they became *ashamed of their faith.*"[6] Under such circumstances, Catholics felt justified in condemning public education, and the members of the hierarchy, collectively and individually, began to urge the establishment of Catholic schools as the only remedy to what they considered to be an objectionable educational situation. If the common schools had been religiously acceptable to Catholics, they would have patronized them, since "in common with our fellow citizens, we pay our taxes for the erection and maintenance of those schools." "But," as one Catholic bishop declared,

5 Horace Mann to Frederick Packard, July 22, 1838, cited in Raymond B. Culver, *Horace Mann and Religion in the Massachusetts Public Schools* (New Haven: Yale University, 1929), p. 266.

6 Proceedings of the First Plenary Council of Baltimore (1852), cited in Bernard Julius Meiring, "Educational Aspects of the Legislation of the Councils of Baltimore, 1829–1884" (unpublished Ph.D. thesis, Berkeley, University of California, 1963), pp. 141–42.

"we hold that it is better far to suffer any earthly loss, rather than to jeopardize our faith or that of our children."[7]

Both contemporaries and historians have agreed that John Hughes, the dynamic and militant immigrant bishop of New York, was a leading figure in the attack against this Protestant-oriented public education and a prime mover in the establishment of the Catholic parochial school system in the United States. From 1840–42 Hughes engaged in a bitter struggle with the public schools of New York City. Under the control and management of the privately controlled and semi-Protestant Public School Society, the city's schools had adopted all of the "sectarian" features so vigorously denounced by Catholics. For three years this acrid conflict involved the schools, the churches, and city and state politics and kept New Yorkers in a state of religious, social, and political tension. So sharp was this controversy that Mann singled it out as corroborative evidence of the "disastrous consequences of implicating the great and universal interests of education, with those of particular religious sects."[8]

When Hughes failed in his campaign to make the public schools religiously acceptable to Catholics, he unsuccessfully sought public funds for his few Catholic schools. Once Catholics were denied this aid, Hughes decided to abandon public education and devote his remaining energy and talents to the establishment of a privately financed parochial school system in New York. So adamant was he in this policy that whenever he appointed a new pastor to a parish church, he insisted that the priest "proceed upon the principle that, in this age and this country, the school is before the church."[9] Hughes was one of the first bishops to urge the development of a Catholic school system as an integral part of the American Catholic Church; his educational vision was officially implemented four decades later. In *Are Parochial Schools the Answer?*, a controversial volume that has recently stirred the Catholic educational world, Mary Perkins Ryan credits the New York bishop with being a seminal thinker and an initial founder of a diocesan parochial school system in the United

7 *An Address to the Impartial Public, on the Intolerant Spirit of the Times, Being the Introduction to the Miscellanea of M. J. Spaulding D.D.* (Louisville: Webb & Levering, 1854), p. 33, cited in Meiring, "Councils of Baltimore," pp. 162–63.

8 Horace Mann, *Fifth Annual Report*, Facsimile Edition (Boston: Dutton and Wentworth, 1842), pp. 68–69.

9 John J. Considine, *The History of Canonical Legislation in the Diocese and Province of New York, 1842–1861* (Washington, D.C.: Catholic University of America, 1935), pp. 18–19.

States. "The Third Plenary Council of Baltimore in 1884 fully endorsed Bishop Hughes' policy," declares Ryan, "by decreeing that every pastor was to establish a school within two years . . . and Catholic parents were required to send their children to these schools wherever they were available. . . ."[10] It seems clear, therefore, that Hughes's struggle with the public schools was not simply a local problem. On the contrary, it evidenced genuine and general Catholic dissatisfaction with public education, and his final solution served as an example for other Catholic bishops.

This volume, then, is a study of the New York school controversy of 1840–42, with Bishop John Hughes and Governor William Seward emerging as the dominant and often paradoxical figures. It was in New York that the parochial school seed took deep root; it was here that this seed was carefully nourished; and it was from New York that the pollen from the growing plant spread to other Catholic dioceses throughout the country. Attention given to the New York dispute thus has great historical value, since its repercussions transcended the local scene and crucially affected the development of Catholic education in the United States. Although this volume is an interpretive study of the school conflict, it espouses no particular cause and endeavors only to clarify a misunderstood part of American educational history.

It is a pleasure for me to acknowledge an intellectual and personal debt of gratitude to those who gave generously of their time in reading all or part of this manuscript. David Austin helped me to make the crucial decision and encouraged me to pursue this study, even when the good bishop and I were no longer on speaking terms; Lawrence Cremin taught me the meaning of historical research and, for good reason, reminded me of Ellwood Cubberley's background; Gordon Lee first whetted my appetite for the history of education as a field of study. My regard for these three friends is reflected in the dedication of the book. Mother M. Benedict, Robert Cross, Henry Perkinson, Timothy Smith, Michael Swanson, Harvey Wish, and Carl Wittke read the entire manuscript as rigorous but gentle critics and offered invaluable suggestions for its improvement; Gary Fenstermacher responded to my many queries with his penetrating insights about human nature and human motivation; Glyndon Van Deusen helped to sharpen my understanding of William Seward

---

10 Mary Perkins Ryan, *Are Parochial Schools the Answer?* (New York: Holt, Rinehart and Winston, 1963), pp. 33–34.

without necessarily agreeing with all my conclusions; the Reverend Henry J. Browne graciously permitted me to read his unpublished manuscript of the life of Hughes; the Reverend Neil McCluskey's letters and writings gave me a deeper appreciation of American Catholic educational history; Solomon Bluhm allowed me to examine his collection of source materials dealing with New York City education during the 1840's and 1850's; my mother, sister, and brother-in-law suffered me during the dark days; my niece helped me by just being there. The strengths of this study are due in large measure to the contributions of these friends and colleagues; its weaknesses are mine alone.

I wish to thank the staffs of the following libraries and institutions for their invaluable assistance in my search for primary sources as well as for their patience and graciousness when neither was warranted: Catholic University Library, Columbia University Library, Fordham University Library, New York Historical Society, New York Public Library, New York University Library, Rush Rhees Library of the University of Rochester, St. Joseph's Seminary, and Columbia University's Teachers College Library. Finally, I wish to thank Case Western Reserve University for a grant-in-aid which made possible my re-examination of the William Seward and Thurlow Weed Papers at the University of Rochester.

Parts of this volume appeared initially in the *History of Education Quarterly*, IV (1964), VI (1966), and in *Pennsylvania History*, XXXII (1965), and I wish to acknowledge the permission of the editors of those journals to use my articles herein.

Vincent P. Lannie

New York University
January, 1968

⤙ Contents ⤚

I.	Prelude	1
II.	The Catholics' Petition	29
III.	The Bishop Assumes Command	51
IV.	The Great Debate	75
V.	The School Book Issue	103
VI.	The Secretary's Solution	119
VII.	Temporary Postponement	145
VIII.	The "Church and State" Party	166
IX.	A Balance of Power	188
X.	Smooth Sailing in the Assembly	204
XI.	The "Midnight Deed" of the Senate	226
XII.	The End Is the Beginning	245
	Bibliography	259
	Index	271

PUBLIC MONEY AND PAROCHIAL EDUCATION

⤙ I ⤚

Prelude

i

While Bishop John Hughes begged Catholic Europe for financial aid and personnel assistance for his New York diocese, the Catholic bishops of the United States assembled in Baltimore to evaluate and improve the state of American Catholicism. Convened in May, 1840, this Fourth Provincial Council of Baltimore focused particular attention on the education of Catholic youth.[1] And not without good reason. American education was in ferment, and its progress centered upon the emerging common school. Horace Mann in Massachusetts, Henry Barnard in Connecticut, Calvin Wiley in North Carolina, Samuel Lewis and Calvin Stowe in Ohio, Caleb Mills in Indiana, and John D. Pierce in Michigan were beginning to achieve encouraging results from their efforts to promulgate common school education in their respective states. They believed that in a republic every child should have the advantage of a publicly supported, publicly controlled, and non-sectarian education. The primary object of a common school education was "to give every child . . . a free, straight, solid pathway, by which he could walk directly up from the ignorance of an infant to a knowledge of the primary duties of man, and would acquire a power and an invincible will to discharge them."[2]

[1] A Provincial Council is "an assembly composed of the archbishops and the suffragan bishops of a province." Peter K. Guilday (ed.), *The National Pastorals of the American Hierarchy (1792–1919)* (Westminister, Maryland: Newman Press, 1954), p. lx. In 1840, the province was Baltimore and its suffragan sees were New York, Philadelphia, Boston, and Bardstown. Seven Provincial Councils were held in Baltimore between 1829 and 1849.

[2] Mary Peabody Mann and George C. Mann, *Life and Works of Horace Mann* (Boston: Lee and Shepard, 1891), II, pp. 387–88.

Common school education professed to be Christian but not sectarian. The fundamental and common elements of Christianity unequivocally belonged in the curriculum, while abstruse and controversial theological doctrines had no place in the school. The medium through which youths were instructed in this non-denominational Christianity was the Bible. No true Christian, regardless of his sectarian beliefs, questioned its salutary influence, reverent heritage, and literary excellence. The Scriptures embodied the precepts necessary to transform an impressionable and pliable youngster into a morally mature and Christian adult. The Golden Rule and the Decalogue were the ethical principles requisite for the moral and spiritual development of Christian children. Peculiar sectarian tenets merely clouded the simplicity and vitality of the Christian message and consequently had no place in the common school. On the other hand, when the student's intellectual and moral faculties became more refined as he entered into the maturity of adulthood, then he could embrace the sect of his choice freely and rationally.

Horace Mann was a pre-eminent apostle of religious non-denominationalism in the public schools. Since he believed that the primary aim of education was the child's moral and religious development, this end could be implemented most effectively by using the Bible without note or interpreter "because it breathes God's laws and presents illustrious examples of conduct, above all that of Jesus Christ."[3] While Mann favored the presence of religious instruction in the schools, he insisted that it include only that body of Christian beliefs which did violence to no one's conscience. The home and the church were free to engraft their own sectarian tenets upon the school's common core foundation. Strongly influenced by his own Unitarianism, the essence of Mann's religion was an ethical Christianity devoid of the theological differences which separated the numerous sects. "The Religion of Heaven" alone belonged in the schoolroom, while the discordant creeds of men were to be deferred for the more mature mind. Since Christianity was essentially ethical, Mann had little difficulty in compiling a cluster of truths denied by no Christian: love God; follow the Golden Rule; live justly, love mercy, and walk humbly; assist orphans and widows; honor one's parents, keep holy the Sabbath, and neither bear false witness nor covet; and finally, act honestly, with respect for the dig-

[3] Neil G. McCluskey, *Public Schools and Moral Education* (New York: Columbia University, 1958), p. 70.

nity of mankind. "As educators, as friends and sustainers of the Common School system," declared Mann on one occasion, "our great duty is . . . to give to all so much religious instruction as is compatible with the rights of others and with the genius of our government—leaving to parents and guardians the direction, during their school days, of all special and peculiar instruction respecting politics and theology. . . ."[4]

Mann was not alone in his advocacy of nondenominational Christianity in the common school. In 1837, the same year that Mann assumed his position as secretary of the Massachusetts Board of Education, Samuel Lewis, the first state superintendent of common schools in Ohio, issued to the Legislature his *First Annual Report*, which supported the nondenominational solution to the problem of religion in the public school. Because this was a Christian and republican people, Lewis believed that the schools should "inculcate sound principles of Christian morality" which did not impinge upon sectarian differences. Since there was "a broad, common ground, where all Christians and lovers of virtue meet," Lewis urged teachers "to train up the rising generation in those elevated moral principles of the Bible" as well as "all the social and relative duties, with proper inducements to correct action."[5] A few months before the Fourth Council of Baltimore met, the Reverend Horace Bushnell, a liberal Congregational minister, published an article, "Christianity and Common Schools," which defended the Scriptures as an integral part of the common school curriculum while denying the legitimacy of sectarian teaching. "Nothing is more certain than that no such thing as a sectarian religion is to find a place for the Bible as a book of principles, as containing the true standards of character and the best motives and aids to virtue." If a parent desired more than this for his child, he would have to do it himself in his own home. "To insist that the state shall teach the rival opinions of sects and risk the loss of all instruction for that," concluded Bushnell, "would be folly and wickedness together."[6] The Public School Society, which administered education in New York City, maintained a point of view consistent with

4 Mann and Mann, *Life and Works*, pp. 289–90. Cf. McCluskey, *Public Schools*, p. 70, and Raymond B. Culver, *Horace Mann and Religion in the Massachusetts Public Schools* (New Haven: Yale University, 1929), p. 266.

5 Samuel Lewis, *First Annual Report of the Superintendent of Common Schools* (Columbus, Ohio: S. Medary, 1838), p. 7.

6 Horace Bushnell, "Christianity and Common Schools," *Common School Journal of Connecticut*, II (January 15, 1840), 102.

those of Mann, Lewis, and Bushnell. In their *Annual Report* for
1838, the trustees of the Society disassociated themselves from sectarianism in their schools and supported nondenominationalism
as the only type of religious instruction compatible with the purpose and genius of the common school. But though sectarian instruction belonged "to the parents and guardians" of students,
the trustees emphasized the importance of "religious impressions in
early youth." As a result, the Society's schools "uniformly opened
with the reading of the scriptures, and the class books" recognized
and enforced "the great and generally acknowledged principles of
Christianity."[7]

By 1840, then, religious and moral instruction in the common
schools generally embraced the nondenominational approach. As
the fundamental medium of Protestant belief and devotion, the
Bible pervaded common school education, while the inculcation of
the general principles of Christianity carefully avoided theological
conflicts among the Protestant sects. Although many Protestants
argued that morality could not easily be separated from theology,
in practice this was essentially done by stressing moral teaching at
the expense of specific doctrine. Many Protestants came to accept
non-sectarian Christianity only slowly, continued to distrust it, and
erected and sustained a whole network of Sunday schools, in part
to supplement it. Thus, among Protestants there developed a "dual
pattern" of schooling for their youngsters. On the one hand, the
common school stressed the reading of the Bible and general Christian morality while, on the other hand, denominational Sunday
schools taught specific sectarian tenets which completed the child's
moral and religious instruction. "As public schools taught only
'common Christianity,' " declares William Bean Kennedy in *The
Shaping of Protestant Education*, "in the eyes of many churchmen
denominational instruction became more and more important."[8]

This state of affairs was part of the educational panorama which
confronted the assembled bishops at Baltimore when the Fourth
Provincial Council officially opened on May 16, 1840. While they
acknowledged that an education completely under Catholic auspices was the ideal, they never jointly condemned common school
education as such. But they voiced the fear that certain school prac-

7 *Thirty-Third Annual Report of the Trustees of the Public School Society of
New York* (New York: Mahlon Day, 1838), p. 7.
8 William Bean Kennedy, *The Shaping of Protestant Education* (New York:
Association Press, 1966), p. 31.

tices posed a threat to the faith and morals of Catholic children. They could not conscientiously permit Catholic attendance at schools which they considered a danger to the religious faith of their children. Since it was "evident that the nature of public education in many of these Provinces is so developed that it serves heresy, as well as that the minds of Catholic children are little by little imbued with the false principles of the sects," the bishops urged the clergy to "see to the Christian and Catholic education of Catholic children with all the zeal they have, and diligently watch that no Protestant version of the Bible be used, nor hymns of the sects be sung, nor prayers be recited."[9] Catholics were not permitted to read any version of the Bible which had not been approved previously by "a responsible and authorized member of the tribunal of the Church."

Since the Scriptures read in the common schools, especially the King James Version, did not enjoy Catholic sanction, the Council rejected them as not being the authoritative word of God and forbade all Catholics to use and study them. Moreover, the reading of the Bible without note or comment "implied acceptance of the principle of private interpretation, even if such a dogmatic tenet was not professedly held by the teacher or other person doing the reading."[10] Catholics had always believed that the Church alone has the divinely commissioned right to interpret the Bible. As a result, the bishops rejected the principle of private interpretation on two grounds: the principle denied the Church's authority and commission to teach infallibly; and secondly, the right of interpretation was given to the individual rather than to the Church "which the Saviour established to teach all nations, during all days to the consummation of the world." The Council also objected to the participation of Catholic children at public school religious exercises and further denounced the use of objectionable textbooks and library books which openly and at times insidiously "misrepresent our principles. . . , distort our tenets. . . , vilify our practices and. . .

9 John Murphy (ed.), *Concilia Provincilia Baltimori* (Baltimore: John Murphy Company, 1853), p. 171. Cf. Appendix VI.

10 William Kailer Dunn, *What Happened to Religious Education?* (Baltimore: The Johns Hopkins University, 1958), pp. 267–68. Cf. Guilday, *National Pastorals*, pp. 131–33. The bishops were also skeptical as to whether the use of the Bible as a school text aided the religious training of students: "It is thereby exposed to that irreverent familiarity which is calculated to produce more contempt than veneration; it is placed side by side with mere human productions, with the fables of mythology and the speculation of a vain philosophy; it is thus too often made the subject of a vulgar jest, it sinks to the level of taskbooks, and shares the aversion and the remarks which are generally bestowed upon them by children." *Ibid.,* 133–34.

bring contempt upon our Church and its members."[11] Such books had been assailed by previous Councils and individual churchmen, and the assembled bishops reiterated this condemnation in the strongest possible language.

Because there were not sufficient Catholic schools to instruct all Catholic children, the hierarchy felt obliged to take every possible step to protect those Catholic children who attended the public schools from these offensive practices. Thus, the bishops attempted to neutralize the Protestant orientation of the public schools and render them religiously palatable for Catholic students. But the Council went beyond this negative accommodation and reiterated the First Provincial Council's (1829) determination to establish schools "in which the young can be taught the principles of faith and morals, while being instructed in letters."[12]

During the eleven years between the First and Fourth Provincial Councils, many bishops became convinced that public education would not abandon its Protestant character. They concluded that Catholic children could not retain their distinctive religious convictions within religiously alien public schools. Though not initially opposed to common school education, the generally unsympathetic response to repeated Catholic complaints forced the bishops to adopt this position. Although the First Provincial Council had called for the establishment of Catholic schools, the bishops in 1840 urged a far more reaching and comprehensive "separate system of education for the children of our communion." In very candid language, they stated their reasons for arriving at this decision: " . . .we have found by a painful experience, that in any common effort it was always expected that our distinctive principles of religious belief and practices should be yielded to the demands of those who thought proper to charge us with error." They judged that the dogmatic beliefs of the Catholic Church could never be reconciled with a heterogeneous and fluid Protestant theology. Catholic Christianity was true Christianity and had to be guarded carefully against any possible taint of corruption. In reaching this decision, the bishops made it clear that it did not result from "any unkind feeling to our fellow citizens; it is not through any reluctance on our part, to contribute whatever little we can to the prosperity of what are called the common institutions of the coun-

---

[11] Guilday, *National Pastorals*, pp. 131–32, 134.
[12] Murphy, *Concilia*, p. 47. Cf. Appendix IV.

try. . . ."[13] On the contrary, concern for the religious welfare of Catholic children attending public schools caused them to embark upon a different educational direction.

The Catholic hierarchy was obviously faced with an inescapable dilemma. To permit Catholic children to jeopardize their faith by attending public schools was tantamount to a neglect of the bishops' religious obligations. And yet, to undertake the development of an independent system of Catholic education confronted them with almost insurmountable financial and personnel difficulties. How would the predominantly immigrant Catholic population supply the material resources necessary to erect and support a school system when it was scarcely able to maintain a subsistence standard of living? The Catholics' inability to build new churches or even to support existing houses of worship was noted by Hughes in a letter to the Leopoldine Society of Austria which described the depleted financial resources of his diocese: "If they could appropriate to the building of churches or other necessary institutions what they are obliged to pay for those already erected the case would be very different. But unhappily, what should belong to the present and the future is already mortgaged to the past."[14] And who was going to staff these schools? Although the number of religious teachers was increasing, it was still insufficient to satisfy the needs of any diocese. The bishops met this dilemma by resorting to the exigency of accommodation. They would "educate as many Catholic children as they could in Catholic schools while striving to protect the faith of those Catholics who were in public schools."[15]

ii

On Saturday, July 18, 1840, the *British Queen* navigated slowly and majestically into New York harbor after sixteen and one-half days

13 Guilday, *National Pastorals*, p. 134.

14 Report of Bishop John Hughes to the Leopoldine Society (April, 1840), New York Archdiocesan Archives. This report was written while Hughes was traveling in Europe in search of money and personnel for his diocese. The Leopoldine Society, founded in 1829 in honor of the Austrian archduchess Leopoldina, had as its specific purpose the promotion and support of Catholic missionary activity in the United States. Cf. Benjamin J. Blied, *Austrian Aid to American Catholics, 1830–1860* (Milwaukee: Benjamin J. Blied, 1944).

15 Jerome E. Diffley, "Catholic Reaction to American Public Education, 1792–1852" (unpublished Ph.D. thesis, Notre Dame, Indiana, University of Notre Dame, 1959), p. 270. Cf. Michael H. Lucey, "Efforts to Regain State Support for Catholic Schools," *Catholic World*, 93 (August, 1911), 599.

on the open sea. Its eighty-seven passengers included the United States Minister to Spain, General J. H. Eaton and his family, and John Hughes, Roman Catholic bishop of New York. Hughes had left Rome in March and then embarked upon a whirlwind tour of some of the principal cities in continental Europe, including "Florence, Lucca, Pisa, Leghorn, Bologna, Modena, Ferrara, Venice, Trieste, Vienna, Presburg in Hungary, Munich, Stuttgard, Strasburg, and on so to Paris." Late in May he departed from the French capital and crossed the channel to England. After a week's stay in London, Hughes travelled to Ireland, whose people "have been crushed by an apostate nation, which prospers withal. But God is just and merciful."[16] He remained in Ireland until July 1, when he boarded the *British Queen* for the return voyage to America.

Hughes arrived in New York under very different circumstances from the first time when he had crossed the Atlantic, as an immigrant lad many years before. Born on a small farm in County Tyrone, Ireland, in 1797, he emigrated to the United States in 1817 to begin a new life in a country "in which no stigma of inferiority would be impressed on my brow, simply because I professed one creed or another."[17] An ocean voyage and a new country did not diminish the youth's childhood desire to enter the ministry. After a year of working at odd jobs and another year of waiting for admittance to the seminary, Hughes was accepted at Mount St. Mary's at Emmitsburg, Maryland, and ordained a priest in 1826 in Philadelphia. He spent all of his priestly ministry in Philadelphia, first in St. Joseph's Church and later in St. John's Church, which he established in 1832. When the elderly and sickly bishop of New York, the Reverend John Dubois, petitioned Rome for a coadjutor bishop in 1837, Hughes received the appointment and was consecrated a bishop on January 7, 1838, in St. Patrick's Cathedral.[18]

---

16 *New York Freeman's Journal*, July 18, 1840; Hughes to Frenaye, (Dublin, June 1, 1840), cited in John R. G. Hassard, *Life of the Most Reverend John Hughes, D.D.* (New York: D. Appleton and Company, 1866), pp. 219–20.

17 Hassard, *Life of Hughes*, p. 20.

18 Dubois was the president of Mount St. Mary's when Hughes applied for admission. Impressed with the youth's determination and enthusiasm, Dubois hired him as a gardener. In return for this labor, Hughes received room, board, and private tutoring to prepare him to enter the seminary as a regular student. After one year of this accommodation, the reluctant gardener relinquished his flowers and vegetables to become a full-time student and pursued the traditional divinity course in philosophy and theology. In 1826, the same year that Hughes was ordained, Dubois was made the third bishop of New York.

Barely two weeks after Hughes's consecration, Dubois suffered a paralytic stroke, which incapacitated him for some time. After a second attack sustained by Dubois, who did "not recover so fast this time as after the first," the attending physicians confided to Hughes that their patient would never recover completely and that the end could come at any time. During the next two years Dubois experienced recurrent attacks, which not only paralyzed his body but, more pitiably, began to affect his once renowned intellect. Nevertheless, he still exercised absolute ecclesiastical control of his diocese. A bad situation was made worse as the infirm bishop became increasingly pathological concerning the maintenance of his episcopal authority and dignity. The coadjutor was placed in the unenviable position of shepherding the diocese with none of the shepherd's attendant authority.

Matters became so bad that Hughes sought advice in a confidential letter to Archbishop Samuel Eccleston of Baltimore. He believed that he would be morally culpable if he remained silent any longer. Dubois' health was not improving, and he suffered increasingly recurrent memory lapses. "In a word, his mind is so relaxed that, whatever he was heretofore, he is that no longer." Chaos had descended upon the diocese as episcopal government had practically collapsed. Dubois never sought his coadjutor's opinion or assistance, "but on the contrary seems glad of every opportunity to prove to himself and others that he does not stand in need of it. The consequence is that I see and hear things which require to be remedied [but am] unable to apply the remedy." The situation could not be allowed to continue for "I fear the consequences will be disastrous." Hughes's solution obviously envisioned his superior's resignation, and "I think if the matter were urged upon him by Bishop [Benedict] Fenwick [of Boston], he would resign."[19]

As the situation worsened, the harried subordinate found it necessary to inform the Roman authorities of the abuses resulting from Dubois' debilitation:

He is now better, now worse. His faculties both of mind and of body are impaired: his memory especially fails him. . . . Devoted to him with

19 Hughes to Eccleston (New York, October 29, 1838), New York Archdiocesan Archives, St. Joseph's Seminary, Yonkers, New York. Henceforth, the New York Archdiocesan Archives will be identified as NYAA. Cf. Hughes to Purcell (New York, February 24, 1838), NYAA; Hughes to Frenaye (New York, February, n.d., 1838), cited in Hassard, *Life of Hughes*, p. 187; Hughes to Purcell (New York, March 18, 1838), NYAA.

my whole heart, as he is to me, I have made no attempt to interfere in the government of the diocese, except in the way of advice and persuasion, which are of little avail, because he is very set in his purposes. . . . I write of these things . . . not that any authority for governing the diocese may be taken away from him, or conferred upon me; but in order that you may be informed of the state and circumstances of ecclesiastical affairs.[20]

Although Hughes did not urge that episcopal jurisdiction be withdrawn from the ailing prelate, the implication was obvious, and his letter certainly had this effect. During the summer of 1839 Rome forwarded its decision in a letter to Dubois. The Holy See was not only aware but solicitous of the bishop's health. In order to facilitate his physical improvement and provide for the welfare of the diocese, Dubois was felicitously but firmly informed that his jurisdiction over the New York diocese was henceforth suspended. The young coadjutor was directed to exercise full jurisdiction over the diocese. In an attempt to soften the severity of the blow, Dubois was permitted to retain the exercise of a certain of his episcopal powers, such as the celebration of pontifical mass, the administration of the sacrament of confirmation, and the conference of major orders upon aspirants for the priesthood. Further salve was applied to the wound in that the new administrator was admonished never to permit Dubois' episcopal dignity to be slighted in any way. The Roman cardinal who wrote the letter exhibited a keen knowledge of human nature when he assured Dubois that Hughes had only the highest admiration and loyalty toward him.[21] -Although Dubois obediently acceded to Rome's decision, he never expressed agreement with its wisdom. This highly charged episode unfortunately precipitated a marked coolness in Dubois toward the younger man. During the closing years of his life, the Frenchman remained civil but definitely aloof in his relations with Hughes. Physically they dwelt in the same house but they were never one in spirit and in comradeship. Hughes attempted to mollify his friend for the sting of his episcopal loss, for he understood the enormity of Dubois' mortification resulting from the deposition. "But in his infirm state of

---

[20] Hassard, *Life of Hughes*, p. 199.
[21] Fransoni to Dubois (Rome, June 1, 1839), NYAA. For a slightly different and melodramatic account of this incident, see Hassard, *Life of Hughes*, pp. 199–200.

mind," comments Hassard, "[Dubois] could not conquer a natural repugnance toward 'Mr. Hughes,' as he persisted in calling him."[22]

Under Dubois, vigorous and dynamic direction was absent in New York. On the other hand, Hughes possessed an energetic leadership which increased to command national attention both within and without Catholic circles. His writings reveal the man and his personality, for they are usually clear, always forceful, and frequently interspersed with Irish humor. Orestes Brownson, a critical and controversial contemporary of the bishop, rightly ascribed the principal defect of Hughes's intellect to his "habit of taking practical views of all questions, and of acting according to circumstances. In discussing a question he rarely states distinctly the principle on which the question turns, and gives it only in his practical solution, from which it is not always easy to gather it."[23] Never a theorist but always practical in his views, Hughes dedicated his long episcopacy to a defense of his church and his immigrant flock against all critics and detractors.

Unbending in will and indefatigable in contest, Hughes welded the Catholics of his diocese into a durable unit to protect their interests and resist the thrusts of nativism. Under the leadership of Hughes and other immigrant bishops, a previously quiescent American Catholicism began to manifest a militant and more aggressive character. Catholics now questioned their traditional role as a suffered minority and openly—often belligerently—began to demand their political and civil rights.[24] In *The Protestant Crusade, 1800–1860*, Ray Billington labels this emergent crusading spirit as one of "arrogance" and styles Hughes as the man primarily responsible for its emergence: "Ill-suited by temperament and training to any compromise policy, he was blindly loyal to the Catholic Church and strove constantly to make that church stronger and better. There

---

22 Hassard, *Life of Hughes*, p. 200. Dubois lingered on in this illness until his death on December 20, 1842, at the age of seventy-eight.

23 Henry P. Brownson (ed.), *The Works of Orestes A. Brownson* (Detroit: Thorndike Nourse, 1882–87), XIII, p. 497.

24 A perceptive analysis of the rise of "aggressive" Catholicism during this period and its consequent influence on the development of American Catholic culture is found in Thomas T. McAvoy, "The Formation of the Catholic Minority in the United States, 1820–1860," *Review of Politics*, X (1948), 13–34. Culturally, McAvoy contends, "the policy of Hughes set back the progress of the Irish immigrant at least a generation" because it delayed the assimilation of the Irish into American culture.

can be no doubt too that his actions and utterances aroused considerable resentment among Protestants."[25]

Certainly, Hughes did not adequately understand the Protestant tenor of his adopted country and its deep suspicion of Catholicism. For his was the "true" faith, and Protestant "heresy" was its deadly enemy. Catholic newcomers to the United States especially had to be protected from an active Protestant proselytism and insulated against a pervasive Protestant environment if they were to retain their traditional faith. Because of a fundamental suspicion of an unsympathetic and often hostile majority, Hughes unfortunately, though perhaps understandably, adopted a defensive mentality and never seriously attempted to integrate his predominately immigrant flock into the mainstream of American life. This immigrant hypersensitivity, together with an aggressive and abrasive personality and a militant Catholicism, played an important role in shaping the direction of the bishop's long episcopal career. His stewardship of a hated church and a despised flock, his school controversy with the Public School Society, his entry into the arena of partisan politics, his lecture on "The Decline of Protestantism, and the Cause," and his determined threat to use force to protect his churches against a potential nativist mob—these must be understood as component parts of the policy of a zealous and often contentious churchman who championed an uncompromising Catholicism and vigorously defended the socially unacceptable immigrant. Inevitably, this policy roused to action an already alarmed Protestantism and added fuel to the quickening anti-Catholic conflagration of the 1840's and 1850's.

On October 14, 1839, Hughes published a pastoral letter which announced that Dubois' resignation resulted from advanced age and infirm health. He also asked New York Catholics to support the establishment of a new college and seminary, first called St. John's and renamed Fordham in the early twentieth century. Two days later, he was bade *bon voyage*, and the *Louis Philippe* carried him off to Europe to seek aid for his diocesan ventures, especially to recruit more priests to minister to his expanding flock and to solicit additional funds and a competent faculty for St. John's.

Although Hughes was in Europe while the Council was in session, New York diocesan officials kept him abreast of its proceedings.

[25] Ray Allen Billington, *The Protestant Crusade, 1800–1860* (New York: Macmillan Company, 1938), p. 290.

Certainly he would read the Council's pastoral letter and decrees upon his return to New York. During his absence, and even before the Council had convened, a school controversy had erupted in New York City which involved Catholic educational interests and public school policy and which dealt with many of the issues raised by the bishops in the Council. Interestingly enough, the Council's deliberations and decisions played no direct role in the emergence of this dispute. Rather, it was Governor William Seward's annual message to the New York State Legislature in January, 1840, which directly precipitated the conflict. Nevertheless, the conclusions of the Council provided Hughes with guidelines in his subsequent formulation of the Catholic position in the school dispute. Indeed, the Sixth Decree urged the clergy to enlist "the help of those who have authority to use a fitting remedy" to rectify what the bishops considered an intolerable school situation. Under the leadership of the clergy, Catholics were asked to invoke the principle of religious freedom to right this alleged wrong. During the troubled years ahead, the bishop of New York never forgot this episcopal injunction, nor did he allow anyone else to forget it.

iii

In 1838 New Yorkers went to the polls to choose a governor. Thurlow Weed, editor of the *Albany Evening Journal* and a powerful Whig political boss frequently called "The Dictator," was certain that Whig triumphs in 1837 presaged another victory in the fall election. Weed had long been a close friend and political mentor of William Seward, and his support of Seward was the deciding factor in the Whig convention's choice of a nominee. To insure certain victory, Weed engaged the services of a young and talented newspaper editor, Horace Greeley, to publish a campaign paper for the Whigs. General resentment against the Democrats, a strong political machine engineered by Weed, and the editorial talents of Greeley produced a substantial Whig victory and the election of Seward as governor of New York.

Approximately a month after his election, Seward received several communications which deplored the condition of New York's system of common schools. Henry Van Der Lyn, an upstate lawyer who was interested in the progress of the state's education, wrote that evil days had fallen upon common school education. "The common schools are . . . much neglected, & invoke the aid of your wisdom & experience." The lack of adequate teacher education had much to do with the ineffectiveness of the schools. Good schools were impossible without able teachers, and Van Der Lyn supported his contention with Victor Cousin's injunction that " 'as is the Master, *so* is the School.' " The solution to this defect was the establishment of normal schools, and New York would do well to examine the examples of Prussia, France, and Massachusetts with their expanding systems of teacher-training institutions. Prussia's "40 teacher's Seminaries, France with 30, & Massachusetts with one, incite this great State, to imitate their wisdom & profit by their experience."

Van Der Lyn linked the lack of good teachers to the impotency of the superintendent of common schools, "who is a mere nominal, ineffective appendage in the office of the Secy. of State." To combat this inertia, he urged the appointment of an independent educational superintendent whose office would more or less parallel the Prussian or French Minister of Education. The voice of the state's chief educational officer would then "be heard in the schoolrooms, to inspire a sense of the value of knowledge, to remove difficulties, correct evils, excite diligence, & put in execution, all the improvements suggested by wisdom & confirmed by experience." If these recommendations were carried out, Van Der Lyn prophesied that New York would rise to national and perhaps to international intellectual, moral, and religious leadership. With the right kind of direction, these reforms could easily and effectively renovate the state's system of education. And Van Der Lyn was certain that the new governor was the right man for the job. "Our evil days, We hope are past, & we confidently look to your Patriotism, public spirit, & enlightened benevolence, for an era of intellectual light, prosperity, & happiness."[26]

Van Der Lyn's concern was highlighted by a survey undertaken by the American Society for the Diffusion of Useful Knowledge. The Society reported that an extensive six-month investigation of educational conditions in the principal towns in western New York showed that "about one third of the children in those towns do not avail themselves of the advantages of the present system of Education, & are without any means of instruction." The report charged

[26] Henry Van Der Lyn to Seward (Oxford, New York, December 3, 1838), Seward Papers, University of Rochester. Henceforth, the Seward Papers will be identified as UR.

that the state's present district school system was outmoded and no longer able to meet the needs of a rapidly increasing population. Echoing Van Der Lyn's plea for centralization as an antidote for this deteriorating educational situation, the Society urged the creation of a state board of education and the appointment of a secretary to the board. Since "some of the Eastern States" had already begun this process of educational centralization, they could serve as excellent models and guides. "The passage of a law organizing a Board of education with a Secretary whose sole duty should be to devise and put into practice plans for the improvement of common schools," concluded the Society, "would go far to correct the errors & supply the deficiencies of our present system."[27]

Both Van Der Lyn and the American Society for the Diffusion of Useful Knowledge advocated the centralization of New York education patterned upon New England and even European prototypes. A board or ministry of education was indispensable, and a chief educational officer—minister, superintendent, or secretary—had to possess "great endowments, & extensive experience, & with a whole mind & heart [be] intent on advancing the cause of education." But even this new administrative structure would not succeed unless normal schools were established to prepare teachers for the common schools. And it was only the state's chief executive who could exercise the moral persuasion and marshal the necessary support to effect the needed reform. "The people will hail with delight, the chief Magistrate, who by wise institutions, exalts the minds of his fellow citizens, & prepares them to uphold & perpetuate the public Liberty."[28] The whole problem was thus thrust upon Seward, who proceeded to give top priority to educational matters during his stay in office.

Very early in January, 1839, Seward delivered his *First Annual Message* to the State Legislature. After recommending a state system of internal improvements—a subject discussed in detail in each of Seward's reports—he turned his attention to the progress of education in New York State. Although the state's system of public instruction was by no means unsuccessful, the governor thought "that its usefulness is much less than the state rightfully demands, both as a return for her munificence and a guaranty of her institutions." Im-

---

[27] John T. Gilchrist to Seward (New York, December 7, 1838), UR; James Brown [*et al.*] to Seward (New York, December 7, 1838), UR.

[28] Henry Van Der Lyn to Seward (Oxford, New York, December 3, 1838), UR.

proved educational facilities were imperative if Americans were to achieve responsible citizenship and cherish their republican heritage. Seward was convinced that only a superior education could effect "the improvability of our race"—an elevation that was infinite in dimension. Careful not to deprecate the past merit of the state's educational efforts, he tempered his critical remarks by noting that "all that is proposed is less wonderful than what has already been accomplished." He did not want the legislators to misconstrue these observations as platitudes doomed to quick oblivion, and forewarned that "education is the chief of our responsibilities." In fact, Seward predicted that during his administration "improvement in our system of education will be wider and more enduring than the effects of any change of public policy."[29]

William Seward did not suddenly become interested in education. On the contrary, his educational views were an integral part of a thoughtfully constructed philosophy of life. His social and intellectual creed rested upon two fundamental beliefs, from which he never fundamentally wavered: the Judeo-Christian doctrine of the unity of mankind under the Fatherhood of God; and the Enlightenment's assertion of man's natural and inalienable rights as expressed in the Declaration of Independence. In answer to a correspondent whose "reflections upon the subject of education" seemed to him "as just as they are liberal," Seward summarized these principles in clear and concise language:

[I] regard the human race as constituting one family, having the same heavenly parentage, the same earthly rights, and the same ultimate hopes. The earth, which for convenience of human government, is divided into territories, states and empires, is the common home of all that family; and every one of its members seems to me to have a natural right to seek happiness wherever it shall seem most likely to be found. This is the spirit of Dr. Franklin's beautiful motto 'Where liberty dwells this is my country.' Free inter-communication between members of the human family tends to promote benevolence, humanity and improvement, and from these result human happiness. Wherever any human being goes, there, in my judgment he is entitled to security and protection of his inalienable rights to life and liberty, and happiness, if he does not by misconduct endanger the rights of others. Physical and moral enjoy-

29 George E. Baker (ed.), *The Works of William Seward* (New York: J. S. Redfield, 1853), II, pp. 206, 208.

ment none will deny him, but his rights of conscience are even more sacred.[30]

This line of reasoning included all human beings—Caucasians and Negroes, Protestants and Catholics, native Americans and naturalized citizens. It is not surprising that the Seward who in time became the champion of Negro freedom and rights was the same Seward who had long before espoused the civil rights and religious liberties of Catholic immigrants. In fact, a decade before he applied the "higher law" doctrine to slavery, he had employed a variation of this controversial principle to defend the rights of the newly arriving immigrant class—a position as unpopular then as was his abolitionism of a later period. When a Whig politico wrote a letter that enunciated a typically negative reaction toward the Irish and rebuked the governor for his over-solicitousness for these newcomers, which was causing discord within Whig party ranks, Seward sent a sharp reply that defended his attitude and actions toward the immigrant:

Why should an American hate foreigners? It is to hate such as his forefathers were. Why should a foreigner be taught to hate Americans? It is to hate what he is most anxious his children should become. For myself, so far from hating any of my fellow citizens, I should shrink from myself if I did not recognize them all as worthy of my constant solicitude to promote their welfare, and entitled of right by the Constitution and laws, and by the higher laws of God himself, to equal rights, equal privileges, and equal political favor, as citizens of the state, with myself.[31]

After this statement of general principle, Seward responded to a series of charges against the Irish by specifically enumerating what he considered to be virtues of the Irish:

I think that the Irish population to whom you allude are useful, well-meaning, and as a mass, inoffensive, and religiously-disposed citizens. I think them more generous, liberal and disinterested than most other classes of the community, reposing more than others upon the consolation of their religion, and less disposed to force its tenets upon others. I think them eminently and proverbially grateful, confiding and devoted. I believe the institutions of their adopted country are as dear to them as

[30] Seward to Mrs. M. P. Mann (Albany, May 5, 1842), UR.
[31] Seward to Harman C. Westervelt (Albany, March 25, 1840), UR. For a negative Whig reaction to Seward's views "respecting our Irish 'fellow citizens,'" see Harman C. Westervelt to Seward (New York, March 19, April 18, 1840), UR.

to us who are native citizens. . . . I believe the history of the Irish people shows that their loyalty has continued faithful [sic] under great exaction, oppression and privations than would have wrought up to frenzy any other People. I believe them less exacting of this government than any other portion of our population.[32]

Seward's educational views and subsequent recommendations emerged directly out of this framework of thought and formed an essential part of his broader social and political philosophy. He favored the development of an educational aristocracy in the sense that "education increased the power of those who enjoy its advantages." Such an aristocracy would forge an enlightened citizenry whose power and influence would increase in proportion to its level of educational competency. Throughout history, society had been effectively partitioned into two inequitable social classes. Seward was convinced that the absence of universal education was the principal factor that sustained the mass-class relationship in society. Essentially an equalizing instrument, Seward's educational aristocracy was to eliminate or at least to neutralize class monopoly through the medium of mass education.

The antidote to class was to grant the advantages of education to the mass. Not only Seward's insistence that all his fellow citizens were "worthy of my constant solicitude to promote their welfare" but a trip to Ireland in 1833 gave him impressions that reinforced his commitment to treat the newly arriving immigrants as equal to the native-born. He traced Ireland's poverty and misery directly to the illiteracy of the people, which he thought was a deliberate policy prescribed by her English Protestant masters. As a result, he was compelled to favor the immediate dissolution of the union between England and Ireland. Unless "the repeal shall take place, the people will never be enlightened and educated" sufficiently to govern themselves. Even Irish Protestants opposed any measures which proposed to educate the predominantly Catholic population for fear that when competently instructed, "they will demand their natural and inalienable rights. . . ."[33] Seward's Irish experience deepened his conviction that the newcomers' civil and political rights entitled them to a republican education that would not only aid them in their individual aspirations but would also help to assimilate them as

---

32 Seward to Harman C. Westervelt (Albany, March 25, 1840), UR.

33 Baker, *Works of Seward*, III, p. 523. Cf. III, pp. 147, 210; II, p. 199; Seward to William Palmar (Albany, December 17, 1840), UR.

loyal and participating citizens in their adopted land. Precisely because immigrants needed more intensive instruction concerning the complexities of republican institutions did they especially require schools "in which their children shall enjoy advantages of education equal to our own. . . ."

Seward was quite serious when he announced that educational improvement was to be his principal gubernatorial task. Van Der Lyn's criticism, buttressed by the suggestions of the Society for the Diffusion of Useful Knowledge, had alerted him to the limited effectiveness of New York State's system of common schools. These correspondents had commended New England as an educational model, and Seward was already in communication with Henry Barnard during the summer of 1839. Since Connecticut had an "enviable distinction in having been the first of the states to found and adequately endow common schools," Seward sought and received a copy of the Annual Report of the Connecticut Board of Commissioners of Common Schools as well as Barnard's "first annual report as Secretary of the board." The governor assured Barnard that he would carefully study both documents in an attempt to improve his own state's educational stature.[34]

In July, 1839, Seward visited New York City to deliver an Independence Day address at a Protestant Sunday school celebration. His eloquence was directed less to the political birth of the nation and more to the important role of education in the democratization of the young republic. The Sunday school movement was an integral part of this educational responsibility, orated the governor, since "Sunday schools and common schools are the great levelling institutions of the age." While Seward was in the city and again when he returned in the fall, he investigated the city's school system, which was not part of the state's district system of education but was administered by the Public School Society. Founded in 1805 as a private, philanthropic, and Protestant-oriented organization, the Society was the principal recipient of common school funds and thus exercised a virtual monopoly over the city's public schools. Originally known as the Free School Society, its name was changed to the Public School Society in 1826. The Society was controlled by a fifty-member board of trustees, while an executive committee composed of five especially elected trustees, the officers of the Society—presi-

---

[34] Seward to Henry Barnard (Albany, June 28, 1839), UR.

dent, vice president, treasurer, secretary—and the chairmen of several subcommittees exercised a general supervision over the Society's work and appointed teachers and assistants for all of its schools.[35] Although Seward found these schools well managed and "excellent in most respects," he discovered that large numbers of Catholic parents boycotted them on the grounds that they constituted a serious threat to their children's religious faith. The Protestant version of the Bible was read without note or comment, Protestant prayers were recited and hymns sung, and volumes critical of Catholicism were sometimes used as text and library books. Weed thought that this "condition was [further] aggravated in most instances by the misfortunes or infirmities and neglect of such parents."[36]

Although Seward expressed interest in centralizing the state's system of education, the report that many children in western New York were without formal education and the deteriorating situation in New York City concerned him even more. He concluded that immediate steps were needed to counteract this state of affairs. For if immigrant children were to grow into adult illiterates, they would eventually become public liabilities and never effectively enter the mainstream of American life. Poverty, ignorance, and vice would stalk them and their children constantly, and the whole inevitable process would begin anew. When Seward returned to Albany, he discussed this crises with his "father confessor," the Reverend Doctor Eliphalet Nott, the Presbyterian president of Seward's alma mater, Union College, who was said to "have great influence" on him. Seward's conversations with Nott as well as with Weed crystallized his educational remedy, which was promptly incorporated into his 1840 message to the Legislature. He expressed shock that a large number of children, especially those in the larger cities of the state, did not enjoy the advantages of a common school education either because they were orphans or because "the de-

35 *Twenty-Ninth Annual Report of the Trustees of the Public School Society of New York* (New York: Mahlon Day, 1834); *Thirty-Seventh Annual Report of the Trustees of the Public School Society of New York* (New York: Mahlon Day, 1842). By 1840, any citizen who paid ten dollars could become a member of the society for life. The members of the Common Council, the mayor, and the recorder were *ex officio* members and trustees of the society.

36 Harriet A. Weed (ed.), *Autobiography of Thurlow Weed* (Boston: Houghton, Mifflin and Company, 1883), p. 483. Seward declared that before his legislative message of 1840, he "had never heard of the New York Public School Society [,] its jurisdiction [,] its powers or its funds. . . ." Seward to Samuel Luckey (Albany, November 29, 1840), UR.

pravity of parents, or other forms of accident or misfortune seem
to have doomed [them] to hopeless poverty and ignorance."

With the New York City school situation obviously paramount in
his mind, Seward designated immigrant children for special consideration. These children, who lived primarily in the populous
cities of the state—New York was the largest of these cities—were
normally deprived of a public education "in consequence of prejudices arising from difference of language or religion." Because
society had to be as solicitous for its immigrant children as it was
for its native-born, the governor proposed "the establishment of
schools in which they may be instructed by teachers speaking the
same language with themselves and professing the same faith. There
would be no inequality in such a measure, since it happens from the
force of circumstances, if not from choice, that the responsibilities
of education are in most instances confided by us to native citizens,
and occasions seldom offer for a trial of our magnanimity by com-
mitting that trust to persons differing from ourselves in language or
religion." Since America was a land of opportunity for the "oppressed of every nation," declared Seward in defense of the wisdom
of this recommendation, "we should evince wisdom equal to such
generosity by qualifying their children for the high responsibilities
of citizenship."[37]

Since many of New York City's Catholic children did not attend
the public schools on religious grounds, Seward urged the establishment of schools that would be acceptable to this minority group and
staffed with teachers who spoke the same language and professed the
same religious faith as their pupils. Such schools would be administered by Catholic officials but supported with public funds. Therefore, under Seward's plan the existing Catholic schools would become part of the state's common school system—Catholic public
schools—even though they retained their private charters and religious affiliation. Public funds would thus be appropriated to fi-
nance denominational schools which Catholic children could attend
without violating their religious convictions. In a letter to a friend,
Seward reiterated his horror upon discovering that so large a number of "foreign" children did not attend school. He could never
permit such a condition to continue, since he had long believed

---

[37] Francis Wayland to Eliphalet Nott (Providence, September 8, 1841), UR. Nott
sent this letter to Seward with a note which reads in part, "I seem to be considered
your father confessor. . . ."; Baker, *Works of Seward*, II, pp. 215–16.

that "no system of education could answer the ends of a republic but one which secures the education of all." As governor of New York, he intended "to turn the footsteps of the children of the poor foreigners from the way which led to the House of Refuge and the State-prison, into the same path of moral and intellectual cultivation made so smooth and plain for our own children."[38]

Whether this recommendation was "unfortunate and ill-advised," "dangerous," or "enlightened," Seward did not submit it in order to gain Irish-Catholic votes.[39] Not all his actions originated from partisan political objectives, especially since he held such strong views concerning human rights and the need for an educated citizenry in a republic. At the same time, it cannot be denied that Seward was a political animal whose veins pulsed with the intrigue and excitement of partisan politics. He was certainly aware that his educational recommendation would do him no harm politically with Irish-Catholic voters. Several Irish-Catholic Whigs from New York City who perennially saw hopeful signs that their countrymen were about to abandon the Democratic party, as well as several of Seward's close confidants, wrote him repeatedly that the city's Catholics were indebted to him for his "liberal sentiments . . . as expressed in his Public documents" and would remember him at the polls.[40] Even Hughes subsequently promised the governor that

[38] Seward to Mordecai M. Noah (Albany, August 29, 1840), UR; Frederick Seward (ed.), *Autobiography of William H. Seward from 1831 to 1834 with a Memoir of His Life and Selections from His Letters from 1831 to 1846* (New York: D. Appleton and Company, 1877), p. 502.

[39] Nevertheless, several of Seward's contemporaries attributed purely political motives to this proposal. Cf. Bayard Tuckerman (ed.), *The Diary of Philip Hone, 1828–1851* (New York: Dodd, Mead and Company, 1889), I, p. 371, II, pp. 21, 153; Thomas L. Nichols, *Forty Years of American Life* (London: John Maxwell and Company, 1864), II, p. 75. At the present time, John W. Pratt is the leading advocate of this viewpoint. For Professor Pratt's position and my sharp disagreement with it, see John W. Pratt, "Governor Seward and the New York City School Controversy, 1840–1842," *New York History*, XLII (October, 1961), 351–64; Vincent Peter Lannie, "William Seward and Common School Education," *History of Education Quarterly*, IV (September, 1964), 181–92; John W. Pratt, "Religious Conflict in the Development of the New York City Public School System," *History of Education Quarterly*, V (June, 1965), 110–20; Vincent Peter Lannie, "William Seward and the New York School Controversy, 1840–1842: A Problem in Historical Motivation," *History of Education Quarterly*, VI (Spring, 1966), 52–71.

[40] Hugh Sweeny to Seward (New York, September 16, 1840), UR; Hugh Sweeny to Seward (New York, September 17, 1840), UR; Robert B. Minturn to Seward (New York, April 10, 1840), UR; Nicholas Devereux to John Canfield Spencer (Utica, April 2, 1840), UR; James Kelly to Seward (New York, April 10, 1840), UR; Francis O'Donoghue to Seward (Newburg, October 10, 1840), UR; Patrick Carberry to Thurlow Weed (Auburn, January 14, 1840), UR.

should he ever seek national office, his name would be "cherished with a peculiar regard by the Catholics of the present generation throughout the United States."[41]

While Seward obviously did not reject any potential electoral increase due to Catholic gratitude, he did not use education as a political lever to gain this vote. In this area of his thinking, he never allowed his broader philosophical perspective to be submerged by political expediency. When a Whig correspondent who was critical of Seward's favorable attitude toward the Irish advised him that the "most judicious method of securing the Irish vote, if such are really your Exceys [*sic*] intentions, is to check animated disposition to impertinence, by letting them almost exclusively alone," the governor lost no time in writing a very candid and caustic reply. He denied categorically that he was a party to any Whig efforts "to secure the votes and influence of the Irish." Although his educational views and sympathy with regard to "foreigners may be erroneous, they are not insincere." Seward assured his correspondent that he was firmly committed to this view and reminded him that

although I have been several years in political life, no different sentiments have ever been expressed by me, but on the contrary on all occasions both here and in letters from Ireland. When at least I could have had no ambitious purposes or political schemes, I published the same and kindred opinions. And you have for further proof of my assurance that now, on review of every word I have written or spoken, there is not one which under the influence of sense of official responsibility, I would consent to obliterate.[42]

Although Seward was a practical and highly effective partisan politician, his educational stance and advocacy of immigrants' rights were grounded upon a genuine and encompassing social and political philosophy. In fact, he remained the immigrants' constant friend all during his long and tumultuous political career both in New York and in Washington. To offer a political motive for his educational recommendation, therefore, is to question seriously the integrity and honesty of his broader philosophy.

As a matter of political fact, Seward's plan won him no appreciable increase in the Catholic vote but rather earned him Whig defections and Protestant censure. The Democratic party prepared to create

---

41 Hughes to Seward (New York, August 29, 1840), NYAA.
42 Harman C. Westervelt to Seward (New York, March 19, 1840), UR; Seward to Harman C. Westervelt (Albany, March 25, 1840), UR.

political capital by equivocating upon the issue, while a sizable portion of city Whigs adamantly opposed the plan and used every means at their disposal to prevent its adoption. Politically, the Whigs had nothing to gain from supporting a measure that would benefit their Irish protagonists, who were consistent in their Democratic voting habits. Since the Whigs had to contend with these naturalized Americans at the polls, frequently unsuccessfully, they were unwilling to extend them any advantages. While the press condemned Seward, the Protestant pulpit thundered its anathema against him. He was branded as the ravager of the common schools, the enemy of Protestantism, and the subverter of free American institutions. Nativist ministers warned that the governor's proposal would in effect support the Roman Church with public funds and permit papist priests to instruct Protestant children. Moreover, he was accused of "sapping the foundations of liberty" and betraying innocent children "to the wiles of the Scarlet Lady." One who was in league with the pope and a disguised Jesuit deserved to be denounced for "plotting the ruin of the state."

If Seward's proposal had been motivated by political considerations, the strong Whig opposition and lack of general support would have been more than sufficient for him to abandon it. An ambitious politician devoid of strong principles and convictions does not risk popular and party antagonism by going against the political tide. But Seward did precisely this. He did go against the tide and never abandoned his basic concern for the education of all the state's youth. Political retaliation did not deter him since he could not "refuse to take the position to which my political principles lead." If people did not respect his views, they could vote for another but could not ask him to violate his conscience:

If any man, whether Whig or otherwise, will withhold his favor from me, because . . . I believe that the State owes it to herself and to a just regard for the stability of her institutions and the happiness of her People to afford to all the destitute children in the Commonwealth advantages of moral and religious education, and that that education, if it cannot be otherwise conferred, may rightly be conferred by the employment for the purpose of teachers professing the same language and religious creed with these children of poverty and misfortune . . . , then let that favor be withheld. Such was not the Whigism we derived from our forefathers of the Revolutionary Age nor is such the Whigism that I shall teach to my children.[43]

[43] Seward to Westervelt (March 25, 1840), UR.

It seems quite clear that Seward never expected such an explosion of hostile reaction against his proposal, especially in view of his conversations with Nott and Weed. Apparently, he discussed the content of these conversations with several of his confidants. Since "Mr. Seward did not enjoin silence" in this matter and since one of these friends, George Wardner, regarded the incident "as a curious piece of political history," he repeated the "substance" of Seward's remarks to an interested correspondent years later, in 1856:

Having the approval of the high priest of Presbyterianism [Nott], the Nestor of that Church, one of the oldest, and ablest and wisest and best of protestant divines, I [Seward] had not the least apprehension of exciting religious feeling, or provoking a bigoted resentment; and having also the approval of the shrewdest politician of the day [Weed], I had as little apprehension of a political outbreak. The result showed that I had underrated both the strength of political hatred and the malignity of political malice. If my recommendation had been adopted, it would have cost the State but a few hundred dollars to support, perhaps, a dozen schools. My charitable intentions . . . raised a religious and political hail storm from whose pelting I fancy I shall never escape. All I can say is that I do not believe Dr. Nott meant to counsel me to my hurt, and I am sure I meant no harm to the public.[44]

"It appeared that he [Seward] had underrated the power of nativism in his own party," declares John W. Pratt, "as well as the durability of the Irish-Democratic alliance."[45]

But to say that Seward underestimated the intensity of nativist feeling in the Whig party and misjudged the allegiance of the Irish to the Democratic party is not to say that he was unaware of this religious and political state of affairs. He was much too astute a politician to misread completely the political signs of the time. He recognized—not as perceptively as he might have—the generally hostile or at least unsympathetic attitude of most Americans toward immigrants and Catholics. From a practical point of view, therefore, Seward's educational recommendation was certainly not good politics. A shrewd and ambitious politician, he would not have risked the loss of thousands of Whig supporters in a difficult attempt to woo an indeterminate number of Irish-Catholic voters into the Whig fold. On the contrary, it was precisely because Seward believed— perhaps naively so—that education was much too important an issue to become involved in partisan politics that he could and did offer

44 George Wardner to Alexander G. Johnson (Windsor, Vt., September 5, 1856), UR.
45 Pratt, "Governor Seward," 357.

his proposal. Although he knew that there would be some adverse reaction to it, he did not foresee accurately its vehemence or its persistence. It is quite possible that because Seward was such a good politician, he never attempted publicly or privately to justify his action as sound political strategy.

Although Seward believed that it was inevitable for a person in public life "to be misrepresented by one's opponents and to be misunderstood by one's friends," it is evident that he displayed an unusual sensitivity to criticism and smarted at charges that his recommendation was motivated by political considerations. Nor could he understand the basis for such criticism. He had sought a system of schools that would provide an education for the state's children. His concern was not directed specifically toward Protestant or Catholic children but rather toward the education of all youngsters in order that they might mature into intelligent and responsible citizens of their state and country. With this in mind, Seward declared, "Knowledge taught by any sect is better than ignorance. I desire to see children of Catholics educated as well as those of Protestants, not because I want them to be Catholics but because I want them to become good citizens. In due time, these views will prevail notwithstanding the prejudices that have assailed them.[46] Seward never recognized any valid constitutional objections to his plan, either serious or "trifling." He simply considered the end—universal education—as sufficient to justify his means. Even though political realities eventually forced him to modify his original proposal, he retained a persistent belief in the righteousness of his action. His only purpose in proposing the recommendation had been to make New York State's "system of education as comprehensive as the interests involved, and to provide for the support of the glorious superstructure of universal suffrage—the basis of universal education."[47]

Although Seward viewed himself as educationally and socially in advance of his times, he nursed a deep hurt and bitterness at the adverse reaction accorded to his proposal—especially by his own party. "The school question is a fiery ordeal," a dejected governor wrote to a correspondent in 1841, "which the wisdom and magnanimity of the Whig party require me to pass alone. They can however

46 Seward to William Palmar (Albany, December 17, 1840), UR.
47 Frederick Seward, *Autobiography*, pp. 502-3. Cf. Jacob Harvey to Seward (New York, March 2, 1842), UR.

discover no faltering in my steps and a brief time will suffice to shew that I am unharmed."[48] One of Seward's good friends, Jacob Harvey, an Irish Protestant and Whig, encouraged him in his educational plan and attempted to apply balm to Seward's wound with heroic sentiments:

But what I admire especially, is your fearless advocacy of the Negro, the Indian and the Irishman, at a time when you were to suffer not gain popularity with your own party, and to obtain the abuse of your opponents. Depend upon it, that when you retire from public life to the 'otium cum dignitate,' you will dwell with far more solid pleasure upon the aid which you are now giving to the glorious cause of humanity and justice, than upon the most triumphant political victory you ever gained.[49]

In response to these and other positive sentiments praising "the generous and honorable service" he had "done the state as its governor," Seward replied that these "opinions are all that a public man can carry out of office worth relying upon except the consciousness of having striven to perform his duties with some advantage to his fellow men."[50] By no means an impartial observer, Seward's son, Frederic, perhaps grasped the true spirit of his father's conviction when he wrote that Seward "believed the principle to be right; and not less so because it was unpopular for the moment. He should adhere to it, [and] let. . . [his gubernatorial re-election in 1840] go which way it might."[51]

With Seward's patent encouragement, the leaders of the New York Catholic community wasted little time before petitioning the city's Common Council for a share of the common school fund for

48 Seward to Samuel P. Lyman (Albany, June 7, 1841), UR. Seward was chagrined further by the hostile reaction of the Whig press to his plan. "I found, however, to my surprise, that the proposition encountered unkind reception. A press that should have seconded it, perverted my language and assailed my motives. My surprise was followed by deep mortification when I found that a considerable portion of the press of the political party to which I belonged, adopted the same perversion, and condemned the policy recommended." Frederick Seward, *Autobiography*, pp. 502–3.

49 Jacob Harvey to Seward (New York, April 26, 1841), UR. Hughes was a close friend of this Irish Protestant. "Such a nice man," the bishop conceded, "that I cannot help hoping he will get to heaven some how or another." Hassard, *Life of Hughes*, p. 329.

50 Henry Dana Ward to Seward (New York, June 7, 1842), UR; Seward to Henry Dana Ward (Albany, June 10, 1842), UR.

51 Frederick Seward, *Autobiography*, p. 502.

its schools. This petition quickly precipitated a school crisis that eventually embroiled the city and state in a torrent of religious polemic, political ambivalence, and physical violence. Indeed, "Joshua" Seward had blown his trumpet, and the walls were soon to come tumbling down.

⌐◦ II ◦⌐

The Catholics' Petition

i

While the State Legislature assessed Seward's educational recommendation, Hughes had already left a generous Paris and was entrained for Rome and a private audience with the pope. During the bishop's three-month stay in the Eternal City, the Catholics of New York seized the initiative to act upon Seward's proposal.[1] Although Catholic New York was temporarily devoid of episcopal leadership, diocesan affairs were administered by Hughes's two vicars general, the Reverend John Power and the Reverend Felix Varela. Neither of these clergymen missed the significance of Seward's recommendation, and Power particularly was moved to quick action. He was acquainted with the Catholic hierarchy's position on education because he had represented Dubois at the First Provincial Council of Baltimore in 1829 and had served the Second Council of Baltimore in 1833 as a consulting theologian. Thus, his educational ideas mirrored the developing Catholic position, and his viewpoint was substantially identical with the one Hughes would champion before long. A short time before Hughes returned to New York, Power wrote a lengthy letter to the recently established Catholic weekly, the *New York Freeman's Journal*. Not only did he detail the Catholic philosophy of education but he also sharply attacked the alleged abuses and inadequacies of the city's public

[1] Pratt apparently believes that the Roman Catholic leadership had previously been consulted concerning the governor's message, since he asserts that "the offer was not unexpected." Pratt, "Governor Seward," p. 355. However, the fact that Catholics petitioned for a share of the common school fund simply indicates that they correctly interpreted Seward's message.

schools. These schools, argued the vicar general, were centers of deism and Protestant sectarianism, housed numerous school books which misrepresented Roman Catholicism, and offended Catholic religious sensibilities. He documented his accusations by dwelling upon the role of the Bible in the schools. Each day a scriptural selection was read from the King James Version with no interpretive commentary by the teacher. Here was a demarcating principle which emphasized the essential difference between the Catholic Church and the Protestant sects: "The Catholic church tells her children that they must be taught their religion by AUTHORITY—the Sects say, read the bible, judge for yourselves. The bible is read in the public schools, the children are allowed to judge for themselves. The Protestant principle is therefore acted upon, slyly inculcated, and the schools are Sectarian."[2] As a result, Power concluded that Catholics could not conscientiously send "their children to those schools, in which every artifice is resorted to in order to seduce them from their religion."[3]

While Power was charting a course of action to implement Seward's recommendation, he received a letter in late January from the Reverend Joseph Schneller, who was the pastor of St. Mary's Roman Catholic Church in Albany. A political savant, he numbered among his confidants Seward and several influential members of the State Legislature.[4] Schneller informed Power that his legislative intimates had strongly insinuated that in view of the governor's suggestion, the time was right for Catholics to seek a share of the common school fund. They had assured him that a Catholic petition would find a favorable reception.[5] Upon Power's receipt of this letter, his deliberations promptly materialized into decisive action. He invited the trustees of all the Catholic churches in the city to a meeting to determine a plan of action to achieve this end. Although Schneller's remarks were enthusiastically received by the majority

2 *New York Freeman's Journal*, July 11, 1840.

3 *New York Freeman's Journal*, July 11, 1840.

4 Richard H. Clarke, *Lives of the Deceased Bishops of the Catholic Church in the United States* (New York: Richard H. Clarke, 1888), II, p. 100.

5 Clarke, *Lives of Bishops*, II, p. 100; Lawrence Kehoe (ed.), *Complete Works of the Most Rev. John Hughes, D.D.* (New York: American News Company, 1865), I, p. 41; Hassard, *Life of Hughes*, p. 227; Edward M. Connors, *Church-State Relationships in Education in the State of New York* (Washington, D.C.: Catholic University of America, 1951), p. 17; Edwin R. Van Kleeck, "The Development of Free Common Schools in New York State" (unpublished Ph.D. thesis, New Haven, Yale University, 1937), p. 165.

of the assembled trustees, the older and more skeptical members, long accustomed to few favors from a hostile Protestant majority, questioned the accuracy of these assurances. In order to verify Schneller's conclusions, the trustees advised their vicar general to go to the state capital and there assess the actual situation. Power's quick trip to Albany and encouraging talks with friends of the governor substantiated the Albany pastor's communication. Satisfied with these legislators' "honesty of purpose" and pledge of success, Power returned downstate to report his findings to the trustees.

After a recess of less than two weeks, during which Power and the Catholic leadership determined a number of specific stratagems to be pursued, the trustees reassembled on February 17 at St. Peter's Church on Barclay Street. The purpose of this meeting was to draft a petition seeking a portion of the common school fund and dispatch it to the Common Council of New York City. State law necessitated that this application be submitted to the municipal government. The fifth section of an 1824 statute "relating to the common schools in the city of New York" vested the Common Council with the power and discretion to distribute common school moneys among New York City schools:

The institutions or schools which shall be entitled to receive of said school moneys, shall, from time to time, and at least once in three years, be designated by the Corporation of the City of New York, in common council convened, who shall also have power to prescribe the limitations and restrictions under which said moneys shall be received by said institutions or schools, or any of them.[6]

Brief and to the point, the petition represented the eight Catholic churches in the city—all of which supported free schools.[7] These schools instructed approximately three thousand boys and girls. No

[6] *Laws of New York*, November 19, 1824, ch. 226; Report of the Committee on Arts and Sciences and Schools, on the Petition of the Officers and Members of the Roman Catholic and Other Churches, in the City of New York, for an Apportionment of School Moneys, to the Schools Attached to Said Churches, *Document No. 80, Journal and Documents of the Board of Assistants of the City of New York*, April 27, 1840, pp. 335–55. Henceforth, this report will be referred to as *Document No. 80* and the *Journal and Documents of the Board of Assistants of the City of New York* will be identified as the *Journal and Documents of the Board of Assistants*.

[7] *Document No. 80*, p. 356, Petition of the Trustees of the Several Roman Catholic Churches in the City of New York. The following churches were named in the petition: St. Patrick's Cathedral, St. Peter's Church, St. James' Church, St. Joseph's Church, Transfiguration Church, St. Paul's Church, St. Mary's Church, and St. Nicholas' [German] Church.

fee was collected for attendance at any school, and all expenditures, including teachers' salaries, were assumed by the respective congregations. But financial difficulties had practically exhausted the funds necessary for their continued maintenance. To prevent the closing of these schools, the trustees sought financial relief from the Common Council. Since the trustees denied that any state or city law barred the city government from granting their request, they urged "that your Honorable Body will be pleased to designate your petitioners as entitled to a share of the Common School Fund of this State."[8] Catholic unanimity was emphasized when the trustees decided that each of the eight churches should submit a supportive petition to the Common Council. Although each petition reiterated the collective appeal, that from St. Peter's Church added that since no public school was situated in the westerly section of the city below Barclay Street, the parish school "has at all times been, and now is attended by children whose parents are of other denominations than Catholic . . . who have been cheerfully received and taught without reference to their religious belief."[9] When the Board of Assistant Aldermen, the lower branch of the Common Council, received these Catholic petitions, it referred them to its Committee on Arts and Sciences and Schools for study and subsequent recommendation.[10]

[8] *Document No. 80,* p. 357.

[9] *Document No. 80,* p. 359, Petition of the Members of St. Peter's Roman Catholic Church. This petition was "signed by George Pardow, John Foote, Edmund Derry and Two-Hundred and Seventy-Nine Others." The petition declared that between four and five hundred children attended this school.

[10] *Journal and Documents of the Board of Assistants,* February 17, 1840, p. 182; March 2, 1840, p. 201. Cf. *Proceedings of the Board of Aldermen of the City of New York,* March 2, 1840, p. 320. Henceforth, the *Proceedings of the Board of Aldermen of the City of New York* will be identified as the *Proceedings of the Board of Aldermen,* and the *Documents of the Board of Aldermen of the City of New York* will be referred to as *Documents of the Board of Aldermen.*

The Common Council was the legislative branch of the city government. It was a bicameral body consisting of a Board of Aldermen and a Board of Assistants [Assistant Aldermen]. Each ward of the city elected one alderman and one assistant alderman for a term of one year. The annual election for these officials occurred on the second Tuesday in April, and they were sworn into office on the second Tuesday in May. Each board met in separate chambers, elected its own officers, and kept a journal of its proceedings. Any law, resolution, or ordinance of the Common Council could originate in either board. When one board passed a law, resolution, or ordinance, it could be approved, rejected, or amended by the other. Executive power in the city was vested in a mayor, the heads of departments, and other executive officers. An Act to Amend the Charter of the City of New York, April 7, 1830, *Manual of the Corporation of the City of New York,* 1854, ch. 122, pp. 24–28. The city charter was amended again in 1849.

During March, the Board of Assistant Aldermen received petitions for a share in the common school fund from two other denominational groups in the city—the Scotch Presbyterian Church and the Jewish community.[11] Both petitions employed essentially the same rationale. Although they had not previously intended to seek a *pro rata* share of the common school fund, they would demand a proportional amount for their schools if the Common Council should accede to the Catholic claim. "If your Honorable Body shall determine to grant their [Catholic] request, and thus establish the principle that this fund, though raised by *general tax*, may be appropriated to *church* or *sectarian* schools," reasoned the Scotch Presbyterian Church, "then your memorialists respectfully but earnestly contend, that they are entitled to a rateable portion thereof. . . ."[12] Representing two "Hebrew" congregations, the Jewish petition argued that the basic Catholic argument—mounting financial difficulties—had even more validity in the Jewish case. Both religious groups insisted that they should participate in the school fund, "provided your Honorable Body determine to appropriate it with reference to religious faith."[13] Ostensibly seeking a share of the school money, these memorials obviously did not support the Catholic position. The language of these documents strongly suggests that both religious groups opposed any division of the school fund among denominational schools. Nevertheless, if the Council should act favorably upon the Catholic petition, they wanted to be included in the distribution of funds. Later on, Hughes characterized both petitions as "in fact, prayers against our rights—remonstrances—and should be classed with them. . . . The Committee [on Arts and Sciences and Schools] should not therefore call them petitions, but should class them where they properly belong, with the remonstrances, for as such they were intended to operate." Hughes intimated that these petitioners in effect blackmailed the Common

11 *Document No. 80*, pp. 363–64, Memorial and Petition of the Scotch Presbyterian Church in the City of New York; pp. 364–65, Memorial and Petition of the Hebrew Congregations in the City of New York. Cf. *Journal and Documents of the Board of Assistants*, March 16, 1840, pp. 225, 227.

12 *Document No. 80*, p. 363.

13 *Document No. 80*, p. 365. The president of Congregation Shearith Israel on Crosby Street was M. L. Moses, and Moreland Micholl was the president of Congregation Benai Jeshurim, located on Elm Street. Some authors refer only to the Crosby Street congregation. Cf. Alexander M. Dushkin, *Jewish Education in New York City* (New York: Bureau of Jewish Education, 1918), p. 44; Ellwood P. Cubberley, *Public Education in the United States* (Boston: Houghton Mifflin Company, 1919), p. 178; Lucey, "Efforts," p. 600.

Council "against granting the relief we ask, as, in that event, they will also demand a share." Although the bishop could not quite be sure that such was their "design," he concluded that such was "the effect in point of fact."[14]

Alarmed at the implications of the Catholic position, several of the city's Protestant churches—Methodist Episcopal, Baptist, Presbyterian, and Dutch Reformed—promptly forwarded to the Common Council vigorous dissents from the Catholic position. The Methodist Episcopal Church contended that the state had authorized only public schools to receive school moneys, and any submission to this Catholic claim "would be a perversion of the Public School Fund." Taking its cue from the Scotch Presbyterian Church's position, the Methodist remonstrance warned the Common Council that if it should accede to the Catholic demand, the communicants of this church would have no other course but to "ask and claim that an equitable proportion of said Public School Fund be appropriated to the Methodist Episcopal Church, to enable them to resuscitate their former school, and erect others, to be managed and conducted by them as they, in their discretion, may judge proper."[15] The Baptist church on East Broome Street believed that any division of the school fund would destroy the effectiveness of the highly esteemed public schools. Certainly these schools were "better calculated to promote the education of the rising generation, than it could be done if entrusted to the great diversity of religious sects, into which the people are divided."[16]

[14] Kehoe, *Works of Hughes*, I, pp. 88–89. Some authors have implied that the petitions of the Scotch Presbyterian Church and the Jewish congregations substantiated the Catholic request and were in complete agreement with it. Cf. Lucey, "Efforts," p. 600; James A. Burns and Bernard J. Kohlbrenner, *A History of Catholic Education in the United States* (New York: Benziger Brothers, 1937), p. 158; Burton Confrey, *Secularism in American Education—Its History* (Washington, D.C.: Catholic University of America, 1931), p. 128. Quoting A. Emerson Palmer, *The New York Public School* (New York: Edwin C. Hill Company, 1908), p. 96, Dushkin declares that "the Hebrew Congregation on Crosby Street joined in the [Catholic] petition." Dushkin further asserts that he has "not been able to verify this statement [of Palmer] either in the records of the New York Common Council, or in the Reports of the Board of Education, or in the minutes of the Congregation." *Jewish Education*, p. 45, note 34. If Dushkin had consulted *Document No. 80*, he would have obtained the desired verification.

[15] *Document No. 80*, p. 380, Remonstrance of the Members of the Methodist Episcopal Church. Cf. *Journal and Documents of the Board of Assistants*, March 16, 1840, p. 227.

[16] *Document No. 80*, p. 382, Remonstrance of the "East Broome Street Baptist Church."

The Reformed Dutch and Reformed Presbyterian churches reminded the Common Council that no governmental agency was empowered to grant support or preferential treatment to any religious sect. Because of imagined religious disabilities, the Catholic clergy exhorted their congregations not to send their children to the public schools. Instead, Catholics established their own schools, in which the inculcation of sectarian religious instruction was an integral part of the curriculum. It was for the support of these denominational schools that Catholics were demanding a share of the common school fund. These churches warned that admitting the Catholic contention would be an unwarranted decision, "directly contributing to the support and perpetuation of the faith and practice of a particular religious sect; an act which would be at variance with the whole spirit of our civil institutions."[17] Thus, any favorable action extended to the Catholic petition "could be regarded in no other light than preferring one religious creed to the disparagement and injury of all others."[18] Nor could Catholics invoke justice in their behalf. The common schools were open to all members of the community regardless of creed or social status. If Catholics declined to avail themselves of this right, then they, in fact, voluntarily relinquished their lawful prerogative to a free public education. "Unless they would make sectarian dogmas the ground of civil legislation," the public authorities could not alter the law merely to satisfy peculiar Catholic sensibilities. As long as no disabilities were imposed upon Catholics which prohibited their attendance at common schools, "and so long as their own sectarianism and exclusiveness alone deprive them of the common privilege, we need not ask if their petition is reasonable—if it is just."[19]

Dire consequences were predicted should the Common Council approve the Catholic petition. Confusion among the people, sec-

[17] *Document No. 80,* p. 390, Remonstrance of the Consistory of the Reformed Presbyterian Church.

[18] *Document No. 80,* p. 385, Remonstrance of the Ministers, Elders and Deacons of the Reformed Protestant Dutch Church in the City of New York.

[19] *Document No. 80,* p. 385. Cf. pp. 387–89, Ministers, Elders, and Deacons of the Reformed Dutch Church in Broome Street. Whether the New York State law of 1824 forbade the distribution of public moneys for denominational schools remained a bone of contention between Catholics and their opponents. The remonstrance of the Reformed Presbyterian Church did not appear to be absolutely certain about such a proscription: "Would not the granting of the petitions against which we remonstrate be a virtual, if not a literal, violation of the law for the direction of this matter made and provided?" *Ibid.,* p. 391.

tarian jealousy and strife, and unrestrained competition between denominational school systems were prophesied as ominous results. Many of the city's denominations would most certainly demand their legitimate share of the school fund, "and thus the business of general education would be mainly directed by religious bodies as such." Such a consequence would no doubt sound the death knell of common school education or at least seriously minimize its effectiveness. To preclude these predicted results, both churches urged the Common Council to reject the Catholic request.

The Catholic proposal met its most formidable bastion of resistance in the powerful and highly respected Public School Society. Since the Society was the principal recipient of common school moneys in the city, it was to be expected that its trustees would resist any division of the fund. To no one's surprise, it quickly appointed a committee to draft a sharp reply to the Catholic petition. Although a preliminary rejoinder was hastily written in the latter part of February, the Society submitted on March 2 a more detailed and carefully documented remonstrance to the Common Council.[20]

The trustee's reply focused its attention upon the circumstances which led to the passage of the state law of 1824. It conceded that the prior statute of 1813 had permitted the city's denominational schools to share in the allocation of the school fund. This permissive legislation continued until a controversy arose concerning the Bethel Baptist Church's legitimate use of its portion of the common school fund.[21] Alarmed at this incident, the Society urged the Legislature to remedy such alleged abuse. After carefully investigating all the facts relevant to the case, the State Assembly's Committee on Colleges, Academies, and Common Schools concluded its report with a recommendation that transcended the immediate case in question:

[20] *Minutes of the Free (Public) School Society of the City of New York, 1805–1853* [MSS in the New York Historical Society], Executive Committee, February 20, 1840; Board of Trustees, February 24, 1840. Henceforth, these minutes will be identified as *PSS: Executive Committee* or *PSS: Board of Trustees*. Cf. William O. Bourne, *History of the Public School Society of the City of New York* (New York: Wm. Wood and Company, 1870), pp. 179–86. The Society's preliminary reply was entitled "Remonstrance of the Trustees of the Public School Society," *PSS: Board of Trustees*, February 24, 1840. The second and more complete rejoinder was entitled "Remonstrance of the Public School Society by Their Executive Committee," *PSS: Executive Committee*, March 5, 1850.

[21] For an analysis of the Bethel Baptist Church episode, see Bourne, *History of Public School Society*, pp. 48–75, and Charles J. Mahoney, *The Relation of the State to Religious Education in Early New York, 1633–1825* (Washington, D.C.: Catholic University of America, 1941).

This [common school] fund is considered by your committee purely of a civil character, and therefore it never ought, in their opinion, to pass into the hands of any corporation, or set of men who are not directly amenable to the constituted civil authorities of the government, and bound to report their proceedings to the public. Your committee . . . respectfully submit whether it is not a violation of a fundamental principle of our legislation to allow the funds of the State, raised by a tax on the citizens, and designated for civil purposes, to be subject to the control of any religious corporation.[22]

The substance of the Committee's conclusion was consequently incorporated into the statute of 1824, which nullified the act of 1813 and conferred upon the Common Council of New York City the right to designate which "societies and schools" would participate in the common school fund. The Common Council followed the direction of the Legislature, insisted the trustees, and concluded "that the common school fund should be distributed for civil purposes only as contradistinguished from those of a religious or sectarian description."[23] Thus, from 1824 all denominational schools were excluded from any further participation in the common school fund, and the Common Council adopted "the great principle of non-sectarianism . . . as the basis for subsequent appropriations from this fund."[24] Henceforth, the common school fund was to be used exclusively for the benefit and support of common school education. Only those schools were classified as common which were available to children of every religion and class and conducted in such a manner that no one could reasonably object. But such was not the case with the Catholic schools. The inculcation of Catholic doctrine was an essential and indispensable part of their instruction. As a result, the Society's remonstrance reasoned that "all unbelievers in Catholic doctrines are unwilling, and may with good reason object, to send their children to such schools."[25] Indeed, the letter as well as the spirit of American constitutional principles condemned any effort whereby the general community "should be taxed to support an establishment in which sectarian dogmas are inculcated whether that establishment be a school or church."[26]

Apart from legal grounds, the Society believed that practical con-

22 *PSS: Executive Committee*, March 5, 1840.
23 *PSS: Executive Committee*, March 5, 1840.
24 *PSS: Board of Trustees*, February 24, 1840.
25 *PSS: Board of Trustees*, February 24, 1840.
26 *PSS: Board of Trustees*, February 24, 1840.

siderations alone sufficed to deny the Catholic petition. Not only were the Society's schools open to all children without any form of social or religious discrimination but they were flourishing and annually increasing in number and quality. As a result of a rapidly increasing student body, the Society had sometime before concluded that the proceeds from the common school fund were inadequate to maintain the high-level quality of its schools. Therefore, the trustees had urged the "largest tax-paying citizens" to petition the Common Council to assess them an additional property tax to be used for "free and common education." This memorial was favorably acted upon, and a tax of one-eightieth of one per cent was imposed upon the city's residents. This additional sum accounted for more than three-fifths of the entire sum of school money for the city. And yet, estimated the trustees, even this increased income did not completely cover the financial needs of the public schools. If denominational schools were allowed to participate in the school fund, a large part of the Society's needed revenue would be frittered away upon the fragmented educational efforts of the various sects and the cause of general education would receive a mortal wound. Not only would these sectarian schools be too numerous and diversified for adequate governmental supervision, but the emphasis which would be given to the inculcation of specific creeds and dogmas would no doubt result in widespread neglect of their pupils' secular education.

Catholics boasted that their schools were open to all students without regard to religious persuasion. Yet this very assertion, the remonstrance contended, further strengthened the Society's rejection of the Catholic petition. For if the Catholic request were heeded, Catholic schools would enjoy an unheralded opportunity to proselytize at public expense by exerting a subtle and insidious influence upon the unformed and susceptible minds of Protestant children. The Society further argued that the Catholic clergy had rejected its schools not because positive religious doctrines were taught, but precisely because the peculiar tenets of the Church of Rome were not taught in these schools. Catholics were seeking a portion of the common school fund, concluded this lengthy remonstrance, so that their schools might effect a fusion of sectarianism and secular learning. Therefore, the Common Council was urged not to accede to the Catholic petition. Indeed, unless the Council were prepared to reject the Catholic application, the Society would request a hearing before the City Council to justify its position.

At the conclusion of this remonstrance, the trustees attached an extract from a meeting of the Commissioners of School Money.[27] The Society had previously communicated with these school officers concerning the dangers inherent in the Catholic petition. The commissioners sustained the Society's contention that the Catholic petition was both unconstitutional and inexpedient. In fact, they unanimously resolved that "schools created and directed by any particular religious society should derive no aid from a fund designed for the common benefit of all the youth of this city, without religious distinction or preference."[28] A copy of this resolution was forwarded to the trustees of the Society "with permission to make such use of it, sustaining the common school system unfettered by sectarian connections, as in their opinion, may best promote that object."[29]

In addition to the remonstrances of the Public School Society and the various Protestant churches, a number of private citizens' groups likewise recommended the defeat of the Catholic proposal. These four remonstrances added nothing new to the argument, since they merely repeated the basic theses advanced by the other plaintiffs.[30]

All of these remonstrances unequivocally repudiated the constitutionality and legality, expediency and practicality of the Catholic petition. Practically speaking, even the Scotch Presbyterian and Jewish petitions sustained the remonstrances' rejection of the Catholic claim. And yet, when the Catholic petitions are collectively analyzed, it is apparent that the Catholic leadership did not put forth any telling arguments to substantiate its position. A deteriorating financial situation was the single argument used by the Catholic

27 *PSS: Executive Committee*, March 5, 1840. There were seventeen Commissioners of School Money who were appointed by the Common Council. Their duty was to visit all schools in the city that participated in the common school fund and report their condition to the Common Council as well as to the state secretary of state, who was ex officio superintendent of common schools.

28 *PSS: Executive Committee*, March 5, 1840.

29 *PSS: Executive Committee*, March 5, 1840. Samuel Gilford, Jr., the chairman, and M. B. Edgar, secretary, signed this copy in behalf of all the commissioners.

30 Remonstrance of Lockwood Smith and Two Hundred and Nine Other Citizens, *Journal and Documents of the Board of Assistants*, March 16, 1840, p. 227; Remonstrance of William Holmes and Sixty-One Other Citizens, *ibid.*; Remonstrance of Gilbert Coutant and Six Hundred and Ninety-Seven Others, *ibid.*; Remonstrance of S. Devereaux and Others, *ibid.*, March 30, 1840, p. 360. Although the assistant aldermen's *Journal* recorded all four of these remonstrances, *Document No. 80* includes only the remonstrances of Lockwood Smith and William Holmes, pp. 381, 383.

trustees in their request for financial relief. They maintained that there were no legal proscriptions barring the Common Council from granting their request. Catholics were seeking a solution to a financial problem "as by law, and in the judgment of your Honorable Body, they may be entitled to, on complying with the requirements of the Statutes of this State, and the Ordinances of your Body."[31] None of their later complaints against the public schools—the lack of positive religious teaching, the reading of the Protestant Bible without note or comment, the use of sectarian prayers and hymns, the presence of objectionable school books—were mentioned in these petitions. Even their appeal to the inviolability of conscience and the rights of citizenship appears to be almost deliberately omitted. Why?

Power, it should be remembered, had returned from Albany with glowing reports about the feasibility of Catholics receiving financial aid for their schools. State politicians, undoubtedly including several from the city, had intimated that the time was opportune for the approval of a Catholic request for funds. Therefore, sound strategy combined with a knowledge of human nature surely must have dictated that a straightfoward, inoffensive, and condescending petition should be sent to the Common Council. The Catholic position would not have been strengthened had its petition included disparaging remarks concerning principles and practices in the city's common schools—especially since the Public School Society

[31] *Document No. 80*, p. 357, Petition of the Trustees of the Several Roman Catholic Churches in the City of New York. The trustees of St. Mary's Church and the Public School Society sent their pleas to the Board of Aldermen as well as to the assistant aldermen. These documents were subsequently withdrawn in order to present them to the Board of Assistants, which was considering the subject. Cf. *Proceedings of the Board of Aldermen*, March 2, 1840, p. 320. In other parts of the state, the governor's message was also understood to favor public funds for denominational schools. The State Senate received petitions from the town of Oswegatchie and from Oswego "praying for an act to carry into effect the recommendation of the governor for establishing schools for educating foreigners' children . . . with teachers of their own religious faith." *Journal of the Senate of the State of New York*, March 3, 1840, p. 218, and March 7, 1840, p. 229. Of course, counter-remonstrances were sent to the same body (April 13, 1840, p. 380). Henceforth, the *Journal of the Senate*, and the *Documents of the Senate of the State of New York* will be identified as *Documents of the Senate*. The State Assembly also received similar petitions and remonstrances during this period. Cf. *Journal of the Assembly of the State of New York*, April 11, 1840, p. 913. The petition for distribution of the school fund among the different religious denominations came from Oneida County while citizens from Erie remonstrated against it. Henceforth, the *Journal of the Assembly of the State of New York* will be identified as the *Journal of the Assembly*, and the *Documents of the Assembly of the State of New York* will be identified as *Documents of the Assembly*.

was so highly esteemed by the vast majority of New Yorkers. Furthermore, since every member of the Common Council was an ex officio trustee of the Society, Catholics would certainly have dimmed their prospect of success had they publicly criticized the Society and the city's educational system. Trusting in large measure the reports from Albany, the Catholic leadership no doubt elected to draft a simple and factual request devoid of any controversial material. The petitioners concentrated upon their future needs and enumerated the difficulties that were being encountered by the struggling Catholic schools. Nor was any allusion made to Seward's recommendation, which had served as a catalyst for the Catholic petition. Finally, it is quite possible that Catholic strategists had not foreseen the almost universal rejection of their request by a majority of New York City's churches, a militant and formidable Public School Society, and several public-spirited groups.

ii

Early spring of 1840 witnessed a rise of discord within Catholic ranks which seriously impaired their unity and hindered the effectiveness of the Catholic movement in this initial stage of the school dispute. Two Catholic papers in New York engaged in a journalistic controversy which publicly voiced Catholic dissatisfaction with the public schools and allowed the entry of partisan politics into the picture. The *Truth Teller*, a Democratic Catholic weekly edited by the layman William Denman, expressed strong opposition to the Whig governor's educational proposal. The paper believed that the common school should impart secular knowledge and moral training, while the church and the home should instruct children in their respective religious creeds. Brandishing a somewhat adolescent nationalism, this Irish-American journal vigorously objected to the use of any language but English in the public schools. Instruction imparted in foreign languages merely served as a ruse to foster European traditions and distinctions that were alien to a free and democratic society.[32]

Although the *Catholic Register*, an "exclusively" religious Catholic weekly founded by Varela in 1839, supported Denman's resistance to foreign languages in the public schools, it chided the *Truth Teller*'s championing of the city's schools. Varela enumerated Cath-

---

[32] *New York Truth Teller,* February 15, 1840.

olic dissatisfaction with these schools: Catholic children had to read the Protestant Bible without note or comment or with "heretical" interpretations; anti-Catholic books filled many shelves of the public schools; and teachers often humiliated Catholic children by insulting their religious beliefs and ethnic background. As a result of this unsatisfactory situation, Catholics were obliged to avoid attendance at these schools. Because Varela believed that Catholic schools were an integral part of the state's common school system and so designated them as "Catholic Public Schools," he editorialized that approval of the Catholic petition would foster the cause of education in New York City.[33] Catholic children who did not attend the public schools would thus be able to receive an education in schools which no longer posed a threat to their religious principles. Public support of Catholic schools would involve no preferential treatment, since all denominations would enjoy the same prerogative. The *Register* concluded by enunciating a principle which would henceforth become a rallying cry for the Catholic school position:

We are of the opinion that our government should spread education without forcing the professors of any religion to act against their conscience, or to decline the benefit offered them, if we can call it a benefit, at least gratuitous, what is abundantly paid for by those who receive it. True liberality and real tolerance would be shown by obtaining the object which is the education, without interfering with any body's principles of religion, but at present it is not the case in regard to Catholics.[34]

The *Truth Teller* denied any opposition to the justice of the Catholic claim. Although its editor had long editorialized in behalf of public funds for Catholic schools, he maintained that Seward's recommendation was a step in the direction of a union of church and state.[35] On the other hand, Varela countered that if Denman supported the Catholic viewpoint, then, *ipso facto*, he had to support the governor's plan.[36]

33 *New York Catholic Register*, February 20, 1840.
34 *New York Catholic Register*, February 20, 1840.
35 *New York Truth Teller*, February 22, 1840.
36 *New York Catholic Register*, March 5, 1840. Varela agreed with Denman's viewpoint concerning school instruction in foreign languages. He considered this particular recommendation an insignificant part of Seward's program. As the school dispute progressed, the question of language was ignored by both sides and, in fact, the governor eliminated all mention of it in his annual message in 1841.

While the columns of both Catholic papers fumed with charge and counter-charge, it was almost inevitable that partisan politics should enter into the picture. Some of the local politicians of both parties—especially Democratic strategists—attempted to subvert this Catholic effort for their own political ends. They apparently succeeded in transforming some of the Catholic school meetings into boisterous and rowdy political rallies. Hassard has succinctly and vividly described the chaos that slowly enveloped Catholic efforts to press for their request:

The meetings were characterized by intemperate language, and disorder almost amounting to violence. The people most interested in the movement—that is, the poorer class of Catholics—were fast becoming the dupes . . . of those 'political underlings who had been accustomed to traffic in their simplicity.' The respectable priests who, from motives of pure charity and patriotism, had inaugurated the movement, were being shoved aside by ambitious and unprincipled partisans. Not only the success of their effort to obtain justice, but the good name of the Catholic body, was imperilled by these noisy assemblies.[37]

City Whigs were not to be outdone. On Sunday, April 12—just three days before the April municipal elections—Whig enthusiasts distributed copies of Seward's speech to the Hibernian Society at Albany to the congregation of St. Peter's Church. Four days later, the trustees of the church published a denial of any complicity in this action and expressed regret that a house of worship should have been profaned by political electioneering. The *Truth Teller* could not resist branding the Whigs as sacrilegious defilers of a house of God in order to gain political advantage. A week later the paper continued its broadside against this Whig attempt "to thrust Federalism down the throats of Irish Catholics as if it were a gilded pill."[38] Even a mediating visit by Schneller to the city could not mend the serious breach in Catholic unanimity. The intrusion of political partisanship and journalistic discord forged an excellent weapon for the opposition. Varela vainly tried to minimize the importance of this internal dissension by observing "that the members of the Catholic Church have proved by their conduct that Catholicity is independent from every party, and Catholics are such as always form one undivisible body whatever may be their division as to

---

37 Hassard, *Life of Hughes*, p. 228.
38 *New York Truth Teller*, April 18 and 25, 1840.

politics."[39] At a time when Catholics desperately needed Power's leadership and guidance, his name was infrequently mentioned in the Catholic press. No doubt his absence and silence were due to the serious illness which incapacitated him over a month and a half during this very crucial period.[40]

iii

While this vitiating rupture made the Catholic camp a house divided against itself, the Common Council had carefully been studying the Catholic petition and countering remonstrances. The Board of Assistant Aldermen's three-man Committee on Arts and Sciences and Schools, responsible for making a recommendation on this question, thoroughly understood the magnitude of the question as well as its controversial repercussions. In order to help clarify some of the knotty questions, the committee held an open hearing on March 12 and invited apologists from both sides to present their points of view. A Catholic delegation and a group of trustees from the Public School Society appeared before the committee. The Catholic representatives stated their objections to the city's public schools and cited their reasons for requesting a share of the common school fund. Although they acknowledged that Catholic doctrine was an integral part of their schools' curriculum, they agreed to limit this religious instruction to after-school hours should the Common Council grant their request. The Society denied the Catholic allegations and reiterated its position that any appropriation of school money for the support of sectarian education was contrary to the purpose of the school fund, hostile to the spirit of the Constitution, and contradicted the principles of free republican government.

Six weeks after this one-day hearing, on April 27, the three-man committee reported its findings to the board. After the committee summarized the protagonists' points of view, it declared that its conclusions were predicated upon the solution of two interrelated questions:

FIRST: Have the Common Council of this city, under the existing laws relative to common schools in the city of New York, a legal right to ap-

39 *New York Catholic Register*, May 28, 1840.
40 *New York Truth Teller*, April 18, 1840.

propriate any portion of the School Fund to religious corporations? SECOND: Would the exercise of such power be in accordance with the spirit of the Constitution and the nature of our Government?[41]

All factions agreed that the Common Council possessed the legal authority to designate the "institutions and schools" which would be permitted to share in the distribution of the common school fund. But which associations belonged under the designation of "institutions and schools?" The committee addressed itself to these questions.

In 1813 the State Legislature passed an act relative to common school education in New York City. This statute enjoined the city Commissioners of School Moneys to distribute school funds to the Free [Public] School Society, a number of other philanthropic institutions, and "such incorporated religious societies in said city, as now support or hereafter shall establish, Charity Schools within the said city, who may apply for the same."[42] The committee emphasized that "incorporated religious societies" were expressly designated as legal recipients of the public treasury. Thus, under this 1813 legislation denominational education benefitted from the assets of the school fund. But in 1824, as a result of the Bethel Baptist Church controversy, the Legislature repealed the 1813 statute and substituted "An act relating to common schools in the City of New York" which delegated sole authority to the Common Council to determine future recipients of the common school fund:

The Institutions or Schools which shall be entitled to receive of said School Moneys, shall from time to time, and at least once in three years, be designated by the Corporation of the City of New York, in Common Council convened, who shall also have power to prescribe the limitations and restrictions under which said moneys shall be received by said institutions or schools, or any of them.[43]

Thus, in 1824 the legislative power to designate beneficiaries which were entitled to receive school funds was transferred to the Common Council. But did the Council have unlimited discretion in this matter or was it restrained by specific legal limitations? Although the law of 1813 had specified "incorporated religious societies" as recipients of school money, it was superseded by the re-

41 *Document No. 80*, pp. 338–39.
42 *Document No. 80*, p. 341.
43 *Document No. 80*, p. 342.

voking legislation of 1824, which directed that only "institutions
or schools receive funds. There was "something peculiar in the
language of the repealing act of 1824" which fully satisfied the
three-man committee "that the Legislature intended, ever after, to
exclude Religious Corporations from the reception of the School
Monies."[44] These three assistant aldermen reasoned that if the
Legislature in 1824 had intended to include "incorporated religious
societies" in the distribution of common school funds, it would have
employed identical or similar language to that used in the act of
1813. Since the later statute had abrogated the earlier act *in toto*,
the aldermen's report argued that the Legislature had nullified that
law "with the full intention that religious societies, as such, should
no longer receive any portion of the School Money from the Public
Treasury, even for the purpose of supporting Common Schools."
The committee asserted that its opinion was "confirmed by the
almost universal opinion of the People of this City, from 1824 to the
present time."[45]

Once it had reasoned the Board of Assistant Aldermen through
these legal and verbal subtleties, the committee weakened its position in discussing the jurisdiction of the Common Council. It admitted that the Council's authority to designate recipients of common
school funds was limited. Although the aldermen had previously
concluded that the city government could not legally include "incorporated religious societies" in its distribution of school moneys,
they acknowledged that such a legal prohibition was "not reduced
to the form of a positive legal enactment." They personally believed
that this proscription was so intended by the act of 1824 and so
interpreted "to the present time." But since the law did not specifically prohibit such a possibility, the Common Council's "power to
apportion the fund among societies of that character [religious] is
at least very questionable." Nevertheless, the committee cautioned
the Council "that a prudent regard for the obligations of duty
should prevent the exercise of so doubtful a power in any case whatever."[46]

The second part of this report sought to determine whether favorable action on the Catholic petition contradicted the legal requirements and intentions of both the state and national constitu-

44 *Document No. 80*, p. 343.
45 *Document No. 80*, p. 344.
46 *Document No. 80*, p. 344.

tions. In agreement with the federal constitution, the New York constitution guaranteed every citizen the "free exercise and enjoyment of religious profession and worship, without discrimination or preference. . . ."[47] Both constitutions explicitly prohibited a legal establishment of religion as well as a union of church and state: both affirmed universal freedom of conscience and worship; and both implicitly reasoned that the proceeds from public taxation should not benefit any denomination or religious organization. In the case before the committee, the Catholic petitioners solicited public support for schools which were established, controlled, and administered by a religious corporation. Teachers were chosen and syllabi prescribed by the trustees of this private religious society. Administrative directives decreed the Catholic catechism as the manual to be employed in teaching religious instruction. To this extent, therefore, the committee believed that the petitioners' schools were "incorporated religious societies."

A more perceptive analysis of the relationship of the Catholic request to constitutional provisions necessitated a knowledge of the financial sources which comprised the common school fund. Three sources funneled money into this fund: the proceeds from the sale of state lands; the interest accruing from the United States Deposit Fund; and a special annual taxation of one-eightieth of one per cent requested by New Yorkers themselves. Now the Catholic petitioners argued that they were taxpayers who annually contributed a ratable sum to the school fund, and were on that account entitled to a *pro rata* share of the fund. It was in answer to this fundamental and recurring argument that the aldermen presented a lengthy and precise rebuttal that is sophisticated and remarkably contemporary in its analysis. Conceding that Catholics did contribute to the state's general tax assessment, the committee argued that Catholics

. . . are taxed not as members of the Roman Catholic Church, but as citizens of the State of New York; and not for the purposes of religion, but for the support of civil government. . . . Admit the correctness of the [Catholic] claim, that the Common Council of the City, or the Legislature of the State, may rightfully appropriate the Public Money to the purposes of religious instruction of any kind, in any school, and the consequence will be, that the People may be taxed by law, for the

47 *Document No. 80*, p. 346.

support of some one or other of our numerous religious denominations. . . . By granting a portion of the School Fund to one sect, to the
exclusion of others, a 'preference' is at once created, a 'discrimination'
is made, and the object of this great Constitutional guarantee is defeated. . . .[48]

Would constitutional difficulties be removed by allowing all
religious denominations to participate in the revenues of the common school fund? The committee was quite sure that the Catholic
petitioners would readily agree to such a solution. But the aldermen
rejected the argument that no preference meant no establishment:

An extension to all other denominations of the bounty asked for by the
petitioners, would be not only impracticable—but would be, equally . . .
repugnant to the principles of our Government. If the doctrines of all
the religious denominations in the state, were taught, in the slightest
degree, at the expense of the people, under the authority of law, there
would still be a legal religious establishment, not confined to one or a
few sects, it is true, but covering many. Taxes, under such a system, would
still be raised for religious purposes; and those who professed no religion, or belonged to no sect, would be taxed for the benefit of those
who did. It is immaterial, in the eye of the law, whether a citizen pro-
fesses any or no religious faith; he is still a citizen, and as such, is entitled
to the free enjoyment of whatever opinions he may entertain: and there
is no difference, in legal principle, between taxing him for the purpose
of educating the young in the doctrines of many churches, to which he
does not belong, and taxing the Catholic for the benefit of Protestant
schools, or taxing the Protestant for the support of Catholic Seminaries.
The rights of conscience are the same, in the one case as in the other; and
the cases are identical in principle, although, in the one instance, but
few may deem themselves injured, and in the other, thousands may
complain of the violation of their rights, as free citizens. No government
can rightfully deprive any, the humblest being, of the rights which he
may derive from nature as a man, or of those which he possesses as a
citizen, under the Constitution of his country.[49]

Not only did constitutional principles proscribe one denomination from receiving public funds, but this prohibition included all
denominations and all religious groups. The state maintained a
strict neutrality with regard to religion or irreligion, and no group
could legally be taxed to support the religious education of any

[48] *Document No. 80,* pp. 349–52.
[49] *Document No. 80,* pp. 349–52.

association—Protestant, Catholic, or "nothingarian." The committee insisted that the same constitutional principles would be violated whether public moneys were distributed to one sect exclusively or to all sects equally. Thus, the principles of "single-establishment" and "multi-establishment" were both denied any constitutional validity by the aldermen.

After briefly restating the more cogent arguments of the Public School Society and the other remonstrances, the committee concluded its report by recommending that the Board of Assistant Aldermen reject the Catholic petition (as well as the other two petitions) for a share in the common school fund. Catholics simply did not possess a valid claim for a participation in the school fund in their capacity as an "incorporated religious society." In addition, "religious instruction is no part of a common school education." This recommendation was promptly approved, with only one vote cast in dissent.[50]

Newspaper reaction to the school question and the board's verdict was rather limited when compared with future journalistic response. But two newspapers did comment briefly upon the assistant aldermen's decision. The *New York Observer*, a vehemently anti-Catholic religious weekly, quite expectably praised the board's decision, which it incorrectly thought was "by an unanimous vote." Nevertheless, it warned its readers not to relax their vigilance against any renewed Catholic prosecution of this proposal, "lest in some unsuspecting hour their jesuitical wiles should prove successful and their political ascendency be secured."[51] Since the majority of the city's Roman Catholics were loyal sons of Jefferson and Jackson, the Democratic *Evening Post* could ill afford to alienate them by its editorial comments. Simple narrative had to suffice in place of praise.

---

[50] *Journal and Documents of the Board of Assistants*, April 27, 1840, p. 402. The vote was sixteen to one. O'Neil voted negatively, while the following voted affirmatively: Balis, Deming, Potter, West, Anderson, Conner, Vandervoort, Campbell, Howe, Dodge, the president (Nathaniel Jarvis, Jr.), Timpson, Spader, Graham, Potter, and Lee. On the motion of Graham, 2,000 copies of this report were ordered to be printed with the accompanying petitions and remonstrances.

[51] *New York Observer*, May 2, 1840. Subsequent to this decision, both contemporary accounts and historians have maintained that the assistant aldermen adopted the committee's report unanimously. But the official proceedings of the Board clearly state that O'Neil voted against the adoption of the report: "The ayes and nayes being called on Mr. Graham's motion, the Report was adopted by the following vote, and the Committee was discharged. Affirmative—16; Negative—1 [O'Neil]." *Journal and Documents of the Board of Assistants*, April 27, 1840, p. 402.

However, the paper did congratulate the Committee of Aldermen for presenting such "an able report on the subject," and thought its analytical disposition of the constitutional question quite "conclusive."[52] Earlier during the year the *Post* had editorialized that if the city's public schools could not satisfactorily embrace children of all denominations, then perhaps the whole system of common school education should be destroyed. And yet, warned the paper, such would be the practical result if the common school fund were divided among the different denominations "to be expended by them in such plans of education as shall promote or diffuse their peculiar views."[53]

When Hughes returned from his European trip, he paid his respects to the aldermen's report. With regard to the committee's distinction between "incorporated religious societies" and "institutions or schools" of the nullifying act of 1824, the bishop remarked that he would not quibble over such subtle nuances. "If they [the Board of Assistant Aldermen] will deny it to us as a 'Society,' " declared Hughes, "they are still authorized to grant a share of the public fund to 'Institutions or Schools,' and Catholic schools can certainly, equally with others, be embraced under one of those terms." He expressed utter contempt for the committee's contention that Catholics were not taxed as members of a church but as citizens of the state. "That is," Hughes chided, "we are citizens when they come to us to gather the taxes, but we are Roman Catholics when we look for a share of the fund thus contributed." Catholics did not demand public funds as Catholics to support their religion, but only in their civil capacity as citizens to support their schools. On the contrary, "we would be amongst the very first to resist such an application of those moneys."[54] As citizens, Catholics desired school funds to support schools in which religious instruction would occur only after school hours. Thus, public moneys would not be used to promulgate specific sectarian doctrines. Hughes branded the whole report as a deliberate attempt to cloud the real issue with worn-out clichés and half-truths, and thus dismiss the Catholic petitioners. He could not permit this nor would he.

52 *New York Evening Post*, May 12, 1840.
53 *New York Evening Post*, February 29, 1840.
54 Kehoe, *Works of Hughes*, I, p. 87.

⌒⌐(III)⌐⌐

The Bishop Assumes Command

1

After disembarking from the *British Queen* on July 18, 1840, Hughes quickly immersed himself in diocesan affairs, particularly the deepening school controversy. He had been away from his diocese just over nine months, which was longer than he had intended, "but not longer than has been essential for the purpose of my journey."[1] During his travels in Europe, he had received copies of Varela's *Catholic Register*, which kept him abreast of diocesan affairs. Thus, he had some knowledge of the checkered Catholic movement of the preceding six months. But as late as June 1, just one month before he departed for New York, his letters indicate that his principal educational interest still focused on the progress of St. John's College and Seminary. Although Hughes expressed keen disappointment that this project had been delayed, he was sure that the delay was due "to causes different from any want of zeal on the part of the Catholics of the city and diocese." But he was not discouraged. St. John's would soon open its doors, especially since "I have been as successful in the object of my visit to Europe as I could have anticipated."[2] Now, however, the bishop was home and ready to resume the episcopal reins of Catholic New York.

Even before Hughes's arrival, the Catholic leadership had scheduled a meeting to be held in the schoolhouse connected to St. Patrick's Cathedral on July 20—just two days after his return. Hughes was very anxious to attend the meeting, at which Power was president, and a prominent layman, Dr. Hugh Sweeney, chairman. At

1 Hughes to Varela (Dublin, June 1, 1840), cited in Hassard, *Life of Hughes*, p. 221.
2 Hassard, *Life of Hughes*, p. 221.

Hughes's suggestion, both men summarized the origin and progress of the Catholic movement.[3] In his address to the meeting, Hughes denounced the intrusion of partisan politics in the Catholic struggle for school aid and warned that he would allow neither political considerations nor political factions to hinder the prosecution of this cause. Hassard has wryly observed that although the vast majority of the bishop's audience enthusiastically endorsed these remarks, "we can imagine that there were others who listened to him with less satisfaction."[4] Although he was not as yet familiar with all the facts in the case, consultations with his clergy convinced him that attendance at the public schools constituted a proximate danger to the religious faith of Catholic children. He resolved this crisis into the following alternatives: Catholics should either submit to this unpalatable situation, or they should attempt to change it with every legitimate means at their disposal. But if Catholics concurred with his conviction concerning the evil effects of the city's public schools, as surely they must, then they could not in good conscience permit their children to attend these schools. Their only alternative, as he saw it, was to petition the Common Council anew to remedy such injustice. After delivering these remarks, Hughes returned to his seat as the audience stamped its seal of approval upon his spirited suggestions with heavy applause.

The moment Hughes concluded his speech, the Catholic movement assumed a new and revivifying spirit which quickly dissolved all former dissension and discouragement. Hughes's effervescent personality and indefatigable energy took hold of the Catholic school effort and imbued it with confidence and direction. No longer could any doubt be raised as to the leadership of the Catholic forces. Leadership had been not too subtly wrested from the Catholic laity and its clerical advisors. There is certainly no doubt that journalistic discord, political intrigue, and previous failure before the Common Council influenced the bishop's peremptory assumption of command. Writing to the Leopoldine Society in

---

[3] Kehoe, *Works of Hughes*, I, p. 42. In his introductory remarks, Kehoe refers only to Power's speech. But when the bishop rose to speak, he thanked both Power and Sweeney for their explanatory remarks. It is certain that Hughes conferred with some of his clergy during the weekend of his return (*ibid.*, p. 45). Although Power and Varela were not mentioned by name, it is reasonable to suppose that the bishop would confer with his two administrative assistants who had exercised diocesan jurisdiction during his absence.

[4] Hassard, *Life of Hughes*, p. 229.

Vienna, he reasoned that only his episcopal authority could eliminate dissension within the Catholic ranks: "Immediately after my
return from Europe I thought it advisable to take up this [school]
problem because several meetings for the purpose of discussing the
subject publicly had been arranged and there was a division of
opinion among Catholics. I have however, succeeded in uniting
them."[5] Although Power and Varela attended subsequent meetings
which continued to be chaired by prominent laymen, it is clear
that Catholic strategy and decision-making became the prerogative
of the bishop of New York. Implementation of episcopal policy
often was delegated to interested and competent laymen. But public, official responsibility and direction of the Catholic school claim
remained with Hughes alone.

Although the bishop had not expected the school issue to erupt
during his absence from New York, it was a topic that had long been
on his mind. Burns asserts that Hughes would have preferred not
to engage in the controversy. It was only because he realized the
extent of the Catholic commitment to this cause that Hughes concluded that it was too late to retreat, argues Burns, "and with char-
acteristic resolution and energy he at once threw himself into the
fight and assumed the leadership of the Catholic forces."[6] Yet,
Hughes had declared from the outset that whether or not the school
question had come up before his return, it had always been his
intention to draw Catholic attention to it. In fact, had not Catholics
previously banded together, he would not have been home three
weeks before he would have organized his flock into action, for the
school question had been a thorn in his episcopal side even before
his departure for Europe.[7] But since he had to determine his juris-
dictional relationship with Dubois while simultaneously attending
to other diocesan problems, he had never found time to devote his
complete attention to the issue. Circumstances during his absence
had merely precipitated the inevitable. Hughes had not initiated the
agitation, but he adopted the movement and adapted its prosecution
according to the needs and alleged rights of his people.

Hughes's assumption of leadership resulted in a well organized
series of bi-weekly meetings in the basement of St. James' Church on

5 Report of Bishop John Hughes of Basileopolis (New York, 1842), pp. 75–82, NYAA.
6 James A. Burns, *The Catholic School System in the United States* (New York:
Benziger Brothers, 1908), p. 364.
7 Kehoe, *Works of Hughes*, I, p. 42.

James Street "in order to reach a fundamental and matured decision" and then implement the decision.[8] During late summer and early autumn, he addressed numerous protest meetings of Catholics at which he denounced the city's public schools and asserted the right of Catholics to share in the common school fund.[9] These gatherings provided Hughes with a forum to present the Catholic viewpoint concerning the religious and moral as well as the legal and political aspects of the school question. He had quickly concluded that the first Catholic petition had been neither adequately explained nor capably prosecuted. Thus, Hughes attributed the first Catholic failure to the fact that the public did not really understand the Catholic position. Nor would they until Catholics ably demonstrated the rationale of their claim. He conceded that he was acting as a publicist for the Catholic position for "I published my views in the public newspapers and I called attention to the injustice which we would otherwise suffer."[10]

Although the Public School Society's trustees claimed that its schools were free from sectarianism, Hughes argued that, even more dangerously, deism remained in the public schools to challenge the religious faith of Catholic children; for the exclusion of sectarianism meant the concurrent exclusion of Christianity and their replacement by deistic rationalism. According to Hughes, there could be no Christianity without sectarianism, for if Roman Catholicism, Methodism, Episcopalianism, Presbyterianism, Lutheranism, *et al.* were removed from the schools, then Christianity would cease to exist in them. Sectarianism and Christianity were one and the same; the one could not exist without the other. In Hughes's mind, no other alternative was possible. He wondered how the Society could exclude Christianity from the schools of a country which prided itself upon its Christian heritage. Even the Society's incorporating charter

8 In his report to the Leopoldine Society, Hughes erroneously stated that "meetings were held twice a week in St. James' Church." Apparently, St. Patrick's schoolhouse was too small to hold the large number of Catholics who attended these meetings, and the large basement of St. James' Church was then chosen as the new meeting center. All subsequent meetings of Catholics under the direction and guidance of Hughes were held there for the rest of the year. Cf. Bourne, *History of Public School Society*, p. 187.

9 During this four-month period, Hughes held eight meetings: July 20, 27; August 10, 24; September 7, 21; October 5, 19.

10 Report of Bishop John Hughes of Basileopolis (New York, 1842), pp. 75–82, NYAA.

emphasized that one of its primary duties was to instruct students in "the principles of religion and morality."

The bishop went beyond what he called the theoretical exclusion of sectarianism in the public schools. He insisted that in practice these schools were permeated with a plethora of sectarian practices and reading matter. Protestant prayers were offered and Protestant hymns sung; the Protestant version of the Scriptures was employed in all the schools; the reading of the Bible without note or comment fostered the Protestant doctrine of private interpretation of Holy Writ; and school and library books were replete with panegyrics of Protestant heroes and denunciations of Catholic personages. It was inevitable that Hughes concluded that the city's public schools were propped upon a deistic and infidel base and had a sectarian and Protestant implementation. Indeed, he did not believe he violated the canons of logic when he simultaneously denounced the public schools as centers of Protestantism and of deism. Such a combination repulsed the religious sensibilities of Roman Catholic orthodoxy. It was not that Catholics did not want to attend the city's public schools but that they could not conscientiously do so. Catholics "found a system supported by the community in general which gave instruction to the children of their [Protestant] neighbor, who knew not or cared not how it operated on the religious training of his child; while the Catholic who did care for the interests of his child's religious principles could not, for that reason, conscientiously partake of its advantages."[11]

Since every American citizen enjoyed the right of religious freedom and free conscience, Hughes appealed to constitutional guarantees to bolster his position. Religious liberty countenanced the discharge of one's duty toward God according to individual conscience. Certainly, the right of conscience sanctioned every man to educate his own children. Catholic educational philosophy advocated not only an intellectual education, but also the discipline of the will and the cultivation of the other mental faculties. In such an education, religious instruction played a significant role, since Catholicism rejected the principle that permitted a child's mind to remain a religious *tabula rasa* until he was mature enough to select a religious commitment. Since Catholics could not conscientiously attend these public schools, Hughes denounced as un-

11 Kehoe, *Works of Hughes*, I, p. 53.

just a system which compelled a man to contribute toward the support of an educational system which weakened the religious faith of his child. He insisted that Catholics claimed nothing for themselves which was not the right of every other religious denomination. In addition, a moral code embedded in a religious foundation would surely assist impressionable youngsters to be "more upright in their intercourse with their fellow-men, more mindful of the sacred relations of the marriage state, and more attentive to their social duties."[12]

Hughes's interpretation of the educational legislation of 1824 was different from that of the Public School Society. It was not the intention of the Legislature to tax New Yorkers for the support of a school system that was boycotted by Catholics, who comprised approximately one-fifth of the city's population. Even a superficial reading of the law, admitted the bishop, revealed that no religious body had a legal right to demand educational funds, although the Common Council enjoyed the discretionary power to grant such aid "if in the judgment of this Honorable Body the circumstances of the case entitle them to it." He reminded the public that alteration of the school law had resulted from the "misappropriation" of school funds by one particular religious group—the Bethel Baptist Church. The sole intent of the Legislature's new statute was to preclude any future fraud in the distribution and use of common school funds. To this end, the Legislature entrusted the city fathers with jurisdiction to specify future recipients of school moneys. Hughes was quite sure that this was the legislative way of voicing the following injunction: "Here is [an] abuse; if it is connected with that system let it be abolished; but we leave the Common Council of New York to determine what schools shall be entitled to the money."[13]

Hughes accused the Public School Society of being principally responsible for the defeat of the first Catholic petition before the Common Council. The Society had challenged the petition on the ground that use of public funds for Catholic schools directly aided and promoted a religious organization. He thought it rather incongruous that such an objection would come from a private corporation whose very charter championed both religious and moral

12 *Works of Hughes*, I, p. 45.
13 *Works of Hughes*, I, pp. 74, 137.

instruction within its schools. In addition, the Society did not represent any state or city agency, and received educational funds only because the Common Council had designated it as a legitimate recipient of common school moneys. Since the Society had cornered the lion's share of the common school fund, Hughes thought it not surprising that this private educational organization would strongly resist any rupture in its monopoly. Under such circumstances, he felt that he had to take some action immediately.

An integral part of Hughes's master plan was so to publicize the Catholic position that the community at large could not possibly misinterpret its motivation and goal. To this end, he asked a committee of eight Catholic laymen to draft "an address to the Catholic community and the public at large, on the injustice which is done to the Catholics, in their civil and religious rights by the present operation of the Common School System."[14] As the episcopal chairman of this committee, he was certainly the guiding hand if not the actual architect in composing the "Address of the Roman Catholics to Their Fellow Citizens of the City and State of New York." Certainly, the document exhibited the sharp Hughesian style and argument.[15]

"We are Americans and American citizens." This patriotic assertion was often repeated by Roman Catholics in their written documents and public speeches. Like any new immigrant group, the Irish Catholics of the 1840's suffered from what may be called a collective inferiority complex concerning the legitimacy of their newly acquired citizenship. There was no doubt a subconscious suspicion that adopted citizenship was not quite as authentic as native citizenship. Although legally this was not the case, the predominantly Protestant society of the period was far from solicitous in its treatment and acceptance of poor Irish immigrants who prided themselves as being spiritual sons of the Church of Rome. Irish Catholics often were victims of a discrimination that was either blatantly

---

14 *Works of Hughes,* I, p. 56. The following laymen were appointed to this committee of eight: Thomas O'Connor, James W. McKeon, Hugh Sweeney, James W. White, James Kelley, Gregory Dillon, B. O'Connor, and John McLoughlin. Hughes worked closely with this committee in drafting the Catholic address.

15 *Works of Hughes,* I, pp. 57–65. Cf. Address of the Roman Catholics to Their Fellow Citizens of the City and State of New York, *Document No. 20, Documents of the Board of Aldermen,* August 10, 1840, pp. 310–23. Hassard, *Life of Hughes,* p. 230, declares that the address was "written by the bishop." Cf. *New York Observer,* September 5, 1840; *New York Freeman's Journal,* September 26, 1840.

unofficial or subtly sanctioned by public authority—simply because they were former sons of the old sod and spiritual adherents of the pope. Thus, in the opening words of the Catholic address, the committee emphasized the obvious fact that Catholics were American citizens and proud to be so. True, most of them were not citizens by birth but rather by choice, "which we deem an equal evidence of our affection and attachment to the Laws and Constitution of the country." Psychologically it was essential to underscore the equality of the naturalized citizen with the native American. Such an equality included civil and legal rights—rights which Catholics believed were being violated within the educational sphere. The Catholic address argued for no more than equality but no less than equality. "We hold, therefore, the same idea of our rights that you hold of yours. We wish not to diminish yours, but only to secure and enjoy our own. Neither have we the slightest suspicion that you would wish us to be deprived of any privilege, which you claim for yourselves."[16]

The substance of the address reiterated the basic Catholic contentions. The legislative act of 1824 had not proscribed sectarian schools from a participation in the common school fund. The public schools had eliminated Christian teaching and had substituted the "sectarianism of infidelity." This new sectarianism was enjoying the very advantages which were denied to all Christian denominations. New Yorkers were asked this loaded question: "Are you willing that your children, educated at your expense, shall be educated on a principle antagonistic to the Christian religion?" Opponents to the Catholic position had argued that generally accepted Christian principles of morality should be taught in the public schools while specific religious tenets be assigned to the home and church. But the Catholic address insisted that only positive religious truth could be the foundation stone of morality both in and out of school. Without any religious sanction, moral principles would be flagrantly violated, since no authoritative source could be invoked. Long and sorrowful experience with the city's public schools had convinced Catholics that their children's religious faith would be endangered if they attended these schools. Indeed, existent school practices merely supported Catholic conscientious scruples. The reading of the Protestant version of the Bible elevated the Protestant belief

16 *Works of Hughes*, I, pp. 57–58.

of private interpretation, while school books abounded with ambiguous and false statements against the Catholic Church.

To counteract this situation, Catholics were forced to establish their own schools so that their children would receive a "complete" education without any danger of losing their religious faith. Because of the expense involved in establishing and maintaining these schools, Catholics had applied for a portion of the school moneys. This money was not to be used to support their church but simply to give Catholic children a well-rounded Christian education. Catholics thought it unjust that they had to pay taxes which helped support a system of schools they rejected. Despite what they considered a just claim, Catholics "are denied our portion of the school fund, simply because we at the same time endeavor to train . . . [our children] in principles of virtue and religion. This we feel to be unjust and unequal." Although Catholics suffered under the unconstitutional limitation of double taxation, they still would not permit their children to attend the public schools. As a result, a large number of Catholic children received no education, since the few Catholic schools could not possibly enroll every child. Nevertheless, illiteracy was preferable to infidelity, for "much as we dread ignorance, we dread this much more."[17]

The address conceded that if the public schools were operated on the principle of religious neutrality, Catholics could conscientiously send their children to these schools. But Hughes and his committee believed that such neutrality was an impossibility. This Catholic position was rather significant in the light of the development of this school dispute as well as the road that American public education traveled on its way to religious neutrality. Not only was this remarkable passage a poor prophecy but in many ways it fostered the progress of the very neutrality it contended was unachievable:

If the public schools could have been constituted on a principle which would have secured a perfect NEUTRALITY of influence on the subject of religion, then we should have no reason to complain. But this has not been done, and we respectfully submit that it is impossible. The cold indifference with which it is required that all religion shall be treated in those schools—the Scriptures without note or comment— the selection of passages, as reading lessons, from Protestants and prejudiced authors, on points in which our creed is supposed to be involved—the comments

17 *Works of Hughes*, I, pp. 60, 62, 64.

of the teacher, of which the Commissioners [of School Money] cannot be cognizant—the school libraries, stuffed with sectarian works against us—form against our religion a combination of influences whose action it would be criminal in us to expose our children at such an age.[18]

The Catholic address closed with a stern warning to all Americans that if Catholic rights were allowed to be trampled upon, "the experiment may be repeated to-morrow on some other." The decay of American freedom was not an instant's work but a long series of slowly eroding encroachments upon each citizen's civil and religious rights. "Should the American people ever stand by and tolerate the open and authoritative violation of their Magna Charta, then the Republic will have seen the end of its days of glory."[19]

Hughes received unanimous support when he read this address to a meeting of Catholics on August 10. As he read the document, he was interrupted time and again with loud and extended rounds of applause. The audience was his. Like the proverbial wounded tiger, Catholics had not died but had merely been nursing their wounds. Now Hughes had restored their health and revitalized their courage. A Catholic bandwagon was beginning to roll, headed once again in the direction of the Common Council.

But the road to the Common Council was not a smooth one. The Public School Society did not falter in the face of this latest Catholic maneuver. Refutation was in order and refutation it would be. Two and one-half weeks after five thousand copies of the Catholic address were distributed, the Society's trustees examined a carefully prepared reply at a special meeting of the Executive Committee on August 27. After several minor revisions, the committee approved the document and ordered the publication of the *Reply of the Trustees of the Public School Society to the Address of the Roman Catholics*.[20] Needless to say, this reply rejected every Catholic charge. Call it what they would, Catholics were seeking public taxation for the support of their religious establishment. Such use of public

18 *Works of Hughes,* I, p. 63.
19 *Works of Hughes,* I, pp. 64–65.
20 *PSS: Executive Committee,* August 27, 1840. Cf. Reply of the Trustees of the Public School Society to the Address of the Roman Catholics, *Document No. 20, Documents of the Board of Aldermen,* August 27, 1840, pp. 324–35. The Executive Committee amended the original reply by an addition and an omission. The members struck out a paragraph proposing to grant the use of Public School Society buildings on Saturdays for religious instruction. The addition reminded citizens that teachers of all religious denominations, including several Roman Catholics, were employed at that very time in the Society's schools.

funds, declared the trustees, violated national and state constitutional principles. Both the statute of 1824 and the decision of the Board of Assistant Aldermen had substantiated this point of view. Such a proscription applied not only to Catholics but to all religious denominations and groups. The trustees chafed that their schools should be charged with teaching infidelity while at the same time condemned for using the Bible to instill moral principles into the minds and hearts of pupils. They felt that the very presence of the Bible in the public schools absolved them not only from the unfounded charge of fostering infidelity, but also eliminated any possible sectarian jealously which would have developed "had they attempted to enforce the peculiar views of any who deduce their religious doctrines from the Scriptures. . . ." Formal religious instruction was not taught in the public schools, nor was it ever so intended. But this policy in no way vitiated the trustees' genuine interest in the development of students' religious literacy and culture. In order to facilitate religious training, the Society had long permitted religious groups to conduct Sunday school classes in public school buildings. This invitation had been extended to all denominations, including Roman Catholic, and the offer was still operative. Even in the selection of teachers a scrupulous religious impartiality was observed. Only a candidate's academic qualifications and moral character, not his religious profession, constituted the criteria for hiring a teacher. Indeed, the public schools included teachers of various religious denominations "including six or seven of the Roman Catholic faith."[21]

The Society found one Catholic argument particularly difficult to understand. Catholics scored the public schools because their exclusion of sectarianism in reality banished positive Christianity. At the same time, however, Catholics voiced opposition "to the admission of sectarianism of any kind, whether Christian or anti-Christian in the schools that are supported by the State."[22] If the Catholic claim for public funds were to be granted, Catholic schools

21 *PSS: Executive Committee*, August 27, 1840. Hughes declared that these six or seven teachers were merely nominal Catholics, the type of Catholics children become after having attended the public schools; "that is, Catholics who have no feelings in common with their church—Catholics who are ashamed of the name, because in the schoolbooks and from the teachers they hear of its professors only as 'Papists,' and of the religion itself only as 'Popery.' It is such as these, I fear that pass as Catholics, though I only know of one who is worthy of the name." Kehoe, *Work of Hughes*, I, p. 129.
22 Kehoe, *Works of Hughes*, I, p. 60.

would be supported in part by the state. If Catholics were logical, religious instruction would have to be eliminated from their schools. And if this were so, reasoned the trustees, there would be no essential difference between Catholic and public schools. "If they teach 'science without religion,' will it not, according to their own showing, produce 'enlightened villainy,' and be liable to the awful consequences which they predicate of the system denounced?" Such a situation would cancel the need for Catholic schools, since their very *raison d'être* would not be fulfilled. On the other hand, if Catholic schools included religious instruction in their curricula, they could not be legitimately "supported by the State."[23] Such public aid not only would clash with Catholic opposition to sectarianism in state-supported schools but also would tread upon constitutional principles in a republican country.

Hughes and the Catholic leadership never effectively answered this allegation. The Catholic position opposed any form of sectarianism in state-supported schools. Catholics were willing to support schools that exhibited a "perfect NEUTRALITY of influence on the subject of religion. . . ." But Hughes, it should be remembered, thought that such religious neutrality was not possible. This pattern of reasoning must be understood within the milieu of American society in the 1840's. The predominant Protestant culture produced a system of common schools that manifested this culture and tradition. These Protestant-oriented schools incorporated a plethora of religious practices and reading material even though, theoretically, they excluded sectarian teachings from their classrooms. It is within this historical framework that the Catholic paradox can best be understood. The public schools' dissemination of the "sectarianism of infidelity," argued Hughes, violated their claim of religious neutrality and prevented Catholics from attending these schools. Since the trustees nullified their principle of religious neutrality by inculcating infidelity in their schools, Catholics insisted that instruction even in the least perfect form of Christian sectarianism was better than "nothingarianism." Neutrality in religion was the ideal; practically, however, instruction in Christian principles—call it sectarianism if you will—was preferable to instruction in deistic infidelity. Thus, the Catholic rationale amounted to this kind of reasoning: sectarianism should not be a part of the

23 *PSS: Executive Committee,* August 27, 1840.

public school's curriculum; if it was a part—and Catholics sincerely believed so—Protestant sectarianism was preferable to deistic sectarianism. Because Catholics argued in this way, Hughes perceived no legitimate reason why each denomination should not receive a proportionate share of school funds to educate its young people to become good citizens and devoted sons of the church.

By this time Hughes had lost his respect for the Public School Society, and his review of the trustees' reply was rather cursory, since "it was not worth while to pursue the subject further." However, his vicar-general, John Power, did address himself briefly to this Catholic dilemma. While he did not deny that Catholic schools were religious establishments, he believed that the city's public schools also deserved this label. The Society's schools were as much religious institutions as Catholic schools, since the trustees had acknowledged that "a kind of Scriptural religion is taught therein. . . ." It follows that if Catholic schools were denied a portion of the school funds because they were religious institutions, then certainly the city's public schools, " 'religious establishments' on the principles marked out by the trustees themselves," should also be refused any share in the common school fund.[24] It is quite obvious that at this point both sides were speaking but neither was listening. What Power, Hughes, and other Catholics regarded as sectarianism in the public schools, the Society and its supporters called non-sectarian religious and moral instruction. What the Society and many Protestants branded as sectarian instruction in the Catholic schools, Catholics labeled as Christian teaching. Each side accused the other of favoring and sponsoring sectarian instruction— infidel, Protestant, Catholic—and each vehemently repudiated the other's charges. This divergence is essential to understanding the whole school question. They could never hope to resolve the issue because they started with a disparate set of postulates, and their choice of words and nuances further blurred the issue. The more they examined and studied the school question, the more their mutual miscomprehension became centrifugal.

While the Catholics charged and the Society counter-charged, the Protestant and Catholic presses became more involved in the controversy and began to editorialize their positions. In the early part of September, the *New York Observer* vigorously attacked sev-

[24] *New York Freeman's Journal,* October 24, 1840.

eral of the Catholic assumptions. At the outset, it agreed with Catholics that sectarian school books had no place in the public schools. "If any book, directly or indirectly, holds up the doctrines of any sect to ridicule, or insidiously teaches those doctrines in preference to others, that book must be abandoned." But the *Observer's* accord ended here since the Bible was another question altogether. Only Catholics and infidels questioned the necessity of retaining the Scriptures in the schools. Since the Bible embodied the substance of the Christian creed, unbelievers thought it unjust to support a school system in which a sectarian book was employed. On religious grounds, Catholics scored the reading of the Protestant Bible without note or comment. "Thus Herod and Pilate are united in a common object: . . . the expulsion of the Word of God from the common schools of this country." The *Observer* thought that the Catholic argument of common school infidelity was feigned and "a fair and vivid specimen of modern Jesuitism. . . ." The editorial concluded by assuring its readers that as long as the Protestant majority ruled, the Catholic claim for public school moneys for sectarian purposes would never be sanctioned.[25] The *Christian Advocate and Journal*, the organ of the Methodist church, concurred in the *Observer's* attack on the Catholic address and position. It supported the Society's contention that the public school system could not possibly be infidel, since Bible reading was a daily school exercise. Surely, none but Catholics would object to the Bible, since only Catholics rejected the pure and unadulterated Christianity contained in its pages. Thus, the *Advocate* viewed Catholic objections to the King James Version as "the artful policy employed by the enemies of our common Christianity to exclude the sacred volume from a place among the books of instruction in our schools."[26]

The Episcopalian weekly, *The Churchman*, presented a very interesting case, since it neither completely condemned nor commended the Catholic position. In an article entitled "End of Education," the journal emphasized what it considered to be the "grand error" of public school education. Substantially in agreement with the Catholic complaint, the author contended that while the public schools were successful in the secular instruction of their students,

25 *New York Observer*, September 5, 1840.
26 *Christian Advocate and Journal* (New York), April 24, 1840.

they ignored their moral and spiritual development. The result of this "partial development," deplored *The Churchman,* was that "the harmony of man's nature has been neglected." The Roman Church had long insisted on the education of the whole man—his intellect, conscience, and will. The Episcopalian communion which gloried "in a purer theology and a more untrammelled philosophy" than the corrupted papal church was asked to see and accept the wisdom in such a position.[27] The same issue of *The Churchman* carried an accompanying article which dealt specifically with the Catholic address. Acknowledging numerous deficiencies in the city's public schools, the author believed that Catholic complaints and fears were exaggerated. Nevertheless, he exhibited a remarkably clear comprehension of the Catholic position. Without any of the customary polemic, the author succinctly summarized Catholic dissatisfaction with the city's public schools:

The 'Address' assumes as a fundamental position, that neutrality of influence on the subject of religion cannot be secured by the present system of public school instruction. It argues that a new sectarianism, antagonist to all *Christian* sects, has been generated in the public schools of New York, and that the advantages which are denied to, what it terms, Christian sectarianism of every kind, are necessarily transferred to infidel sectarianism.

The Churchman's concluding observation evinced surprise not so much "in the *nature of* their claim, as in the *boldness* with which it is advanced at this time."[28]

The Episcopalian author should have known that the *Freeman's Journal* would not allow this last remark to go unanswered. Objecting to the term "Romanist," the editor sought the grounds upon which the Protestant writer objected to the Catholic claim. The article, in fact, did not specify the claim as essentially unjust but objected only to "the *boldness* with which it [was] advanced" at that time. Perhaps *The Churchman* decried such Catholic "*boldness*" because of its traditions of Anglican supremacy and English persecution of Roman Catholics. But in this country, the *Freeman's Journal* reminded its Protestant rival, there was no such thing as " 'Canterbury high, sir' . . . . It may shock his traditional notions of

27 *The Churchman* (New York), August 22, 1840.
28 *The Churchman,* August 22, 1840.

Legislative pre-eminence to see Catholics asking for their rights in any thing but a creeping attitude. . . . The Churchman may think it hard, but we cannot help it."[29]

Toward the end of August, Hughes forwarded a copy of the Catholic address to Seward as an example of Catholic unanimity on the school question. In this first of many subsequent letters to Seward, Hughes not only promised to visit him in person at Albany but also revealed a genuine admiration for the state's chief executive. In addition, the bishop ever so subtly intimated that the governor would yet reap a political harvest from his enlightened and liberal educational principles:

> In the name of the Catholics of this state, as well as prompted by my own feelings, I would convey to you the expression of my gratitude for the high, liberal and true American views which Your Excellency has entertained and expressed officially on the subject of popular education. . . . I have reason to believe that should our country call you yet to higher trusts in the Republic, your name will ever be cherished with a peculiar regard by the Catholics of the present generation throughout the United States.[30]

Hughes was careful to add that his flock was politically divided, and that his responsibility was to shepherd all Catholics regardless of their political allegiance. Seward forwarded his answer just three days after he had received Hughes's communication. He regarded the bishop's letter as an expression of a generous spirit with regard to education. He expressed great satisfaction in reading the Catholic

29 *New York Freeman's Journal*, August 29, 1840. No doubt the editor of this journal found the source for his retort in Hughes's remarks on *The Churchman's* stand, which were delivered before a Catholic meeting on August 24. Kehoe, *Works of Hughes*, I, p. 68. The *New York Freeman's Journal*, September 26, 1840, analyzed the Public School Society's reply under the title, "An Appeal to the Prejudices of the Community." Later in the controversy, *The Churchman's* position moved closer to the Catholic one. In fact, some years after the school debate had been terminated, in 1851, this journal editorialized support for the Catholic position: "Where was the harm of allowing each division of the great mass in this country, 'calling themselves Christian,' to establish and maintain and govern its own schools? . . . . The old law distributing the school money among *all* free schools in proportion to the numbers of the scholars was just in principle, and if defective in execution and liable to abuse, it was not difficult to find and apply the remedy." *The Churchman* (New York), December 6, 1851. The *Christian Advocate and Journal* (New York), December 18, 1851, retaining its original position of opposition to the Catholic claim, expressed strong disapproval of *The Churchman's* position and warned that "the new coalision [*sic*] of Romanist and High-Church influence will not be able to shake that [public school] system from its foundations."

30 Hughes to Seward (New York, August 29, 1840), NYAA.

address and congratulated Hughes's "circumspection in avoiding the danger of exciting prejudices incident always to every effort to reform manners or morals." Seward assured Hughes of his complete support and sympathy for the Catholic claim. Not only did he regard a visit by the bishop as an anticipated honor but he also pledged whatever support "it is in my power consistently with other duties and relations to afford." Seward was too astute a politician to bite Hughes's political bait, insisting that he was content with his present gubernatorial position, which completely satisfied his political ambitions.[31]

ii

It did not take any prophetic sense to realize that the Catholic leadership was preparing for a second and more concerted effort to obtain a share of the common school fund. The bi-weekly meetings and the Catholic address had been the ground work for the new thrust which the *New York Observer* accurately predicted would soon come. The Protestant weekly did not have long to wait. At a regular meeting of Catholics held on September 7, Hughes announced that these meetings had accomplished the double task of uniting Catholics and clarifying the issues to New Yorkers. The time had now come for more direct and practical measures to prosecute the Catholic claim. To this end, he formed a five-man committee to prepare a second petition to the Common Council to determine whether it was "still disposed to persevere in denying to the Catholics their rights."[32] Remembering that partisan politics had bred dissension within Catholic ranks while he was in Europe, Hughes decided that the committee would consist of two Whigs, two Democrats, and himself, who professed no political allegiance.

Two weeks later, on September 21, the committee completed its task.[33] This second petition was significantly different from its

---

[31] Seward to Hughes (Albany, September 1, 1840), NYAA.

[32] Kehoe, *Works of Hughes*, I, p. 95. In addition to Hughes, four prominent Catholic laymen were chosen, all of whom had helped to prepare the Catholic address: Thomas O'Connor, Dr. Hugh Sweeney, James W. McKeon, and James Kelley.

[33] Kehoe, *Works of Hughes*, I, pp. 102–7. Cf. Report of the Special Committee to Whom Was Referred the Petition of the Catholics Relative to the Distribution of the School Fund, Together With the Remonstrances Against the Same, *Document No. 40, Documents of the Board of Aldermen*, January 11, 1841, pp. 569–79. Henceforth, this report will be referred to as *Document No. 40.*

predecessor. The first petition had stated financial need as the sole reason for seeking school funds. Catholics then had been careful not to antagonize any segment of the population nor to castigate the Public School Society. But new circumstances and the hardening of positions during the intervening six months had drastically altered the picture. No longer on the defensive, and led by their militant bishop, the Catholics now presented a strongly worded petition which clearly defined their position. For the most part, it reiterated the oft-repeated Catholic arguments. But Hughes and his committee did introduce several new points. Although the trustees of the Society included men of various religious persuasions, the memorial charged that the Society of Friends exercised the controlling religious influence in the city's public schools. A specific Quaker principle, argued the committee, regarded any formal teaching of religion as unnecessary or, at best, as "unprofitable." The Catholic petitioners had often observed that Quaker school children, having had no formal religious training, frequently were "untractable, disobedient, and even contemptuous towards their parents—unwilling to learn any thing of religion—as if they had become illuminated, and could receive all the knowledge of religion necessary for them by instinct or inspiration."[34] But more important to Catholics, they noticed that this type of behavior was frequently emulated by Catholic children who attended the public schools. Though not directly accusing the Quaker influence as the cause of this poor behavior, Catholics charged that children who attended the Society's schools frequently misbehaved in this manner. In addition, the Catholic petition wished to make it quite clear that the Society had obtained its educational monopoly in the face of much opposition. On numerous occasions, the Society's annual reports had unsuccessfully urged the poor to attend the public schools. The trustees even went so far as to "call for coercion by 'the strong arm of the civil power' to supply its deficiency." The very Quaker gentlemen whose pacifism had exempted them from military obligations did not hesitate to seek civil power "for the purpose of abridging the private liberties of their fellow-citizens, who may feel equally conscientious."[35] After this questionable argumentation, the petition concluded by urging the Common Council to designate the eight Catholic schools in the

34 Kehoe, *Works of Hughes*, I, p. 103.
35 Kehoe, *Works of Hughes*, I, p. 106.

city as recipients of common school funds. If the Council wished to question the petitioners in person, the committee suggested a hearing before the entire Council at a time most convenient to it.

As soon as Hughes had read this petition at the September 21 meeting and his Catholic audience had unanimously approved it, the petition was rushed to the Common Council, since the Board of Aldermen was in session that evening. Since their first petition had been rejected by the Board of Assistant Aldermen, Catholic strategists directed this appeal to the other body of the Council. Alderman Graham suggested that the Catholic petitioners be permitted to argue their case before the full Board at the next regularly scheduled meeting. The Board defeated this motion, while approving Alderman Chamberlain's resolution that a special committee of aldermen be appointed to determine the feasibility of granting a formal hearing to the Catholic memorialists. Three aldermen, Chamberlain, Graham, and Jarvis, were assigned to investigate the matter.[36] Now the stage was set for a new struggle. For the moment, however, Catholics had to bide their time while awaiting Council action on their request for a hearing.

As could be expected, the Public School Society quickly sent an official remonstrance against the Catholic petition, just as it had done after the first Catholic petition.[37] Indeed, the Society expressed a certain annoyance with this renewed Catholic agitation since it believed that the subject had been unequivocally resolved by the Board of Assistant Aldermen's negative decision earlier in the year. The trustees' memorial was deliberately brief since they believed that the Assistant Alderman's report had conclusively answered every Catholic argument. However, they did attempt to refute the two new charges that the Catholics had interjected in their petition. If Hughes had become disenchanted with the Society, the Society had just about lost all its patience with the latest Catholic charges. Catholics simply misunderstood the law by establishing an analogy between their situation and the pacifism of the Society of Friends. It was true that the Quaker conscience was respected with regard to the military. But what the Catholic petition had conveniently omit-

[36] *Proceedings of the Board of Aldermen*, September 21, 1840, pp. 277–78.
[37] *PSS: Executive Committee*, September 29, 1840. The same remonstrance committee appointed in February was reappointed and "clothed with full power" to protest the second Catholic petition. This resurrected committee consisted of Messrs. Roger, Mott, Trumble, Halsey, Cornell, Murray, Allen, and Cooper. This remonstrance is found in *Document No. 40*, pp. 586–90.

ted was the fact that the law imposed an equivalent for personal military service in the form of a fine or tax. If a person could not afford the tax, he was imprisoned, and every year people were jailed in New York State for this reason. The trustees were angered at the Catholic allegation of an unwholesome Quaker influence upon public school children. Were the Roman Catholics aware, quizzed the remonstrance, that there were only twelve Quaker trustees among the Society's one hundred trustees? And about half of these twelve had become trustees solely to superintend Negro schools. Furthermore, whereas six or seven public school teachers were Roman Catholics, only two teachers belonged to the Society of Friends. The trustees were baffled concerning the motive which prompted Catholics to put forth such an unfounded and inflammatory charge. They hoped that this explanation sufficed to show that the Catholic allegation was "as unfounded as it is illiberal and ungenerous."

Concerning the other allegation of attempting to force children to attend the public schools, the trustees were shocked at just how far the Catholic petition had distorted the real meaning of the Society's annual reports. By quoting out of context, Catholics "so arranged and commented upon [them] as to convey a meaning directly opposite to the one intended and clearly expressed in the original documents."[38] The trustees admitted that on numerous occasions they had urged the city to force roaming and vagrant children to attend some "public or other daily school." Their intention was not so much that these children attend a specific school as that they go to some school. The Society could not understand how the Catholic petition could twist this intent into an abridgement of civil liberties and proof that the public schools lacked the confidence of the poor. Should the Council agree to hear the Catholic petitioners, the trustees concluded by asking to be heard at the same time as the Catholics.

The Public School Society was not alone in its dissent. The "pastors and churches" of the city's Methodist Episcopal Church formed a committee of three to prepare a further remonstrance against the Catholic claim.[39] This Methodist committee repeated the Society's irritation at the continued Catholic activity and expressed dismay "that the clear, cogent and unanswerable arguments, by which the

[38] *Document No. 40*, p. 589.
[39] *Document No. 40*, pp. 580–85.

former application for this purpose was resisted" had not as yet convinced the papists. In the main, this remonstrance restated the denomination's previous opposition to the Catholic claim: a division
of the school fund would engender discord and ruthless proselytism
within the New York community; the public school system would in
effect be destroyed; the same amount of money would be needed to
educate fewer children as was used to educate the majority; and
much of the so-called objectionable reading material in the schools
merely recorded the truth about the dark Catholic past. On a new
note, however, the remonstrance questioned whether those who paid
taxes had to derive personal benefit from them. If people were not
required to pay taxes unless they directly profited from them, why
then were Quakers and others who conscientiously opposed war
obliged to pay taxes which were used partly for military appropriations? The remonstrance argued that a citizen did not have to benefit
directly from the payment of his taxes, for a citizen profited from all
governmental levies, even if only indirectly. Every advantage gained
by the whole community, after all, redounded to the individual
good. Applying this principle to the school dispute, the Methodist
committee employed Jeffersonian language in arriving at its conclusion:

So it is believed the public interest requires the education of the whole
rising generation; because it would be unsafe to commit the public
liberty, and the perpetuation of our republican institutions, to those
whose ignorance of their nature and value would render them careless
of their preservation, or the easy dupes of artful innovators; and hence
every citizen is required to contribute in proportion to his means to the
public purpose of universal education.[40]

The remonstrance concluded by engaging in some lively polemic.
Methodists had hoped that the democratic influences of American
institutions would have tempered the intolerance and exclusiveness
which had historically characterized Romanism. But the continued
Catholic sectarianism in the United States had, they said, destroyed
such a utopian illusion. Methodists, the committee barbed, calmly
accepted the Catholic exclusion of all "heretics" from heaven "for
we were sure they did not possess the keys, notwithstanding their
confident pretensions." Neither was there any complaint when the
papists refused Protestants admission into purgatory, since it was

[40] *Document No. 40*, p. 582.

a figment of their imagination and thus entitled to remain the exclusive property of the Catholic Church. But the Methodist church did protest against the appropriation of public school funds for the exclusive benefit of the Romanists "or for any other sectarian purposes whatever."[41]

With this increased agitation, the secular press slowly began to open its columns to the dispute, which would soon command maximum coverage. The *New York Herald*'s reporter of religious news noted that the Roman Catholics were in the midst of "moving heaven, earth, and all the saints" for the successful promulgation of their position. With the exception of the Jews, all the other religious denominations were said to oppose the Catholic demand. The writer found it strange and almost amusing that on this question "Jews and Catholics unite, for the first time, in 1840 years."[42] The *Herald* also editorialized its opinions concerning the school dispute. Its controversial editor, James Gordon Bennett, supported the Catholic contention of a disproportionate Quaker influence within the Public School Society. Although one hundred trustees directed the Society's schools, "the practical operation of the management of the society, has became like that of a close [sic] corporation, and the whole business is managed, directed, and controlled by some half a dozen worthy Quakers, very honest and pious men, no doubt, but possessing very peculiar notions on the subject of religious instruction." The *Herald* believed that the Society's attempts to delete anti-Catholic passages from its school books were futile since such efforts would not render the public schools any more acceptable to Catholics. Furthermore, if such expurgations were made for Catholics, the same concessions would have to be granted to other minorities, including Jews and non-believers. Such a situation would inevitably heap contempt upon all religion as well as promulgate infidelity. Echoing Hughes, Bennett insisted that any religion in the public schools was preferable to no religion. Not to foster religious instruction in the schools was to abandon "the brightest part of human existence" and in reality cultivate the "silent progress of infidelity." Since Catholics promised to limit religious instruction to after-school hours and did not object to other denominations participating in the common school fund, Bennett contended that

41 *Document No. 40*, pp. 584–85. The ministers who comprised this committee were Doctors Bang, Bond, and Peck.
42 *New York Herald*, October 1, 1840.

the only feasible course of action was to permit Catholics to receive "their fair proportion of the fund, and educate their children to their heart's content. . . . It is all they want; and it is not an unreasonable request." Certainly, concluded the *Herald*, the school dispute would not be resolved until this was done.[43]

A Whig daily, the *New York Sun*, took a somewhat different approach. It was as unconstitutional to grant the Catholic position as to deny it. The *Sun* attempted to grab this bull by its horns. If a law were passed, reasoned the paper, which exempted Catholics from paying taxes for the support of the public schools, the dilemma would be solved. Public funds would not be used for sectarian purposes and Catholics could attend their own schools without fear of violating their consciences. "Farther than this it appears to us it would be impossible to go; and this it seems should be satisfactory to all."[44]

The Board of Aldermen's special committee presented its report on Monday, October 19. No doubt a hearing for the Catholic petitioners was unusual and perhaps out of order. But the subject was of a "peculiar nature," was highly controversial, and had attracted the "great and absorbing interest" of a large part of the community. Furthermore, the Council needed the opportunity to receive first-hand information on the school question. In this way, the aldermen would acquire "a thorough knowledge of all the facts and reasonings by which the claims of the petitioners are either supported or opposed."[45] In view of these considerations, the committee urged the Board to extend an invitation to the Catholic petitioners and recommended that this privilege be granted to all other interested parties, including the Public School Society. The Board adopted the committee's recommendation and arranged a special hearing for the following Friday afternoon, October 23. However, an unspecified delay occurred and the meeting did not convene until October 29.

At last the Catholics had attained part of their goal. They would have the opportunity to argue the full force of their claim directly before the municipal government. It was true that this government had denied the prior Catholic petition earlier during the year. But at that time Catholics had lacked strong leadership and had been

43 *New York Herald*, October 23, 1840.
44 *New York Sun*, October 15, 1840.
45 *Proceedings of the Board of Aldermen*, October 19, 1840, pp. 308–9. Cf. *New York Commercial Advertiser*, October 20, 1840.

rent with internal dissension. Now in October it was an entirely different scene. Hughes had taken command, had unified a militant laity, and had personally directed a well-planned and effective course of action—all this in four months! The protagonists were about to meet in a show-down of words. Both sides would employ their best minds to argue their respective positions. For Hughes there was no turning back. Whether he was successful or not, he was convinced that Catholic children could never again attend the city's public schools. He discussed this inevitable outcome in a letter he wrote to Bishop Anthony Blanc of New Orleans during the latter part of August. He informed Blanc that he was at that time preoccupied in an effort to sever all Catholic connection with the public schools, since their influence had a corrosive effect upon "our religion." Whether or not the Catholic request would be granted he could not be sure. But whatever the outcome, Hughes had decided that "the effort will cause an entire separation of our children from those schools, and excite greater zeal on the part of the people for Catholic education."[46] Nevertheless, even if Hughes did not quite expect victory before the Common Council, he would not yield without a fight. His whole character and personality rebelled at any thought of meekly surrendering what he felt was a just cause. He would fight the good fight, and if he fell it would be in the thick of battle.

[46] Hughes to Blanc (New York, August 27, 1840), NYAA. Hughes also related that Dubois's health was much improved over the previous year.

⤙ IV ⤚

The Great Debate

i

Thursday, October 29, 1840, loomed large in the minds of many New Yorkers. The day that Catholics had long sought finally arrived. This was the first official confrontation between the opponents to plead the validity of their respective positions. At four o'clock in the afternoon, all the halls and passages leading to the Common Council chamber were thronged with the interested and the curious anxious to attend the hearing. Shortly before the appointed hour, delegates representing the Roman Catholics, the Public School Society, and the Methodist Episcopal Church arrived at City Hall. Some time elapsed before these participants and the aldermen could struggle through the large numbers seeking admission. Observing proper protocol, the Board of Aldermen had invited the assistant aldermen as observers to the hearing.[1] Alderman Purdy presided over the procedural machinery and maintained remarkably good order. Although Hughes was the only official Catholic delegate, Power and a number of laymen accompanied him in an unofficial capacity.[2] The Public School Society engaged the legal services of two prominent lawyers, Theodore Sedgwick and Hiram Ketchum— the latter a long-time trustee of the Society. The Reverend Thomas Bond, a signer of the Methodist Episcopal remonstrance, repre-

1 Although there were sixteen aldermen, only fourteen were present: Elijah Purdy, Caleb Woodhull, Egbert Benson, Daniel Pentz, Robert Jones, James Ferris, Josiah Rich, William Chamberlain, Freeman Campbell, Nathaniel Jarvis, Samuel Nichols, David Graham, Jr., Peter Cooper, and Orville Nash.
2 The five laymen were five of the old faithful: O'Connor, Cooper, Sweeney, McKeon, and Kelley.

sented his denomination.[3] After dispensing with the reading of the minutes and the regular order of business, the chair ruled that Hughes would first address the Board, followed by the Society's attorneys and ending with Bond.

As soon as the Catholic petition and counter remonstrances were read by John Paulding, reader to the Board, Hughes rose to speak on behalf of the Catholic claim. The Catholic bishop of New York stood before the Common Council as the lone spokesman for the Catholic cause. Catholic authors have frequently eulogized Hughes as another Daniel in the lion's den who "stood alone for the Catholics, while arrayed against him was a whole field of talent gathered from the legal profession and the Protestant clergy."[4] He announced that he had obtained the services of a lawyer to advise him on the legal aspects of the case. Unfortunately, at the last minute this anonymous counselor was forced to cancel his appearance at the hearing "by the bursting of a small blood-vessel."[5] Whether or not this was the principal reason, it seems clear that Hughes's monopolization of the Catholic presentment followed a carefully conceived plan. Recalling this incident in his reminiscences eighteen years later, he acknowledged that there were several well-qualified Catholic attorneys who could have served as his legal advisers at the hearing. "But as none of them had studied the question as deeply as myself and as it was almost certain that our views would exhibit discrepancies on minor points, I wished to make the argument so consistent with itself . . . that the adversary could not find a flaw or crevice.

---

3 Kehoe, *Works of Hughes*, I, p. 125, declares that Bangs and Peck, the other two signers of the Methodist Episcopal remonstrance, were also official representatives. This point of view is substantiated by Hassard, *Life of Hughes*, p. 235. Hassard also adds that the Presbyterian and Dutch Reformed Churches were officially represented at this hearing. Actually this was not the case. The only official representatives delegated to speak were Hughes for the Catholics, Sedgwick and Ketchum for the Public School Society, and Bond for the Methodist Episcopal Church. All the other ministers attended as unofficial observers, and on the following day, October 30, a motion was passed that permitted any person who wished to address the Board to do so. As a result, several other Protestant ministers made brief statements which denounced the Catholic petition.

4 Billington, *Protestant Crusade*, p. 147; John G. Shea, *History of the Catholic Church in the United States* (New York: John G. Shea, 1886–92), III, pp. 527–28.

5 Kehoe, *Works of Hughes*, I, p. 141; Hassard, *Life of Hughes*, p. 234. It should be noted, however, that at least one of the laymen who accompanied Hughes, James McKeon, was also a lawyer who subsequently submitted a legal brief which supported the Catholic petition. Cf. *New York Freeman's Journal*, December 12, 1840.

Hence I deemed it expedient to monopolize all the speaking. . . ."[6]

Hughes added little in his speech before the Common Council. He attempted to answer his opponents' charges while trying to catalog and synthesize the Catholic position. Catholics had never contended for public funds for their sectarian needs, "for to this money, for such a purpose, we have no right." The law of 1824 had not forbidden religious bodies to receive school funds but had simply transferred discretionary designative power from the State Legislature to the Common Council. Roman Catholics opposed neither public school education nor the presence of the Bible in these schools. However, they did oppose the sectarianism and infidelity found there as well as the use of the Protestant version of the Bible. Would not Protestants likewise object to the presence of the Catholic version? Yet when Catholics emphasized their dissatisfaction, they were denounced as enemies of the Bible. "But to object to their version," maintained Hughes, "is not to object to the Holy Scriptures." American constitutional principles contained no law concerning particular religions but placed the rights of conscience above everything else, "granting equality to all, protection to all, preference to none."[7] Catholics championed equality and protection and not preference. Thus, they resented having to support schools which violated the religious convictions of their children. If schools which inculcated religion surrendered their right to use of school funds, then Hughes insisted that the Society's schools were no more entitled to common school moneys than were other denominational schools. Not only did these schools implant sectarian instruction, but, worse yet, they propagated the sectarianism of infidelity.

The Catholics of New York City numbered one-fifth of the total population. But if one considered that the rich usually sent their children to private schools and countless numbers attended no school at all, Hughes estimated that among the poorer class that most required the assistance of the common schools, Catholics probably comprised one-third or more. Yet, by refusing to allow variations in the common school system, the Public School Society and other groups were depriving Catholic children of the benefit of an

6 Henry J. Browne, "The Archdiocese of New York a Century Ago: A Memoir of Archbishop Hughes 1838–1858," *Historical Records and Studies*, XXXIX–XL (1952), pp. 150–51. Henceforth, this article will be referred to as Browne, "Memoir."

7 Kehoe, *Works of Hughes*, I, pp. 134, 138.

education that the state intended to confer on every youngster. Since Catholics would not attend the public schools as long as the Society retained its educational monopoly, they sought common school funds for their own schools. They did not oppose other sects' participating in this fund although Hughes did not foresee such an eventuality. Since all the remonstrances against the Catholic petition had expressed complete satisfaction with the present school system, he thought that the public schools would continue to be well attended. As far as Catholics were concerned, however, they received absolutely no benefit from these religiously alien schools. Hughes ended his address by appealing to the Board of Aldermen not to "take from Catholics their portion of the fund by taxation, and hand it over to those who do not give them an equivalent in return. Let those who can receive the advantages of these schools; but as Catholics cannot, do not tie them to a system which is intended for the advantage of a class of society of which they form one-third, but from which system they can receive no benefit."[8]

For more than two hours, Hughes reviewed the school issue before an alert, if somewhat hostile, audience. Hassard gratuitously observes that the bishop ably demonstrated that his opponents' arguments "were either founded on false premises or directed against a false issue." On the contrary, his long, rambling discourse was more a refutation than a well-organized, well-prepared argument. With no legal counsel, Hughes devoted little time to the Common Council's legal right to support the Catholic petition. His lack of legal training resulted in a rather superficial treatment of this question which undoubtedly weakened the Catholic case in the minds of those aldermen who were lawyers. This was very poor strategy since the Society's lawyers, especially Sedgwick, emphasized the legal case against the Catholic request. Had the bishop outlined a careful and more orderly defense of the Catholic position, he would have made a greater impression than he did. Were it not for the abusive tactics of Hiram Ketchum and the polemical harangues of some of the Protestant ministers, Hughes would indeed have made a very poor showing before the Council.

In explaining this substandard performance, Hassard insists that the bishop realized that his primary task was to overcome the pre-

8 Kehoe, *Works of Hughes,* I, pp. 142–43.

judice of his audience and answer the misrepresentations of his opponents. The Council's right to grant the petition seemed so obvious as to place it above dispute. But the fact that it was not so obvious was precisely the reason it was such a bone of contention. Hassard further maintains that Hughes really had no expectation of success before the Board of Aldermen since "right or wrong, he felt certain that they would decide against him." Since his presence before the Council was merely a preliminary gesture before the Catholics appealed to the State Legislature, Hughes "was more anxious therefore to disabuse the public mind of false impressions respecting the purpose of this Catholic movement, than to defeat the ministers and lawyers who had come here to meet him."[9] The problem with this explanation is that the germ of truth contained in it has been magnified into the entire rationale. It completely ignores Hughes's militancy whenever the rights of his church or his flock were involved. Since he was never known to shrink from controversy, it seems inconceivable that he should have played down this golden opportunity to present the Catholic position before the city fathers and the general public—especially since he had fought so hard to get this hearing. It seems that on this point Hassard "doth protest too much!" It must be admitted, however, that Hughes's principal rebuttal on the following day was much more positive and direct—and thus much more successful.

Without any intermission, Thomas Sedgwick, a prominent New York attorney, arose to address the Board on behalf of the Public School Society. His clear and logical two-hour speech traced the history of common school education in New York State and endeavored to show that sectarianism had been carefully excluded. The statute of 1813 which had permitted incorporated religious societies in New York City to receive school moneys was repealed in 1824. Since that time all denominational groups had been denied school funds, and the Common Council did not possess the legal right to authorize appropriations to any religious organization. If the Catholic petitioners determined to get educational funds, Sedgwick argued that only the Legislature had the power to amend or change the existing law. He insisted that he harbored no hostility toward the petitioners because they were Catholics. Even if antagonism to Catholicism did exist, Sedgwick stressed that "most as-

[9] Hassard, *Life of Hughes*, pp. 235–36.

suredly I am not its mouthpiece." His own conscience and principles forced him to speak out against the Catholic claim for school funds. He summarized the Society's main arguments and labeled as illogical the Catholic charge that the city's public schools were at once sectarian and infidel. Neither proposition had any validity since they were mutually exclusive. A child could not very well develop as a Protestant and an infidel at the same time.

That Sedgwick argued as a non-Catholic is apparent in his analysis of the content of a common school education. He delineated three possible types of education which could be adopted by the state: secular, moral, and religious. A secular education would instruct the child to read and write and receive what the state called " 'a purely English education.' " A moral education would imbue the youngster with those fundamental moral principles accepted by all Christians regardless of sectarian differences. A religious education would be equivalent to the inculcation of specific sectarian doctrines of the various denominations. Thus, Sedgwick's conception of a moral education was essentially the same as Horace Mann's —an education which instructed all children in the fundamental ethical norms which were the basis of all religions. From the very beginning, common schools had tried to impress their students with these great and universal moral precepts. But they had never intended to impart Episcopalianism, Methodism, Catholicism, Unitarianism, or any other sectarian creed. Indeed, "the State intends to give a 'secular' and moral but not a religious education; the State does not intend to give a sectarian education, and this is precisely what the reverend gentleman [Hughes] does intend to give."[10]

Sedgwick broached a question which was hotly debated in various parts of the country: was the education of children a proper sphere of governmental concern? In his speech, Hughes tended to reject this proposition on the ground that the public schools separated children from their parents and thus deprived parents of their offspring. Sedgwick rightly interpreted Hughes to deny any state interference in the education of children since it was primarily and antecedently a parental right. But if the bishop's premise were sound, reasoned Sedgwick, then the whole common school system ought to be abolished. For if the state did not possess any educational prerogatives, then no school taxes should be collected, and the exist-

10 Bourne, *History of Public School Society*, p. 229.

ing funds should be diverted to other channels. But right or wrong, the attorney maintained that such was not the understanding of New Yorkers:

They have said that there is a portion of every population that does not sufficiently appreciate the advantages of education voluntarily to secure them; they know, or think that they know, by experience that such parents, unless compelled, will not properly attend to the interests of the child, and therefore the people of the State say, 'We will interfere; no man shall come up to his majority and claim the right of voting, without that education which shall prepare him, at least in part, to exercise that right. He shall have at least a portion of that instruction, without which he is a firebrand in the midst of a magazine.' This matter, therefore, no longer admits of argument. The question to be argued here is, not whether the father and the mother are the best judges of the interests of the child in this point of view. . . . The postulate in this case is, 'The State requires its children to have some kind of education.' [11]

After enunciating these basically Jeffersonian and Mannian educational principles, Sedgwick scored Catholic resistance to the Protestant Bible, which was read without note or comment in the public schools. Although Protestant and Catholic biblical versions differed on doctrinal points, he believed that they both contained the same fundamental ethical principles of Christ. Since the public schools wished to teach precisely these universally accepted moral precepts, Sedgwick suggested that a single collection of biblical extracts could be compiled which would satisfy both Protestants and Catholics. Such a compromise had been adopted in a similar dispute in Ireland. In the highly advanced American society, concluded the attorney, a common ground could certainly be found on which both parties could agree.

Although the press reported a factual account of Sedgwick's discourse, no paper praised it. This apparent conspiracy of silence has continued in the subsequent historical analyses of this school dispute. Hughes, however, expressed more respect for Sedgwick's presentation than for that of any of the other participants at the hearing. Not only was he able, perspicacious, and conciliatory, but the bishop credited him with having spoken with "frankness and sincerity." Catholics respected Sedgwick as a sincerely motivated opponent who was not animated by any religious or ethnic prejudice

11 Bourne, *History of Public School Society*, pp. 228–29.

but by a profound and personal conviction in the value and necessity of a non-sectarian common school system. On the other hand, the Whig and nativist presses hitched their star to Sedgwick's colleague, Hiram Ketchum, who was an able lawyer and a long-time trustee and advocate of the Public School Society. Ketchum was obviously the person upon whom the Society placed its greatest reliance and confidence for success. Ketchum rose to address the assemblage.

At the very outset he reiterated his colleague's denial that the Society opposed the petitioners because they were Catholics. For the past eighteen years, Ketchum had fought all sectarian claims for participation in the school fund. During this time petitions had been received from the Episcopalians, the Dutch Reformed Church, the Baptists, and the Methodist Church. The same proscriptions which barred these petitions necessarily excluded the Catholic request. Ketchum and the ministers who followed him denounced Hughes for holding bi-weekly meetings to prosecute the Catholic claim. The implication was that the bishop had harangued his people in order to enlist popular support for the Catholic demand. The attorney evinced shock that a "mitred gentleman had been greeted by cheers, and his flock 'cheered' him on in his attempt to inflame the passions of his people." It debased the episcopal dignity of the "mitred gentleman" that he should have descended into the arena and inflamed popular prejudice in an attempt to sway the judgment of the Board. "If I, or any other, man, had been passing St. James', at the times these meetings were held," barbed Ketchum, "we would have supposed that they were political meetings, and that possession of the hall was taken by either the 'Whigs' or the 'Democrats.' "[12]

Ketchum and Sedgwick presented essentially the same argument, though there were different emphases and minor differences. Religious pluralism precluded any man's being taxed for the support of any religion. The study of the religious base of morality was therefore delegated to the church and the home. Ketchum did not take as advanced a position as his colleague, since he denied the state's right to coerce anyone to attend school. He did sanction the state's obligation to provide a secular and moral common school education which would be acceptable to those who availed themselves of its advantages. Common schools excluded the inculcation of any form of sectarianism, though they did disseminate Christian

12 Bourne, *History of Public School Society*, p. 240.

moral principles which all denominations accepted without question. But this common core nondenominationalism was not equated with the exposition of creedal dogmas: "We don't teach purgatory; we don't teach baptism or no baptism; we don't teach any thing that is disputed among Christians." The common school did teach, however, that "God's eye sees all you do; and if you steal, or lie, the retribution of eternal judgment will follow you." As a result, "We have the right to declare moral truths, and this community gives us that right—not the law, but as my friend says, public sentiment. . . . We thus undertake in these public schools to furnish this secular education, embracing as it does, not solely and exclusively the common rudiments of learning, but also a knowledge of good morals, and those common sanctions of religion which are acknowledged by every body."[13] A respecter of conscience, Ketchum denied the validity of the Catholics' alleged conscientious scruples. The Catholic conscience could not possibly be infringed upon by having a Catholic child attend a school which taught reading, writing, and ciphering. If a Catholic protested this instruction, he might as well have conscientious scruples against apprenticing his son to a Protestant lawyer to study law. What reasonable conscience, furthermore, would repudiate the school's inculcation of sound moral precepts and universally accepted Christian teachings? How could such instruction compromise the faith of Catholic children or make them irreverent to their parents?

Because Catholics rejected the Protestant Bible without note or comment, Ketchum did not think that "we [should] give up this Bible. . . . It would be a very hard thing." The Bible was a sacred part of the American religious and political tradition, and its absence usually connoted spiritual darkness and political despotism. He discounted Sedgwick's suggestion of a "common Bible" of extracts on the ground that this compromise in Ireland was on the verge of collapse, since a dissenting minority of the Catholic hierarchy had appealed to the pope in this matter. Ketchum rued the day that a foreign potentate should dictate to Americans whether or not the Bible should be read in their common schools. This remark evoked a broad smile on Hughes's face. Angered by the bishop's reaction, Ketchum exclaimed that though the "mitred gentleman" might smirk, he could not ignore the inescapable logic of these conclusions.

---

13 Bourne, *History of Public School Society*, pp. 242–43.

"Though the mitre may be placed by a foreign power on the head of him that wears it, I know there is a feeling in the American bosom—be it Catholic or Protestant—that will not allow a foreign potentate, either directly or indirectly, to interfere."[14]

Not only did public school education discharge the Jeffersonian maxim, but Ketchum extended the principle by urging the common schools to take the lead in the great Americanization program that was just beginning in the United States. This was the era of a growing immigrant influx which would soon inundate American shores. If America were to serve as an asylum for the oppressed foreigner, this public school advocate expected the newcomer to give his heart to his adopted country:

If he comes with an Irish heart, let it become an American heart; let him stand by America, and by her children, enjoying the same rights as they enjoy, and growing up with them, amalgamate with them, and interchanging the same kind and benevolent feelings together. . . . I ask the gentleman [Hughes] if they cannot come in and place their children side by side with ours, and let them feel that in the schools there are no partialities. . . .[15]

Ketchum admitted that the Public School Society was a corporation. But it was bound by law to report its proceedings yearly to the Common Council and at stated times to the Legislature. It was a corporation which had control of a great fund to discharge for the good of the state. In answer to Hughes's charge that the Society enjoyed an educational monopoly, Ketchum reminded his clerical opponent that the Society had repeatedly volunteered to transfer all of its real estate to the Common Council. Furthermore, the trustees received no salary for their services. These selfless public servants had nothing to lose but their arduous duties and long hours. If the Council found the trustees inadequate, new ones should be chosen; if the Catholic petition were granted, new ones would not be needed, since the Society would then lose its effectiveness. It was the Board's responsibility to decide, though "I hope, sir, the prayers of the petitioners will not be granted."[16]

When Ketchum had taken his seat, the Methodist Episcopal representative rose to discuss his Church's attitude on the question.

14 Bourne, *History of Public School Society*, pp. 246–47.
15 Bourne, *History of Public School Society*, pp. 246–47.
16 Bourne, *History of Public School Society*, p. 249.

Hughes quickly jumped up and asked the Board for permission to reply briefly to the Public School Society's representatives. Since the hour had struck ten—the aldermen and the audience were certainly fatigued after five and one-half hours of continuous discourse —the Chair granted the bishop's wish, though not before Bond waived his precedence. Everyone was certain—at least they hoped— that Hughes's extemporaneous remarks would consume less time than Bond's prepared speech. The bishop categorized both lawyers as presenting a choice between two alternatives: either the Catholic conscience must be ignored or the public school system be destroyed. One or the other had to result, and Sedgwick and Ketchum had obviously decided to dismiss the legitimacy of conscience. Hughes was not the enemy of the Bible because he did not reverence a Protestant version nor permit Catholic children to read it. Furthermore, he branded Ketchum's picture of a harmonious American society as an illusion. Although Hughes theoretically assented to this vision, in practice he rejected the possibility of its implementation. To be sure, such a society insured harmony among Protestants, but it left no room for Catholics. He emphasized his skepticism by recalling Ketchum's remarks about papal authority and spiritual allegiance. Moreover, he denounced the personal slur that he suffered from the captious Ketchum. Hughes had held regular meetings because he believed that Catholics were victims of religious and political injustice. As chief pastor in New York, he declared that his duty was to seek a remedy for this situation. And besides, this was an internal Catholic matter and none of Ketchum's business. With this stern lecture, Hughes relinquished the floor. After a short but acid exchange between Hughes and the treasurer of the Public School Society over the question of anti-Catholic school books, Bond once again stood up to speak. And once again he was to be thwarted. The hearing had been in continuous session for over six hours and the hour was well past ten. Participants, judges, and spectators were obviously tired and hungry. Alderman Benson proposed that the hearing be recessed until the following afternoon. The Council quickly approved the motion, and the Chair declared the session adjourned until Friday at 4:00 P.M.[17]

If Thursday had been a contest between Hughes and the Public School Society, Friday augured as a religious debate between the

[17] *Proceedings of the Board of Aldermen*, October 29, 1840, p. 327.

Protestant churches and the Scarlet Lady of Rome. Although the hearing was scheduled to reconvene at four, serious delay was once again encountered. Newspaper accounts and word of mouth further transformed this emotionally charged question into a *cause célèbre*. As on the previous day, many hundreds of persons gathered around City Hall long before the designated hour and obstructed entrances, corridors, and halls. Once again the participants experienced considerable difficulty entering the council chamber. The room was quickly filled to capacity, and some of the persistent even resorted to standing in the alcoves of the large chamber windows. When the large door was closed, hundreds of disappointed spectators had failed to gain entry. Further delay was experienced when unsuccessful attempts were made to acquire larger accommodations in order to satisfy the great numbers excluded from admittance.[18] As the hour of five approached, Alderman Graham finally assumed the Chair as the *locum tenens* of the president, Elijah Purdy. Since this second session matched the religious representatives against each other, both sides rallied reinforcements. Seated near Bond were many Protestant clergymen of his denomination, among them the Reverend William Brownlee of Maria Monk fame. Even Hughes was accompanied by several prominent New York Catholic clergymen, including Power and his scholarly curate, the Reverend Constantine Pise, as well as the ever faithful laymen. Graham called the meeting to order, and at long last Bond rose to address the Board on behalf of his denomination.

The minister's one-and-one-half-hour speech added heat but no light to the dispute. As a result, Bond set the tone for the remainder of the hearing. An educational inquiry degenerated into a religious debate about theological doctrine and biblical interpretation, which, as Graham remarked, were entirely irrelevant to the issue. Bond repeated the charge that Catholics demanded public funds for sectarian purposes, since their schools inculcated religious instruction. If religion was taught, sectarianism was taught. Catholics themselves affirmed that the two were inseparable, "and if so, then will not the public money be used for sectarian purposes?" Like Ketchum, the Methodist clergyman denied the validity of the Catholic appeal to conscience. The public schools could not possibly

18 *Proceedings of the Board of Aldermen,* October 29, 1840, pp. 327–28; Bourne, *History of Public School Society,* pp. 252–53; *New York Observer,* November 7, 1840; *New York Freeman's Journal,* November 7, 1840.

violate the Catholics' consciences, since their children were not compelled to attend these schools. If the Common Council were to grant the Catholic petition, "it will not be to their conscientious objections that you yield, but to the alleged injustice of compelling them to contribute to a public benefit from which they, as a sect, derive no advantage."[19] Such an eventuality would force the Council to apply the same relief to any group which could not conscientiously avail itself of the advantages offered by the public schools. The rest of Bond's long discourse was a harangue filled with abstruse theological dialectic and nativist polemic.

Bond was the last authorized speaker of the hearing. As it was only about six-thirty in the evening and as it was known that several of the city's Protestant ministers wished to make statements, Graham asked the Board its pleasure in this matter. Alderman Rich moved that any person who wished to address the Board be permitted to do so after presenting his name to the Chair. This resolution was adopted, and the following ministers submitted their names to the Chair: the Reverend David Reese, a Methodist preacher and medical doctor; the Reverend Knox of the Dutch Reformed Church; the Reverend Bangs, another Methodist minister; and the Reverend Gardiner Spring of the Presbyterian Church, who spoke only in his own name. A group of Catholic laymen led by Hugh Sweeney appeared as a Catholic committee but relinquished their time allotment to Hughes to allow him to answer these new critics.[20] Hughes naturally consented to this arrangement, especially when it was determined that his rebuttal would conclude the hearing.

By emulating Bond's inclusion of religious discord and nativist polemic, the ministers, as a group, unfortunately impaired the quality of the discussion. Insisting that neither Romanism nor the Board was on trial, only Reese refused to descend into the morass of religious bigotry. The real issue was "whether any denomination—whether any portion of the community—shall have the exclusive control, though it be but of a single dollar, of the money raised by public taxation for the public benefit."[21] Instead of mobilizing his people against the public schools, Reese thought Hughes would

19 Bourne, *History of Public School Society*, pp. 255, 267.
20 Bourne, *History of Public School Society*, p. 268. Bourne is the sole authority for this statement. This Catholic committee is mentioned neither in the *Proceedings of the Board of Aldermen* nor in any of the contemporary newspaper accounts.
21 Bourne, *History of Public School Society*, p. 268.

have rendered a public service had he instructed them that opposition to the Catholic petition "is not opposition to the Roman Catholics" but to the principle of appropriating public moneys for the exclusive control of private or special groups.

Knox saw the ever present paradox when Catholics argued that the public schools were both infidel and sectarian at the same time. Since the Catholic bishop pledged that his schools would impart no religious instruction during the regular school day, the Dutch Reformed preacher wondered why Hughes would not permit his children to attend the common schools and receive Catholic religious instruction afterward. Knox did not believe that the religious milieu in the public schools was "adverse to feelings of reverence for Catholic peculiarities." The mingling of children of different creeds did not weaken a child's faith but rather strengthened it. He argued that religious diversity necessarily demanded greater religious toleration. When his own youngsters encountered children of different creeds, they simply informed their father: "We think we are right and they are wrong, and we let it pass."[22] Another Methodist champion, Bangs, urged the state to compel vagrant and schoolless children to attend the public schools. This coercive action of the state would really be an act of compassion, since these vagrants would be snatched from the streets and their concomitant vices, and taught to become Christian gentlemen and competent citizens. Lastly, speaking in his own name and as an American Protestant, the lone Presbyterian cleric, Gardiner Spring, did not camouflage his antipathy toward Catholicism. Unlike any other speaker at the hearing, he opposed the petition the more because it emanated from the Roman Church: "I do view it with more alarm on account of the source from which it comes." So intense was his feeling against Catholicism that "if there was no alternative between infidelity and the dogmas of the Catholic Church," he said, "I would choose, sir . . . , to be an infidel tomorrow."[23]

When Spring had finished his painfully candid tirade, Graham announced that the hearing's concluding remarks belonged to the Catholic petitioners, who were represented by their bishop. Ketchum observed to the Chair that should Hughes introduce any new material, the Public School Society should be given the opportunity

22 Bourne, *History of Public School Society*, pp. 273–74.
23 Bourne, *History of Public School Society*, pp. 276–77.

to respond. At about 8:00 P.M., Graham asked the bishop to deliver his summation.

Since Hughes knew that this would be his last chance to crystallize the Catholic position, he ranged far and wide in cataloging the whole gamut of Catholic complaints, arguments, and answers. Although he agreed with Reese that religion was not on trial before the Common Council, no one could deny that in practice it was a major consideration. Despite denials to the contrary, he insisted that the Catholic petition was resisted primarily because it was a Catholic petition. Indeed, Hughes publicly acknowledged Spring's frankness in stating his religious dispositions. He had listened to seven able and educated gentlemen of law, medicine, and theology speak at length against the Catholic claim. With all due respect for their eruditeness and sincerity, Hughes asserted that they had not successfully refuted one Catholic argument. They had all employed the same fallacious premises, and thus the Catholic position remained as unshaken as the rock of ages. "There must . . . be something powerful," declared the bishop, "in our plain, unsophisticated, simple statement, when all the reasoning brought against it leaves it just where it was before."[24]

After reiterating the Catholic position concerning the Bible in the public schools, the relationship between morality and religion, the legal meaning of the statute of 1824, Catholic payment of taxes to help support the common schools, and the presence of anti-Catholic books in these schools, Hughes devoted considerable time to analyzing the most vulnerable Catholic argument: that the public schools were simultaneously centers of infidelity and Protestant sectarianism. Several speakers, including Sedgwick and Knox, had trenchantly scored this apparent inconsistency. Hughes readily admitted that his contention revealed a superficial breach in logic. But Sedgwick and others had omitted, according to the bishop, the crucial element that substantiated his charge. To prove his point, he compared the reasoning used in the report of the Board of Assistant Aldermen, which had denied the first Catholic petition and the various assertions of the Public School Society:

In the document which emanated from the Board of Assistants last spring, they say that the smallest particle of religion is a disqualification, and that 'religious instruction is no part of a common school education.'

24 Bourne, *History of Public School Society*, p. 280.

Now, was it the intention of your honorable body to exclude all religion? . . . . And yet that very decision, I ask you, if we are not authorized to interpret as proof of the charge, that the system has a tendency to infidelity? For, banish religion, and infidelity alone remains. And, on the other hand, we find the gentlemen of the Public School Society themselves repeatedly stating that they inculcate religion, and give religious impressions, and I say it does them credit; for, as far as they can, they ought to teach religion. It would be better if they did for those who are satisfied with THEIR religious teaching. This explanation will set us right in the minds of your honorable body. It is first said, no religion is taught, and then it is admitted that religion is inculcated; and next, our petition is opposed because it is alleged that, if our prayer be granted, religion will be taught. What weight, then, is the objection of the Public School Society entitled to, if this be the fact? And where is our inconsistency? If there is a dilemma, to whom are we indebted for it but to the report of the Board of Assistants on the one hand, and to the testimony of the Public School Society on the other? Let us not, then, be charged with inconsistency.[25]

Once again, this charge of "inconsistency" can be traced to the protagonists' different frames of reference. Hughes defined religion as being inseparable from specific denominational doctrines, and denied that it could be equated with generally accepted Christian moral principles. Because sectarian doctrine was indispensable to Hughes's definition of religion, any attempt to separate the two would result in infidelity. Moreover, unless moral prescriptions rested upon a solid base of Christian doctrine, they had no absolute validity as guides of conduct. On the other hand, the Public School Society, the Board of Assistant Aldermen, and many Protestants disagreed with the bishop's definition. For them, there was a real distinction between religion defined as a central core of moral principles, and religion characterized as a formal creed of established doctrinal beliefs. Moral religion, Horace Mann's "Religion of Heaven," referred to a nondenominational Christian code of ethical standards, while doctrinal religion or sectarianism, Horace Mann's "creeds of men," comprised different doctrinal beliefs which divided Christianity into numerous and often hostile denominations and factions. Thus, although Hughes argued that ethics and doctrine could not be divorced, his opponents countered that it was both proper and necessary to do so in the public schools.

25 Kehoe, *Works of Hughes*, I, pp. 150–51.

Hughes's contention, therefore, was consistent within his singular definition. He believed that the Public School Society's effort to eliminate sectarian doctrine from the public schools was equivalent to the inculcation of infidelity, while its practice of teaching a common core Christianity was in effect the teaching of sectarian Protestantism. Within their dualistic definition, however, the Society and the Board of Assistant Aldermen were equally consistent. Since sectarian doctrines had been removed from the common schools, these schools were now non-sectarian and inoffensive to children of all religious faiths. When the Board of Assistant Aldermen excluded religious instruction from the public school curriculum, religion meant specific doctrinal beliefs such as the sacramental system, the trinity, episcopal polity, predestination, that is to say, sectarianism. But religion defined as common core Christian morality was retained in the schools, defending them from charges that they were hotbeds of infidelity. Indeed, the Society's advocacy of common school religion was limited to the teaching of these generally accepted Christian norms of behavior.

What Hughes defined as religion, the Society and assistant aldermen labeled as sectarianism; what the latter regarded as nondenominational Christianity, Hughes scorned as sectarianism. Because Hughes viewed religion holistically, it could never be separated from sectarianism. Because the Society, the aldermen, and others denied this unity, morality and doctrine could be and were treated as separate commodities. Moral instruction, in their opinion, certainly belonged in the public schools, while sectarianism definitely did not. This difference was basic, and the two positions never met. It was not that either side was right or wrong. They simply started from different premises and proceeded on their separate ways—equal but separate.

Catholics had objected to the sectarian character of the public schools. But critics asked how Catholics could teach religion in their schools and not call them sectarian. As on numerous occasions, Hughes compromised his position on this point. "We do not intend to teach religion," he said, during regular school hours. In order to guarantee this pledge, he volunteered to submit all Catholic schools to the same inspection procedures as the public schools. If it were ever demonstrated that Catholics violated this proscription, he would have his schools excluded from further school aid. In an argument so reminiscent of the present time, Hughes insisted that "there is neutral ground on which our children may learn to read and cipher." At least Catholic schools would substitute reading lessons which did not attack Catholicism. And yet, unwittingly perhaps, Hughes exhibited a propensity for Catholic subjects. He would teach his children that when American liberty was planted, "it was watered with Catholic blood." In place of Protestant apologies, his children would read selections on the Magna Carta, which had been wrung from the tyrant King John by the Catholic bishops and barons at Runneymede. Instead of "the deceitful Catholics" burning John Huss, Catholic children would study the life of Charles Carroll, who was one of the architects of American liberty. The use of these lessons could not be constituted as inculcating religion. Certainly, they would spare Catholic children from reading anti-Catholic literature. One thing was certain: Ketchum's "melting pot" concept was beyond the scope of the city's public schools. The Public School Society simply contended for too much when it sought "to shape religion and balance it on a pedestal as to make it suit every body and every sect."[26]

Hughes had one task left to complete. Ketchum's insulting remarks had roused his ire. He told the Board that when he entered its chambers, he expected to be treated as a gentleman by gentlemen. It was apparent that Ketchum had not intended to accord Hughes the respect due his office. It seems certain that Ketchum had employed the courtroom technique of fixing his gaze upon Hughes during his entire speech. Quipped Hughes, "he has no ordinary countenance—and addressed me so solemnly, that I really expected every moment he would forget himself, and say 'the prisoner at the bar.' " The chamber rocked with laughter. This reception only sharpened the bishop's closing remarks: ". . . and whilst I recognize and respect the 'human face divine,' because God made it to look upward, I may here observe, that it has no power to frighten me, even if it would be terrible; and therefore I was not disturbed by the hard looks which he gave me."[27] The *Freeman's Journal* expressed partisan satisfaction over Hughes's dissevering process. "The

26 Kehoe, *Works of Hughes*, I, pp. 156, 158.

27 Kehoe, *Works of Hughes*, I, p. 154. Apparently, Ketchum's personality and courtroom behavior irritated others besides Hughes. That staid chronicler of the times, George Templeton Strong, described Ketchum as "that foolish fat bag of unfragrant flatulence . . . who thinks himself like Daniel Webster." Allan Nevins and Thomas Halsey (eds.), *The Diary of George Templeton Strong 1835–1875* (New York: Macmillan Company, 1952), I, p. 250.

dignified yet most caustic retort with which in his closing argument he fairly annihilated Mr. Ketchum . . . who had been very personal in his speech, was most excellent." But the reporter was quick to add that a knowledge of the "very peculiar manner of Mr. Ketchum" was essential to gain a "full appreciation and enjoyment of this passage in his speech."[28]

Hughes had finished his rebuttal. He had been speaking continuously for over three and one-half hours. It was past eleven-thirty. Nevertheless, in a very impolitic move, Ketchum demanded time to reply to the bishop. The Chair refused to recognize him, but nevertheless he began to speak. After interposing once unsuccessfully, Graham finally called Ketchum out of order, and at last he reluctantly relinquished the floor. Graham announced that the next official meeting of the Board would convene the following Monday. With this statement, the Chair adjourned the hearing—a few minutes before midnight.[29] The Catholics had presented their case. The Catholics had had their day in court.

There was no dearth of newspaper reaction to the "great debate." Editorial opinion was fairly predictable. Most of the secular and Protestant press lauded the remonstrators, while the *Freeman's Journal* thought Hughes had achieved a notable victory. Bennett's *Herald* printed a factual report of the hearing while continuing his paper's generally conciliatory attitude toward the Catholic claim.[30] The Catholic *Truth Teller* retained its aloofness to the Catholic position by printing the bishop's speech without any editorial commentary.[31] The *Commercial Advertiser* commended "the argument of Mr. K[etchum] to the public attention" as the product of a "strong, clear, and logical mind" and with which it was in complete agreement.[32] Spring's preference for infidelity to Catholicism evoked sharp denunciation in both the *Freeman's Journal* and *The Churchman*. The Catholic weekly was shocked that such blasphemy could emanate from a Christian minister. The editor thought that such

---

28 *New York Freeman's Journal*, November 7, 1840.

29 Representatives of the various groups were desirous of submitting written legal opinions on the subject. They were instructed to do so at the Monday meeting of the Board. James McKeon submitted a legal brief on behalf of the Catholics. *New York Freeman's Journal*, December 12, 1840.

30 *New York Herald*, October 30 and November 2, 1840.

31 *New York Truth Teller*, November 14, 1840.

32 *New York Commercial Advertiser*, December 4, 1840. Cf. *New York Commercial Advertiser*, October 30, 1840.

a deistic statement could only have been uttered because the "reason and understanding, and every religious principle" which Spring was expected to possess "appeared to be . . . utterly consumed by the bigotry of his heart. . . ." Spring's hostility to Catholicism in reality exhibited "the spirit that Catholics have to encounter in some quarters in the prosecution of their attempts to obtain simple justice."[33]

As might have been expected, the nativist *Observer* devoted considerable coverage to the entire proceeding. Though Hughes's speech was praised as "ingenious, respectful and as able as an indefensible position would allow a skilful pleader to make it," the paper lauded Ketchum's speech as "one of the most eloquent forensic efforts to which it has ever been our pleasure to listen." The *Observer* emphasized the unanimity of Protestant opposition to the Catholic claim while lamenting the fact that such a brilliant man as Hughes should use his many talents on behalf of a superstitious papism. "No one could hear him without painful regret that such powers of mind, such varied and extensive learning, and such apparent sincerity of purpose were trammelled with a false system of religion."[34] The *Freeman's Journal*, on the other hand, viewed the hearing as "a glorious and triumphant vindication of the Catholic name and Catholic principles." The bishop so overwhelmed his calumniators and their sophisms with a driving "force of eloquence and argument and fact," eulogized the paper, that "the principles of Catholics . . . have been vindicated in a manner that will never be forgotten. . . ."[35]

By far the most interesting editorial commentary was expressed in the newspaper *The Churchman*. Much against its own inclination, it felt necessitated to justify in part the Catholic position. The editor agreed with Sedgwick and Ketchum that the state had the duty to provide a moral education for the children of the state. But he differed with them concerning the standard of morality the Legislature had adopted. Some criterion had to exist, or morality could never have an absolute validity. The Society's representatives had essentially preached a natural code of morality. They denied that the Legislature had provided any religious standard for the inculcation of Christian morals. This opinion clashed diametrically

---

[33] *New York Freeman's Journal*, November 7, 1840.
[34] *New York Observer*, November 7, 1840. Cf. *New York Observer*, December 19, 1840.
[35] *New York Freeman's Journal*, November 7, 1840.

with *The Churchman*'s position. It contended that it was the design
of the Legislature of a Christian country "to prescribe Christian
doctrine as a rule or standard of its system of moral education." In
denying this position, Sedgwick and Ketchum "yield to Bishop
Hughes his premises; and yielding him his premises, they put it out
of the power of the reasoning portion of the community to escape
from his conclusions." The only way to avoid Hughes's conclusions,
reasoned the editor, was to admit that the Legislature had designed
Christianity as the religious base of all moral instruction. Unless this
be acknowledged, *The Churchman* could take "no issue with Bishop
Hughes; but we are obliged to confess that we see no reason why the
Romanists should be left to lose the benefits of the public fund,
except on condition of conforming to a standard which the legislature has not prescribed."[36]

The "great debate" was over and nothing had changed. The
Catholics had not converted their opponents; the remonstrators had
not convinced the Catholics; the Protestant journals had not persuaded the Catholic papers; the Catholic weeklies had not satisfied
a generally hostile secular press. Partisans remained staunch in an
unswerving devotion to their respective causes. True, *The Churchman* had argued a certain dogmatic difficulty which precluded its
acceptance of the majority opinion. But it was only a voice crying
in the wilderness. The Catholics had debated their case. Now they
had to wait for the verdict. In the interim, however, strenuous attempts were made to reconcile the two apparently irreconcilable
positions.

ii

About two weeks after the "great debate," the Public School Society
urged the Board of Aldermen to appoint a committee to visit the
city's public schools in order to dispel what they considered to be
unfounded slurs upon their schools.[37] Not only did the Board ap-

---

36 *The Churchman* (New York), December 12, 1840. Cf. *The Churchman* (New York),
December 19, 1840.

37 *Proceedings of the Board of Aldermen*, November 16, 1840, pp. 352–53. In addition, the Society submitted another document to the Board which objected to certain
remarks Hughes made about certain school books the trustees had given him for
examination. The Society's objection as well as Hughes's detailed answer were published in the *New York Herald*, November 28, 1840.

point such a committee, but it also invited a select number of Catholic and Society representatives to accompany it on its visitation. In addition, this three-man committee was asked to study the arguments of the recent hearing and submit its recommendations concerning subsequent Council action. The committee was further empowered to attempt an accommodation between the Society and the Catholic leadership.

Toward the end of November or the beginning of December, the committee spent two days visiting a number of schools, without prior notification, including three Catholic schools. As soon as the committee completed its investigation, it asked Society and Catholic officials to designate special authorized personnel for some hard bargaining sessions in an attempt to effect a compromise. Both groups promptly accepted the invitation, with Hugh Sweeney and James McKeon as the Catholic representatives, and Mott, Halsey, and Rogers comprising the Society's delegation. Meetings were held throughout December with both sides submitting a series of proposals. The Society's trustees reiterated their pledge to remove all objectionable text and library books from their schools. They further promised to do all in their power to prevent any school incident calculated to offend the religious feelings of Catholic children. The Catholic representatives, on the other hand, offered to operate their schools along the same general lines as the public schools. They volunteered to place all their expenditures under the direct supervision of the Society, to conform their curricula and discipline along the lines of the public schools, and to hire only those teachers certified by the Society as fully qualified and of unimpeachable moral character. They further offered to have their schools inspected by authorized local or state officials and to permit them to examine the teachers, books, and curricula of these schools. Catholics agreed to administer their schools according to state and city law "to guard against abuse in the matter of common school education." Finally, they promised that no Catholic religious instruction would occur during regular school hours, nor would any derogatory remarks be permitted against the creeds of different denominations.[38]

---

[38] *Document No. 40*, p. 565. Cf. Hassard, *Life of Hughes*, pp. 238–39. In addition, the Catholic representatives conceded to the Public School Society the right to hire qualified candidates for the Catholic schools provided the Catholic trustees accepted the new teachers. These compromise propositions of both sides were officially written down and dated December 19, 1840.

As might have been expected, these compromise efforts came to an impasse and died quickly. Although Catholics conceded more than the Society did in this eleventh-hour attempt, neither side compromised its basic position. The Society reiterated its stand on the book issue, while the Catholic petitioners emphasized the administrative aspects of their schools. But objectionable school books were only one Catholic complaint against the public schools and not the most important one. The trustees refused to concede one cent of public funds for Catholic schools. And this was precisely the crux of the Catholic position. Since both sides were willing to compromise only the non-essentials, an accommodation was not reached and, in fact, never was achieved.

The days following the "great debate" passed swiftly into weeks, months, and a new year. Although the *Freeman's Journal* cautiously hoped for success, this optimism was not shared by Hughes or other Catholic leaders. They all predicted an adverse decision, and their pessimism proved not to be unfounded. Ten weeks after the Council hearings, on January 11, 1841, the special committee of aldermen presented its recommendations to the Board.[39] Its report was essentially an apotheosis of the Public School Society and a rejection of the Catholic petition. The public schools were characterized as eminently qualified to implement the state's policy of providing universal education. The aldermen were favorably impressed with the efficient administration of the schools and the advanced intellectual progress of their pupils. The various classes examined "exhibited an astonishing progress in geography, astronomy, arithmetic, reading, writing, etc.; and indicated a capacity in the system for imparting instruction, far beyond our expectations." Satisfaction was expressed that a nondenominational morality was successfully integrated within the secular curriculum.

Investigation of the three Roman Catholic schools, on the other hand, revealed them to be "lamentably deficient in accommodations, and supplies of books and teachers: the rooms were all excessively crowded and poorly ventilated; the books much worn as well as deficient in numbers, and the teachers not sufficiently numerous." The committee did concede that additional funds would raise the standards of the Catholic schools at least to the level of the public schools. Catholics must have been chagrined when the aldermen

[39] *Proceedings of the Board of Aldermen*, January 11, 1841, p. 115.

reported that school book passages to which Hughes had so strenuously objected, remained "entirely unobscured in the books used
in one of the Catholic schools."[40] This disclosure certainly lessened
the effectiveness of this Catholic argument. The *Observer* reveled
that such a revelation placed the Catholics in a very awkward position "and demonstrated their *consistency* in clamoring so loudly
against Protestant books."[41] The aldermen bluntly declared that
their compromise efforts were obstructed by the Catholics' rejection
of any terms "which did not recognise the distinctive character of
their schools as Catholic schools, or which would exclude sectarian
supervision from them entirely. . . ." And then the heart of the
matter! Although Catholics had the right to boycott the public
schools, the Common Council was not justified in subsidizing this
separatist activity by granting Catholic schools a share in the common school fund. Catholic schools had a right to exist but lacked
a right to public maintenance:

They have an unquestionable right to pursue such a course, if the dictates of conscience demand it of them; and they have a just claim to be
sustained by the Common Council in the exercise of that right, but they
cannot justly claim public aid to carry out such intentions, unless they
can show that the public good would be promoted by it, and that such
public aid can be extended to them without trespassing upon the conscientious rights of others; but if any religious society, or sect, should
be allowed the exclusive right to select the books, appoint or nominate
the teachers, or introduce sectarian peculiarities of any kind into a
public school, the exercise of such a right, in any one particular, would
very clearly constitute such school a sectarian school, and its support at
the public expense would, in the opinion of the Committee, be a trespass
upon the conscientious rights of every taxpayer who disapproved of the
religion inculcated by the sect to which such school might be attached;
because they would be paying taxes for the support of a religion which
they disapproved.[42]

The report concluded by recommending that the Board of Aldermen reject the Catholic petition for school funds and that the committee be discharged from any further consideration of the subject.
By an overwhelming vote of fifteen to one the aldermen approved

40 *Document No. 40*, pp. 560–62.
41 *New York Observer*, December 5, 1840. Cf. *New York Sun*, January 13, 1841.
42 *Document No. 40*, pp. 567–68.

the report, denied the Catholic petition, and discharged the three-man committee.[43]

Press reaction to the Council's decision continued its familiar partisanship. Most of the secular dailies applauded the report as one which "will reflect credit on the Committee." The Protestant press also lauded the Board's action. "It [was] with no ordinary gratification" that the *Observer* expressed its profound satisfaction at the rejection of the Catholic petition. The editor hoped that Catholics would finally realize that they could never obtain school funds for their sectarian purposes any more than politicians, desirous of Catholic votes, could expect to be elected by allying themselves with "a conspiracy to put public money in the hands of Roman Catholics for their exclusive use. . . ." Just as it had warned its readers after the rejection of the first Catholic petition, the *Observer* once again counseled them to beware of future Catholic incursions to divert schools funds since the "spirit that has made this attempt on the integrity of our institutions . . . is a spirit that never slumbers. . . ."[44] Mirroring Hughes's position, the *Freeman's Journal* hurled its most partisan broadsides against the report, the Public School Society, and the aldermen themselves. It was not surprising, declared editor James W. White, that "gentlemen who are so tender, and such partizans [*sic*], of the monopoly of the Public School Society" should have devoted a substantial part of their report to eulogizing the Society and its schools. This "iniquitous" report was characterized "as weak and superficial in its discussion of the great question that was presented by the petition of the Catholics as it is unjust and unsound in its conclusions." Because the committee defended the quality of public school instruction from attacks which Catholics never made, the *Freeman's Journal* insisted that the report ignored the principal Catholic arguments and thus never came to grips with the main issue. But the paper was sure of one thing: "that with the Public Schools, as at present constituted, they [Catholics] will never have any connection." The editorial concluded by encouraging its readers not to be disheartened. Catholics

---

[43] *Proceedings of the Board of Aldermen*, January 11, 1841, p. 115. The vote was as follows: affirmative—Purdy, Balis, Woodhull, Benson, Jones, Rich, Chamberlain, Campbell, Hatfield, Jarvis, Smith, Nichols, Graham, Cooper, and Nash; negative—Pentz, As a result of his dissenting vote, Pentz became a favorite of the city's Catholic population.

[44] *New York Observer*, January 16, 1841. Cf. *New York Observer*, February 6, 1841.

may have lost a battle, but the war was far from over. Catholics would persevere in their crusade for justice with renewed spirit and energy. The friends of free education according to the dictates of conscience had "only made a beginning."[45]

Hughes was disappointed with the verdict but not surprised and certainly not ready to concede final defeat. Although the Common Council had denied Catholics their rights, Hughes proclaimed that "we are triumphant over them, for logic and truth are with us." He complained that so much time at the hearings had been wasted in theological controversy that "not one half hour was given to the only question which the Common Council should have permitted to come before them—namely, are the rights of this portion of the citizens violated or not? If so, are there in our hands, as the public guardians of liberty, the means to apply a remedy? Just and impartial judges would so have stated the question, and have discarded all theological discussions."[46] Years later, as he reminisced upon the "great debate" with a certain degree of pride, he reflected that nearly everyone "admitted that I had the best of the Argument so far as truth and justice, and logic were concerned. But those who made this concession remarked also, that popular prejudice was so strong against my position, that if I had a giant's strength I should still be unable to stem the torrent."[47] Browne writes that the debate "resulted in a logical and moral victory for the bishop" while Burns and Kohlbrenner insist that "the merits of the case were lost sight of in the heat and acrimony of the debate before the council."[48] Both Billington and Connors believe that the nativist attacks on Catholicism during the hearing presaged the inevitable outcome since "it was obvious that prejudice was to rule rather than reason."[49] In his study of *Political Nativism in New York State*, Louis Dow Scisco maintains that nativism became activated in response to this Catholic movement. "Anti-foreign and anti-Catholic sentiment rallied behind the Public School Society as representing Amer-

45 *New York Freeman's Journal*, January 16, 23, 1841.

46 Kehoe, *Works of Hughes*, I, p. 243.

47 Browne, "Memoir," p. 151.

48 Henry J. Browne, "Public Support of Catholic Education in New York, 1825–1842: Some New Aspects," *United States Catholic Historical Society, Historical Records and Studies*, XLI (1953), 35; Burns and Kohlbrenner, *History of Catholic Education*, p. 159.

49 Billington, *Protestant Crusade*, p. 147; Connors, *Church-State Relationships*, p. 28.

ican ideas of undenominational education."[50] Although there is truth in all these statements, it must be remembered that nativist hostility alone did not defeat the Catholic petition; for if Catholics enrolled under the banner of conscience, it must be remembered that non-Catholic Americans also had consciences and were guided by them. Regardless of the defects of the public schools and the validity of certain Catholic charges, the Catholic solution seemed sectarian, unconstitutional, and un-American to the majority of the citizens of that day.

In all of the arguments against the Catholic position, one fact came to the surface clearly and repeatedly: the Catholic request for common school funds was equivalent to a demand for public funds for religious purposes. This is certainly the reasoning that forced Hughes to repeat *ad infinitum* that school moneys would not be used to advance the cause of Catholicism in the United States. But, in fact, the bishop was never able to convince the Common Council or the majority of his fellow citizens. Anti-Catholic sentiment and nativist opposition certainly increased the difficulty of Hughes's task. But his basic contention was not, nor has it ever been, accepted by the majority of the American people.

The battle was over and also just beginning. The *Freeman's Journal* sounded the clarion call for Catholics to stand firm in their resolve while the *Observer* warned loyal American Protestants to be on the alert for new Jesuitical schemes. Exactly one month after the Council's adverse decision Hughes addressed a meeting of Catholics at which he told his audience "that the aldermen are not competent judges in this matter, inasmuch as they are ex-officio trustees or members of the Public School Society . . . and jointly they form a monopoly which threatens to mould and subjugate the minds of our children to their peculiar notions." Since the Legislature had given the Common Council discretion to allocate school funds in New York City, an appeal to the city government was but "a preliminary step to going before the Legislature."[51] Catholics were sure that their chance for success was far better in Albany. From the first they had received encouragement from Seward and several state legislators. Nor was this Catholic stratagem a well-guarded secret. Even before the Common Council had issued its decision, the Pub-

[50] Louis Dow Scisco, *Political Nativism in New York* (New York: Columbia University, 1901), pp. 32–33.
[51] Kehoe, *Works of Hughes*, I, pp. 244, 236.

CARL A. RUDISILL LIBRARY
LENOIR RHYNE COLLEGE

lic School Society had anticipated this Catholic maneuver by ap-
pointing "a delegate or committee" to go to Albany to resist all
Catholic efforts to obtain school funds for the support of their
"sectarian schools."[52] During the remainder of this school dispute,
both sides would match wits in the political environment of the
state capital. Both sides were in the process of regrouping for the
next phase of the battle. The intricacies and in-fighting of partisan
politics would once again come to the foreground. Truly did the
Observer prophesy that the "Roman Catholic claim is destined to be
a question of absorbing interest."[53]

52 *PSS: Board of Trustees*, November 1, 1840.
53 *New York Observer*, February 6, 1841.

⌒⟨ V ⟩⌒

The School Book Issue

i

During most of 1840, including the period of the "great debate," Hughes and the Catholic leadership contended that numerous public school books were either patently anti-Catholic or subtly Protestant oriented. Both text and library books were alleged to include historical statements calculated to disparage Catholicism in the eyes of Catholic children. "These passages were not considered as sectarian, inasmuch as they had been selected as mere reading lessons, and were not in favor of any particular sect, but merely against the Catholics."[1] Hughes further taunted the Public School Society for using school books which contained the word "popery" since this term was traditionally employed to express contempt toward Roman Catholicism. It was indefensible, he argued, for the Society to expose Catholic children to such derogatory terminology regarding their religion.

On numerous occasions, Hughes analyzed those public school books which portrayed the Catholic Church in an unfavorable light.[2] And there is no doubt that he had ample evidence to document his case. Wittke writes that "Catholic protests against prejudiced textbooks were frequently justified."[3] In *The Protestant Cru-*

[1] Kehoe, *Works of Hughes*, I, p. 62.

[2] Hughes addressed himself to the textbook issue during most of the Catholic school meetings held is 1840 and 1841. Cf. Meetings of July 20 and 27, August 10 and 24, October 5 and 19, 1840; June 16, 1841. He also gave considerable attention to objectionable school books in his speeches before the Common Council on October 29 and 30, 1840.

[3] Carl Wittke, *We Who Built America* (New York: Prentice-Hall, Inc., 1945), p. 479.

sade, 1800–1860, Billington substantiates Hughes's contention when he declares that school books "all were blatantly Protestant in sympathy and many were openly disrespectful of Catholicism."[4] Nor did the Public School Society deny the presence of such books and, save for the extremist elements, all the interested parties agreed that a legitimate grievance existed.

Nevertheless, it is important to understand Billington's distinction. He identifies two classes of books: those which "were blatantly Protestant in sympathy" and those which "were openly disrespectful of Catholicism." This second group of books could never be justified under any circumstances and was rightly condemned. The first class, however, requires more critical analysis, although Hughes was warranted in attacking even these volumes. The very orientation which permeated the public schools of this era pervaded the school books of the period. American education had indeed a long Protestant heritage. Since the population had always been predominantly Protestant, the schools quite naturally mirrored this tradition. School children read the Protestant Bible, offered Protestant prayers, and sang Protestant hymns. Furthermore, schools used textbooks which were steeped in this heritage. Reading selections were culled almost exclusively from American and European Protestant authors. As a result, Protestants usually emerged as righteous heroes while Catholics were painted as inquisitorial villains. It is not surprising that the Protestant milieu facilitated and supported such an undesirable, though understandable, state of affairs. Even educational reformers such as Horace Mann envisioned a nondenominational Protestantism as an integral part of the emerging common school. The country was Protestant, and its inheritance was Protestant. Consequently, there was no reason for the common school to develop a different pattern. It is certainly not difficult to understand why the majority of Americans demanded Christian—not sectarian—schools in a Christian country. This Christianity, however, was Protestant Christianity which frequently denounced the alleged sectarianism and exclusiveness of the Church of Rome. Although such a situation could not withstand twentieth century scrutiny, it was more easily understood when viewed through the myopic eyes of the 1840's.[5]

4 Billington, *Protestant Crusade*, p. 144.

5 A neglect of Billington's distinction as well as insufficient attention given to the Protestant milieu of the period are the principal flaws in the otherwise informative

Hughes's crusade against these school books generally attacked those volumes which distorted history to the discredit of Catholic Europe, as well as sectarian and "infidel" books.[6] He judged a series of religious and historical textbook selections as definitely repugnant to Catholic sensibilities. A "Dialogue Between Fernando Cortez and William Penn" by Baron George Lyttleton in the *New York Reader* pictured the two colonizers discussing the principles upon which they established their respective colonies. Part of this discussion included the following exchange:

Cortez. It is blasphemy to say, that any folly could come from the fountain of wisdom. Whatever is inconsistent with the great laws of nature, and with the necessary state of human society, cannot possibly have been inspired by God. Self-defence is as necessary to nations as to men. And shall particulars have a right which nations have not? True religion, William Penn, is the perfection of reason. Fanaticism is the disgrace, the destruction of reason.

Penn. Though what thou sayest should be true, it does not come well from thy mouth. A Papist talk of reason! Go to the inquisition and tell them of reason and the great laws of nature. They will broil thee as thy soldiers broiled the unhappy Guatimozin! Why dost thou turn pale? Is it at the name of the inquisition, or the name of Guatimozin? Tremble and shake when thou thinkest, that every murder the inquisitors have committed, every torture they have inflicted on the innocent Indians is

---

study of Sister Marie Leonore Fell, *The Foundations of Nativism in American Textbooks, 1783–1860* (Washington, D.C.: Catholic University of America, 1941). Perhaps Sister Fell's emphasis is best understood by the following selection from her Preface, pp. vi–vii:

> Contents [of textbooks] were confined to excerpts from history or historical selections which were controversial and which represented the attitude of the writer or compiler as far as the Catholic Church and the foreigner were concerned. The excerpts taken, often dealt with specious half-truths skillfully told which in themselves might be difficult to disprove *in toto*. Again false impressions were often created by over-emphasis and stress as well as by a clever searching for unhappy incidents in which Catholics could be placed in an objectionable light.

Cf. Sister Fell's master's thesis, "Bishop Hughes and the Common School Controversy" (unpublished master's thesis, Catholic University of America, Washington, D.C., 1936). Henceforth, her master's thesis will be listed as Fell, "Hughes," while her doctoral dissertation will be referred to as Fell, *Nativism*.

6 Hughes also objected to the presence of anti-Catholic library books in the public schools. He particularly scored *An Irish Heart* which included offensive remarks about Catholicism in general and Irish Catholics in particular. Kehoe, *Works of Hughes*, I, pp. 52–53, 66, 144–45. An unidentified writer trenchantly reviewed other unacceptable library books in the *Freeman's Journal*, September 19, October 24, and December 12, 1840.

originally owing to thee. Thou must answer to God for all their in-
humanity, for all their injustice.[7]

Hughes questioned whether such a lesson was appropriate instruction for Catholic children, who might come to believe that their
church nurtured a generally immoral and illiterate breed of adherents.

Two biographical sketches in the Appendix of Samuel Putnam's
Sequel to the Analytical Reader earned further censure from the
bishop. A short paragraph summarized John Huss's life: "Huss,
John, a zealous reformer from Popery, who lived in Bohemia, towards the close of the fourteenth, and beginning of the fifteenth centuries. He was bold and persevering; but at length, trusting himself
to the deceitful Catholics, he was by them brought to trial, condemned as a heretic and burnt at the stake."[8] A biographical sketch
of Martin Luther was written as a panegyric of the Reformation:
"Luther, the great reformer, was at first, a Benedictine [sic] monk.
He lived toward the close of the fifteenth and beginning of the six-
teenth centuries. The cause of learning, of religion, and of civil
liberty, is indebted to him, more than to any other man since the
Apostles."[9] Hughes insisted that "deceitful Catholics" were not
responsible for the Bohemian's death, and employed a rather defensive approach in refuting the alleged intellectual renaissance
attributed to Luther and the Protestant Reformation.

One textbook which Hughes found particularly odious was Lindley Murray's *Sequel to the English Reader*, especially its selections
on Martin Luther and Archbishop Cranmer. The "Character of
Martin Luther," written by a Dr. Robertson, who was a Presbyterian minister, attempted to present an impartial analysis of Luther's character. But his Protestant affinity and the whole spirit of the
age transformed the author's stated neutrality into a glowing por-
trait of the reformer:

Luther was raised up by Providence to be the author of one of the greatest and most interesting revolutions recorded in history. . . . Zeal for

---

[7] *New York Reader, No. 3* (New York: 1819–40), pp. 201–5; Kehoe, *Works of Hughes*,
I, pp. 115–16; Fell, *Nativism*, p. 64; Fell, "Hughes," pp. 36–37. This volume was the
third in this series, which was used from the lowest grade to the eighth year.

[8] Samuel Putnam, *Sequel to the Analytical Reader* (New York: 1824), p. 266; Kehoe,
Works of Hughes, I, pp. 72, 105, 109, 147–48, 156, 191; Fell, *Nativism*, p. 62; Fell,
"Hughes," p. 38.

[9] Putnam, *Sequel to the Analytical Reader*, p. 296; Kehoe, *Works of Hughes*, I, p.
72; Fell, *Nativism*, p. 62; Fell, "Hughes," p. 38. This selection incorrectly labeled Luther
as "a Benedictine monk" when he actually belonged to the Augustinian Order.

what he regarded as truth, undaunted intrepidity to maintain it, abilities both natural and acquired to defend it, and unwearied industry to propagate it, are virtues which shine so conspicuously in every part of his behaviour, that even his enemies must allow him to have possessed them in an eminent degree. To these may be added, with equal justice . . . , purity, and even austerity of manners . . . , sanctity of life as suited the doctrine which he delivered. . . . Accustomed himself to consider everything as subordinate to truth, he expected the same deference for it from other men. . . . To rouse mankind, when sunk in ignorance or superstition, and to encounter the rage of bigotry armed with power, required the utmost vehemence of zeal, and a temper daring to excess. A gentle call would neither have reached nor have excited those to whom it was addressed. . . .[10]

If these excerpts indicate that Robertson's attempts at impartiality were not very successful, yet his efforts in this direction should not be ignored. Although he tried to mitigate Luther's weaknesses by urging that they be judged "by the principles and maxims of their own age, not by those of another," the author did not neglect to identify these faults:

By carrying some praiseworthy dispositions to excess, he bordered sometimes on what was culpable, and was often betrayed into actions which exposed him to censure. His confidence that his own opinions were well founded, approached to arrogance; his courage in asserting them, to rashness; his firmness in adhering to them, to obstinacy; and his zeal in confuting his adversaries, to rage and scurrility. Regardless of any distinction of rank or character, when his doctrines were attacked, he chastised all his adversaries indiscriminately, with the same rough hand . . . ; he discovered, on some occasions, symptoms of vanity and self-applause. . . .[11]

Hughes would concede only one point in Robertson's characterization. Martin Luther indeed had a character! However, people etched that character very differently. He thought that no Catholic could represent Luther as a prophet who had purified a superstitious church. It seems doubtful, however, whether Hughes would have

---

10 Lindley Murray, *Sequel to the English Reader* (New York: 1845), pp. 63–65; Kehoe, *Works of Hughes*, I, pp. 51, 66, 69, 71, 109, 156; Fell, *Nativism*, p. 7; Fell, "Hughes," p. 37. Henceforth, Murray's book will be listed as Murray, *Sequel*.

11 Murray, *Sequel*, pp. 64–65. Sister Fell's developing historical reflectiveness tempered her former stricture of this selection. In her master's thesis, she wrote that this description "eulogizes Luther." She restricted the scope of her criticism in her doctoral dissertation by declaring that the "selection read like an apologia for the extremes that were found in Luther's character."

sanctioned any positive picture of Luther. He displayed this bias in his complaint that this reading lesson had not been written by a Catholic author. The implication was quite obvious—a Catholic would have portrayed a very different Luther. Such was the caliber of the historical and religious writing of the day.

Hughes categorized the "Execution of Cranmer, Archbishop of Canterbury," written by the English historian Hume, as distorted history of the worst kind. Although he never specified his objections to this essay, except to say that Hume's historical veracity could not be trusted, his criticism could have been leveled against the following passage:

Queen Mary, determined to bring Cranmer, whom she had long detained in prison, to punishment; and in order more fully to satiate her vengence, she resolved to punish him for heresy, rather than for treason. . . . Bonner, bishop of London, and Thirleby, bishop of Ely, were sent to degrade him; and the former executed the melancholy ceremony, with all the joy and exaultation which suited his savage nature. The implacable spirit of the Queen, not satisfied with the future misery of Cranmer, which she believed was inevitable, and with the execution of that dreadful sentence to which he was condemned, prompted her also to seek the ruin of his honour, and the infamy of his name.[12]

At first, said Hume, human weakness made the archbishop acknowledge his error. Either because he discovered that Mary intended to execute him regardless of his confession or because he "had repented of his weakness," Cranmer subsequently retracted his recantation. "Amidst the insults of his enemies," he was promptly led to the stake. Immediately, he thrust his right hand into the flames "till it was consumed" while he penitently shouted: " 'This hand has offended.' " Hume concluded his panegyric by describing Cranmer as "a man of merit; possessed of learning and capacity, and adorned with candour, sincerity, and beneficence, and all those virtues which were fitted to render him useful and amiable in society."[13]

12 Murray, *Sequel*, pp. 74–75.
13 Murray, *Sequel*, pp. 74–75. Other historical selections to which Hughes objected included another reading selection, an American history book, and a volume on world geography. The reading selection, written by Hume, was entitled "The Character of Queen Elizabeth," and was found in Lindley Murray, *The English Reader* (Bridgeport: 1830), pp. 95–96. Salma Hale's *History of the United States* (Cooperstown, New York: 1842), p. 11, included the following excerpt which annoyed Catholics: "The Religious Wars which afflicted France in the 16th century, induced that illustrious statesman, Jasper Coligni, the head of the Protestant sect, to project, in 1502, a settle-

Hughes would have replaced this reading lesson with a chapter from the Catholic historian Lingard which illustrated the struggle of the English barons and the Catholic bishops against King John, culminating in the issuance of the Magna Charta.

So-called sectarian and "infidel" books and selections comprised the second type of school reading challenged by Hughes. *Lessons for Schools, taken from the Holy Scriptures, in the Words of the Text, without Note or Comment* was cited as a direct threat to the religious faith of Catholic children. "Without note or comment" troubled Catholics, since it implied approval of the Protestant doctrine of private interpretation of Scripture. Since the message of this volume directly contradicted Catholic teaching concerning the interpretation of the Bible, Hughes classified the book as sectarian and completely unacceptable to Catholics. He was particularly annoyed by the following selection, which was brought to his attention by Power:

It was Sunday morning. All the bells were ringing for church, and all the streets were filled with people, moving in all directions, and here numbers of well-dressed persons, and a long train of charity children were thronging in at the wide doors of a handsome church; there a number equally gay in dress were entering an elegant meeting-house. A Roman Catholic congregation was turning into their chapel; every one crossing himself, with a finger dipped in holy water, as he went in.

The opposite side of the street was covered with Quakers, distinguished by their plain and neat attire, who walked without ceremony into a room as plain as themselves, and took their seats, the men on one side, the women on the other, in silence. A spacious building was filled with an overflowing crowd of Methodists, while a small society of Baptists assembled in the neighborhood.

Presently the services began. Some of the churches resounded with the solemn organ, and the murmuring of voices following the minister in prayer; in others a single voice was heard; and in the quiet assembly of the Quakers not a sound was uttered.

Mr. Ambrose led his son Edwin round these assemblies; he observed

---

ment in America, to which his brethren might retire from the persecutions of the Catholics." Finally, there was this selection from Conrad Malte-Brun's *A System of Universal Geography* (Philadelphia and Boston: 1832), V, p. 292:

Superstition prevails not only at Rome but in all the States of the Church. The inhabitants observe scrupulously all the ceremonies of religion omitting nothing connected with form or etiquette, although apparently destitute of true devotion. Confession is a practice which all follow more from custom than from Christian humility, and rather to lull the conscience than to correct vice.

them all with great attention, but did not so much as whisper lest he
should interrupt any one. When he was alone with his father, 'Why,'
said Edwin, 'do not all people agree to go to the same place and to worship God in the same way?'

'And why should they agree?' replied his father. 'Do you not see that
people differ in a hundred other things? Do they all dress alike, and
eat and drink alike, and keep the same hours, and use the same di-
version?'

'In those things they have a right to do as they please,' said Edwin.

'They have a right, too,' answered his father, 'to worship God as they
please. It is their own business, and concerns none but themselves.'

'But has not God ordered particular ways of worshiping him?'

At this point of the story, Hughes wryly commented that Edwin had
more sense than his father. Edwin's father answered his son's question: " 'He has directed the mind and spirit with which he is to be
worshiped, but not the manner. That is left for every one to choose.
All these people like their own way best.' "[14]

It is not too difficult to understand the bishop's rejection of such
a rationale. An immigrant church in a hostile environment, the
Catholic Church struggled to preserve what it considered to be
the true and integral Christian faith. No quarter could be given
to error. In addition, life in a frequently antagonistic religious and
social milieu forced the Catholic hierarchy and clergy into mili-
tantly defending a religious faith so closely identified with the un-
welcome Irish immigration. Catholic religious unity together with
an unsympathetic Protestant majority combined to render this vi-
gnette completely unacceptable to members of the "one, true
Church." It is not surprising that Hughes identified the theme of
this selection with deism, for there was no valid comparison between
the choice of dress and the choice of religion. One was trivial and the
other essential; one was temporal and the other eternal. He would
have none of this for his young flock since it was "too early for
them to judge for themselves." This selection concluded with a
picture of persons of different creeds united in a common effort to
comfort a stranger who "fell down in the street in a fit of apoplexy
and lay for dead." Edwin and his father looked on. " 'Here,' said Mr.
Ambrose, 'is a thing on which mankind is made to agree.' "[15] This
was defective reasoning, thought the bishop, not because it endorsed

14 Kehoe, *Works of Hughes*, I, pp. 46–47, 51–52, 151.
15 Kehoe, *Works of Hughes*, I, pp. 46–47, 51–52, 151.

noble human actions but because it de-emphasized their religious base. Invoking the memory and authority of George Washington, Hughes declared that Catholics could never sanction "morality without religion."

Hughes rejected three additional reading selections because they did not clearly proclaim, at least in his judgment, the divinity of Jesus Christ and the supernatural origin of Christianity. There was no doubt that the "Character of Christ" eulogized his many virtues:

> ... he possessed and practiced every imaginable virtue. ... His manner was gentle, mild, condescending, and gracious. ... Over his own passions he had the most complete command. ... He endured the cruelest insults from his enemies. ... Nor was his wisdom inferior to his virtues. ... The doctrines he taught were the most sublime ... and his answers to the many insidious questions that were put to him, showed uncommon quickness of conception, soundness of judgment and presence of mind. ... He was ... the wisest and most virtuous person that ever appeared in the world.[16]

But Christ was never called divine. Hughes thought it rather liberal of the author to attribute such outstanding virtues to the "blessed Lord and Saviour Jesus Christ." He thought that such a description could just as well have been applied to any of the Greek philosophers. In fact, any deist or atheist could have employed such language and remained perfectly consistent with his beliefs or lack of beliefs. The same criticism was leveled at the other two selections: "Character of the Great Founder of Christianity" and "Spirit and Laws of Christianity Superior to Those of Any Other Religion."[17] Christ was the "Great Founder of Christianity" but not God; Christianity was superior to "Any Other Religion" but not divine. What was perhaps most exasperating, bemoaned Hughes, was that they were both written by a Scotch Presbyterian minister.

On every count—blatantly anti-Catholic themes, misrepresentation of the Catholic Church and its history, and sectarian and infidel influences—Hughes found these books unfit to be present in the city's public schools. Most of the selections had been written by Protestant and often anti-Catholic authors. Why did not the Public

---

16 Lindley Murray, *Introduction to the English Reader* (Philadelphia: 1847), pp. 109–10; Kehoe, *Works of Hughes*, I, p. 51.

17 Murray, *Sequel*, pp. 127–31; Kehoe, *Works of Hughes*, I, p. 51. Two other selections of the "sectarian" type were "Conversations on Common Things" and "The Ten Virgins." Kehoe, *Works of Hughes*, I, p. 120.

School Society, asked Hughes, use books and selections written by Catholic authors? After all, it was an acknowledged fact that a large part of human progress emerged under Catholic auspices. Philosophy, government, the sciences, the humanities, education—all were eminently represented by qualified Catholic scholars. Indeed, the vaunted superiority of the Protestant achievement was merely a poor reflection of Catholic ingenuity and creativeness. Hughes demanded that the Society rectify this state of affairs. Otherwise, he would never permit Catholic children to attend schools which used such reading material as instructional media.

ii

The Public School Society was certainly aware of Catholic complaints with regard to the school book issue. As early as 1834, Catholic dissatisfaction had been evidenced when Dubois had objected to certain volumes. At that time the Society had offered to remove objectionable passages, but the matter was soon dropped when no active co-operation was received from the bishop.[18] When this objection was renewed in 1840, the Society made a similar effort to enlist the co-operation of the Catholic clergy in remedying the situation. During most of the year, the trustees employed every possible means to render school books acceptable to Catholics. And yet in his volume on *Public Funds for Church and Private Schools*, Richard J. Gabel blandly ignores these facts when he asserts that the "Public School Society, after twenty years of lip service to the doctrine of separation of Church and State, finally discovered that its textbooks were partisan. . . ."[19] On the other hand, Edward M. Connors' analysis of *Church-State Relationships in Education in the State of New York* affirms that the "trustees of the society had seemed sincerely bent on reaching agreement with Catholic leaders on the schoolbook issue."[20] An examination of the Society's records and correspondence clearly substantiates Connors' conclusion.

After Catholics had first petitioned the Common Council in early 1840, the Society had begun a series of tedious negotiations with

18 Bourne, *History of Public School Society*, pp. 160–63.

19 Richard J. Gabel, *Public Funds for Church and Private Schools* (Washington, D.C.: Catholic University of America, 1937), pp. 704–5.

20 Connors, *Church-State Relationships*, p. 22. Bourne devotes chapter eleven to an analysis of the school book issue. Bourne, *History of Public School Society*, pp. 324–49.

Catholic officials concerning the school book problem. These negotiations had started while Hughes was still in Europe and continued
after his return.

At a meeting of the Board of Trustees on March 24, Lindley
Murray, the Society's vice president, reported that Varela had written the Society for a set of reading books used in the public schools.
Not only did the Board agree to send the books, but it unanimously
resolved "to remove every objection which the members of the
Catholic Church may have to the books used or the studies pursued
in the Public Schools."[21] The trustees assured Varela that any suggestions he offered would receive the Society's careful and serious
consideration. After examining the school books for two weeks,
Varela set down his views in a letter to the Society. He severely
criticized *Lessons for Schools, taken from the Holy Scriptures, in
the Words of the Text, without Note or Comment.* Such lessons,
believed the vicar-general, were in essence advising Catholic children: "Your Church is wrong in giving the Bible always with notes;
disregard her, and read the Scriptures without any note or comment,
and find out a religion for yourself."[22] The very title of the volume
acknowledged the Protestant principle of private interpretation and
thus established the sectarian nature of the public schools. Varela
also disapproved of certain selections in Malte-Brun's *A System of
Universal Geography* as well as the questionable sketch on Martin
Luther found in Lindley Murray's *Sequel to the English Reader,*
"which, no doubt, will please the Protestants, but imply an attack
against the Catholic Church."[23] Upon receipt of Varela's letter, the
trustees decided, on May 1, to appoint a five-man committee to examine all public school text and library books for offensive and
slighting remarks against Catholicism, and to confer with "such
persons of that Church as may be authorized to meet them in reference to such alterations."[24]

This committee immediately sought an interview with the other
Catholic vicar-general, John Power, to discuss the school book question. A meeting was held on May 14 during which both sides can-

21 *PSS: Board of Trustees,* March 24, 1840.

22 *PSS: Board of Trustees,* March 24, 1840. This letter is marked "A" in the
Appendix of the Society's report of September 25, 1840.

23 *PSS: Board of Trustees,* September 25, 1840.

24 *PSS: Board of Trustees,* May 1, 1840. J. Smyth Rogers, Joseph B. Collins, Samuel
F. Mott, James F. Depeyster, and Robert Hogan were appointed to the committee.

didly expressed their points of view. Power's unexpected rigidity certainly dampened the committee's hope for a satisfactory solution of the disputed issues. Despite his pessimistic attitude, Power agreed to examine a collection of school books used in the public schools and communicate his conclusions to the committee.[25] But the committee waited in vain for the expected response. For nearly two months, Power's office remained silent on the question. Finally, in an obvious case of high-handedness and affront, Power ignored the Society and expressed his opinions in a letter to the *Freeman's Journal.* In his long catalogue of objections to the public schools, Power castigated the Society for allowing school libraries to shelve anti-Catholic and sectarian books. Such books were placed within the reach of Catholic children, suggested the clergyman, "no doubt for the very laudable purpose of teaching them to abhor and despise that monster, called Popery."[26] This remark was understandably resented, and the committee expressed its annoyance in a reply forwarded to Power during the early part of August. Especially in view of its prior meeting with him, the committee expressed shock that Power should have imputed such dishonorable motives to the Society. Nevertheless, the committee gracefully tried to explain Power's conduct, using his own words as an excuse: "[pressing duties] of so heterogeneous a nature . . . leave me but little time to arrange my

[25] At this meeting the trustees explained to Power the circumstances under which *An Irish Heart* had entered public school libraries. It was one of a series of books published by the Temperance Society. The trustees had read and investigated the first few volumes of this series, and had found them to be adapted to the reading ability and needs of children. Since it was assumed that subsequent volumes of this series would continue in the same high quality, new titles were promptly ordered for the public schools. In this way, *An Irish Heart* gained admittance into the Society's schools. Some time later a Catholic trustee discovered the anti-Catholic tone of the book and had it immediately removed from all public school libraries. Power appreciated these unfortunate circumstances and observed that under similar conditions this volume might just as easily have entered Catholic school libraries. Despite the Society's explanation, Hughes still scored the trustees for permitting *An Irish Heart* to enter their schools. When he renewed this charge before the Common Council in October, 1840, Samuel Mott, the treasurer of the Society, explained the circumstances surrounding this volume and insisted that Hughes had known the full story. Since Power had been given the facts months before the bishop appeared before the Council, it seems certain that he should have related them to Hughes. For Hughes's analysis of *An Irish Heart*, see Kehoe, *Works of Hughes*, I, pp. 52–53, 66, 144–45. Cf. footnote 6.

[26] *New York Freeman's Journal*, July 11, 1840. The committee incorrectly stated that this edition was published on July 12, 1840. *PSS: Board of Trustees*, September 25, 1840, Appendix C.

thoughts to my own satisfaction on any subject."[27] But the committee's grace did not prevent it from offering Power a lesson on the social amenities:

[The Committee] now submit to your more calm and deliberate consideration whether, pending an examination of the school-books, with a view to their expurgation, in which you promised cooperation, it would not have been more consonant with propriety and the generally acknowledged courtesies of life, if you had suspended your public denunciations of a large body of your fellow-citizens until they had furnished evidence of 'bad faith,' by refusing to expunge—as they assured you they would do—everything in the school books which might be pointed out as objectionable by yourselves [sic] and associates in religious faith.[28]

Power certainly deserved this stricture and, in fact, made no further gesture to correspond or co-operate with the committee or the Society in general concerning any question.

When Hughes returned to New York in July from his European trip, the Catholic leadership and the Society were already leveling charges against each other over the school book issue. Getting nowhere with Varela and Power, the Society's book committee arranged an interview with Hughes sometime between August 27 and September 15. It seems quite probable that only one member of the committee, Robert Hogan, almost certainly a Catholic, actually met with the bishop. A set of school books which Hughes requested was promptly sent to him. The trustees hopefully thought that the bishop had sought these books so that he might co-operate with the committee. With high hopes, it urged Hughes to submit to the Society a detailed list of passages he thought to be objectionable. The committee expressed its conviction that a Catholic clergyman, and especially a bishop, could better identify unacceptable passages than any non-Catholic.[29] Hughes responded promptly and curtly. Much to the dismay of the committee, he noted that he had not asked for the school books in order to participate in the trustees' expurgation efforts. His numerous and pressing duties did not leave him sufficient time for this purpose. However, he did remind the Society that in spite of all its efforts, the article on John Huss which he had desig-

---

27 *PSS: Board of Trustees*, September 25, 1840, Appendix C.
28 *PSS: Board of Trustees*, September 25, 1840, Appendix D
29 *PSS: Board of Trustees*, September 25, 1840, Appendix G. The committee conveyed to Hughes its disappointment that Power had cut off all communication with the Society.

nated as objectionable "eighteen months ago . . . has remained un-touched up to this time."[30]

It was evident that Hughes did not intend to co-operate with the Society in its expurgation attempts. Nor was this a new attitude on his part. In 1837, he had written a letter to Bishop John Purcell of Cincinnati in which he counseled against any collaborative efforts with Protestants, especially on school matters:

In these coalitions there is no advantage. If we join them for instance in education, they will not expunge their abominable books. And if they should yield to correct some things, they will retain others. What has been excluded will be more than compensated by the implied sanction of what will be retained.[31]

Part of Hughes's lack of co-operation no doubt stemmed from his increasing suspicion of the Society and its motives. He believed that its gestures toward textbook expurgation were merely hollow overtures which offered no permanent guarantee. What was deleted at one time could easily be restored at another time. New and perhaps more objectionable passages could enter the schools as fast as designated selections were removed. In addition, there was no assurance that the Society would honor its pledge or that future trustees would continue this policy. Finally, Hughes wanted to make it clear that Catholics had not initiated the Society's expurgation process. Fifteen years later, the bishop reminisced to Charles Carroll that

so far from having insisted on having certain passages in the elementary books of the public schools of that time expunged or buried under black lines, I told them [trustees] distinctly that I looked upon books as public property which they had no right to destroy or efface. They mutilated these books on their own responsibility. But neither at my request nor with my approval.[32]

The Society failed completely in its attempt to enlist Catholic co-operation in solving the school book question. Varela never pursued his initial inquiry; Power remained incommunicado after his impolitic letter to the *Freeman's Journal*; and Hughes carefully pursued a "hands off" policy. Regardless of its efforts, the Society failed to get even a semblance of Catholic co-operation. Connors is there-

30 *PSS: Board of Trustees*, September 25, 1840, Appendix H.

31 Hughes to Purcell (Philadelphia, June 27, 1837), cited in Hassard, *Life of Hughes*, p. 178.

32 Hughes to Carroll (New York, October 16, 1855), NYAA. Cf. Kehoe, *Works of Hughes*, I, pp. 104–5, 113, 130.

fore right in concluding that "with little consistency the bishop and his vicar general [Power] continued to assail the society publicly on the schoolbook issue."[33] Although the Society sincerely desired to remove offensive matter from its school books, it erred in thinking that such efforts would end Catholic hostility to the city's public schools. This was the fatal flaw in the Society's policy. To the Society, it was an end; to the Catholics, it was a beginning. Their primary goal was public funds for their schools. And as the scene of the school dispute shifted to Albany, the school book issue became less and less important in the midst of more important priorities. In a perceptive analysis of the significance of the Society's attempts at school book expurgation, the *Herald* characterized its efforts as "supremely ridiculous, for it is well known that it will not bring the Catholics and public school trustees one inch nearer together. The Catholics say openly that they will not be satisfied with mere negatives—they must have something positive."[34] There seemed to be a lack of genuine understanding between the protagonists concerning their respective positions. Lines of communication between them broke down, and all formal and informal channels quickly came to an end. The Society reluctantly but correctly concluded that it could no longer rely on the goodwill and co-operation of Catholics in its expurgation efforts.

Nevertheless, the Society felt that the expurgation of offensive school books was quite essential and decided to proceed alone in this process. Catholics were frankly told that if the Society's subsequent efforts did not meet their expectations, they had only themselves to blame. The school book committee appended to its recommendations a list of selected passages which they judged to be offensive to Catholics. Corrections and erasures were advised for Murray's *English Reader* and *Sequel*, the *New York Reader*, Putnam's *Sequel*, Malte-Brun's *Geography*, Hale's *History of the United States*; and "without Note or Comment" in *Lessons for Schools, taken from the Holy Scriptures, in the Words of the Text, without Note or Comment*[35] was to be deleted. The revision of these volumes was quickly expedited; objectionable passages were stamped out with ink from a wooden block, and page leaves were pasted together. In some cases, a volume was completely discontinued as a school book. But as the textbook issue ebbed, frayed and mutilated

---

33 Connors, *Church-State Relationships*, p. 22.
34 *New York Herald*, October 23, 1840.
35 *PSS: Board of Trustees*, September 25, 1840.

volumes were gradually replaced by new copies which included the controversial passages. Thus, in the 1844 edition of Murray's *Sequel*, the selections on the "Character of Martin Luther" and "Execution of Cranmer, Archbishop of Canterbury" were erased, with the pages remaining blank. But in the very next year, a new printing of the *Sequel* found both selections restored in their unexpurgated form, thus apparently justifying Hughes's fears.[36]

Many Protestants quickly surmised that the trustees' expurgation work was initiated to placate Hughes's demands. In view of this misconception, the trustees passed a resolution which placed complete responsibility for the enterprise upon the Society itself. The Catholic hierarchy and clergy had never pressured the trustees in their expurgation efforts. On the contrary, the trustees were motivated by an earnest desire to remove all obstacles which prevented "the cooperation of every portion of the community with them in the business of public education."[37] Despite the Society's denial, suspicion of Catholic coercion persisted long after the school dispute had subsided. As late as 1854, Hughes was still branded as the episcopal villain in an article in the *Princeton Review*:

To what an abyss of degradation was the Empire State led down by her puny politicians, when she submitted all her school books to be expurgated by Bishop Hughes! . . . May this infamy remain ever without a parallel, and may those blackened books be soon committed to the flames, and replaced by others luminous with Protestant Christianity! Nothing short of this can ever efface the stigma which mars the lofty brow of that great state.[38]

Never the prime issue with Catholics, they quickly discarded the school book issue in their quest for more positive results—a share in the common school fund. Hughes's subsequent references to objectionable reading material merely served to accentuate Catholic disenchantment with the public schools as a whole. Once the school question became a state matter, the subject of school books was seldom heard in the protagonists' arguments. Catholics played for bigger stakes and employed new tactics to achieve their goal. And the Public School Society as well as interested Protestants reacted promptly and directly to every new Catholic stratagem.

36 Murray, *Sequel*, pp. 63–65, 71–73, 74–75, 84–85.
37 *PSS: Board of Trustees*, November 1, 1840.
38 Charles Hodge, "The Education Question," *Princeton Review*, XXVI (1854), 536.

⌣⟨ VI ⟩⌣

The Secretary's Solution

i

During the period between the "great debate" and the Common Council's decision in January, 1841, the United States held its national and state elections. Long before the November election, Seward was assured that many Irish Catholics "who have never . . . voted for any but the regular Democratic candidates" had decided to vote for his re-election. Although Seward could expect defections among his "old [Whig] friends as they call themselves," he could count on three thousand new Catholic voters who "unanimously denounced and renounced Van Burenism and pledged themselves to support Seward and Harrison!"[1] By the end of August, a confidant reassured the governor that the Whigs would sweep the state and New York City, provided Catholics did not attempt to pressure candidates publicly to support their school claim. If they did, Protestants would react adversely and the Whigs would be defeated. To prevent this possibility, Seward was asked to convert Hughes to this political course—though not without offer of political reward:

I hope you will now, use your influence with Bishop Hughes and Power and *desire, nay, urge*, them, not to ask for a pledge in favour of an equal distribution of the school fund, if they do, we are gone, they can leave that matter in your hands, or they may suggest a name or two to run on the assembly ticket, & keep still about it, it can be done without creating the least difficulty, in the world, but as sure as our Catholic friends

[1] James Kelly to Seward (New York, May 22, 1840), UR; James Kelly to Seward (New York, June 2, 1840), UR; William Clark to Seward (New York, September 11, 1840), UR.

push this matter, I care not how just, the protestants will rise up, as a body, and oppose it.[2]

Either Seward did not try or his efforts were unsuccessful. Less than two weeks elapsed between the "great debate" and the important elections. During this time, the school issue remained a hot political question—an issue that further divided Protestants and Catholics and alienated more Whigs from the governor.

Although New York in common with the rest of the country voted against the "used up" Van Buren and for "Tippecanoe and Tyler too," Seward won re-election only by riding the coattails of the national ticket. His plurality of five thousand was just half his winning margin in 1838, and had not Harrison won a big victory in New York, Seward would most certainly have been defeated. Attacked by Whig and Democrat alike, Seward's majority was substantially reduced by Whig defections and Irish-Catholic reluctance to desert the Democratic party. City Whigs particularly resented the governor's educational recommendation and did little to aid him in his bid for re-election. On the other hand, the Democrats warned Irish voters that Seward's school proposal would never be approved because his own party, notorious for its opposition to immigrants, refused to support the measure. "It appeared that he [Seward] had underrated the power of nativism in his own party," concludes Pratt, "as well as the durability of the Irish-Democratic alliance."[3] A double-edged sword was thus thrust against Seward. Protestants were urged to vote against him because he was pandering to the Catholic clergy while Catholics were exhorted to remain loyal to the Democratic party since the Whigs would never enact the governor's recommendation. The Whig chronicler, Philip Hone, attributed Seward's close election to the "ill-judged favour which he has shown the Catholics, by which he has lost many of his friends, and not gained the votes of those whom he sought to propitiate."[4] The *Observer* thought it a "well known fact that the suspicion of Gov. Seward's partiality to the Roman Catholic pretensions nearly lost him his election. . . ."[5]

Although most of Seward's contemporaries attributed his poor

---

[2] Marshall Owen Roberts to Seward (New York, August 30, 1840), UR.

[3] Pratt, "Governor Seward," p. 357.

[4] Bayard Tuckerman (ed.), *The Diary of Philip Hone, 1828–1851* (New York: Dodd, Mead and Company, 1889), II, p. 52.

[5] *New York Observer*, February 20, 1841.

electoral showing to his unpopular educational views, he challenged this post-election appraisal. He admitted that the Irish throughout the state generally voted against his candidacy, but he denied that the lack of Irish support "alone, or chiefly, effected our loss. . . ." His canvass of the returns indicated that very few foreigners resided in such counties as Delaware, Otsego, Putnam, Chemung, and Tioga, and yet "those counties all gave increased majorities against us." Instead, Seward traced his poor showing to the anti-Catholic and anti-foreign nativism of his own party, for "Irishmen abandoned the Whig Party, because they were alarmed for their rights." The large Irish anti-Whig vote was not directed toward him personally, since it was well known that "the adopted citizens in mass have long been opposed to the party to which I belong." Although the Whig party refused to deal equitably with adopted citizens, he could neither sanction nor defend such a policy. If he refused to censure publicly those "Americans in both parties" who misrepresented him on the school question, he did insist on having the last word. The hypersensitive Seward bluntly charged that "if I were to say with whom lies the fault of Irishmen voting in mass against the candidates of the Whig party, I should say that the fault was with my countrymen."[6] To a correspondent who strongly intimated that Hughes and the Catholic clergy had instigated "the Catholics against us," Seward sternly replied that "I *know* this [charge] to be untrue, totally untrue. . . . Bishop Hughes is my friend. I honor, respect, and confide in him."[7] When Hughes heard "the reports that have gone forth of the interference of the Catholic clergy in the late contest," he quickly wrote to Seward. He knew of only one case, "a Priest in Greene County," and he had since suspended him from his clerical duties. To emphasize this point, Hughes informed the governor that he had recently held a clerical meeting at which he warned his priests that he would "not overlook any interference of theirs in such matters."[8]

Other correspondents informed Seward that the Democrats not only distorted and misrepresented his educational position but also promised "the Catholics generally and particularly their clergy, that they . . . would do more for them if they obtained the ascendancy in the state than you had even proposed in your message, in the mat-

6 Baker, *Works of Seward*, III, pp. 386–87.
7 Seward to Benjamin Silliman (Albany, November 15, 1840), UR.
8 Hughes to Seward (New York, November 29, 1840), UR.

ter of the School fund."[9] Although the Erin Conservative Association of the City of New York denounced Whig defections from Seward and promised him continued electoral support, several anonymous letters warned the governor in rather caustic and insulting terms that his educational proposal had nearly cost him reelection and intimated that adherence to this position would consign him "to the walks of private life."[10] In a post-election issue of the Whig campaign paper, *The Log Cabin*, Horace Greeley admitted that Seward "ran considerably behind the other Whig candidates" principally because he suggested "a modification of the law regulating the Distribution of the School Fund." Because such a view was construed to be favorable to Catholics, Greeley concluded that the school issue became enmeshed in the "no popery" crusade and thus cost Seward thousands of Whig votes. He defended the governor's proposal and scorned those Whigs who deserted Seward at the polls. "God forbid that we ever lie at the mercy of such friends!"[11]

In his letter defending the Catholic clergy against the charge of political interference in the November election, Hughes sympathized with Seward over the loss of the Irish vote. Not only did Hughes lash out against secret societies among his people which "required that their members shall be of one political party [Democratic]," but he also promised to make a "holy war" against the *Truth Teller*, which had misled so many Irish Catholics:

We are almost ruined by the havoc which politics have made among our ignorant and misled people. But I trust that the bad influence which has too long been exercised on them by a vile print in this city affecting great zeal for their country and their religion, but in reality an injury to the character of both, will soon be at an end. I shall make a holy war on these miserable traffickers on their credulity.[12]

The bishop identified his own political sentiments when he expressed regret at the desertion of Seward at the polls as "a poor encouragement for a public servant who wishes to be guided by high, and large statesmanlike views—instead of that low & selfish policy, which the great interests of the *whole* are so liable to suffer."[13]

9 Benjamin Birdsall to Seward (New York, November 9, 1840), UR.

10 Lawrence W. Power to Seward, New York (November 14, 1840), UR; "A Conservative" to Seward (New York, November 12, 1840), UR; "A True Whig" to Seward (New York, November 11, 1840), UR.

11 *The Log Cabin*, November 9, 1840.

12 Hughes to Seward (New York, November 29, 1840), UR.

13 Hughes to Seward (Nov. 29, 1840), UR.

Seward was obviously heartened by Hughes's magnanimous and yet partisan comments. His quick reply had political overtones though it was couched in lofty sentiments:

There is much to rejoice for in the prospect of a release of all classes of citizens from the controlling power that has so long established the creed of political orthodoxy. For myself I am content to abide my vindication, and I trust yet to have the support of all good men in attacking ignorance and vice although for a time through misapprehension the hands of some have been raised against me.[14]

This exchange of letters certainly indicated that prelate and governor were moving closer to one another in mind and action.

On January 5, about one week before the Common Council rejected the Catholic petition, Seward delivered his third annual message to the Legislature. Once again, he devoted considerable attention to the state's educational progress. Once again, he combined his concern for the downtrodden immigrant, a literate citizenry, and a comprehensive school system into a unified statement. Although Seward acknowledged the excellence of New York City's public schools, he could not ignore the thousands of unschooled children who still roamed the streets of the city. It was imperative that this blight be removed "unless we assume that society consents to leave it without a remedy." He was not satisfied with the Public School Society's contention that its schools offered a free public education to all the city's children. An educational system "that does not accomplish what it proposes" was a defective system. As a result, Seward branded the system as "deficient in comprehensiveness, in the exact proportion of the children that it leaves uneducated; that knowledge, however acquired, is better than ignorance; and that neither error, accident, nor prejudice, ought to be permitted to deprive the state of the education of her citizens."[15] Education was essential for both foreign and native children since both groups would eventually possess the right of suffrage and the obligation of responsible citizenship.

Despite this educational ideal, Seward's concrete proposal stopped short of his previous recommendation. "I have no pride of opinion," he announced, "concerning the manner in which the education of those whom I have brought to your notice shall be secured. . . ."[16]

14 Seward to Hughes (Albany, December 3, 1840), NYAA.
15 Baker, *Works of Seward*, II, pp. 279–80.
16 Baker, *Works of Seward*, II, p. 279.

The important question was not "how or by whom shall instruction be given" but that it be given. Nevertheless, in an attempt to vindicate his former position, the thin-skinned governor indicated that no one had yet challenged the efficacy of his plan "nor has any other plan been proposed." On the contrary, "the same evil remains as before." There is no doubt that the city's unsatisfactory educational troubles still bothered Seward very much. But even though he was a reformer, he was also a seasoned politician—and his former recommendation had nearly cost him his political life, and his party the loss of the state. It seems evident that in this message Seward was seeking a compromise solution which at the same time would not betray his convictions. What was needed was an arrangement whereby Catholic children could conscientiously attend the public schools without destroying the essential integrity of the city's educational system. Neither the contented Protestant majority nor the dissatisfied Catholic minority could possibly reject such an accommodation. Alleviation of Catholic complaints without the use of public funds for their schools was certainly the answer to Seward's dilemma.[17] He could then shelve his controversial proposal, his political stock would quickly soar, and his educational goals would remain intact.

The Whig *Commercial Advertiser*, a strong advocate of the Public School Society, could find no fault with Seward's remarks. Everyone agreed with him that "all proper means should be taken to secure the full advantages of our common schools to every child in the state, of exotic birth, as well as native." Seward's retreat from his initial position pleased the paper and he was praised for avoiding "both the rocks of Scylla, and whirlpool of Charybdis."[18] Since the *Observer* was not quite sure whether the governor had really acquitted himself on the school question, it warned him that the people of the state would never vote for a man who favored the use of their money for the support of sectarian schools of any denomination.[19] On the other hand, an Irish-Catholic Whig from upstate New York characterized Seward's educational statement as "the language of the Patriot, the Statesman, and the Philanthropist." He was eulogized as the vindicator of the "wrongs and sufferings of an oppressed, brave, and generous people" who desperately needed the blessings

---

[17] Cf. Pratt, "Governor Seward," p. 358; Billington, *Protestant Crusade*, p. 150.
[18] *New York Commercial Advertiser*, January 8, 1841.
[19] *New York Observer*, February 20, 1841.

of an education "so essentially necessary for the maintainance [*sic*] of our republican form of government."[20]

ii

On February 11, exactly one month after the Common Council's decision, a large Catholic gathering crowded into Washington Hall to determine future strategy. After Power had delivered some introductory remarks, Hughes rose to address the audience. In a taunting mood, he counseled his flock to subdue its cheering lest Ketchum confuse this meeting for a Whig or Democratic political rally. After all, observed Hughes, he "is not obliged to reason like other men, and if he should pass by and reason so, the fault will be yours for cheering, and not his for foolish reasoning." He spent considerable time in reviewing the history of the school controversy, interspersing his analysis with humor, sarcasm, and even an Irish anecdote. But he was basically an optimist who came not to mourn defeat but to encourage his disheartened Catholics and devise the next phase of battle.

What, then, remains for us to do? We must not fold our arms and rest. We must take measures. . . . I trust that no such defeat as we have experienced—the defeat of justice by authority—shall make you give up your principles. Spread it abroad that you ask no favor—no preeminence —no boon from their honors of the Common Council, but that you have rights and these rights you claim. Let them reserve their favors for those who want them. This is the ground on which the question will meet with respect, both from your brethren in faith, and your fellow-citizens at large. This is a question of right; and though a whole Board should be found to bend the knee to the Baal of bigotry, men will be found who can stand unawed in its presence, and do right.[21]

20 David Nagle to Seward (January 11, 1841), UR.

21 Kehoe, *Works of Hughes*, I, pp. 242–45. The Common Council's decision reminded Hughes "of a story I once heard of the times when, in Ireland, law and justice were set at open defiance, and every petty tyrant had the right to trample on his neighbor, provided he himself were the minion of the government. A poor man was taken up by one of these petty despots, and cast into prison, where he remained for a considerable time, ignorant of his crime and his destiny, not knowing whether he was to be sent to the gallows or the convict ship. But after a month or so of suspense, the little tyrant came, and marching his prisoner to the door, gave him a push and kicked him out, when the poor man, finding himself abroad and at liberty once more, turned round and very emphatically said, 'Thank your honor.' The aldermen have treated you somewhat similarly, and I hope you will all say with becoming gratitude, now that you are out of their hands, 'Thank your honors'" (pp. 243–44).

Everyone in the audience knew that the men who would "do right" were the state legislators. When the bishop finished his address, one of the laymen made a motion to form a "Central Executive Committee on Common Schools" which would organize meetings in each ward of the city to protest the existing public school situation.[22] In addition, each ward would appoint a two-man committee to obtain signatures for a forthcoming petition to the Legislature. Each ward committee would effect on a ward level any measures recommended by the central committee. After these resolutions were adopted unanimously, an additional resolution was passed which expressed Catholic appreciation to Alderman Pentz for his independent action in voting against the report of the Common Council.

In the weeks following, the central and ward committees energetically pursued their respective duties. Ward protest meetings were held and seven thousand signatures appended the petition to the Legislature, "several of which were those of liberal Protestant gentlemen."[23] At first the central committee appointed a delegation to carry the petition to Albany and deposit it in friendly hands. Later on, political expediency and sound strategy made the committee ask the noted Catholic attorney and influential politician, Joseph O'Connor, to perform this duty. O'Connor accepted the responsibility, and toward the end of March he traveled to Albany and entrusted the petition to Gulian Verplanck, a Whig senator from New York County who was admittedly sympathetic to the Catholic cause. Since O'Connor did not personally know Verplanck, he carried a letter of introduction from the Reverend Charles Constantine Pise, Power's curate, who was on friendly terms with the state senator. Pise's letter stressed the fact that all children should be instructed in the knowledge of their duties and rights as citizens "of this one glorious Republic." "The children of foreigners are *Americans*," declared the clergyman, who was confident that Verplanck did not wish them "to be deprived of the only sure support of their morals—Education with Religion." They would not come to the common schools, and Catholic schools were so overcrowded that they educated only one out of every fifty Catholic children. Many ignorant and preoccupied parents, moreover, did not insist upon their children's education. After a useless *"controversy about dog-*

22 *New York Freeman's Journal*, February 13, 1841. James McKeon, Hugh Sweeney, Robert Hogan, James White, and Thomas O'Connor were named to the committee.
23 *New York Freeman's Journal*, April 3, 1841.

mas," the Common Council rejected the Catholic petition and made "an appeal . . . to the wisdom of the state legislature." Pise assured Verplanck that his cordial reception of O'Connor would be appreciated by "the body Catholic generally" as well as deepen their own friendship.[24]

O'Connor quickly expedited his task and reported to a meeting of Catholics on April 3 that Verplanck had promised to present the Catholic petition to the Senate as soon as possible. He also conferred with the secretary of state and *ex officio* superintendent of common schools in New York State, John C. Spencer, who "had expressed himself in a very friendly manner." In comparison to the city aldermen, he found the Albany legislators to be "honest, liberal, honorable men—men of both political parties, who publicly and fearlessly acknowledged that there was something wrong in the city of New York—that there was here an unnatural corporation, such a one as should not exist under a republican government."[25] When another speaker urged his listeners to support only those legislators favorable to the Catholic cause, O'Connor sharply dissented against the introduction of partisan politics into what he felt was a moral issue. He was convinced that only bipartisan support would ensure a favorable hearing for the Catholic claim. Hughes reiterated O'Connor's admonition against interjecting politics into the school question even though he thought it a self-evident proposition "that if I appoint a man to provide for the public table, and he sets on it what I cannot eat, that then my duty is to withhold from him my future support."[26] In the November elections, Hughes would act upon this principle. Thus, whether O'Connor and Hughes knew it or not, the school question was entering the arena of state politics.

On March 29, 1841, Verplanck submitted to the Senate a "memorial of Citizens of New York for an amendment of the common school laws."[27] The memorial was deliberately not introduced as a specifically Catholic petition but rather as one from the "citizens of New York." The *Observer* warned that this new Catholic maneuver before the Legislature was the beginning of a Catholic political party. "The 'Church and State party' is now fully and fairly in the field . . . with the new but bold inscription on their banners, '*the*

---

24 Charles Constantine Pise to Gulian Verplanck (New York, March 23, 1841), Gulian C. Verplanck Papers (MSS in the New York Historical Society), Letter P, No. 48.
25 *New York Freeman's Journal*, April 3, 1841.
26 *New York Freeman's Journal*, April 3, 1841.
27 *Journal of the Senate*, March 29, 1841, p. 244.

people's money shall be ours.' " The weekly expected the Public
School Society to react promptly with a strong remonstrance against
the Catholic claim, and presumed that it would "see that every
citizen has an opportunity of signing his name to a firm and manly
protest against the monstrous demands, which these enemies of our
free and equal institutions have made. . . ."[28] The *Observer* did not
have long to wait. Even before the paper had alerted the Society,
its trustees resolved to urge the Legislature to reject the Catholic
petition. The trustees further decided to prepare a remonstrance
against the petition and circulate it throughout the city for signatures. At another meeting held on the same day that the Senate received the Catholic petition, the trustees appointed a four-man
committee to go to Albany whenever circumstances required it.[29]
Although the Society had not circulated its remonstrance by April
5, its committee had already gone to Albany and had arranged a
meeting with a legislative committee for April 9. The trustees
deemed it politic to delay further action until after this meeting.

As soon as Verplanck submitted the Catholic petition to the Senate, it was read and promptly referred to the state's chief educational officer, John C. Spencer, for his scrutiny and recommendation.
During the month that Spencer studied the question, New York
City prepared for its municipal election for the mayoralty, Common
Council membership, and numerous minor offices. No one doubted
that the school question would figure in the outcome, and all political eyes focused upon Alderman Pentz's campaign for re-election. As
early as February, the *Christian Advocate and Journal* had cautioned that the Catholics had not abandoned their claim and "will
unite in an effort to change the complexion of the next Common
Council." Much too astute to attempt the election of a Catholic
majority, Catholics would seek to elect a sufficient number of "nominal Protestants or real infidels . . . who will answer their purpose
quite as well. . . ." The paper felt that the only secure antidote
against such a possibility was "personal pledges previously given by
the candidates to resist the claim to any sectarian appropriation
of the public school fund."[30]

Although Whigs were generally united against the Catholic po-

---

28 *New York Observer*, February 20, 1841.

29 *PSS: Board of Trustees*, March 29, 1841. The members of this committee were
Rogers, Rockwell, Averill, and Mott. Cf. meeting of February 19, 1841.

30 *Christian Advocate and Journal* (New York), February 3, 1841.

sition, city Democrats were divided between nominating or renom-
inating either pro-Catholic candidates or those committed to the
recent decision of the Common Council. The same day that the
Democratic party held ward meetings to make its nominations, the
city's "blank walls, pumps and posts" were plastered with large
handbills and posters urging Catholic Irishmen to attend the primary meetings to insure the nomination of candidates sympathetic
to the Catholic position on the school question:

Catholics Arouse! The Time is at hand when your fair and just proportion of the School Fund may be secured—the voice of the people is to
be heard at the ballot box—It Will Be!! But you must be sure of your
men—Attend the Primary Meetings This Night—show your strength—
present your candidates—combine—agitate! agitate! agitate!!! The united
Irishmen of New York, a body of at least *Ten Thousand* citizens, have
rights and the power peaceably to maintain them—they have been deceived and misled by their *friends* long enough—trust none but yourselves
—select committees who will nominate candidates *favourable to your interests*—move together unitedly and you will achieve this great end—*the
balance of power is in your hands*—Use It! You form a majority of the
Democratic Party—assert your rights—press forward—insist upon a representation on the committees—you have offered sound and unanswerable
arguments, and have been deceived—DEMAND now that your claims be
listened to—agitate for CATHOLIC EMANCIPATION, and such are
your numbers that the battle will be won. A CATHOLIC.[31]

Another handbill specifically called upon Catholics to vote for
Pentz:

Catholics Arouse! To the Rescue! Irishmen to your posts!! The friends
of an equal distribution of the School Fund are called upon to rally!
Come early to the polls and deposit your vote for Daniel C. Pentz, the
friend of the Catholics; he openly proclaims that he is in favor of an
equal distribution of the School Fund. Daniel C. Pentz was the only
member of the Common Council who dared proclaim to the world
that he was willing we should have a share of the School Fund. Irishmen, if you would have your children educated, come and vote for
Daniel C. Pentz.[32]

While the Whig press gloried in this apparent internal Democratic
division, the city's Democratic organ, the *Evening Post*, branded

---

[31] *New York Commercial Advertiser*, March 18, 1841. Cf. *New York American*, March
18, 1841.
[32] *New York Observer*, May 1, 1841.

these handbills as "a device of the Whigs, designed to injure the Catholics themselves, and distract the Democratic party. It is hardly necessary to add, that the plot is so well understood that it will have no effect."[33] In fact, the editor had been assured by a prominent Catholic gentleman that Catholics had nothing to do with the handbills and placards in question.

On election day, April 13, New Yorkers elected a Democratic mayor and Common Council. Pentz, however, was soundly defeated by the voters of his ward, even though they solidly supported Robert H. Morris, the Democratic mayoralty candidate. Most of the city newspapers rightly felt that Pentz's vote on the school question caused his defeat. The *Freeman's Journal* regretted that people voted against the alderman "because he had the manly courage to vote in favor of our claims for justice." Had Catholic voters acted on the same premise, they could have defeated two-thirds of the aldermen who had denied their request. Commenting on this electoral retaliation, the *Freeman's Journal* voiced a thinly veiled threat in the form of a rhetorical question:

If the Catholics and other friends of the Freedom of Education should, at any future time, follow the precedent and example which have thus been established for them by the partizans of the Public School Society, could those advocates of a Monopoly in the business of disciplining and instructing the youthful minds of the State, make it a cause of complaint?[34]

In a few months there would be nothing rhetorical about this question!

iii

On April 26, Spencer reported his analysis of the Catholic petition to the Senate. In his study of the question, he had elicited the viewpoints of the New York City delegations of both legislative houses. The Albany correspondent of the Democratic *Evening Post* accused Spencer of trying to place principal responsibility for his report upon legislators from the city: "Nearly the whole winter he has been coquetting with different members of the New York delegation, to shift the responsibility of acting in this matter from his

33 *New York Evening Post*, March 19, 1841.
34 *New York Freeman's Journal*, cited in the *New York Observer*, April 24, 1841. Cf. *New York Observer*, April 17, 1841.

shoulders to theirs, but finding them, no doubt, rather intractable for this purpose, has finally consented to out with the matter himself. . . ."[35] Spencer quickly wrote a sharp letter to the editor denouncing this charge. He had conferred with city legislators in an attempt to find a common ground of agreement "as would insure a harmonious action on a subject of acknowledged importance and difficulty, a successful result, and an adjustment that would be permanent."[36] He accepted full responsibility for his report even though there is little doubt that he had conferred with Seward and Verplanck on the matter. Several hours before the Senate received his report, the secretary of state wrote a short note to Verplanck which evidenced a certain anxiety that the Senate might react unfavorably to it. Among those legislators not well acquainted with the subject, Spencer detected "a bias against doing anything which may be considered favorable to the Roman Catholics." Too many tended to ignore the broad educational principles of the question and made it an issue between Protestants and Catholics. Spencer thought the question so important that he urged Verplanck to have the report read in the Senate in order that "much prejudice . . . be removed by such a course."[37]

After Spencer summarized state and city educational legislation as well as Catholic objections to New York City's public schools, he made it clear that the academic merit of the Public School Society and the energetic devotion of its trustees was not sufficient cause to dismiss the petitioners' charges. The dispute was not simply a quarrel between Catholics and the Society. The more fundamental question was whether the Society was successfully expediting the Legislature's charge to furnish the means of education to all of New York City's youth. From the outset, the secretary doubted that the Society was accomplishing this task:

On the contrary, the views which will be subsequently presented, afford strong ground for the belief that the education of a much larger number than now are, or under any circumstances may be expected to be pro-

35 *New York Evening Post*, April 28, 1841.

36 *New York Evening Post*, April 30, 1841.

37 Spencer to Verplanck (Albany, April 26, 1841), Gulian C. Verplanck Papers (MSS in the New York Historical Society), Letter S, No. 133. Spencer thought that his report would be in great demand and suggested that additional copies be supplied by the Senate. Verplanck agreed with this recommendation, and upon his motion the Senate ordered one hundred additional copies of the report printed. Cf. *Journal of the Senate*, April 26, 1841, p. 359.

vided for by the Public School Society, or any one society, will be secured by inviting the cooperation, and stimulating the exertions of all who are disposed to engage in the enterprise.[38]

Quoting from his own annual educational report for 1840, Spencer cited specific statistics to prove the Society's limited success. Outside of New York City, there were 592,000 children in the state between the ages of five and sixteen. Of these, 549,000 attended public schools. In New York City, there were 62,952 children within this age bracket. Of these, 30,758 went to public or private schools. As a result, a greater percentage of city children lacked an education than was the case in the state as a whole. Moreover, the Society enrolled 22,955 of the 30,758 children who attended school in the city. In reality, however, the average actual attendance of public school pupils numbered only 13,189. "With these facts before us," reasoned Spencer, "it must be admitted that the Public School Society has not accomplished the principal purpose of its organization, and for which the public funds have been so freely bestowed upon it—the education of the great body of the children of the city."[39]

In addition to charging that education under the Society's auspices was not comprehensive in reaching New York children, Spencer also supported the Catholic charge that the Society was a closed corporation without any direct responsibility to the citizenry. The Society was not subject to any governmental supervision except the nominal jurisdiction of the Common Council. Although school buildings were purchased with public money, they remained the private property of this private corporation. Spencer admitted that if these schools were left unoccupied, there would be few physical facilities for education in the City. But abuses would have to be flagrant before the Common Council ever decided to withhold public funds from the Society. Such a measure would drive "into the streets the multitude of children who now occupy these houses." An integral element of republican government included the people's right to manage the affairs of government. And this right extended into the field of public education. As a result, "thousands of citizens of New York demand the right of controlling through responsible public agents, the education of their children, and the

[38] Report of the Secretary of State upon Memorials from the City of New York, Respecting the Distribution of the Common School Moneys in That City, Referred to Him by the Senate, *Document No. 86, Documents of the Senate*, April 26, 1841, p. 6.
[39] *Document No. 86*, p. 18.

application of common funds to which they have contributed for a common object."[40] Only such a system could ever command the confidence and cooperation of all citizens. Although Spencer acknowledged the efficiency, integrity, and honesty of the Society's trustees both individually and collectively, he subtly implied that the days of the Society's educational monopoly were numbered. He suggested that the trustees yield to the inevitable before a rising tide of hostility negated even the meritorious past of the Society.

Spencer used Protestant and Catholic disagreement as a springboard to discuss the whole area of religious education in the public schools. The constitution and laws of New York State were neutral concerning the religious affiliation of citizens. Since citizens had the right to control public institutions, including public education, they also possessed the right to determine the religious character of these institutions. The state intended only the intellectual training of children and left moral and religious instruction to the church and the home, and Spencer believed that this was a rather unrealistic approach. This was a Christian nation, and "public sentiment would be shocked by the attempt to exclude all instruction of a religious nature from the public schools: and that any plan or scheme of education, in which no reference whatever was had to moral principles founded on these truths, would be abandoned by all." In fact, such an attempt was quite impossible. No books or other reading material existed which did not include, either directly or indirectly, some principle of religious faith. Thus, religious instruction was a necessary corollary of public education.

Spencer did not exclude the Society's schools from this analysis. They imparted religious instruction because the Society viewed education as incomplete without the inculcation of moral and religious principles. Indeed, they required Scripture readings and instruction in Christian nondenominationalism. The trustees, it is true, professed an eagerness to exclude sectarianism and any practice or book construed to be religiously offensive. Nevertheless, substantially in agreement with Hughes's position, Spencer charged that any kind of religious instruction was necessarily sectarian. Since the divisions in Christianity had established mutually opposing theological positions, there were few if any religious beliefs commonly accepted by all denominations. Religious instruction always favored

[40] *Document No. 86*, p. 15.

one set of beliefs over another. "Even the moderate degree of religious instruction which the Public School Society imparts, must therefore, be sectarian. . . ." Nor did Spencer believe that the absence of religious instruction was a valid alternative to sectarianism. "On the contrary," declared Spencer, "it would be in itself sectarian, because it would be consonant to the views of a peculiar class, and opposed to the opinions of other classes."[41]

The superintendent realized that these views posed a difficult dilemma: "that while some degree of religious instruction is indispensable, and will be had, under all circumstances, it cannot be imparted, without partaking to some extent of a sectarian character, and giving occasion for offence to those whose opinions are thus impugned." In an attempt to cut this Gordian knot, Spencer invoked a principle which he called "absolute non-intervention." He based this principle upon his interpretation of the first amendment to the constitution. No law could be passed "respecting an establishment of religion or prohibiting the free exercise thereof." Such a prescription could be enforced only if government scrupulously abstained from legislation on any religious matter. Spencer felt that his principle was in perfect harmony with the first amendment. In fact, non-intervention had long been in operation throughout the state except for New York City. No common school officer was permitted to legislate respecting the nature and extent of religious instruction in the schools. Religious control was "left to the free and unrestricted action of the people themselves, in their several districts." State law provided only for the organization and management of district schools and left other matters to local home rule. "The practical consequence is, that each district suits itself, by having such religious instruction in its school as is congenial to the opinions of its inhabitants. . . ."[42]

New York City's difficulties had arisen from the violation of this principle. Since the Public School Society maintained an educational monopoly. "absolute non-intervention" would work only when it removed its own brand of religion from its schools. These schools could never inculcate religious instruction without offending particular religious beliefs. Since Spencer rejected the removal of all religious instruction as an alternative, he recommended that

41 *Document No. 86*, pp. 9, 13.
42 *Document No. 86*, p. 10.

such instruction be left to the choice of parents "in small masses."
In this way, each school district could successfully inculcate religious
instruction without wounding anyone's feelings.

The Society had tried unsuccessfully to be all things to all men at
all times. "It is because it embraces children of all denominations,
and seeks to supply to them all, a species of instruction which is
adapted only to a part, and which, from its nature, can not be
moulded to suit the views of all, that it fails, and ever must fail, to
give satisfaction on a subject, of all others the most vital and the
most exciting."[43] Because Spencer viewed the basic deficiency as
organizational, he also saw the basic remedy as organizational.
Therefore, his report urged the Senate to extend the state district
school system to New York City. Such a plan would break the
Society's monopoly by means of decentralized local rule. Each city
ward would elect commissioners of public schools who would act as
a board and have general jurisdiction over all public schools in the
city. Immediate management and control of the schools would remain with their trustees or officers. The board would be aided by a
city superintendent of schools who would be a full-time and well-
paid city official. New schools could be opened as district schools
whenever a sufficient number of responsible citizens organized to
establish and manage them. The commissioners would distribute
school moneys on a pro rata basis to the schools under their jurisdiction for the exclusive use of teachers' salaries. Tuition or rate-
bills would be required though the children of the poor would be
exempt from such payment. Under such a system, the majority of
each district school would exercise control over the kind and extent
of religious instruction which would be given to its children. However, if any school during the school day diverted its secular instruction exclusively to a narrow sectarianism, the commissioners
could dissolve the school and withhold its share of school money.
Spencer emphasized that the schools of the Society as well as other
operational schools would remain intact and on an equal basis with
other district schools.

An objection to this plan was the possible increase of religious
dissension and sectarian rivalry. Spencer rejected such an eventuality since each school would act independently and not come into
contact with other schools. Although he admitted that, since school

43 *Document No. 86*, p. 11.

funds would be distributed in proportion to a school's enrollment, competition to register students would develop, he welcomed such rivalry. As competition sharpened, the schools would improve their faculties and enrich their instruction in order to attract more students. In the end, the real victors would be the students, who deserved the best possible education.

Spencer's report clearly vindicated the Catholic position since under this plan, Catholic schools would become part of the common school system of the state and thus be entitled to public funds. The educational monopoly of the Public School Society would come to an end, and its new position would be as an equal among equals. In any district where the majority did not support the Society, it could establish a new district school which would be supported with public funds. Since most Catholics lived in ghetto areas of the city, district schools established within these neighborhoods would certainly embrace Catholicism as their religious instruction. Spencer was convinced that he had supplied the solution to the school dispute. True, the Society would lose its educational primacy, but it would still own and control most of the city's educational facilities, thus having a *de facto* monopoly. Although Catholic schools were not allotted school funds, in practice district schools with a Catholic majority would be equivalent to Catholic schools. In reality, Spencer's recommendations, especially his principle of "absolute nonintervention," would have established sectarian public schools without specific denominational control. Successful operation of such a system of schools would have made separate Catholic schools completely unnecessary.

While Roman Catholics applauded Spencer's report, the Public School Society was put on the defensive for the first time. Seward was not in Albany when Spencer forwarded his report to the Senate, and the secretary may have made a tactical error in not first consulting with the Society. One of Seward's city advisers, Robert B. Minturn, had been trying to get several trustees to go to the state capital to judge whether some compromise formula could be effected. Just when "Ketchum, Mott, and some others" had agreed to go to Albany, "intelligence came in that *the report had been presented to the Senate.*" Minturn feared there was "no hope of any compromise," and he was right.[44] On April 30, the trustees memor-

---

[44] Robert Bowne Minturn to Seward (New York, April 26, 1841), UR.

ialized the Senate against Spencer's report and asked for a hearing before that body "in opposition to the statements, the principles and the arguments contained in said report."[45] Since the Senate had referred Spencer's report to its Committee on Literature, this committee received the Society's request. It agreed to a hearing for the Society but opened it to include Catholic representatives as well. On May 8, the hearing was held with Hiram Ketchum once again representing the Society and James McKeon and Wright Hawks appearing for the Catholics.[46]

For the most part, Ketchum's speech was a restatement of his remarks before the Common Council. Once again he summarized state and city educational legislation, including the Bethel Baptist Church controversy and the law of 1824. That decision had been accepted by every denomination except the Catholic Church. Catholics had regularly petitioned the Common Council for public funds and the aldermen had repeatedly denied their request. It was obvious that the "citizens" petitioning before the Legislature were overwhelmingly Roman Catholics. "I believe I may safely affirm that, if not exclusively, it [the petition] is almost altogether signed by Roman Catholics."[47]

As he had done before the Common Council, so now he attempted to refute each of Spencer's contentions. Although Ketchum did not deny the private corporate charter of the Public School Society, he insisted that it was responsible to the people through their elected representatives. The Legislature had granted the Society its charter and it continued to function only because of the Common Council's financial support. The Council and school commissioners were agents of the people who "supervise and direct and control and give daily bread to the Public School Society, whom they make their almoners to do this work under their eye. . . . What principle of republicanism dear to the heart of any man is violated by this?" Publicly disposed and philanthropically motivated, the trustees volunteered to organize and superintend the public schools "without

---

45 *Journal of the Senate*, April 30, 1841, p. 380.

46 *New York Evening Post*, May 10, 1841; *New York Freeman's Journal*, June 5, 1841; Hassard, *Life of Hughes*, p. 242; Bourne, *History of Public School Society*, p. 373. Although the committee did not issue a report on the meeting, several newspapers subsequently printed Ketchum's complete speech in their columns. Cf. *New York Commercial Advertiser*, June 10, 1841; *New York Evening Post*, June 14, 1841.

47 *New York Commercial Advertiser*, June 10, 1841; *New York Evening Post*, June 14, 1841.

money and without price." Ketchum believed that voluntary public service was preferable to service performed by salaried officials. He thought it unwise for the public to reject this service since such men desired to devote themselves to philanthropic enterprises and so "in a quiet way accomplish something for the benefit of mankind."[48] As to the Society's property holdings, Ketchum repeated the Society's offer to deed all its property to the Common Council and then lease this property for its educational enterprises.

Ketchum acknowledged that a large number of children in New York City did not attend the public schools. With the exception of Catholics, this condition did not stem from dissatisfaction with the public schools. Many parents saw no need to send their children to school while many youngsters refused to attend any school. He conceded this difficulty but predicted that "nothing but legal provision can make them [attend school], and probably, we are not prepared for a resort to force." Furthermore, Ketchum challenged Spencer's statistics. The annual school report numbered 32,194 children who did not attend school in New York City in 1840. But the Public School Society reported its enrollment at nearly 23,000. The 8,000 who attended Roman Catholic schools raised the number of school children to 31,000. If this total number were deducted from the 62,952 children between five and sixteen, the number remaining would be 31,952, which was a smaller number than the 32,194 children recorded by the report! Ketchum reminded the committee that this number did not take into account the large number of children who attended the city's private schools. He calculated that in his own seventeenth ward there were over 1,000 students who attended private schools. Thus, he said, "I doubt whether the persons who took the census were remarkably accurate or particular in obtaining information respecting the attendance of children in schools."[49]

Spencer had asserted that while the Society's schools had enrolled 22,955 students in 1840, the average actual attendance dropped to 13,189. Ketchum did not so much deny these figures as explain the disparity. He admitted that the difference between students who attended school and the number on the register was twenty per cent; "that is to say, twenty children out of one hundred do not attend the

48 *New York Commercial Advertiser*, June 10, 1841; *New York Evening Post*, June 14, 1841.

49 *New York Commercial Advertiser*, June 10, 1841; *New York Evening Post*, June 14, 1841.

schools daily." Many of the ordinary reasons such as illness and bad weather explained part of this absence although other causes were unjustified. Some parents refused to send their children to school before the age of six while others terminated their children's education at eleven or twelve to get them ready for employment. Thus, in addition to the specific reasons which kept children home on a given day, there were many youngsters under six and over eleven not sent to school by their parents at all; "So that, in this calculation, you do not arrive at a result which shows you the number of children actually left uneducated. It is difficult to decide this point."[50]

The heart of Ketchum's rebuttal dealt with Spencer's proposals for religious instruction in the public schools. In specific terms, he denounced the superintendent's solution. Under Spencer's plan, reasoned Ketchum, a school organized in the heavily Catholic sixth ward would choose trustees who would no doubt select Catholicism as that school's brand of religious instruction. In poignant terms, Ketchum defended the rights of a religious minority in a religiously pluralistic society:

Now suppose that, in any given district, there should be about five hundred Roman Catholic children, and two hundred Protestant children. These Protestant children are compelled to worship according to the opinions of the majority; that is to say, they are compelled to be taught religion according to the doctrines of the Roman Catholic Church. I ask you, gentlemen, if that is not the tyranny of the majority? The Secretary admits that a majority of the people, in a given district, has a right to indicate what religion shall be taught in the district school; and to that religion, or that form whatever it may be, the minority must submit. Thus, in a given district, the Protestant shall be taxed for the support of the Roman Catholic religion; or, on the other hand, the Roman Catholics shall be taxed for the support of [a] definite Protestant religion; and thus, by abandoning the present system, we are to form and create a system which will overcome the difficulty. Is this reasoning like an American statesman? I deny the Secretary's proposition. I affirm it is false and erroneous from beginning to end.[51]

Ketchum denied that common school money could ever be employed to teach sectarian doctrines. A minority of one was a sufficient

50 *New York Commercial Advertiser*, June 10, 1841; *New York Evening Post*, June 14, 1841.
51 *New York Commercial Advertiser*, June 10, 1841; *New York Evening Post*, June 14, 1841.

majority to protest the inculcation of denominational tenets in the public schools. This minority had the legal right to say, " 'I will not pay my money to teach the Roman Catholic religion; I will not pay my money to teach the Protestant religion; I will not pay my money to teach the doctrines of Tom Paine. . . .' "

In opposition to Spencer's plan, Ketchum urged the Senate committee to continue the present religious accommodation in the public schools of New York City. "I affirm that the religion taught in the public schools is precisely that quantity of religion which we have a right to teach. It would be inconsistent with public sentiment to teach less; it would be illegal to teach more." He sustained the schools' right to teach generally accepted moral principles and nondenominational Christianity. Such principles were legitimate in the schools since they were accepted throughout the country. "Beyond that, no such right exists; because, the moment you go beyond that, you trample upon the conscience of this or that man, whose conscience you are bound to respect." Emphasizing the schools' obligation to teach commonly accepted ethical and religious principles, Ketchum insisted that the Society's schools "neither say nor do anything to interfere with the peculiar sentiments of any sect or denomination." Ketchum concluded his remarks by urging the Senate committee to leave the public schools of New York City undisturbed. The people of the city well understood the situation and had expressed their will through the decision of the Common Council. "Why not leave the matter to us, the people of the city of New York?"[52]

iv

During all this time, Hughes maintained a discreet public silence. More than anything else, he did not want to abet the opposition's claim that the petition of the "citizens of New York" was in reality a Catholic document. He held no public meetings and made no public statements. Nevertheless, Hughes was in regular communication with Seward, Spencer, and others sympathetic to the Catholic cause. He was pleased with Spencer's views and hailed the report

[52] *New York Commercial Advertiser*, June 10, 1841; *New York Evening Post*, June 14, 1841. The speeches of Hawkes and McKeon were neither printed nor preserved. Thus, when Ketchum's address was later published in the press, Hughes decided to answer him publicly. Cf. chap. 7, sec. 3.

as "a blow . . . from which the Public School Society will never recover."[53] Writing to the secretary, Hughes praised Spencer's "statesmanlike Report" as entitling him to "the deep and respectful gratitude of every man that loves the first principles of the American Constitution. . . ." He expressed apprehension "lest you like the governor should be made to suffer for having been the friend of a measure which would place us on a level with our fellow citizens of other religious denominations."[54]

A short correspondence between Hughes and Seward revealed a minor disagreement over political strategy. The governor suggested that Hughes call a large public meeting in order to show public support for Spencer's recommendations. Seward thought that such a move would help mobilize and consolidate legislative support. With perhaps greater political astuteness than the governor, Hughes opposed the meeting because it would emphasize Catholic unanimity on the school question:

1. It must be called by Catholics, and Catholics would principally compose it. 2. It would give the opponents of the measure the opportunity which they desire of making this appear a Catholic question. If the meeting could be called & had without this feature of Catholicism's being mixed up with it, then indeed it would be serviceable. But I fear this is impossible.[55]

He felt that the tide of public opinion was turning against the Society "as being an anomaly in the midst of our Institutions—as something undemocratic if not anti-republican." Since principally "Catholics" and "foreigners" would attend this rally, Hughes feared that anti-Catholicism and antiforeignism would raise their ugly banners against the Catholic "claims of justice and equal rights." As a result, he was of the opinion "that now at least *we* should not awaken the false but imputed sectarianism of this important question." In a very pragmatic vein, Hughes reminded his political friend that, after all, "*success* is the criterion by which the soundness of a public measure is judged and decided on."[56]

Although Seward's answer tacitly acceded to Hughes's course of

[53] Hughes to McCaffery (New York, May 6, 1841), cited in Connors, *Church-State Relationships*, p. 33.

[54] "Letter of Archbishop Hughes on the School Question, 1841," *American Catholic Historical Researches*, XXII (1905), 262.

[55] Hughes to Seward (New York, May 11, 1841), UR.

[56] Hughes to Seward (May 11, 1841), UR.

political expediency, it also evidenced a more consistent and high-minded approach to the school question than that of his episcopal friend. He did not doubt that Hughes's course was politically wise. Yet he pointedly reminded the bishop that he always confided "in the intelligence of the People" and never "feared at any time to avow distinctly and maintain in action and argument the principles and measures which are involved in the effort to extend the system of common school education to all the children in the State." Even if Catholics alone objected to the public schools, Seward would uphold their right to complain. "If Catholics only are offended in conscience I maintain that that offence ought not to be continued by [the] authority of law." Since he had decided to retire at the end of his present term of office, he reaffirmed "all I have before promulgated concerning the policy of this country in regard to foreigners and the education of their children."[57] Although participation in the political wars caused his views to be misunderstood and maligned, Seward was certain that history would vindicate the justice and liberality of his position.

The *Commercial Advertiser* acquired a copy of Seward's letter, and published it on June 8, 1841. The paper reiterated its censure of the governor's position on the school question and insisted that only Catholics were dissatisfied with the public schools, because they did not inculcate sectarian doctrine. The task of the schools was to teach only the core of generally accepted moral and religious beliefs, while parents were to decide whether their children entered "the kingdom of Heaven as good Catholics, or good Baptists, or Methodists, or Presbyterians." Catholic objections were neither reasonable nor theologically justified, but rested upon the hierarchy's desire "to build up and maintain a separate Catholic empire within the bosom of our country." Such Catholic exclusiveness thwarted the effectiveness of the public school's Americanization program for immigrants, which was "that, when they settle down among us, they shall no longer look upon themselves as members of this or that foreign nation, but become AMERICANS."[58]

The *Commercial Advertiser* extended its sharp criticism to Spencer's plan. Along with many New Yorkers, the paper "did not antici-

---

[57] Seward to Hughes (Albany, May 13, 1841), UR.
[58] *New York Commercial Advertiser*, June 8, 1841. Cf. *New York Freeman's Journal*, June 19, 1841.

pate such a document from such a source." Since the secretary's report substantially endorsed Seward's educational views, the editor believed that the entire public school structure was in danger. In its place, the decentralized district schools would become "subservient to the detestable politics of Tammany Hall, in which every political and religious faction will thrust a mischievous hand, 'and chaos will come again.' "[59] Although the district plan worked in rural areas, it would be disastrous in New York City and would transform the "order and beauty" of the public schools into utter confusion. A letter to the *Evening Post* warned that, if the city were divided into districts or "masses," there would be numerous districts "in which persons cannot be found who have the talent, the time, and the disposition, to superintend the schools, and watch them with the vigilance, which their welfare demands." It was common knowledge, declared the writer, that many rural district schools were neglected by their trustees. Moreover, this elective district system would inject partisan politics into the management of the schools and bestow teaching positions "as a reward for party drudgery and political services."[60]

The Democratic *Sun*, on the other hand, was favorably impressed with Spencer's proposals. The genius of the secretary's plan was that "it neither builds up or tears down any creed, nor does it have any thing to do with matters so foreign to the business of legislating for the equal benefit of all; but it leaves everything in the hands of the people. There is where it should be left."[61] Predictably enough, the *Freeman's Journal* described Spencer's report as "masterly and statesmanlike." It applauded the recommendations as founded upon true republican principles. The editor thought it refreshing that the report attacked the Society's educational monopoly and private corporate character. An important principle, ignored by the Society, endowed citizens with the right to manage their own affairs. Even De Tocqueville, "in his celebrated work on America," lauded this principle as "the grand preservative of a Democratic spirit and of permanent national prosperity." The *Journal* lashed out against the editorial policy of the *Commercial Advertiser* on the school

---

[59] *New York Commercial Advertiser*, April 29, 1841.

[60] *New York Evening Post*, May 3, 1841. This letter was signed "Howard." Another critical letter, signed "J.S.R.," was printed in the *New York Commercial Advertiser*, May 5, 1841. Additional adverse remarks are in the *Advertiser*, May 4, 1841.

[61] *New York Sun*, May 7, 1841.

issue and criticized the anonymous letters in the paper as well as those in the *Evening Post.* The editor prophesied that the Public School Society's sun was slowly beginning to set: "The popular spirit is awakened, and their star is no longer in the ascendant."[62] The Society's star was indeed ebbing, but it was not yet extinguished.

62 *New York Freeman's Journal,* May 8, 1841. Cf. May 1, 1841.

⏤✦ VII ✦⏤

Temporary Postponement

i

Despite Ketchum's denunciation of Spencer's report, the Senate Committee on Literature submitted to the Senate on May 11 an "Act to extend the benefits of common school education in the city of New York" which included the essential proposals of the secretary of state.[1] Under the provisions of this act, each city ward would elect a commissioner of common schools at the yearly municipal elections. These ward school-commissioners would possess the same powers and have the same duties and obligations as the "commissioners of common schools in the several towns of the state. . . ." Collectively, they would form a board which would choose a chairman and a clerk and keep regular minutes. The board would then "appoint a superintendent of common schools for the city and county, who shall hold his office during the pleasure of the board."[2] This city superintendent would be equivalent to the state's county deputy superintendents, having the same authority and obligations.

Whenever any group of citizens wished to establish a school in the city, it would petition the commissioners to designate the school as a district school. If the commissioners approved the application, they would certify the new school as a part of the district system. The trustees of the new school would possess full authority to govern their school within the framework of state law. They could impose

[1] *Journal of the Senate*, May 11, 1841, p. 416.

[2] An Act to Extend the Benefits of Common School Education in the City of New York, *Document No. 565, Bills of the Senate and the Assembly*, May 11, 1841, sec. 2, p. 2.

a tax based on real and personal property "for building, hiring or purchasing a school house." Students would be subject to rate-bills unless financial circumstances prevented the payment of this tuition. After the deduction of necessary but limited expenses, the common school fund would be distributed to the public schools under the commissioners' jurisdiction. These moneys would be applied exclusively to the payment of teachers' salaries while the schools' others expenses would be met by tuition and a district tax.[3] The schools of the Public School Society would be subject to the same general jurisdiction of the ward commissioners but would remain under the immediate management of their trustees. This act envisioned the Society's schools as city district schools with the same rights, obligations, and pro rata school funds.[4] The bill did not mention religious instruction because, in Spencer's opinion, this aspect of the schools was to be regulated by the trustees of each district school. The Society's subsequent remonstrance to the Senate was thus erroneous in maintaining that this act did "not bear even a

---

[3] *Document No. 565*, sec. 5, p. 3; sec. 14, p. 6; sec. 15, p. 7. The commissioners would approve a new school when they were satisfied that three conditions were fulfilled: "a school at the place specified will promote the interests of education, and not interfere with any school already established, and that the persons applying are sufficient to maintain a reputable school for the instruction of children in the branches usually pursued in common schools. . . ." Necessary board expenses included salaries for the superintendent (not to exceed $2,000 per annum) and clerk (not to exceed $1,000 per annum) and unavoidable board expenses (not to exceed $500 per annum). The ward commissioners would not receive any remuneration for their labor.

The act was quite specific concerning the conditions under which a district school could receive aid. The commissioners

> shall ascertain the whole number of children over five and under sixteen years of age, who attended each school during the year, and who were exempted from the payment of tuition money, and the total amount of such exemption. They shall apportion to each of the said schools, a sum equal to the deficiency in the amount paid or due for the wages of teachers in such school during the year, caused by such exemptions, if the moneys at their disposal are sufficient, and if not sufficient, then such moneys shall be apportioned among the said schools in proportion to the attendance of the exempt pupils, to be determined by the number of half days such exempt pupils shall have attended such schools respectively.
>
> Furthermore, no pupil could be included in the apportionment who pursued studies other than "spelling, reading, writing, arithmetic, English grammar, geography, and history."

[4] *Document No. 565*, sec. 4, p. 2. Other operational schools listed together with the schools of the Public School Society were: "the New York Orphan Asylum school, the Catholic Orphan Asylum school, the Half Orphan Asylum school, the school of the Mechanics' School Society, the Harlem school, the Yorkville Public school, the Manhattanville Free school, the Hamilton Free school, and the school of the Association for the benefit of Colored Orphans. . . ."

remote resemblance to the plan proposed in the late report of the Superintendent.''[5]

The fact that Spencer's recommendations had been formulated into specific legislation deeply concerned the Society. In an attempt to prevent passage of the Spencer bill, the trustees delivered a strongly worded memorial to the Senate opposing both the report and the proposed legislation. At the Society's insistence, New York City's Common Council urged the Senate to defer passage of the pending bill until the aldermen had re-examined the whole school question.[6] At the same time, the Society received welcomed support from the commissioners of common schools in Brooklyn. Some time before, the Brooklyn schools had become part of the district school system. In a report to the Common Council of Brooklyn, the commissioners expressed serious concern at the perceptible retrogression of the city's schools. Praising the Society's schools as worthy of imitation, the commissioners could not "shut our eyes to the fact, that however justly we may be proud of the beauty and healthfulness of our local position, contrasted with our elder and sister city, New York, in our public school system we are far, very far behind her, in all its essential elements." The cause of this disparity and "defective system of our schools results mainly from their being conducted on the isolated district system." This was not a hasty conclusion but a conviction which had matured as a result of trial and investigation. Although the district system was well adapted to a rural or village setting, the commissioners' experience had convinced them that it could never accommodate the peculiarities of a city population.[7] The Society's supporters felt vindicated that another city had judged the district system as inadequate for a city's educational needs.

Perhaps because each passing day increased the chances of the school bill's passage, the Society resorted to a rather clumsy tactic in an attempt to defeat the measure. The Senate had made the school bill the special order of business for Friday, May 22. On the previous day the *Journal of Commerce* had published a letter which pur-

[5] Memorial and Remonstrance of the Trustees of the Public School Society of the City of New York, *Document No. 97, Documents of the Senate*, May 22, 1841, cited in Bourne, *History of Public School Society*, p. 421.

[6] *Journal of the Senate*, May 22, 1841, p. 476; Memorial and Remonstrance of the Trustees of the Public School Society of the City of New York, *Document No. 97, Documents of the Senate*, May 22, 1841, pp. 1–31; *Journal of the Senate*, May 15, 1841, p. 428; *New York Evening Post*, May 17, 1841.

[7] *New York Commercial Advertiser*, May 20, 1841.

ported to criticize Spencer's report. In reality, it was an anti-Catholic diatribe which included a fictitious bill of excommunication allegedly hurled against a recalcitrant Roman Catholic priest in Philadelphia, and it enumerated a number of vile accusations against Catholicism. The letter writer "Americus" reasoned that these allegations were the principles that Catholics wished to inculcate into the minds of their children. "Are not these principles," asked the author, "very essential and their transmission indispensable?"[8] Over thirty copies of the *Journal of Commerce*'s Thursday edition were quickly forwarded to William Rockwell, the Society's agent at Albany. Just before debate began on Friday, Rockwell placed on each senator's desk a copy of the paper with the "calumnious article" marked with black lines so that it could not be missed. Later on, Hughes dared the Society to deny responsibility in this affair, especially since "I have a copy of the papers thus furnished, with the member's name written at the top." Hughes asserted that when Rockwell was confronted with the charge, he "replied that he had done so under instructions."[9] This tactic suggests that the Society's fear that the bill would be passed had frightened it into employing questionable measures.

In spite of the Society's strategy, the supporters of the school bill pressed for quick passage. On the afternoon of May 22, Verplanck successfully motioned the Senate to consider the act. The Senate resolved itself into a committee of the whole and proceeded to debate the bill and adopt several amendments. However, on the motion of Senator Livingston, further discussion was terminated and the bill was laid on the table. Since the Legislature adjourned at the end of

---

8 *New York Journal of Commerce*, May 20, 1841. Cf. Billington, *Protestant Crusade*, p. 151.

9 Kehoe, *Works of Hughes*, I, pp. 187, 197. At the August meeting of the Society's Board of Trustees, Robert Hogan recommended that his colleagues not only condemn Rockwell's action but also request his resignation from the Board. *(PSS: Board of Trustees*, August 6, 1841). The resolution read as follows: "Resolved, that the trustees of the Public School Society reprobate the conduct of a member of the Board who improperly and unauthorisedly placed on the desks of the Senate Chamber of this state a number of the Journal of Commerce of 20th May which contained a gross libel on the religious sentiments of our Roman Catholic fellow citizens. Resolved, that to prove our unequivocal condemnation of an act inconsistent not only with fair dealing, but repugnant to those principles of honourable opposition with which alone the assailants of our Society should be resisted, the individual guilty of it be requested to retire from the Board." Both resolutions, however, were tabled.

May, the bill's advocates pursued the matter. On May 25 the Senate once again considered the amended school bill. Lively and sharp debate ensued among Senators Livingston, Dickinson, Nicholas, Foster, Furman, Denniston, Hull, and Verplanck.[10] Nicholas felt that the bill was too controversial to be passed at this session of the Legislature and moved for its indefinite postponement. Verplanck argued against this motion, for he thought it simple justice to extend relief to thousands of city children deprived of a common school education. Furman replied that such a situation existed because these children refused to attend the public schools. Livingston considered some legislation to be imperative. Not only were more than 27,000 children devoid of a common school education, but the city's public school system was essentially antirepublican and "unnecessarily partial and oppressive." He insisted that everyone who contributed to the school tax had a right to its benefits. Nevertheless, Livingston opposed the present bill because it would destroy all common school education and resurrect sectarian animosity. As a result, he favored the motion for indefinite postponement on three counts: the Common Council had urged a delay on this question; many petitioners had requested this delay; and the great majority of New Yorkers opposed this legislation.

Since the Senate was hopelessly divided on the question, Foster affirmed his intention to support indefinite postponement. Sensing growing sentiment in favor of such a solution, Verplanck spoke lengthily and eloquently for the passage of the act. As debate continued, Denniston introduced a compromise measure. Instead of indefinite postponement, the school bill would be tabled until the next session of the Legislature, which would convene in January, 1842. After Nicholas withdrew his motion for indefinite postponement, the Senate agreed to this temporary postponement by a narrow vote of eleven to ten.[11]

Political partisanship did not control the outcome of this vote.

[10] The content of this debate is a composite taken from the *New York Tribune*, May 27, 1841; *New York Commercial Advertiser*, May 26, 1841; and the *Albany Evening Journal*, cited in the *New York Freeman's Journal*, May 29, 1841.

[11] *Journal of the Senate*, May 25, 1841, p. 498. The vote was as follows: in favor of postponement—Denniston, Ely, Foster, Furman, Hull, Humphrey, Johnson, Livingston, Nicholas, Rhoades, and Taylor—11; against postponement—Dickinson, Hopkins, Hunt, Lee, Moseley, Paige, Scott, Sibley, Strong, and Verplanck—10. Since the Senate had thirty-two members, eleven senators did not vote on this measure.

Seven Whigs and four Democrats voted for postponement while the ten negative votes numbered seven Whigs and three Democrats. The two senators from New York City, the Whig Verplanck and the Democratic Scott both voted against postponement. Furman from King's County voted with the majority while Tompkins from Richmond County abstained from voting. The *Observer* contemptuously declared that the "final vote was not a party one. The names of Whigs and Democrats are mingled promiscuously for and against the bill."[12] Obviously both parties were fairly evenly divided on this explosive issue. No doubt the Common Council's request for postponement influenced several votes, and Nicholas mentioned it as directly influencing his. The supporters of the Public School Society expended a maximum effort to defeat the bill and readily agreed to the postponement. The religious hostility between Protestants and Catholics over the school question undoubtedly influenced the waverers to vote for postponement. These wary politicians preferred to defer any action until the people had expressed their will at the November election. Because their political future was at stake, some senators desired to avoid taking a stand on the question until the election returns were counted. Such reasoning gave them "their cue to defer definite action until after the November elections."[13] At any event, the approaching election loomed prominently in any settlement of the school question.

More than a month before Spencer's report reached the Senate floor, John L. O'Sullivan, a Democratic assemblyman and an Irish Protestant from New York City, had introduced an alternative school bill before the Assembly. On March 15, he introduced "An act to extend and improve the benefits of common school education in the city of New York."[14] When the Assembly decided to refer the bill to its standing Committee on Colleges, Academies, and Common Schools, he moved that his bill be studied by a special Assembly committee composed of the New York delegation. During the rest of March, the Assembly debated the proper agency for the bill. O'Sullivan's political skill finally gained the day, and on the last day of the month the Assembly voted to assign the school bill "to a

12 *New York Observer,* June 12, 1841.
13 Connors, *Church-State Relationships,* p. 34.
14 *Journal of the Assembly,* March 15, 1841, p. 591. Cf. March 8 and 13, 1841. A favorable picture of O'Sullivan is found in the *New York Evening Post,* March 18, 1841.

select committee, consisting of the delegation attending this house from the city and county of New York."[15]

The New York legislators studied the O'Sullivan bill for nearly two months before they submitted their report to the Assembly on May 22. This lengthy report analyzed the dispute between the Public School Society and the Catholics. It traced the history of the struggle through the "great debate" before the Common Council. Although the assemblymen hailed the management and accomplishments of the Society, they believed that Catholics as well as Jews, Unitarians, and even Quakers had legitimate grievances against the city's public schools. They believed that there were two principal defects in the Society which called for revision: its "exclusive monopoly," and the wide discrepancy which existed between its objectives and its practical operation. Established initially as an organization to offer free education to the poor, the Society had gradually expanded its function until it now monopolized public education. Unfortunately, neither of these functions was "performed with the efficiency and success which would attend the operation of a system more directly and distinctly adapted to the one object or the other." On the other hand, school funds could not be given to Catholic or other sectarian schools because of legal objections and public disapproval.

Sensitive to public opinion and possible political repercussions, the New York delegation concluded that compromise was the only solution to the dispute. But adoption of the district school system for the city was not the remedy the legislators had in mind. Leaving the Society untouched, the O'Sullivan bill "authorized the formulation of voluntary associations, on the model of the existing society, entitled to an equal proportional participation with it in the benefit of the [school] fund in question." Each new association would be chronologically designated as "The Second Public School

15 *Journal of the Assembly*, March 31, 1841, pp. 763–64. The complete political maneuverings and debate preceding O'Sullivan's victory can be found under the following entries: March 8, 13, 15, 20, 30, and 31, 1841. The members of the New York delegation at this session were: William Maclay, Paul Grout, Norman Hickok, Edmund Porter, Cornelius Bryson, Solomon Townsend, George Weir, David R. F. Jones, Absalom Miller, Conrad Swackhamer, William McMurray, Abraham Davis, and John L. O'Sullivan. The standing Committee on Colleges, Academies, and Common Schools comprised the following membership: William Duer (Oswego County), William Maclay (New York County), Levi Hubbell (Tompkins County), Isaac Stoddard (Genesee County), and Edmund Elmendorf (Dutchess County).

Society of New York," "The Third Public School Society of New York," and so on. Ward commissioners of public schools would be elected annually at the city elections. They would collectively form a board, select a chairman, and appoint a salaried "Superintendent of Public Schools in the city of New York," whose duties would be purely educational in scope. The ward commissioners would distribute school moneys to each educational society formed under this act, including the Public School Society, on a pro rata basis to be determined by the actual attendance of students between the ages of four and sixteen years. This money would be applied exclusively toward "defraying the necessary expenses incident and contingent to the actual education of scholars" and not for the erection, repair, or rental of school buildings.

Receipt of school moneys would be contingent upon the guarantee that "no peculiar sectarian doctrines or systems of religion shall form any part of the course of education pursued in any such school." Public opinion and common sense would maintain the fine distinction between teaching sectarian doctrines and inculcating general principles of morality and religion. The commissioners would possess the power to withhold public funds from any school which violated or evaded this proscription. The assemblymen doubted that sectarian competition would eventually dissipate the school fund. "The compulsory exclusion of sectarian doctrines or dogmas will preclude any possible motive that could lead to such a result."[16] Catholics would no doubt establish a society under this act to care for their many unschooled children. Employing one of Hughes's arguments, the assemblymen felt that most Protestants

16 Report of the Select Committee Consisting of the Delegation from the City of New York, on the Bill Entitled "An Act to Improve and Extend the Benefits of Common School Education in the City of New York," *Document No. 296, Documents of the Assembly*, May 22, 1841, pp. 27, 29, 31, 34–35. The duties of the newly created superintendent included "full power to visit, at all times, all public schools in the said city participating in the benefits of the aforesaid school moneys; to supervise their expenditure and application of the said moneys; to inspect their buildings, books, courses and modes of education; to advise and suggest in relation to improvements in the same; and to acquire from such schools such periodical returns, in relation to the statistics of their operation, as he may from time to time prescribe. It shall be his duty to make a report, quarterly, to the said board, and at least once a year to the superintendent of common schools, of the state of the schools under his supervision, and to perform all such duties, connected with his office, as may be required from him by the said board of commissioners." His position was identical to the county deputy superintendents of the state.

would continue to patronize the Society's schools, which were unrivaled in organization and academic success.

Like Spencer's bill, this act attempted to break the Society's educational monopoly without impairing its continued effectiveness. Like Spencer's proposals, the O'Sullivan bill strove to make public education palatable to thousands of Catholic children. However, the assemblymen thought it unnecessary to "districtize" New York City's educational system to achieve this end. Under O'Sullivan's leadership, they relied on the establishment of private and philanthropic school societies modeled after the Public School Society. Contrary to Spencer's position, sectarian instruction was prohibited from the school curriculum although the bill did not ban the use of school buildings after regular hours for that purpose. The O'Sullivan bill envisaged a series of private school societies supported by public funds and supervised by publicly elected school officials. On the one hand, Catholics would have schools acceptable religiously for their children. On the other hand, the Society would remain essentially unaffected and public funds would not be used to support sectarian education. O'Sullivan, like Spencer, was convinced that he had blunted the horns of a difficult dilemma.

By the time the New York delegation reported the bill back to the Assembly, Spencer's bill had reached the Senate floor and completely overshadowed its Assembly counterpart. Excitement over the Senate bill was so intense that the O'Sullivan bill receded into the background and never came before the Assembly for debate and consideration. Scant attention was paid it by the respective protagonists. The Society obviously considered the Spencer bill the real threat to its continued existence while Catholics had more to gain by supporting the Senate bill. Solomon Bluhm's study ignores this factor when it contends that the Assembly bill failed because

the contending forces were too uncompromisingly intent on their own special objectives: the friends of the Public School Society to prevent any incursion on what they deemed their mission and domain; the Catholics to establish what they deemed their moral and legal right to a proportionate share of the public school moneys or, at the least, to break the 'monopolistic control' of public education by the Public School Society.[17]

When the Legislature adjourned at the end of May, neither school

[17] Solomon Bluhm, "Genesis and Establishment of New York City's Board of Education, 1840–1855" (unpublished Ph.D. thesis, New York, New York University, 1951), p. 186.

bill had passed either house. Although newspaper reaction to the failure of the Spencer bill was predictably partisan, the press almost completely ignored the fate of the O'Sullivan bill. The Albany correspondent of the *Evening Post* paid it a passing compliment when he judged Spencer's legislation "not as good as the plan of Mr. O'Sullivan. . . ."[18] Reaction to the deferment of the Senate bill, however, was sharp and continuous. The *Commercial Advertiser* was "exceedingly rejoiced" at the postponement. Its editor urged state officials and legislators to visit the city's public schools to ascertain the shallowness of Catholic objections. The paper repeated its warning that Spencer's district plan would involve the ward schools in bitter political warfare and religious controversy.[19] The *Observer* did not take much solace in the postponement since it expected continued Catholic agitation. Although it had in the past been accused of alarmist tendencies over the school question, the editor hoped that its readers now realized the seriousness and relentlessness of the papist drive for public funds. Protestants and other libertarians were asked to make their views known to state legislators lest the latter capitulate to Catholic pressure. Constant vigilance was needed lest Protestant lethargy ensure the enemy's victory.[20]

Greeley's *Tribune* interpreted the Senate's moratorium as an opportunity for all sides to consider their respective positions rationally and attempt a rapprochement. "Let us all look steadily into it, giving each other credit for purity of motive, and anxious not so much to justify and uphold our several views, as to find some ground on which we may all honorably and heartily agree."[21] The *Freeman's Journal* concealed its disappointment at the Senate's postponement and insisted that Catholics had "much to encourage them, in this decision." Rather unconvincingly, the paper argued that the more the Catholic "claim is dispassionately examined, the more it will be found supported by truth and justice." It scored the secular press for its "bigotry and misrepresentation on this subject since the postponement of the New York School Bill by the Senate." Although the *Evening Post*, the *Express*, the *American*, and the

---

18 *New York Evening Post*, April 28, 1841. For some pointed comments on O'Sullivan's bill, see the *New York Evening Post*, March 23, 1841.

19 *New York Commercial Advertiser*, May 26 and June 24, 1841.

20 *New York Observer*, June 12, 1841. Cf. July 10, 1841.

21 *New York Tribune*, May 27, 1841.

Journal of Commerce were roundly censured, the editor saved his choicest broadsides for the *Commercial Advertiser*, which was accused of having "an imbecility of mind on the subject that is really pitiable. . . ." Nevertheless, within this journalistic verbiage, the Catholic weekly set the tone for future Catholic action. The temporary postponement of Spencer's bill "will only inspire us with increasing determination to press for" relief.[22]

At a Catholic meeting on June 1, Hughes pursued this line of reasoning. He believed that a temporary deferment would only make the eventual Catholic victory that much more gratifying. He was confident that the majority of state legislators were sympathetic to the Catholic cause. However, some had concluded that they needed more time to investigate the question and gauge the opinion of their constituents. But Hughes assured his audience that they could expect justice from the Legislature. He reminded them that Catholics were no longer "under the necessity of pleading your cause before a Committee of the Public School Society, commonly known as the Common Council of the city of New York."[23] Although redress was near at hand, Hughes warned his flock not to relax their efforts when victory was so close. In unity there was strength. Before long, Catholic unity and the whole Catholic cause would be put to a sharp test at the polls.

ii

One of the casualties of the school bill's postponement was Ketchum. Early in the year, it became known that there would be a vacancy in the state circuit court. Although several names were prominently mentioned for this position, Ketchum was clearly in the forefront. A lawyer friend of Seward, Samuel Stevens, wrote to the governor outlining the qualifications of a judge. The appointee should be "a *good Lawyer, a sound man*, a man carrying great *moral influence*; he should have all these requisites, they are *each* requisite, particularly, for a presiding judge, in capital cases." After listing these essential requirements, Stevens believed that Ketchum was "the *best* candidate at *present*."[24] Another correspondent defended

22 *New York Freeman's Journal*, May 29 and June 12, 1841.
23 Kehoe, *Works of Hughes*, I, p. 269.
24 Samuel Stevens to Seward (New York, February 5, 1841), UR.

Ketchum's Whigism and championed his candidacy: "All party's [*sic*] have full and entire confidence in his *ample* qualifications to a due discharge of the duties of the office."[25]

Seward did not particularly like Ketchum, especially since he knew that the attorney's educational views were strongly opposed to his own. Although he believed that Ketchum had misrepresented him "to the world as cheating [,] deceitful and double dealing," he would ignore this calumny in considering Ketchum for the position.[26] Seward's New York confidant, Richard Blatchford, urged Ketchum's appointment as politically sagacious and personally high-minded. "[F]or you personally it is one of the most popular appointments and best hits you can profitably make—for the public, none can be better—for the party no one is more meretorious [*sic*]—from you it will be magnanimous & generous. . . ."[27] Reports that Seward intended to appoint Ketchum to the circuit court met with public acceptance, and another correspondent had "no doubt but he is fully competent to discharge the duty incumbent upon him, and will do so impartially & fearlessly to the extent of his power."[28] It seemed quite clear that Ketchum would be appointed to the judgeship.

As soon as Spencer had made his views public, Ketchum hastened to Albany to plead the Society's case against Spencer's report. Soon after Ketchum delivered his blistering attack on the report, his nomination was withdrawn from the Senate. Even Blatchford thought that Ketchum behaved "bad about the Report of Mr. Spencer," and Weed wrote "on his slate 'kill Ketchum.' "[29] Seward had obviously had his fill of Ketchum. Never on personal terms with him, the governor believed that Ketchum's speech had contributed to the defeat of Spencer's bill and had betrayed his liberal treatment toward him. He would not reward a person who had helped to sabotage his administration's school bill. As a result, the Whig leadership offered the position to William Kent, who promptly accepted it. Spencer concluded that such an appointment "will be very acceptable to the public at large as well as our friends, and

25 James Van Alen to Seward (New York, April 16, 1841), UR.

26 Seward to Richard M. Blatchford (Albany, February 6, 1841), UR.

27 Richard M. Blatchford to Seward (New York, January 20, 1841), UR.

28 Thomas Carnley to Seward (New York, January 13, 1841), UR.

29 Richard M. Blatchford to Seward (New York, May 9, 1841), UR.

will be more fatal to Ketchum and his views than any other that could be made."[30]

Seward's high-handed tactics greatly disturbed the Whig press because it appeared that not only the public schools but now even the judiciary and "the rights of the community, and the dignity of the law, and honest manly American sentiments.—are all to be considered as things of little or no regard, when weighed against the importunate claims of the Roman Catholic Church, and a population mainly foreign, however respectable. . . ."[31] The Democratic *Evening Post* branded Seward a "demagogue" and a "miserable and truckling tool" for this arbitrary action.[32] On the other hand, Seward's son defended his father's action as principled and just. As might have been expected, Weed also attempted to justify his pro-

[30] John C. Spencer to Seward (Albany, August 12, 1841), UR. Kent quickly accommodated to his new office, "sitting 10 hours every day, for 4 weeks, & still going." Cf. William Kent to Seward (New York, October 25, 1841), UR.

During most of 1841, the question of the judgeship was of great interest among Whig politicians and candidates for the position. In addition to Ketchum, several others, including David Graham, Jr., of New York City, vied for the position. After Seward vetoed Ketchum and an abortive effort to select John C. Spencer failed, the Whig leadership finally agreed upon William Kent. The correspondence on this question is quite extensive. Richard M. Blatchford early analyzed for Seward the qualities of each of the contenders for the position. Cf. Richard M. Blatchford to Seward (New York, February 14, 1841), UR. Most of the correspondence either strongly supported or opposed Hiram Ketchum. Cf. Thomas Carnley to Seward (New York, January 13, 1841), UR; Richard M. Blatchford to Seward (New York, January 13, 1841), UR; Richard M. Blatchford to Seward (New York, January 20, 1841), UR; Hiram Ketchum to Seward (New York, February 2, 1841), UR; Samuel Stevens (New York, February 5, 1841), UR; James Van Alen to Seward (New York, April 16, 1841), UR; Richard M. Blatchford to Seward (New York, May 9, 1841), UR; Richard M. Blatchford to Seward (New York, June 7, 1841), UR; Richard M. Blatchford to Seward (New York, August 5, 1841), UR. Although David Graham, Jr., had no real support for the judgeship, he nevertheless wrote several letters to the governor outlining his qualifications for the position. Cf. David Graham, Jr., to Seward (New York, February 1, 1841), UR; David Graham, Jr., to Seward (New York, February 4, 1841), UR; Trumbull Cary to Seward (Batavia, February 10, 1841), UR; David Graham, Jr., to Seward (New York, February 17, 1841), UR; David Graham, Jr., to Seward (New York, August 6, 1841), UR; David Graham, Jr., to Seward (New York, September 6, 1841), UR; Seward to David Graham, Jr. (Albany, September 15, 1841), UR. After Spencer refused the position, Kent was finally chosen the new circuit judge. Cf. Thurlow Weed to Seward (no place, August 9, 1841), UR; Horace Greeley to Seward (New York, August 11, 1841), UR; Samuel B. Ruggles to Seward (New York, August 12, 1841), UR; John C. Spencer to Seward (Albany, August 12, 1841), UR; William Kent to Seward (New York, October 17, 1841), UR; William Kent to Seward (New York, October 25, 1841), UR.

[31] *New York American*, cited in the *New York Evening Post*, May 29, 1841.

[32] *New York Evening Post*, May 29, 1841.

tege's behavior and, perhaps, his own. In view of Ketchum's opposition to the administration's school bill, Weed judged Seward magnanimous for even nominating him for the circuit judgeship. Then, "feeling assured of . . . [his] confirmation," Ketchum vehemently attacked the bill before the Senate committee. In "the course of . . . [this] violent harangue against the bill, he charged unworthy motives and discreditable conduct to the Governor. This was going even beyond the point where forbearance ceases to be a virtue. The Governor . . . felt that in this case a rebuke was demanded."[33]

iii

The summer months produced a bitter exchange among a most incompatible triumvirate: Ketchum, Hughes, and the Reverend William Brownlee, who was a leading Presbyterian minister of the city noted for his impassioned anti-Catholic views. During the early part of June several city dailies printed Ketchum's complete speech, which attacked Spencer's plan.[34] Hughes quickly announced that he would review and refute Ketchum's arguments as well as the Society's memorial against the Catholic petition. One of the governor's New York lieutenants, Richard Blatchford, was pleased at this move and wrote Seward that he could not complain "that the war does not open with the right troops."[35] When Hughes's intention became publicly known, Brownlee entered the fray and advised that he would review and refute Hughes's review and refutation of Ketchum. The *Herald's* editor, James Gordon Bennett, lampooned this forthcoming verbal effusion as so much "humbug and nonsense." Referring to this "funny fight," his pointed pen could not resist burlesquing the whole affair as well as the participants. To the question, "What next?" Bennett tauntingly replied: "Why this— as soon as Dr. Brownlee has confuted Bishop Hughes' refutation of Hiram Ketchum's speech on the Catholic Question, we, James Gordon Bennett, shall enter the lists, and confute and review Dr.

33 Frederick W. Seward, *Autobiography of Seward*, p. 536; Harriet A. Weed, *Autobiography of Weed*, p. 485.
34 *New York Commercial Advertiser*, June 10, 1841; *New York Evening Post*, June 14, 1841.
35 Richard M. Blatchford to Seward (New York, June 4, 1841), UR. Cf. Chap. 8, footnote 77.

Brownlee's refutation of Bishop Hughes' confutation of Hiram Ketchum's speech on the Catholic Question."[36] Either Hughes did not read the *Herald*'s satire or, more probably, he remained adamant in spite of it since there was very little love lost between the bishop and the editor. On three warm June evenings he reviewed Ketchum's remarks in Carroll Hall.[37] Numbered among the large gathering which attended the bishop's three-night rebuttal were the lieutenant governor, Luther Bradish, several state senators, and a few Protestant clergymen.

Hughes's rebuttal contained little fresh material. The Catholic position was well known. His opponents had repeatedly remonstrated with the same arguments, and the bishop rebutted with standard answers. But Hughes spoke fluently and eloquently, and he had a distinguished and politically important audience. He conceded that the question of a universally satisfactory school system was difficult in a religiously pluralistic society. At the same time, he argued that nowhere in the United States had religious instruction been proscribed in the schools except in New York City. On the first evening, he summarized the conflict up to that time. His examination spanned the whole question from the Common Council's first denial of the Catholic request in early 1840. In addition to certain disreputable tactics used by the society at Albany, Catholics had to contend with the bitter anti-Catholic prejudice of the Protestant churches. Many ministers whose duty was to preach the gospel of love to all men "have taken up the habit of abusing us, and have rung the changes on this topic, till in some instances some of their audiences—more liberal than they—have left the place disgusted."[38]

---

36 *New York Herald*, June 8, 1841.

37 Kehoe, *Works of Hughes*, I, pp. 183–226. The bishop was scheduled to speak on three successive evenings: Wednesday, June 16; Thursday, June 17; and Friday, June 18. However, a heavy rainstorm "that deluged the city during the entire afternoon and evening" forced a postponement of Friday's speech to the following Monday evening, June 21. The Catholics should have been adjusted to postponements by this time.

38 Kehoe, *Works of Hughes*, I, p. 197. These anti-Catholic clergymen reminded Hughes of a story he had once read. On one occasion, declared the bishop, the author "said that occasionally he was straitened for the price of a dinner, but he could always manage to make a good meal of Cheshire cheese; but it also happened that oftentimes he was in a similar strait in his official capacity, and was called on to preach when he had not a word of a sermon prepared, and then he took 'a fling at Popery.' The people went away edified and delighted. For this reason he says, 'I call Popery my Cheshire cheese!' It seems to me that the occupants of half the pulpits of New York,

The next night Hughes again focused on the municipal phase of the conflict. He reviewed in detail the "great debate" before the Common Council as well as the events preceding the issuance of the Council's negative report. Once again, he claimed that Catholics were denied an impartial hearing before the Council. Since Council members were ex officio trustees of the Public School Society, it was quite obvious to the bishop that they were fundamentally biased, perhaps unconsciously, against the Catholic petition. When the Council had denied them simple justice, Catholics had turned for relief to Albany and the State Legislature. The Society and its staunch counselor objected even to this maneuver. Ketchum's speech emphasized the city phase of the school dispute, declared Hughes, in order "to convey the idea that if there had been anything just, or proper, or true in our claims, it could not have escaped the notice of public officers in New York—the immediate representatives of the people, and that consequently, the Senators should approach the subject with minds already biased, and prejudiced against us."[39]

Hughes's final effort dwelt upon Ketchum's remarks before the Senate. The attorney had asserted the schools' right to teach generally accepted Christian beliefs. "And pray," queried the bishop, "what are we to understand by religion that is not [so] decided? A religion which is vague—a general religion? What is the meaning of these terms? I desire to have a definition of them."[40] Such a nondenominational "general religion" could never have any meaning for Hughes other than synonymity with Protestantism. But anything beyond this "general religion" Ketchum considered sectarian and not permissible in the public schools. The bishop had said nothing new, and Ketchum's subsequent reply added no light.

The Reverend William Brownlee further clouded the issue. Long identified with the Maria Monk fraud, he decided to answer Hughes on Thursday evening, July 8, at the North Dutch Church.[41] A popular and knowledgeable preacher, Brownlee attracted an overflow crowd. But "a great number of Irish and American Catholics" were interspersed among the congregation, ever ready to defend their

are nearly in the same predicament, and would die of inanition, were it not that their stock of 'Cheshire cheese' is still unexhausted."

39 Kehoe, *Work of Hughes*, I, p. 202.

40 Kehoe, *Works of Hughes*, I, pp. 221–22.

41 *New York Commercial Advertiser*, July 8, 1841; *New York Times and Star*, cited in the *New York Commercial Advertiser*, July 9, 1841.

religion at all costs. Such a mixture forboded trouble, which materialized as soon as the clergyman started to speak. The *Herald's* correspondent satirically headlined his story "The Redoubtable Doctor Swallowing the Pope without Pepper or Salt—A Funny Scene."[42]

Brownlee's audience did not have long to wait for his anti-Catholic diatribe. Wherever Romanism flourished, declared the divine in his strong Scottish brogue, knowledge and liberty were absent, spiritual tyranny and civil dictatorship reigned supreme, and the people remained shackled in ignorance and tyrannized by their priests. "Look at Lower [French] Canada," declared Brownlee. "It was settled the same time as New England; one is the land of knowledge, the other of ignorance; one of liberty, the other the reverse. In New England all can read; in Lower Canada a petition was got up, with 8,000 names, to be sent to England [and] of these 7,000 could only make their marks." In the same manner, Catholic Latin America would never attain its freedom until the spiritual and civil legacy of a decadent papism was destroyed. Had the American colonists been subject to the debilitating influence of Romanism, "it would have taken 100 years to gain their liberty instead of seven."

Turning to the school question, Brownlee insisted that Hughes had created an insoluble dilemma by simultaneously assailing the public schools for being dens of infidelity and sanctuaries of sectarian instruction. "But then the Bishop twists and turns so often—that searching out the meaning of the Right Rev. gentleman's mind, is like sifting out chaff. He says no, when he means yes; and he says yes, when he means no—until you don't know what he means." Brownlee artlessly mingled the school question with his favorite clichés. He saw nothing false about the school book lesson on John Huss. It was accurate and true. The Public School Society may have deleted from its readers the phrase "deceitful Catholics . . . although it's an historical fact; they were deceitful." The Catholics had slowly been growing restive. Brownlee's remarks about the "deceitful Catholics" prompted several Catholics to rush precipitously down the aisles toward the clergyman's desk. However, his congregation prevented any manhandling, and the Catholics finally returned to their seats—still ready to defend the honor of their Church.

[42] *New York Herald*, July 9, 1841. The following account is based on the *Herald's* report. No other paper gave coverage to Brownlee's discourse.

But Brownlee was just beginning. In answer to the Catholic complaint that the public schools' lack of discipline undermined parental authority, he insisted that these schools provided the best training grounds for teaching children to tolerate religious differences. To illustrate this point, he presented a hypothetical example of a "sincerely" motivated Protestant youngster attempting to understand his Catholic schoolmate's religion. Brownlee's lesson in religious toleration unfortunately degenerated into a caricature of certain Catholic beliefs:

'Why, John, how can you be so silly as to believe that a bit of wafer is the Lord Jesus Christ? How can you believe such nonsense?' And again: another will say, 'Well, I believe I'll try confession;' he has but two shillings; but he goes to the priest, and says to the priest, 'Well, how much will you charge me for confession?' Says the priest, perhaps, 'I'll charge you two shillings. . . .'[43]

Nor did such a lesson persuade his Catholic "guests." His derision of the Catholic sacrament of the Eucharist evoked a menacing murmur throughout the audience. When he accused priests of charging money to hear confessions, Catholics jumped up in different parts of the church and shouted, " 'It's a lie;' 'you can't prove it;' . . . 'the priest makes no charge;' 'he's an old liar;' 'Maria Monk;' 'turn out;' 'shame' . . . ." Immediately, the imperturbable Brownlee cried out that "we're in a church" and warned his audience that if anyone else interrupted his discourse, he would have him removed from the church. This caused a further clamor and several Catholics were promptly ejected. A sharp wit, the clergyman announced that he would proceed "as soon as the Church is expurgated. There are several going out—we can spare more of them."

For a time, order was restored. But Brownlee continued his harangue, impervious to Catholic religious sensibilities; for Catholics had not been invited to this discourse, and if they did not like it, they could leave. He maintained that Catholics wanted public money for sectarian purposes; that Catholics believed that there was no salvation outside the Roman Church; and that Catholics desired the union of church and state. Brownlee was shocked that Hughes had denied these charges. "Why, can amazement cease?" He referred his audience to Pope Pius' statement that "this is the true Roman Catholic Church, out of which *extra quam* (laughter) there is no

43 *New York Herald,* July 9, 1841.

possible chance of salvation." Feigning compunction, the preacher pleaded "mercy for us poor miserable benighted Protestants (laughter), for so says His Highness Pope Pius, of blessed memory of course, because he's dead and buried a long time ago." In addition, Hughes was accused of desiring a union of church and state in the United States, "for that's what his language means, stripped of all its verbiage." To prove his contention, Brownlee quoted Pope Gregory XVI—"not yet of blessed memory, for he ain't dead"—who allegedly condemned all those who supported the separation of church and state. Since Hughes swore spiritual allegiance to the pope, it was obvious that he was "bound in his heart and soul and conscience . . . to obey the Pope." Either Hughes supported the union of church and state, Brownlee reasoned, or he rejected papal authority, "and he will not break his oath." Once more latent disorder became apparent as several ladies, perhaps fearful of an impending riot, left the church amid cries of " 'Maria Monk,' 'Partridge,' 'Small potatoes,' 'It's false,' 'Turn him out,' 'Shame,' 'Sit down'. . . ."

But "I speak boldly," shouted Brownlee, and he refused to stop. By this time the restive Catholics in the audience lost whatever patience they had left. Brownlee no sooner resumed his discussion than complete bedlam broke loose. The *Herald's* reporter concluded his sparkling article in delightful journalistic style:

Here the noise increased so that we only caught the following:

Dr. B: If by the wrath of Heaven, and by the political juggling we are cursed with such a use of the public money to encourage this religion, and the spirit of foreignism—

(The rest was drowned in a most tremendous uproar and cries of 'pitch him over,' 'shame,' 'turn him out,' 'Maria Monk,' 'd—d old scoundrel,' 'order,' 'sit down,' 'he deserves to have his skull cracked,' etc., and terrible hissing and applause.)

One Catholic jumped up and cried out—'Will you show me that bull of the Pope?' [Bull of Pope Gregory XVI which was alleged to curse all who believed in the separation of church and state.]

Dr. B: I will and read it.

The Doctor began to read it in latin.

(Great Row.)

Voice: Where did you get it.

Dr. B: It was published in a city paper.

Voice: Name the paper, be Jasus [*sic*].

Here the row become [*sic*] so great, that we only heard the Doctor cry out: 'It's false as an emanation from the bottomless pit;' and immediately all the people left the church, and the lights were put out, and the doors closed.[44]

But Catholics had more in store for Brownlee. He had roused their ire and insulted their religion. The next night they waited for him in large numbers at the North Dutch Church, "determined to sustain the honor of the Pope." When he arrived, Catholics refused him entry to the church. As soon as Brownlee's supporters saw what was happening, they rushed to his aid, and a riot developed in front of the church. However, in the midst of this tumultuous excitement, "the Doctor cleared out" in time and escaped any injury.[45] Brownlee certainly helped to enkindle the flames of religious bigotry and sectarian partisanship that blighted the whole school question.

The Protestant divine still had another mission to complete. He published four open letters "To Bishop Hughes, On The Public School Question" during July, August, and September.[46] Once again, he added very little in clarification of the conflict. His first letter reiterated the Society's contention that the New York statute of 1824 had repealed prior legislation authorizing the payment of public moneys to "incorporate religious bodies" for the benefit of Catholic schools. The theme of the second letter asserted that Catholics demanded public funds not as citizens but as an "incorporate religious body" which was no longer permitted by state law. The real Catholic motive was to obtain common school funds to support and propagate the papist religion. Many of Hughes's contradictions and "ludicrous blunders" had arisen from a labored but unsuccessful attempt to conceal this object. If the day should ever come when a governmental agency acceded to the Romanist demand, the clergyman offered this warning: "And mark it well— those who may venture, at any time, so to vote away these moneys, can be sued for its recovery, *personally*. And there are enough of us able and willing to take this step for the recovery of funds appropriated unconstitutionally."[47]

No one denied Catholic children entrance to the public schools, asserted Brownlee in his third communication, except "your Bishop

44 *New York Herald*, July 9, 1841.

45 *New York Herald*, July 10, 1841.

46 *New York Commercial Advertiser*, July 24, July 29, August 12, and September 15, 1841.

47 *New York Commercial Advertiser*, July 29, 1841.

Hughes [who] wantonly rears arbitrary barriers in the way, and actually shuts up, as far as in him lies, the doors of the public schools against you." Catholics voluntarily deprived their children of a public education and thus their alleged "just claims" were fraudulent and unjust. The city of New York opened public school doors to every child of every class. In answer to this public invitation, "you [Hughes] bring up your organized troops, such as those hopeful saints who beautifully figured the other evening in the North Dutch Church; you and they rear a lofty barrier before these open doors of education. . . ."[48] Brownlee's last letter disparaged Spencer's report and characterized the secretary as contriving "very ingeniously" to come to Hughes's aid. At the end of the letter, he urged his Catholic counterpart to review his faulty reasoning and divest himself of all presumption to special sectarian privileges. "Be exhorted, in good earnest, to examine your plans, and look well to it, lest you fall into the Italian error. For your's [*sic*] does smell strongly of the Italian garlic."[49]

Hughes never answered Brownlee's letters and refused to have anything to do with him. As late summer drew to an end, the Brownlee melee had become a memory, albeit an easily awakened one, and New Yorkers turned their attention to the approaching election. The *Freeman's Journal* ineffectively tried to establish a causal relationship between the increase of crime and the multiplication of suicides and a deficient common school system, "which boasts of training the head, but leaves the heart neglected."[50] The summer also saw the publication of the report of the city commissioners of common schools, which eulogized the Public School Society and deprecated the Catholic claim.[51] But the November election was in sight. It would result in a new wave of religious bigotry and political partisanship. And yet, the results of this election would provide the first steps toward a "solution" of the school question.

48 *New York Commercial Advertiser*, August 12, 1841.
49 *New York Commercial Advertiser*, September 15, 1841.
50 *New York Freeman's Journal*, August 21, 1841.
51 Report of the Commissioners on the Public School Money for the City and County of New York for the Year Ending May 1, 1841, *Document No. 26, Journal and Documents of the Board of Aldermen*. This report was printed in full in the *New York Commercial Advertiser*, August 18, 1841, and the *New York Tribune*, September 16, 1841.

⊸ VIII ⊱

The "Church and State" Party

i

Once Spencer's bill had been postponed, Greeley's *Tribune* cautioned the Whig party not to magnify the school question into a passionate bone of contention "so as to defeat our City Ticket in the Fall."[1] However, the Whig editor's counsel fell upon deaf ears. The issue was too charged with tension to recede into the background. Nor would the contending parties allow its demise. Nativists, the Public School Society, and Catholics all realized the significance of the election. They well knew that the fate of the school question would depend upon the political complexion of the next Legislature. And the New York delegation would play a significant role in the outcome. Each actively engaged in partisan politics in a frenzied effort to sway votes and achieve an electoral victory.

The nativists did not wait long to act. On May 30, the American Protestant Union was established to oppose further alleged Catholic encroachments against the public schools.[2] Samuel F. B. Morse, inventor and anti-Catholic controversialist, was chosen president of the organization. At stake in the November election was the New York delegation of two state senators and thirteen assemblymen. Since Catholic fortunes depended largely upon these legislators, the Union decided to act as the election drew near. Union officials canvassed the school views of each candidate in an attempt to distinguish between "safe" and "unsound" men. Such a technique was not novel; prior to the city election in April, the Protestant *Chris-*

---

1 *New York Tribune*, July 26, 1841.
2 *New York Observer*, June 12, 1841; Scisco, *Political Nativism*, p. 34.

166

tian Advocate and Journal had urged that candidates promise personal pledges to resist any rupture in the common school fund.[3] Most of the Protestant press applauded such a procedure, while enthusiasm was also voiced from many Protestant pulpits. Indeed, Brownlee had intimated that politicians sympathetic to the Catholic cause would suffer recriminations at the polls.

Both major political parties were caught in a delicate quandary. Support for the Catholic position by either party would undoubtedly result in mass Protestant defection. The dilemma was not nearly so acute for the Whigs as it was for the Democrats. Nativist in orientation, city Whigs refused to support a position championed by the loyal Democratic Irish Catholics; and this despite the fact that the initial proposal had been suggested by a Whig governor. Seward and the city Whigs remained in constant disagreement during the entire school dispute. Seward and the upstate Whigs did not have to contend with the formidable Irish-Catholic–Democratic coalition that challenged the city Whig machine in every municipal, state, and national election. As a result, the Whigs nominated a ticket pledged to sustain the Public School Society and inserted a plank in their platform which opposed any change in the school system. After a number of changes were made, the following candidates comprised the Whig assembly ticket: Joseph Tucker, John C. Hamilton, Richard Carman, Linus W. Stevens, Cyrus Chenery, Richard E. Mount, Elbridge G. Baldwin, John Coger, Jr., Nathaniel G. Bradford, Charles M. Graham, Jr., William Jones, Horace St. John, and James W. Gerard.[4]

The Whigs experienced some minor internal discord concerning one of their senatorial nominations, Gulian Verplanck. The New York senator had previously expressed his wish not to seek reelection. Nevertheless, the Whigs renominated him, though not without anxiety on the part of the "Friends of the Public School Society." Since he was avowedly sympathetic to the Catholic claim, the Society's supporters argued that a party that officially advocated an educational status quo in the city could not consistently nominate a man committed to its alteration. Fearing that internal dis-

[3] *Christian Advocate and Journal* (New York), February 3, 1841.
[4] *New York Tribune*, October 21, 1841. St. John and Gerard were not initially on the ticket. But when Peter Jay and Edward West declined "an election to the Assembly," the Whig County Convention selected St. John and Gerard to take their places. Cf. October 27 and November 1, 1841.

sension would endanger the entire party ticket, the *Tribune* attempted to soothe fears about Verplanck's "heresy . . . on the Public School question." Greeley insisted that a "respectable" Whig minority agreed with the senator's plan for modification of the city's public schools. And yet, complained the editor, the nominating committee completely ignored this segment of opinion and selected an assembly ticket pledged to the vindication of the Society. Only after two "sound" men had declined to run was "a single candidate from the minority . . . placed on the ticket—a man eminently qualified by everything save heterodoxy on this question." The *Tribune* thought that since fourteen of the fifteen-man Whig delegation were "sound" on the school question, Verplanck's other great attributes would atone for his one political sin. It was unfair for the majority to risk the defeat of the entire ticket, "of which you have *fourteen* members, because those who differ from you have one."[5]

The debate over Verplanck's candidacy was really quite academic. When he returned to the city "after an absence of some weeks," he declined the nomination in accordance with his initial determination not to seek re-election. City Whigs loyal to Seward on the school question put tremendous pressure on Verplanck to seek another senatorial term. Richard Blatchford described this pressure in a letter to Seward: "I saw Verplanck yesterday—We all saw him—We begged—prayed—entreated—but he was obstinate & unrelenting—We coaxed—scolded and swore by turns but to no purpose."[6] When it became obvious that he would not reconsider his decision, the Whigs selected Alderman Morris Franklin of the seventh ward as Verplanck's replacement.[7] Franklin's "safe" nomination in addition to the other "sound" senatorial candidate, Daniel Lord, Jr., marked the Whig ticket as unanimously opposed to the Catholic position.

Although New York Whigs generally agreed on the school question, the national party was in the throes of deep division. The aged

5 *New York Tribune*, October 25, 1841. Cf. October 26, 1841; Frederick A. Tallmadge to Seward (New York, October 23, 1841), UR; David Nagle to Seward (New York, October 28, 1841), UR.

6 Richard M. Blatchford to Seward (New York, October 28, 1841), UR.

7 *New York Tribune*, October 28, 1841. Scisco, *Political Nativism*, p. 35, maintains that "the anti-Catholic feeling" in the Whig party in New York City "was strong enough to force a certain pro-Catholic aspirant off the ticket." The evidence does not sustain this assertion.

William Henry Harrison contracted pneumonia and died on April 1, 1841—just one month after he delivered his excessively long inaugural address. John Tyler, the states' rights Democrat turned Whig, now became the new President of the United States. Although he was the chief executive of the land, Tyler was challenged in his party leadership by Henry Clay. When the President vetoed Clay's bank bill in August, a breach opened between Tyler and his supporters and Clay and his followers. Since most members of Tyler's cabinet were Clay partisans, all save Daniel Webster resigned on September 11. This national split made itself felt on the state and local level where party members described themselves as Tyler or Clay Whigs. New York Whig leaders worried lest this division lead to indifference and recrimination at the November election. If the ward and precinct workers did not campaign energetically and get out the vote, the Whigs would be defeated in a crucial election.

The Democrats, on the other hand, stood to lose valuable support regardless of which position they adopted. Commanding a substantial vote in the city, the party would sacrifice the Protestant vote by supporting the Catholic position and the Irish Catholic vote by endorsing the Public School Society. Early in October, the *Journal of Commerce* reported that the Democratic nominating committees rejected *"the advocates of sectarian schools. . . ."* But the final selections did not completely justify the paper's assessment. Isaac L. Varian and Elijah F. Purdy were nominated for the Senate and the Assembly ticket included the following candidates: John O'Sullivan, Edward Sanford, William McMurray, William B. Maclay, David D. Field, David R.F. Jones, Paul Grout, Conrad Swackhamer, George Weir, Solomon Townsend, Auguste Davezac, George G. Glasier, and Daniel C. Pentz.[8] Since Pentz alone had supported the Catholic petition before the Common Council, his candidacy gave the Whig press a field day. "Mr. Pentz is put on [the ticket] to catch the Catholics," declared the *Tribune*, while the *Commercial Advertiser* warned that, "if Messrs. Pentz and Co. can succeed in their schemes, the Protestants of this city are to be taxed for the support of Roman Catholic Schools, AS SUCH! Are the Protestants of New York prepared for this?"[9] At a Whig rally presided

8 *New York Journal of Commerce,* cited in the *New York Observer,* October 9, 1841; *New York Tribune,* October 20, 1841; *New York Evening Post,* October 30, 1841.
9 *New York Tribune,* October 20, 1841; *New York Commercial Advertiser,* October 19, 1841.

over by the influential Whig politician, Philip Hone, on October
29, the party reaffirmed its support of the Society and its opposition
to a division of the school fund upon sectarian principles.[10]

   The Democratic *Evening Post* feared the effect of the Whig's
"no popery" crusade. It insisted that the whole school question was
of Whig origin. Seward, Verplanck, Spencer, and company were
responsible for its emergence. The editor affirmed that there was not
the slightest chance for Catholics to receive common school funds,
and this was as it should be. The Democratic candidates for the
Assembly, assured the paper, collectively rejected the use of public
funds for sectarian schools. "We have conversed with several of
them, and find a perfect conformity of their views with ours, and
believe that we may answer for the whole of them, that they are
not for allowing any religious denomination whatever to put in a
claim for any portion of the school money." The *Post* urged the
people to ignore Whig allegations and take their regular rest "without any fear of finding themselves under the dominion of the pope
when they wake."[11]

ii

As election day drew near, it became apparent that both political
parties were pledged to support the Public School Society and oppose the Catholic claim. Such a unanimity of opinion tended to null-
ify Irish-Catholic influence at the very time it was most needed.
Hughes realized that if the next city delegation to the Legislature
were unsympathetic to the Catholic position, chances would be
negligible for the passage of any favorable legislation. At this junc-
ture, he decided to play a bold and potentially dangerous hand. As
far back as July, Jacob Harvey, friend both to Seward and to Hughes,
had warned the governor that the school controversy

will inevitably produce a *political* union among the Catholics, finding as
they do, that the only way to produce an effect either in the assembly or
in the Common Council, is thro' the ballot boxes—and as the Catholic
vote is sufficient to kick the beam on either side, one party or the other
will very soon find it necessary to conciliate the umpire. I reject this
state of affairs very much, & have done every thing in my power to pre-

10 *New York Tribune,* October 30, 1841.
11 *New York Evening Post,* October 28, 1841.

vent it, but a few of our worthy Presbyterians were so fearful of Catholicity they would not unbend in certain points, and my exertions went for nothing![12]

Harvey had foreseen what was coming, and at the gathering of Catholics at Carroll Hall on October 25, Hughes underlined the importance of the Catholic vote in the coming election. He had been told that three out of four candidates were hostile to the Catholic application and pledged to preserve the Society. His audience was urged to ignore party labels and cast its vote only for the friends "of the free and unrestricted education of your children." Since the election was so important to future Catholic success, Hughes warned his followers that "if any danger should . . . be approaching, they might expect a call that would be heard throughout New York, and that would rally them in support of the great principle for which they were contending."[13] Most informed people knew what this meant, and an Irish-Catholic Whig wrote Seward that "the die is cast [;] plenty of trouble in the Loco Foco Camp [;] . . . the Irish men of this City . . . have broke [*sic*] the chains that bound them and are determined to be free. . . ."[14] Although certainly interested in these political developments, Seward ignored his correspondent's partisan comments and emphasized his hope that ethnic and religious differences would vanish in the face of general social improvement.

Catholics did not have long to wait for the episcopal call. Four days later and less than a week before the election, on October 29, Carroll Hall was once again thronged with the bishop's loyal supporters. Before the meeting, Weed, Seward's adviser and Hughes's confidant, dined with his episcopal friend as the bishop explained the latest Catholic strategy. After dinner, the Whig boss shrewdly decided not to accompany Hughes to the hall. "I went, however, unobserved, into the gallery, where I listened with intense interest to his bold and telling speech to a crowded and enthusiastic auditory."[15] The audience realized that this meeting meant that the Catholic leadership had made an important decision.

This evening the fighting bishop was at his militant best. Something had to be done to stem the growing political tide against Cath-

12 Jacob Harvey to Seward (New York, July 1, 1841), UR.
13 Kehoe, *Works of Hughes*, I, p. 274.
14 David Nagle to Seward (New York, October 25, 1841), UR.
15 Harriet A. Weed, *Autobiography of Weed*, p. 500.

olics. As their spiritual shepherd, Hughes regarded it as his solemn duty to act. And act he did. He told his listeners that Catholics did not want public funds to promote sectarian purposes. Neither did they seek the introduction of religious instruction into the public schools, although "if such religious influences be brought to bear on the business of education, it shall be, so far as our children are concerned, in accordance with the religious belief of their parents and families." Not only was the public press arrayed against the Catholic request but now the major political parties had left Catholics no alternative but to vote for candidates pledged to the Public School Society. If such candidates were to be elected, Hughes urged his listeners not to be a party to this betrayal of Catholic interests. The Society's supporters could malign the Catholics; they could employ the press to misrepresent their case; they could use unethical means to thwart justice; but they could never tamper with "the unpurchasable votes of their victims." Hughes's solution to this dilemma? "We have resolved to give our suffrage in favor of no man who is an enemy to us and the recognition of those rights, and to support every friend we can find among men of all political parties."

To this end, the Catholic leadership prepared an independent ticket of candidates who "are friendly to an alteration in the present system of public education." Although several of those chosen had been thought to oppose the Catholic claim, the bishop had been reliably assured that "all of them, can be depended on as determined . . . to support the justice of our claims." Once this ticket was ratified, Hughes would consider the decision final and exhort all Catholics to support the approved candidates. This "Carroll Hall" ticket included the following names: Thomas O'Connor and John Gottsberger for the Senate; for the Assembly, John L. O'Sullivan, Auguste Davezac, William McMurray, David R.F. Jones, Daniel C. Pentz, George Weir, Paul Grout, Conrad Swackhamer, William B. Maclay, Solomon Townsend, Tighe Davy, Timothy Daly, and Michael Walsh.[16] The first ten Assembly candidates were on the regular Democratic ticket. The Catholics nominated three new men for the Assembly and two different nominees for the Senate. No Whig candidate was considered "safe" enough to merit Catholic endorsement. After the assembled Catholics approved the proposed

16 Kehoe, *Works of Hughes*, I, pp. 277, 280.

ticket "with the most deafening and uproarious" applause, Hughes incited his audience to remain loyal to their decision:

You now, for the first time, find yourselves in the position to vote at least for yourselves. You have often voted for others, and they did not vote for you, but now you are determined to uphold with your own votes, your own rights. Will you then stand by the rights of your offspring, who have for so long a period, and from generation to generation, suffered under the operation of this injurious system? (Renewed cheering.) Will you adhere to the nomination made? (Loud cries of 'we will,' and vociferous applause.) Will you be united? (Tremendous cheering—the whole immense assembly rising en masse, waving of hats, handkerchiefs, and every possible demonstration of applause.) Will you let all men see that you are worthy sons of the nation to which you belong? (Cries of 'Never fear—we will.' 'We will till death!' and terrific cheering.) Will you prove yourselves worthy of friends? (Tremendous cheering.) Will none of you flinch? (The scene that followed this emphatic query is indescribable, and exceeded all the enthusiastic, and almost frenzied displays of passionate feeling we have sometimes witnessed at Irish meetings. The cheering—the shouting—the stamping of feet—waving of hats and handkerchiefs, beggared all powers of description.) Very well, then, the tickets will be prepared and distributed amongst you, and on the day of election go like freemen, with dignity and calmness, entertaining due respect for your fellow-citizens and their opinions, and deposit your votes. And if you do not elect any of your friends, you will at least record your votes in favor of justice, and in favor of your principles, which must not—cannot be abandoned, and you will be guiltless of the sin and shame and degradation of electing men who are pledged to trample on you if they can![17]

Although Hughes denied any political intent in this move, he did not convince many people. Nor was his motivation in precipitating this unorthodox action difficult to understand. He played this trump card in an attempt to compel the Democratic party, heavily dependent upon the large Catholic vote, to endorse the Catholic position. He took a calculated risk, knowing full well the opprobrium that would descend upon his episcopal head.[18] David Nagle,

[17] Kehoe, *Works of Hughes*, I, p. 283. Hughes did not warn his flock that they were obliged to vote this ticket under pain of sin as was alleged by the *New York Observer*, November 6, 1841.

[18] Billington, *Protestant Crusade*, p. 151; Connors, *Church-State Relationships*, p. 36. Scisco's explanation that "the bishop's purpose was to rebuke the Democratic leaders" is not convincing. Scisco, *Political Nativism*, p. 35.

an Irish-Catholic Whig who was at the meeting, summarized the significance of this meeting to Seward in a telling sentence: "The Sword is drawn and the Scabbard thrown away nor will it be returned till the battle is fought and soon at the Ballot Boxes."[19]

If Hughes anticipated a measure of Democratic capitulation, he was to be sadly mistaken. The city Democrats, faced with an insoluble dilemma, decided to risk the wrath and electoral reprisal of many Catholics by remaining firm in their initial commitment to the educational status quo. The day after Hughes's political entry, the *Evening Post* carried a card to the public signed by ten Democratic Assembly candidates. They wished to remove any misapprehensions concerning their stand on the school question. Not only did they reject the Whig administration's proposals but they also "opposed . . . any appropriation of the School Fund for any sectarian purposes, directly or indirectly" and disclaimed their "Carroll Hall" endorsement.[20]

The Democratic rift presaged a Whig victory and the Whig press immediately unleashed a sharp barrage against the "disclaimer of the ten." The *Tribune* considered the card a grotesque subterfuge compounded "of cowardice, insult and treachery." If the Democratic candidates opposed the Catholic claim as "a perversion of the School Fund to the support of their Church," then they should have been honest enough to state clearly their disapproval.[21] The *Commercial Advertiser* branded the Democratic disclaimer as a "*Stupendous Fraud* which the *Roman Catholics* and *Tammany Men*" were attempting to foist upon the "friends of the *Public Schools*." The paper denounced the card as "*Evasive*: they do not declare themselves opposed to the Roman Catholic project of breaking up the schools under their present admirable organization; but only say that they are opposed to the project *in the shape presented by Governor Seward*. How easy for them to arrive at the object of the *Pope* and his *Bishop* in some other form." "A gentleman of the soundest

19 David Nagle to Seward (New York, October 31, 1841), UR.

20 *New York Evening Post*, October 30, 1841. Cf. *New York Evening Post*, November 3, 1841; *New York Tribune*, November 1 and 3, 1841. The ten who appended their signatures to this communication were: Townsend, Grout, McMurray, Swackhamer, Field, Davezac, Weir, Jones, Sanford, and Glasier. Only the first seven were endorsed by the "Carroll Hall" party while Maclay, Pentz, and O'Sullivan did not sign the card because they were "out of town." However, the undersigned were sure that "those who are absent will concur with them."

21 *New York Tribune*, November 1, 1841.

integrity" had informed the editor that there was perfect accord between the Democratic nominees and Catholics on the school question. Even Hughes had assured his flock that the "Carroll Hall" nominees supported the Catholic position. In fact, after the "denial of the Ten" had been printed, the *Freeman's Journal* published an extra which recommended support for the entire "Carroll Hall" ticket. Unless an understanding had been effected by Tammany and the Catholics, the bishop's organ would not have recommended the "Carroll Hall" ticket "strenuously to the support of the Church of Rome."[22]

Since the disclaimer failed to pledge support to the Public School Society or censure the Catholic claim, the *Observer* branded the communication as totally unacceptable to the Protestant community. Greeley informed his readers that a prominent Catholic had apprised him that the Catholic leadership "had private promises from all these men that they would sustain such an alteration of the School System as Bishop Hughes desires. We believe this is true."[23] In its denunciation of the Democratic card, the *Commercial Advertiser* urged Irish Catholics to abandon the Democratic party because "they have been trifled with by their pretended friends at Tammany Hall." In their hour of need, the deceitful Democratic party betrayed "our Irish fellow-citizens" and "cut them adrift" by its cruel betrayal of Catholic interests. The paper brazenly intimated that Catholics could find truthfulness and honesty of purpose within the Whig party.[24] The *Tribune* carefully noted that the names of Pentz, O'Sullivan, and Maclay rather conveniently did not appear on the disclaimer. Although the "pretence is that they are out of town . . . , in regard to Mr. Pentz it was untrue; Mr. O'Sullivan had conveniently left but the evening before; Mr. Maclay, we believe, had contrived to be out of reach."[25] Greeley insisted that this trio could not possibly concur with the other ten. Pentz's vote in the Common Council was self-explanatory; O'Sullivan still sought passage of his compromise school bill; and Maclay was supposedly an ardent advocate of the Catholic cause.

These three Democrats did not wait long to clarify their respective

---

22 *New York Commercial Advertiser*, November 2, 1841; *New York American*, November 2, 1841.
23 *New York Tribune*, November 3, 1841.
24 *New York Commercial Advertiser*, November 1, 1841.
25 *New York Tribune*, November 1, 1841.

positions. Pentz published a personal card which substantially reiterated the majority's disclaimer. Although he denied any endorsement of "the measures of a particular sect . . . , I am willing to make
such alterations or amendments of the present system as would give
satisfaction to every portion of the community."[26] The *Tribune*
characterized Pentz's response as the height of the "science of twist-
ing and turning." Pentz's attempt to please "every portion of the
community" brought down upon him Greeley's biting satire: "Gal-
lant, fearless spirit! How dare he support what everybody shall be
in favor of? Surely this must be the Heroic Age in legislation and
politics! And now, reader, be good enough to blow aside the fog
and tell us what Mr. Pentz *is* in favor of? Can you satisfy yourself?"[27]
Since Maclay was out of town on special legislative business, "a
confidential friend of his" assured the *Evening Post* that the assemblyman's views fully coincided with the "disclaimer of the
Ten."[28] O'Sullivan expressed his views in a response to the American
Protestant Union's inquiry concerning his position on the school
question. He felt that religion should not enter into the solution of
this question. Although "a Protestant in my private capacity," he
promised to guide his actions only by the principles of the Democratic party. He would never consent to jeopardizing the continu-
ance of the Public School Society nor would he ever support the use
of public funds to establish or maintain schools of a sectarian character. Nevertheless, he thought that the passage of his bill would
"constitute a fair and just compromise of this vexed question." It
would leave the Society intact and at the same time satisfy Catholic
grievances by removing "from the present system that character of
exclusive chartered monopoly, to which the democracy I profess, can
never reconcile itself, and at the same time, greatly extend, elevate
and improve its beneficent action."[29] The *Tribune* characterized this
reply as "timid and apologizing," issued with very little conviction
"in a weak voice."[30]

The Democratic press rushed to its candidates' rescue. The *Evening Post* considered the Carroll Hall proceedings "a plot concocted

26 *New York Evening Post*, November 1, 2, 3, 1841; *New York Tribune*, November
2, 1841; *New York Journal of Commerce*, November 3, 1841.
27 *New York Tribune*, November 2, 1841.
28 *New York Evening Post*, November 1, 2, and 3, 1841.
29 *New York Evening Post*, October 30, 1841; *New York Journal of Commerce*,
November 1, 1841.
30 *New York Tribune*, November 1, 1841.

at Albany, to bring odium upon the democratic ticket, and censure its rejection by the people. . . . The Albany conspirators manifestly expected . . . that the democratic candidates would stand too much in fear of losing the votes of the Catholics" to dare oppose the bishop's ultimatum. On the contrary, they courageously issued a disclaimer which stated their views on the school question. Not a single Democratic candidate favored Seward's proposal to appropriate public school funds to Catholics. "Not one of them is for giving to the sects the money of the people." Employing the offensive Whig strategy, the *Evening Post* accused Whig candidates of standing unpledged on the school issue. The paper refused to believe that intelligent citizens would in conscience award their votes to candidates who did not have the courage to state openly their views on the school question. The Whig nominees were damned as "men who are placed before the public with the staring badge of fraud, concealment, upon every one of them; pigs in huge pokes; candidates concerning whom their own nominating committee declares, that 'no pledges have been asked of them'; candidates who are purposely uninterrogated, in order that they may not be bound by the instructions and wishes of their constituents."[31]

In an article entitled "Are They All All Right?" the *Commercial Advertiser* was "quite sure that the Whig Ticket is sound and true on the school question." The paper assured its readers "that no apprehension need be entertained upon that subject." In fact, the same issue of this paper carried Morris Franklin's reply to the American Protestant Union's inquiry. The Whig senatorial candidate was "decidedly and unequivocally opposed to any system calculated" to injure the status of the Society or divert public moneys for sectarian schools. The *Advertiser's* editor, Colonel William Stone, pledged that the other senatorial candidate, Daniel Lord, Jr., endorsed Franklin's statement. Stone personally knew that "Mr. Lord has been an active advocate of the Public School Society for nearly

---

31 *New York Evening Post*, October 30 and November 3, 1841. Pentz, the most vulnerable of the Democratic candidates, was especially singled out as opposing the use of public funds for Catholic schools. His vote

so often alluded to, given by him when in the Common Council of this city, was not for any such measure, but was given with a view to keep the question open till it could be considered whether any modification of the common school system, as administered in this city, could be devised, which, without allowing the Catholics any separate use of the school money, might reconcile them to the system, and induce them to send their children freely to the schools.

twenty years."[32] But the Whig Assembly candidates, while rejecting the Catholic claim, never issued a special card pledging their endorsement of the Society. They did not think it necessary nor, indeed, was it necessary. It was well known that city Whigs were unalterably opposed to the Catholic position. Not one Whig had been selected by the "Carroll Hall" ticket. The Democratic party was definitely at a disadvantage, and its press endeavored to boomerang its discomfiture to the Whigs' embarrassment.

Once the "Carroll Hall" party entered the field, Hughes predictably drew the wrath of the secular and Protestant press. Even Philip Hone privately recorded "generalissimo" Hughes's movement as a "most imprudent interference with the rights and privileges of native Americans; an unblushing attempt to mix up religion with politics—an unpalatable dish in this country. . . ."[33] The *Observer* announced that Hughes's tactic vindicated its worst fears of the devious design of the papists. It was aghast that an *"ecclesiastic* at the head of his flock actually nominated a ticket . . . , declared his official approbation of it, and enjoined it upon his trembling followers to go to the polls and put *that* ticket into the ballot boxes. . . ." Here was conclusive proof that the Roman Catholic Church was brewing a plot to gain political control of the country. The "mask" was off. "The foot of the Beast was trampling on the elective franchise, and His High Priest was standing before the *ballot box*, the citadel of American liberties, dictating to his obedient followers the ticket they must vote. . . ."[34] Hughes was compared to the Irish leader O'Connell by the *Christian Advocate and Journal*, and was accused of imitating the "bullying braggadocious conduct of the Irish agitator." The paper insisted that no Protestant ecclesiastic could have entered the political field so impudently "without incurring the displeasure, and receiving the indignant rebuke, of the people of his own Church." But the Catholic had no choice, since his creed made him a spiritual slave of the hierarchy "whose power over him is absolute, both as it regards his present happiness, and his future prospects."[35]

The *Evangelist* reprobated the "Carroll Hall" party as a formal and decided movement toward "a union of Church and State"—a

---

32 *New York Commercial Advertiser*, November 2, 1841.
33 Tuckerman, *Diary of Hone*, II, pp. 96–97.
34 *New York Observer*, November 6, 1841. Cf. October 30, 1841.
35 *Christian Advocate and Journal* (New York), November 10, 1841.

charge that was echoed in the West by the Ohio *Presbyterian of the West*.[36] Although *The Churchman* supported the basic Catholic position, its editor disliked Hughes's entry into the political arena. The bishop had an obligation to warn his people about the hostility of public schools to their children's religious faith. But he should have done so "in a manner consistent with the dignity and holiness of . . . [his] office: by the force of reason and persuasion, by calm appeals to the understanding and consciences of . . . [his] fellow-citizens, in the quiet energy of faith, and in the temper of patient endurance."[37] Employing vivid language, the *Commercial Advertiser* fulminated against Hughes's attempt to unite "church and state." In a scorching attack upon Hughes and the "Carroll Hall" ticket, the editor railed at the prelate's episcopal approval of the Catholic party's candidates and appealed to Protestants to defeat every Catholic nominee:

'I will simply say that the decision of this night is to be final!' Mark that! True to its arrogant pretensions in the days of Hildebrand and Ignatius Loyola, when the Roman Church speaks, there can be no appeal—'The Decision is Final'—and mark! it is added, 'without any expression of individual opinion as to the merits or demerits of the names that will be read!' Here, fellow citizens, you have the decree. There is to be no 'individual opinion.' The Church has spoken and let its votaries Tremble and Obey! Will the people of this Protestant country stand this? Will not every denomination be opposed to 'MYSTERY-BABYLON,' arouse themselves to action on this occasion? We shall see.[38]

The Democratic press particularly attacked Hughes's maneuver because it could so rupture the party as to ensure a Whig victory at the polls. The *Sun* labeled the Catholic movement as "desperate," "ill advised," "unfortunate," "rash," and "suicidal." It accused Hughes of haranguing his flock into supporting the "Carroll Hall" ticket. The editor threatened his Catholic readers that should the

36 *New York Evangelist*, November 6, 1841; *Presbyterian of the West*, November 17, 1841.
37 *The Churchman* (New York), November 12, 1841. This weekly found two serious faults with the public schools: "The first is that the State as such, had taken upon itself the education of the people; and the second is, that she had adopted a theory of education which excludes religion, and which is thus virtually ATHEISTIC." The *Princeton Review*, cited in the *New York Freeman's Journal*, November 13, 1841, "would have the Public Schools distinctively and decidedly religious and Protestant."
38 *New York Commercial Advertiser*, October 30, 1841. Cf. *New York Tribune*, October 30, 1841.

bishop's party become a permanent fixture in city politics, Catholics could expect the eventual "repeal or material alteration of our naturalization laws." The *Sun* warned naturalized Catholics that native Americans were extremely sensitive to an attempt at a union of church and state. Because Hughes's "politico-religious party" had aroused "the tenderest chord of our national sensibility . . ., if not at once abandoned by those who have embarked in it, they will have cause to regret it to the latest hour of their lives." Hughes's entry into the political field was adjudged by the editor to be a "national insult." It was hoped that he would "see the folly and danger of the step" he had taken and quickly remedy it. But if Hughes persisted in his foolhardy venture, Catholics were reminded that they owed their bishop only spiritual obedience and could "manage their own wordly affairs without his interference. . . ."[39] The *Evening Post* emphasized Catholic political freedom and urged Catholics to "stand ready to repress, with a firm hand, the intrusion of priestly influence into the sphere of politics." The whole school question was of Whig origin, and Hughes, "a Whig likewise," entered the political arena to make "declarations which, if true, would cause the democratic ticket for the assembly to fail by thousands of votes." The editor felt that Hughes's zeal had greatly outstripped his discretion in entering the Catholic hierarchy in partisan politics. To say that Hughes acted as a citizen and not as a bishop was no answer since

a bishop in any church is more a bishop than anything else, more a bishop than a citizen, and carries with him a clerical and official influence, wherever he goes and whatever he does. The church of Rome is the most strictly organized church in the world, and when her hand is seen in the elections, the jealousy of the community is aroused in an instant.[40]

Regardless of the outcome, the *Post* argued that it had a journalistic obligation to examine Hughes's public statements and "if they deserve it, to contradiction [*sic*] as those of any other man." The paper was sure that Hughes was misled in this matter and was the unwitting dupe of a Whig plot to win the November election. After the bishop's maneuver reached the attention of the independent *Herald*, it predicted a collapse of the city's major political parties

39 *New York Sun*, November 1 and 2, 1841.
40 *New York Evening Post*, October 30, 1841. Cf. November 1 and 2, 1841.

and "the formation of the Protestant and Catholic factions, with all the madness of the last century. We dread the future."[41]

James Gordon Bennett, the fiery editor of the *Herald,* thundered his journalistic anathemas against Hughes with unmitigated fury. The "bold, daring, reckless" abandonment of his priestly calling was viewed with the "most ineffable disgust and his attempt denounced by Whigs, Democrats, and even by the intelligent members of his own church." Although the bishop knew the hopelessness of his political venture, he adroitly pursued his errant course since it was part of a Whig intrigue negotiated "between Governor Seward and Bishop Hughes for nearly two years past." The editor urged all Catholics to confine Hughes and his clergy to their own proper business of "saying masses for the dead—forgiving the sins of the living—giving the sacrament—marrying young couples at $5 a head—eating a good dinner and drinking good wine at any generous table—or toasting their shins on a cold night at their own firesides." If the bishop and his priests went beyond these bounds, the *Herald* suggested that Catholics "do as Queen Elizabeth did, 'unfrock them, by G–d.' " Just before the election Bennett predicted that if Hughes could swing three thousand votes to the Catholic ticket, the Whigs would sweep both senatorial seats and elect three assemblymen, with the Democrats winning the remaining ten Assembly seats. The editor proved to be a remarkably accurate prophet in his forecast.[42]

As a result of the sharp criticism hurled against him and the "Carroll Hall" party, Hughes published a card which sought to justify his course of action. He declared that the press had misrepresented his position. He was neither a Whig nor a Democrat nor a politician of any persuasion. Politics was not his concern, and he had expressly forbidden his clergy to "meddle" in political matters. The Public School Society and its supporters had caused the "School Question" to degenerate into a "political test" by uniting both political parties against the Catholic position. Because Catholics had no real choice in the election, their alternative was "to throw away their votes on a ticket of their own." This was the genesis of the Carroll Hall meeting. "It was not a political meeting" but a large gathering of Catholics "determined to support no man who was

---

41 *New York Herald,* November 1, 1841.
42 *New York Herald,* November 3, 1841.

pledged to the Public School Society." Between these facts and "meddling with politics," the bishop drew "a wide distinction."[43]

The *Evening Post* questioned the logic and accuracy of Hughes's argument. The bishop denied any interference in political matters. And yet, observed the editor, he attended a meeting that nominated candidates for the Legislature and "introduced a ticket . . . which, said he, 'I have approved' " and committed his Catholic audience to support the measure. "This is all; and in this, he sees no meddling with politics." If Hughes considered this to be abstention from politics, the *Post* announced that "the less Bishop Hughes recommends to his clergy to abstain from politics the better."[44] The *Herald* continued this line of criticism and ridiculed Hughes's card as an insult to common sense. The bishop might as well have said that "I am not a Bishop—I did not get my orders from Rome—I am not Bishop Hughes—I am only the poor gardener of Bishop Dubois, with the vestments of the Church put on by way of joke." But if Hughes were guilty of organizing "his church into a political club," so to a greater extent were the political fomenters of both parties who instigated and abetted the prelate's entrance into the political arena—"to substitute a log cabin for the holy altar—and a cider barrel for the holy chalice."[45]

Hughes was not without defenders. Since Catholic rights were threatened with "total destruction," the *Freeman's Journal* understandably lauded Hughes as performing "A NOBLE AND IMPERATIVE DUTY when he appeared at Carroll Hall." His courageous action deserved the gratitude and deep affection of all Catholics "because he stood up for . . . right in the hour of need. . . ." The Catholic weekly reminded its readers that their bishop was a man of strong resolve who was not easily "turned by either violence or falsehood from the course which duty makes clear and unquestionable."[46] The *New York Sunday Times* branded the political accusations against Hughes as "all mere moonshine." The bishop's energetic defense of what he considered to be Catholic rights was not a crime "to merit the

43 *New York Evening Post*, November 1, 1841; *New York Commercial Advertiser*, November 1, 1841; *New York Herald*, November 2, 1841; *New York Tribune*, November 2, 1841; *New York Freeman's Journal*, November 6, 1841.

44 *New York Evening Post*, November 1, 1841.

45 *New York Herald*, November 2, 1841. Among the "miserable political leaders of both political parties," Bennett mentioned Seward, Verplanck, and Weed while the Democrat named was John McKeon.

46 *New York Freeman's Journal*, November 6, 1841.

threats of assassination!—tar and feathers, etc." Although the *Times* editor made it quite clear that he opposed Hughes's contention for school funds, he championed his right to claim such funds. Had he not done so, he would have betrayed his own principles as well as his flock and lost the respect of most honest and liberal citizens. Obviously an admirer of Hughes, the editor eulogized him as "one of the great men of the age," who "finds his rank in the scale of genius with such spirits as Daniel Webster, Henry Clay, and Dr. Channing of Boston."[47]

iii

The approach of election day found the Democratic party "running scared." On election eve, Tammany Hall promoted a "Great Meeting of Adopted Citizens" in an attempt to picture overwhelming Irish-Catholic support for the regular Democratic ticket. The rally was chaired by James T. Brady and the majority of officers had Irish names. Both Brady and Charles P. Daly gave addresses which challenged Hughes's entry into the political field. The bishop's maneuver was censured as a "miserable mistake" engineered by crafty Whigs who led the prelate astray. In a series of resolutions, the participants deprecated any religious group organized to influence popular elections and labeled the clergy's participation in politics as "unbefitting their high and holy avocation." The resolution on education, while substantiating the regular Democratic platform, carefully employed language to mollify Hughes's Catholic supporters:

Resolved . . . , that while the Constitution recognizes no disqualification from the accident of birth or the peculiarity of a religious creed, it necessarily requires that the public schools should be free from sectarian influence, and that for carrying out this great and necessary object, we consider it the duty of the representatives of the people respectfully to receive and deliberately examine the complaints of any class of our citizens, and to secure through the legitimate and constitutional channel, the proper application of a fund raised by equal taxation for the purposes of general education.[48]

---

[47] *New York Sunday Times*, cited in the *New York Freeman's Journal*, November 13, 1841.

[48] *New York Evening Post*, November 3, 1841. Cf. *New York Herald*, November 3, 1841; *New York Evening Post*, November 2, 1841.

Although the *Evening Post* and the *Herald* labeled the meeting a huge success, the *Freeman's Journal* represented the Tammany rally as a further attempt to discredit the Carroll Hall nominations. James T. Brady was blackened as a disreputable Catholic who did not represent the community of practicing Catholics. The bishop's organ printed the letter of "A CATHOLIC" who had attended the Democratic rally. He pictured the alleged "respectable and influential Catholics," especially Brady, as a group of brawling politicians who were Catholics for "that night only" in an attempt to prostitute their religion for partisan political advantage. "The attempt to pass off that meeting as a Catholic one, at which not a Catholic was present except perhaps a few through curiosity, or the men calling it as 'influential Catholics,' must excite our unmitigated ridicule. . . ." As an Irish-Catholic citizen, the writer repudiated "with utter scorn, the idea, that these men could influence a single countryman of mine, who was at all acquainted with the simplicity and justice of our demands."[49]

Another "Great Meeting of Adopted Citizens," this time German Democrats, met to reaffirm their allegiance to the Tammany ticket. John Gottsberger, one of the Carroll Hall senatorial candidates, attempted to justify his conduct. But "his indignant and excited countrymen" refused to listen to him, and he was forced to retire. Instead, the gathering was addressed in both English and German by several regulars who advocated unanimous support for the whole Democratic ticket. The *Evening Post* quoted the *New Era* as declaring that German Democrats bound themselves under the following maxims:

No union of Church with State.
The school fund to be applied to the education of the children of all.
Purification of the school system from sects and ecclesiastical influence.
No distribution of the school fund to particular sects.
The German Democratic Association adopts the ticket of the Nominating Committee at Tammany Hall for the Senate and Assembly.
The whole ticket and nothing but the ticket.[50]

Two days before election day, the *Journal of Commerce* and Morse's American Protestant Union jointly announced the formation of a Union ticket. Essentially the nativist answer to the Carroll

---

49 *New York Freeman's Journal*, November 6 and 13, 1841.
50 *New York Evening Post*, November 2, 1841.

Hall movement, Morse asserted that this unexpected ticket was "formed with the view of testing public opinion on the School Question, and of rebuking priestly dictation. In the expectation of uniting true Americans of both parties, the selection has been made from the nominees of both political parties." Bipartisan in selection, Morse chose candidates from both the Democratic and Whig tickets. The Whig Franklin and the Democrat Varian were nominated for the Senate while seven Whigs and six Democrats were supported for the Assembly. Although the two unendorsed senatorial candidates, Purdy and Lord, Jr., were characterized as men of "respectable moral character" and thoroughly opposed to the Catholic claim, nevertheless, they did not quite fulfill the requirements of the Union party. "For reasons for which he no doubt thought sufficient," Purdy had refused to answer the American Protestant Union's query concerning his position on the school question. Lord's answer, on the other hand, did not satisfy Morse and his committee. Lord opposed the Catholic claim as well as Seward's recommendation and Spencer's bill. But he refused to be the Union's man and if elected, "I wholly decline saying that I will use my influence or give my vote in one way or another." He wanted to be free to examine objectively any proposed legislation before casting his vote one way or the other. "I shall deem myself wholly unfettered by any past expressions of my opinion to vote otherwise than as I shall be convinced."

The three Democratic Assembly candidates not ratified by the "Carroll Hall" ticket, Sanford, Glasier, and Field, received quick Union endorsement. Maclay's past legislative opposition to any change in the city's school system and Jones's and Townsend's disclaimer were sufficient to merit Morse's support. Although it was recognized that all the Whig candidates were pledged against the Catholic position, the *Journal of Commerce* evaluated several of them as "very poorly qualified for the halls of legislation." In fact, however, since the Union party called for bipartisan support, its sponsors realized that they would have to endorse candidates from both parties to attract Whig and Democratic Protestant votes.[51]

---

[51] *New York Journal of Commerce*, November 1, 2 and 3, 1841. The Whig candidates supported were Baldwin, Stevens, Tucker, Bradford, Graham, St. John, and William Jones while the six Democrats were Townsend, D. F. Jones, Maclay, Sanford, Glasier, and Field. The positions of O'Sullivan and Pentz were declared to be "inconsistent with the safety of our public schools." Cf. *New York Evening Post*, November 3, 1841.

It seems clear that the *Journal of Commerce* and Morse hoped that this ticket would channel the large anti-Catholic sentiment in both parties upon its candidates. The Democratic press remained unusually silent concerning this eleventh-hour movement, no doubt delighted that the Union ticket might neutralize the drawing power of the "Carroll Hall" party. Since the Whigs had counted on large numbers of nativist voters, this potential loss stimulated the Whig press to condemn the movement as rash and part of a calculated Democratic plot "to frighten the Irish back to Tammany by the raw—and—bloody—bones of Native Americanism."

The *Tribune* warned its readers not to be deceived by this cheap Democratic trick, and to vote the "Whig ticket, the whole ticket and nothing but the ticket." Greeley characterized Maclay, Townsend, and Jones as "The Tight-Rope Candidates" because they were endorsed by the mutually exclusive "Carroll Hall" and Union tickets. Since they could not honestly support the propositions of both parties, these men were accused of "manifest and double treachery." The Union party had no valid reason to withhold its support from any Whig candidate when they were all unequivocal opponents to any change in the city's school system. And yet, in spite of this, it had endorsed certain "Carroll Hall" nominees who were committed to the Catholic position. The *Tribune* could not understand the Union's position except that "this Protestant Union ticket is an imposture."[52] The *Commercial Advertiser* considered Lord's position on the school question as completely orthodox, his reply to Morse notwithstanding. The paper accused Morse and the *Journal of Commerce* of deliberately suppressing the Whig Assembly candidates' replies to the American Protestant Union's inquiries. Every Whig response sustained the school system "as it is—in its own matchless excellence and simple beauty." Such suppression was denounced as part of a scheme to defeat the Whig candidates. "Why oppose Catholic juggling in one breath," declared the angry editor, "and indulge in Protestant juggling in the next?"[53]

The bitter mud-slinging campaign ended on November 3, election day. A great deal of hatred and misunderstanding had been unleashed, tempers were high, and the city was uneasy. This emotional state of affairs caused the *Sun* and the *Herald* to warn city

52 *New York Tribune*, November 1 and 3, 1841.
53 *New York Commercial Advertiser*, November 2, 1841.

authorities to be prepared for possible election disorders and riots.[54] Although the Whigs were divided on national issues, the contest for the Legislature, especially in New York City, revolved principally about the school question. Upon this issue all the political parties, regular and maverick, waged their bitter campaigns. The *Sun's* election day editorial colorfully and shrewdly analyzed the various parties on the ballot.

Now comes the "tug of war." To-day a contest takes place in New York embracing all the elements of the serious, the curious, the sublime and the ridiculous. It is to be a genuine "scrub race" between Whigs, Democrats . . . , Catholics, Protestants, Native Americans and Abolitionists.

After listing the senatorial candidates of each contending faction, the editorial predicted that the "Carroll Hall" party would be supported only "by those who have no minds of their own, and who allow a priest to control their political action; and also by those who are in favor of overthrowing our republican government, and establishing a hierarchy in its place." Because the voters of New York were presented with "this vast variety . . . , embracing the interests of America, of Europe, and Africa—of white men and black men— of schools, mechanics, and State prisons—of churchmen and laymen— of catholics, protestants, Greeks, and Hebrews—of adopted citizens and natives—and of every man, woman, child, and thing beneath the sun, moon and stars," the *Sun* concluded by urging all "gentlemen . . . [to] walk up . . . quietly, and vote for whom you please— you cannot vote amiss for everybody is nominated."[55] On November 3, New Yorkers went to the polls.

---

54 *New York Sun*, November 2, 1841; *New York Herald*, November 1 and 3, 1841.

55 *New York Sun*, November 3, 1841. The following candidates were on the Abolitionist ticket: for the Senate, Arthur Tappan and Horace Dresser; for the Assembly, Leonard Gibbs, Anthony Lane, John Hill, Adrastus Doolittle, Leonard Crocker, Rufus Hibbard, Charles Fox, Henry Piercy, Thomas Field, Benjamin Wooster, George Barker, Daniel Sands, and William Tracy.

◁ IX ▷

A Balance of Power

i

As soon as the votes were counted, it was apparent that a Democratic landslide had materialized throughout the state. The Democratic party captured both houses of the Legislature from Whig control with a narrow two vote margin in the Senate and a three to one Assembly majority.[1] In New York City, the Democrat Varian and the Whig Franklin won senatorial seats while Tammany Hall captured ten of the thirteen Assembly seats.[2] Every Democratic can-

[1] *New York Tribune*, November 18, 1841. This same issue compared legislative majorities from 1835 to 1841:

			Senate				
	1835	1836	1837	1838	1839	1840	1841
Whigs	4	5	10	14	20	21	15
Democrats	28	27	22	18	12	11	17
			Assembly				
Whigs	18	33	100	82	70	66	33
Democrats	110	95	28	46	58	62	95

[2] The senatorial vote was as follows:

Varian (D)	19,811
Franklin (W)	19,675
Lord (W)	19,584
Purdy (D)	19,522

The assemblyman vote was as follows (* signifies elected):

Whig		Democrat	
*Tucker	16,326	*Townsend	18,385
*Jones	16,315	*Jones	18,375
*Baldwin	16,314	*Maclay	18,274
Bradford	16,310	*Weir	18,242
Stevens	16,285	*Grout	18,196

didate endorsed by the "Carroll Hall" party was elected while each of its own senatorial Assembly nominees polled over 2,000 votes.[3] A comparison of the voting returns demonstrates that Catholics had sufficient electoral strength to defeat four Democratic candidates. The votes cast for O'Connor or Gottsberger easily would have elected Purdy to the Senate. If the "Carroll Hall" party had supported the three defeated Democratic assemblymen, Sanford, Glasier, and Field, as the Union party had done, the entire Democratic Assembly ticket would have been victorious. Instead, the *Journal of Commerce* admitted that "Bishop Hughes and co. . . . succeeded in defeating Messrs. Field, Glazier [*sic*] and Sanford on the Tammany ticket, and thus enabled the Whigs, with the help of the Native American party, to elect Messrs. Tucker, Wm. Jones and Bradford. . . ."[4]

The city vote clearly showed that Catholics held the balance of power in the Democratic party since only those Tammany candidates who had not received Catholic endorsement met defeat. Hughes had effectively shown the city's Democratic leaders that the Catholic vote was a power to be reckoned with in subsequent elections. Even the *Journal of Commerce* acknowledged that the Catholic vote indicated "that Bishop Hughes does not command his

St. John	16,250	*Swackhamer	18,097
Graham, Jr.	16,246	*Davezac	18,064
Coger, Jr.	16,208	*McMurray	17,972
Mount	16,176	*O'Sullivan	17,645
Carman	16,165	*Pentz	16,891
Gerard	16,161	Sanford	16,286
Hamilton	16,158	Glasier	16,232
Chenery	16,093	Field	16,075

These official returns were published in the *New York Tribune* November 12, 1841, and the *New York Evening Post*, November 13, 1841. Bourne, *History of Public School Society*, p. 481, has incomplete returns taken from the *New York Tribune*, November 6, 1841. These figures have the Whig Bradford as the thirteenth elected assemblyman. However, the official returns made the Whig Baldwin the victor over Bradford by four votes.

3 O'Connor received 2,449 votes and Gottsberger 2,422 votes. The three Assembly candidates polled the following votes: Walsh, 2,344; Davey, 2,172; and Daley, 2,168. These figures were published in the *New York Tribune*, November 12 and 13, 1841. Although Abolitionist votes were listed by the city papers, not one paper carried the returns of the Union ticket.

4 *New York Journal of Commerce*, November 6, 1841. Although the incomplete returns listed Bradford as elected, the final results declared Baldwin the victor over Bradford. Cf. footnote two.

followers in vain."[5] The *Evening Post* tacitly conceded Catholic voting strength when it took satisfaction in the fact that the Democratic candidates had done so well despite the party's schism and nativist incursions. "Our ticket had to make head against, not only its regular adversary, the Whig ticket, but also against the tickets of the two religious parties, the one styled the Bishop's ticket, and the other the Union ticket. . . ."[6] Bennett's *Herald*, which had predicted the results fairly accurately, argued that the state returns completely repudiated the mixture of religion and politics. If Hughes hurt the Democratic party in the city, his movement "injured the Whigs immensely in other parts of the State." However, Bennett proved a poor prophet when he predicted that the election "finally and irrevocably settled" the school question "for a century at least."[7]

The Whigs suffered a devastating defeat and they knew it. Two days before the election, Greeley thought that "Every thing looks well with us today" and predicted that "the majority of our whole ticket is pretty sure." Two days after the election, he wrote a letter to Seward filled with thinly veiled sarcasm, which admitted that "all is lost—Senate, Assembly, Canal Commissioners, Canal Board, Tolls, Locks, etc."[8] Seward really did not need Greeley's account to assess the political picture. All over the state Whigs were voicing a despondency toward the future. "We are down, and I fear to remain

5 *New York Journal of Commerce*, November 5, 1841. Those who have written on the subject are sharply divided over the influence of the "Carroll Hall" party on the outcome of the election. Connors, *Church-State Relationships*, p. 37, is rather uncommitted. One group of authors has attributed no real significance to the Catholic vote: Burns, *Catholic School System*, p. 373; Burns and Kohlbrenner, *History of Catholic Education*, p. 160; Bluhm, "Board of Education," p. 217; Edwin R. Van Kleeck, "The Development of Free Common Schools in New York State" (unpublished Ph.D. thesis, Yale University, New Haven, 1937), p. 188; and A. Emerson Palmer, *The New York Public School* (New York: Edwin C. Hill Company, 1908), p. 101. Other authors attribute various degrees of influence to the bishop's political movement: Flick, *History of the State of New York*, VII, p. 51; Florence E. Gibson, *The Attitudes of the New York Irish Toward State and National Affairs, 1848–1892* (New York: Columbia University Press, 1951), p. 73; Robert Ernst, *Immigrant Life in New York City, 1825–1863* (New York: Columbia University Press, 1949), p. 169; John K. Sharp, *History of the Diocese of Brooklyn, 1853–1953* (New York: Fordham University Press, 1954), I, p. 92; John F. Maguire, *The Irish in America*, 4th ed. (New York: D. and J. Sadlier and Company, 1887), p. 435; Pratt, "Governor Seward," p. 361; Scisco, *Political Nativism*, p. 36; and Henry J. Browne, "Public Support," p. 38.

6 *New York Evening Post*, November 4, 1841.

7 *New York Herald*, November 5 and 6, 1841.

8 Horace Greeley to Seward (New York, November 1 and 5, 1841), UR.

so for many years," declared an upstate Whig, and even Weed believed that the Whig party "could not recover from the recent disaster in ten years."[9] Almost accepting defeat, Seward wrote: "Well the rout has come. New York has fallen back to her old position of 1836. . . . the Assembly and . . . Senate is carried by our opponents." Although he disapproved of the formation of the religious parties in New York City, he implied that he was at least partly responsible for their emergence:

I do not speculate upon the strange incidents [in New York City] . . . for I am not in possession of means to judge of their future or permanent effects. I think that they will stand out in history with something of the promise and character of the Witchcraft persecutions in New England and the Negro plot in New York. I shrink from no responsibility of mine in the matter.[10]

And yet, Seward believed that the Whig party once again suffered defeat because of its antagonism to the masses and its refusal to change its ways:

The Whig party was always held at bay because it sympathized not with the masses. It was called into power by the masses when they were reduced to despair. It gave relief and repose and it dies until despair comes again upon the masses. Who ought to complain of this? Not the Whig party for it would not correct, it *could not* correct its constitutional disease! Not those who have relieved a suffering and alarmed country. It is a high honor to be invoked in such a crisis.[11]

Although Seward did not attribute the Whig defeat to "error at Washington," other post mortems placed a share of the responsibility upon the split in the national Whig party. An upstate Whig wrote Weed that "the apathy, or rather, the intentional indifference of the *Whigs* has ruined us. . . ." He attributed this lack of Whig enthusiasm to the Washington scene: "The condition of things at Washington—the course of the Pres. and the breaking up of the Cabinet has paralyzed all energy with hundreds of our best men."[12]

Catholic success at the polls led the *Freeman's Journal* to an-

9 George W. Patterson to Thurlow Weed (Westfield, December 9, 1841), Weed Papers, University of Rochester; Samuel Blatchford to Seward (New York, November 12, 1841), UR.

10 Seward to John C. Spencer (Albany, November 4, 1841), UR.

11 Seward to Thomas C. Reed (Albany, November 9, 1841), UR.

12 Levi Hubbell to Thurlow Weed (Ithaca, November 10, 1841), Weed Papers, University of Rochester.

nounce Catholic determination to regroup politically whenever "occasion may require, to stand forth in defence of equal rights and equal justice to all classes, civil and religious."[13] On November 10, a large number of "Carroll Hall" independents gathered to evaluate the outcome of the election. While attempting to reconcile the Democratic regulars, they did not apologize for their recent action. Since the electoral results far exceeded their expectations, they forewarned Tammany Hall that "if necessity requires it," they would reorganize the "Carroll Hall" ticket and marshal to its standard double the number polled in the late election. Their zeal was unabated "though we would rather that justice should be done without its being again aroused to action."[14] The *Herald* predicted that unless the new Democratic Legislature did "something for these chaps" during the next session, Catholic electoral strength would defeat the Democrats in the city election in April. Employing a Biblical analogy, Bennett warned that, unless the Tammany sachems acted promptly, "the glory will depart from Israel never to return again. It will be a greater loss than that of the ten tribes of Israel, and the defeat will equal that of the ten thousand."[15]

Press and pulpit censure of Hughes's political action drew between three and four thousand of his loyal followers to Washington Hall to pledge to their spiritual leader "their unwavering confidence in your judgment, zeal, and acknowledged ability; and to testify, thus publicly, to the respect which the fearless, independent, and judicious course that you have pursued in relation to this vital question of education, has excited in their minds." The "unholy league" of the Public School Society and spineless politicians left Catholics no other alternative than to form an independent ticket and thus give meaning to their votes. They denounced the press's role in the election as well as the "Catholic" Democratic rally which attacked the bishop's entry into politics. Concerning this last minute "Catholic" repudiation of Hughes's action, the assembled laymen "do here IN THE NAME OF THE CATHOLIC BODY OF NEW YORK, REPEL WITH INDIGNATION THEIR assumption of a right to speak for or represent in any manner the sentiments of that body." In fact, had not Hughes acted promptly in this matter, he would have been remiss in the performance of his episcopal duty. And because he suffered

13 *New York Freeman's Journal*, November 6, 1841.
14 *New York Herald*, November 11, 1841.
15 *New York Herald*, November 11, 1841.

greatly for his action, "you are, sir, thereby DOUBLY ENDEARED TO US ALL. . . . Your heroic devotion, Rt. Rev. Sir, shall not be lost upon us."[16] The laymen promised their bishop unanimous and continuous support in all subsequent attempts to forward the Catholic school claim.

Strongly critical of Hughes's election maneuver, the *Herald* bristled that the prelate's influence over so many Catholics "seems to be undiminished by his extraordinary and mischievous course." It characterized the laymen's support of Hughes as a "miserable affair which was poorly attended." Instead of the *Freeman's Journal's* estimate of a three to four thousand attendance, Bennett insisted that there were not more than five hundred persons in the hall. Of this number there were about one hundred and fifty Protestants who attended out of curiosity, at least one hundred and fifty Irish Catholics who opposed the bishop's political course, "about 100 whigs, who went there to swell the apparent number of the Bishop's supporters," and the remaining hundred were Hughes's personal friends. The *Herald* painted the meeting as a badly arranged and quarrelsome failure with the "intelligent Irish Catholics" conspicuous by their absence.[17]

Immediately after the election and before the Catholic laymen's meeting, Hughes left New York and was away for most of the month. He had previously agreed to deliver a lecture before the Mercantile Library of Philadelphia on the "Life and Times of Pius VII," and he then hastened west to assist at the consecration of Peter Paul Lefevere as bishop-administrator of the diocese of Detroit.[18] Hughes returned to New York at the end of November and penned his response to the laity's endorsement on November 29. This reply attempted to justify his recent actions and to vindicate the Catholic school position. In this letter Hughes explained the rationale that forced Catholics to band together in sheer self-defense:

I hold it as a natural and civil right, that, when a class or profession of men is singled out, denounced, assailed, they should combine for the purpose of self-defence the same weapons which are employed by their oppressors for oppression. If men are singled out to be trampled on as mechanics, they have a right to rally as mechanics, and wield the weapons

16 Kehoe, *Works of Hughes*, I, pp. 286–88. Cf. *New York Freeman's Journal*, November 20, 1841.
17 *New York Herald*, November 12 and 17, 1841.
18 Kehoe, *Works of Hughes*, I, p. 299; *New York Herald*, November 17, 1841.

of assault, for the purpose of repelling the assailants. So in regard to religion, if men are assailed as Methodists or Presbyterians, as Methodists and Presbyterians they have a right to combine and protect themselves. And if in consequence of the exercise of this right a political or even physical contest should ensue, the censure of virtuous judgment, whether from the judicial bench or the public press, should fall on the aggressors against the rights of others; and not on those who in consequence of their being assailed are obliged to stand together in self-defence.[19]

Because the Public School Society, the secular and religious press, and the Protestant pulpit united politically to defeat the Catholics at the polls, the "assailed" Catholics were forced to organize to give meaning to their votes in the election. The only alternative for Catholics was to vote for hostile candidates and then not to complain when these legislators later rejected the Catholic petition. Under such circumstances, Catholics were denied a real choice and thus, said Hughes, "I approved [of the 'Carroll Hall' movement], and were it to be done again, in the same circumstances, I should urge it in language quite as strong as any employed by me on the evening of the 29th of October." The press notwithstanding, Hughes denied that he had become a politician in his pre-election stroke. He believed that his religious calling precluded his participation in partisan politics, and he expected his clergy to observe the same rule. But he could not very easily explain away the "Carroll Hall" party. Therefore, if at any time he appeared to deviate from this rule, it must have been "for the maintenance of some constitutional principle far deeper and more sacred to the welfare of our country than anything involved in mere party politics."[20]

During the many months that Catholics were allegedly denied justice in their religious capacity, Hughes accused the secular press of maintaining a conspiracy of silence. When the stronger Protestant sects attacked the numerically and influentially weaker Catholics "in a manner which turns religion into politics, and politics into religion," the sentinels of the free press were fast asleep. But when the "assailed" Catholics used the same weapons to repel the "assailants," the press suddenly expressed anxiety over the admixture of religion and politics. Now Hughes agreed with the press that the intermingling of religion and politics endangered a free society.

19 Kehoe, *Works of Hughes*, I, pp. 289–90.
20 Kehoe, *Works of Hughes*, I, pp. 291–92.

But in the application of this principle, he argued that those who first employed this principle were the culprits, and not the "assailed" who appropriated it only for their own defense. Although no paper could deny these facts, not one ever raised its editorial voice in protest:

The *Post* came and proclaimed no tidings; the *Sun* was eclipsed; the *Commercial Advertiser* gave no warning; the *American* forgot its name . . . whilst the *Journal of Commerce* was, what I suppose it ever will be, in morals as well as merchandise, the *Journal of Commerce*. Nay, whilst the religious papers, such as the '*New York Observer*,' became political, the political papers, especially the *Commercial Advertiser*, the *American*, and the *Journal of Commerce*, became profoundly religious. Their politico-religious appeals were daily addressed to this 'Protestant country,' this 'Protestant community,' against the unfortunate 'Romanists.' This is known to all their readers. They cannot, and will not deny it.[21]

Hughes believed in the freedom of the press as long as the news was responsibly reported with "knowledge, just judgment and truth." The press was regulated not only by libel laws but also by ethical bounds of decency and objectivity. Although the bishop conceded that he was human enough to be stung by the press's personal insults hurled against him, his episcopal trust transcended human considerations in his quest for educational justice for his Catholic flock. If he contested the school question with perhaps too much zeal, it was "because my own appreciation of what I owed my God and to the flock, which is His, committed to my care, made it my duty to do so."[22]

In this reply, Hughes reiterated what he considered to be the simple justice of the Catholic school case. Catholics conscientiously objected to that "vague, sickly, semi-infidel Protestantism which prevails in the public schools." Because of the religious pluralism of American society, he preferred secular schools to the Protestant-oriented schools of the Public School Society. Of course, Hughes hoped that all denominational schools would be included in the state's common school system and thereby participate in the common school fund. This did not mean the union of church and state or the use of public funds for sectarian purposes. Unless Catholics con-

[21] Kehoe, *Works of Hughes*, I, pp. 290–91.
[22] Kehoe, *Works of Hughes*, I, p. 293.

tinued to press for their constitutional rights, concluded the bishop, "you will be cordially despised, as you ought to be, by your fellow citizens."[23]

The *Herald*'s commentary on Hughes's analysis minced no words. Bennett branded Hughes's principles as alien to the spirit and letter of the Christian message and "fraught with danger." Christ had abrogated the doctrine of "an eye for an eye and a tooth for a tooth." The bishop's principles and political actions were called "contrary to the gospel of which he is a minister." Bennett challenged anyone to find an analogy between Hughes's conduct and that of Christ or the apostles. He accused the bishop of tacitly admitting the legitimacy of physical force to achieve an end. "Does this impudent and ignorant prelate imagine," asked Bennett, "that the respectable Catholics of New York will take up arms and murder the other Christian sects, if he cannot carry his point?" When Hughes attacked the secular press, Bennett did not miss the bishop's deliberate omission of his paper. Hughes was accused of assuming this "studied silence, in not naming the *New York Herald*, as if to show his readers that he never read that paper, when it is palpable from the latter part of his address, that he had conned every syllable of it."[24]

The *Observer* could not wait to denounce the bishop's reply as a manifesto calculated to misrepresent the facts before the public. Contrary to the Catholic assertion, the papists were responsible for provoking the school controversy. All denominations regarded the city's schools as satisfactory until the Romanists decided to test their political power in an attempt to wrest a portion of the indivisible school fund. The paper painted Hughes's allusion to the use of physical force as a favorite theme of the Catholic Church that was often employed by its clergy. The effects of this alleged Catholic principle were obvious, since just a week before "a meeting was proposed by the Protestants to consider the school fund question, and the 'physical contest' friends of the Bishop assembled in such numbers and with such demonstrations of violence, that the meeting could not be held." It was also a " 'physical contest' that resulted in putting one of the Bishop's candidates in jail at the last election."

In addition, Hughes was accused of a "palpable contradiction." He had condemned the *Observer* for becoming political but denied that

---

23 Kehoe, *Works of Hughes*, I, p. 297. Hughes felt for those "poor Catholics" who opposed the Catholic claim "only a sentiment of pity."

24 *New York Herald*, December 1 and 9, 1841.

the "Carroll Hall" movement was a political measure. Protestants were obviously on the side of wrong and Catholics on the side of right. "If we were political," argued the editor, "so were they. But the Bishop in one part of his paper charges us with having become political, and in another denies that he has interfered in politics at all. Here is a dilemma, to escape from which will require a more cunning manifesto than the one before us."[25] In the final analysis, predicted the *Observer*, Catholics would never be satisfied until they received public funds to instruct their children in papal dogmas. On the other hand, Hughes's Catholic-convert lawyer friend, William G. Read of Baltimore, eulogized Hughes's apologia as a definitive primer from which future Catholic immigrants would learn their political obligations and rights.[26]

ii

After the November election, most of the secular press devoted little space to the school question. Election news became old news, and most of the papers awaited the opening of the new Legislature.[27] That is, all except the *Herald*. Bennett pursued a personal vendetta against Hughes and attempted to split the ranks of the American Catholic Church. A former student for the Catholic priesthood who had soured on his ancestral religion, the Scottish journalist published a series of scathing articles against his episcopal opponent that ran over a month. Bennett professed esteem for Hughes despite his political aberrancy. "He is a Bishop of the Church—he is a minister of Jesus Christ—he is a Viceregent of God at the holy altar. In all these attitudes and respects, we honor, we love, we esteem, we pray for John Hughes, and hope that he will repent and be forgiven."[28] But once the bishop left the sanctuary and assumed the politician's role, the editor could only describe him with sentiments

[25] *New York Observer*, December 11, 1841.

[26] William G. Read to Hughes (Baltimore, December 10, 1841), NYAA.

[27] Nevertheless, the *New York Tribune* printed many letters on the school issue during the rest of the year. Especially interesting was the lively debate between "Cato," a Catholic and defender of Hughes's school position, and "Hamilton," who was his unyielding protagonist. For this exchange, see *New York Tribune*, November 16, 23, and 30, and December 4 and 11, 1841. Additional letters can be found in the *New York Tribune*, October 30, November 24, and December 4, 1841; the *New York Evening Post*, November 1, 1841; and the *New York Freeman's Journal*, November 20, 1841.

[28] *New York Herald*, December 3, 1841.

of "utter contempt and profound detestation." This "foolish prelate" and "Abbot of Unreason" was branded as unfit to administer the episcopal office. Bennett's venomous pen reminded readers that Hughes's irregular education had left him without the knowledge and sophistication requisite for the episcopacy:

Although a Bishop of the Catholic Church, he is so ignorant of the first elements of a highly classical education, as to be utterly unable to translate correctly a sentence of the original Greek or Hebrew, and we will venture to say he could not, to save his soul from purgatory for a month, give a correct English version of the Canons of the Council of Trent, under which he acts and possesses power and authority. And yet this is the man who would embroil the Catholics with the American people.[29]

Bennett did not intend to scorn a man's rise from obscurity to prominence. But on the other hand, he felt that Hughes had not sufficiently matured intellectually to manage the complexities of his episcopal office:

But when a plain gardener, at Emmettsburgh [*sic*], with a deficient education, and an intellect half made up of shreds and patches, like a piece of second-hand clothes, brings to the rank and position of a bishop the small intrigue—the vain rivalry—the little arrogance—which might be confessed and forgiven monthly in a tender of kitchen cabbages, we then see incongruity—incapacity and incompetency in its broadest light.[30]

Bennett contended that the bishop's political maneuvers, so reminiscent of the despotic prince-bishops of the Middle Ages, had placed the Catholic Church in an unfortunate light before the American people. If a prelate of any other denomination had attempted Hughes's political machinations, he would have been disciplined immediately and perhaps even removed from office. Since Hughes held his episcopal commission from the pope alone, unfortunately to him alone was he responsible. There was no American "ecclesiastical court" which could punish him for his "ecclesiastical indiscretion." The only course open to New York Catholics was to make a public petition to "the court of Rome" to remove Hughes from his diocese as well as to condemn his meddlesome political activities. If the papacy refused to comply with this request, Bennett proposed a

29 *New York Herald,* November 24, 1841.
30 *New York Herald,* December 4, 1841.

schism from the Roman Church and the establishment of an independent American Catholic Church:

. . . we verily believe it is the duty of the American Catholics to call a general council, to organize their church on an independent footing, make their own laws, appoint their own Bishops, and renovate their holy religion with a fresh spirit and a new infusion of Christianity. As one humble individual, I shall contribute *one thousand dollars* at once for the complete re-organization of the American Catholic Church, beyond the reach or influence of any foreign prince, potentate or power, be he Pope, Patriarch, or Emperor.[31]

Bennett pictured the Catholic Church, with all its dogmas and "drivellings," to be in the last stage of decrepitude. The time was right for American Catholics to throw off the shackles of a totalitarian church with its political intrigue and wordly bishops in favor of a vibrant and independent new world Catholicism presided over by elected American prelates schooled in the principles of free republican government.

Not only did the *Herald* engage in personal defamation and attempt to rend the Catholic Church in America, but it also tried to sow discord between Hughes and his clergy. The paper discerned two contradictory pressures contending for ecclesiastical power in Catholic New York. On the one hand, there was "the scheming, tricky, intriguing French Catholic influence," while on the other, "the honest, straight-forward, open, manly Irish Catholic influence." Although the Irish segment was both qualitatively and quantitatively the superior Catholic element, the French clique enjoyed more weight at Rome. Aided by foreign Jesuits, the French influence held sway at Rome and dominated the ecclesiastical life of Catholic New York. French dominance caused the "unpopular appointment" of Dubois, and his protégé John Hughes, "once his highly respectable and industrious gardener," to be named as coadjutor. The most talented and best equipped clergyman and the unanimous choice of the Irish majority for the episcopal vacancy, the Reverend John Power, co-vicar-general of the diocese, had been vetoed by the French-Jesuit conspiracy and "sacrificed in order that the parvenu of an old imbecile might supplant him." The "miserable truckling and intrigues of Bishop Hughes, and the imbecility of Bishop Dubois" were contrasted with "the learning, the intelligence, the pro-

[31] *New York Herald,* November 6, 1841. Cf. November 5, 1841.

found scholarship, the many noble and amiable qualities of the Rev. Dr. Powers [*sic*], the Rev. Mr. Levins, and the Rev. Mr. Peese [Pise] . . . [who] are the master spirits of the Catholic Church in this city. . . ." Since these priests had the support of Irish Catholics, they were proclaimed as saviors of the Catholic Church in New York from the ruin that Hughes and his French clique "would wish to bring upon it."[32]

Less than a week later, Power and Pise sent a joint communication to the *Herald*'s office which disclaimed any accord with the paper's assertions. They were unaware of discordant clerical parties and expressed their admiration for the Jesuits. They personally esteemed Hughes and "venerate him as a prelate, and duly appreciate his able and triumphant vindication of the 'Common School Question.' "[33] The clergymen's explanation did not satisfy Bennett. Although they professed admiration for their bishop, the editor noted that they did not express support for Hughes's "soiling his holy vestments" by descending into the muddy political waters. Bennett insisted that Hughes had compelled them to exonerate their spiritual superior. The *Herald* was satisfied that Power and Pise discountenanced any subsequent attempts of Hughes "to excite afresh the political ferment at the next elections, and thus to set in array the whole country against the Catholics. . . ."[34]

Because Bennett once again placed these clergymen in a rather compromising position, each of them issued separate cards which categorically denied any discord between them and their bishop. However much Power valued his reputation with the citizenry and the public press, he felt compelled to repudiate any praise bestowed upon him which simultaneously disparaged Hughes, "whom inclination and duty lead [me] to revere and esteem." Pise also rejected any idea of friction between him and his bishop. He unequivocally supported Hughes's efforts to render the public schools palatable for Catholic attendance and had respected the bishop's purity of intention "from my earliest youth."[35] Apparently, Power and Pise could do nothing to convince Bennett, since he accused them of writing their cards under "the insolent and imperious mandate of their Bishop." He expected loyal responses from such learned and

32 *New York Herald*, November 17, 1841.
33 *New York Herald*, November 24, 1841.
34 *New York Herald*, December 1, 1841.
35 *New York Herald*, December 3 and 4, 1841.

sophisticated gentlemen. But once again, he insisted that both replies did not affirm their approval of the "Carroll Hall" movement. Bennett believed that both men were eminently qualified to hold responsible positions in the independent Catholic Church he hoped would emerge. Hughes's star was fading, and eventually he would be removed because of his political jugglery. In such an eventuality, Bennett desired "an accomplished man to supply the vacancy that will then be created, and no man in our opinion, can better occupy the Bishopric than the learned, meek and excellent Doctor Power."[36]

Sensitive to journalistic criticism, Hughes smarted from the *Herald*'s harangue against him. But he answered the "vituperation, calumny, and slander" of the editor with a contemptuous silence. When their feud erupted anew in 1844, Hughes wrote a letter to the mayor of New York in which he branded Bennett as "decidedly the most dangerous man, to the peace and safety of a community, that I have ever known, or read of." Hughes compared the "dangerous and degraded" Bennett in his attempt to sow discord among the Catholic clergy to the "serpent in Paradise who seduced Adam and Eve—although in this case the serpent was foiled." The editor was an enigma who occupied a position which made him too contemptible for public attention and yet sufficiently powerful to cause mischief. If Bennett were "more depraved or less despised," Hughes would not have considered him so dangerous. "If you notice his slanders, and convict him of them, people will say that you lose your labor; inasmuch as 'nobody believes what Bennett says.' If you do not, your enemies will take that up as undeniable—asserted in the newspapers—or, as Colonel Stone [editor of the *Commercial Advertiser*] adroitly expressed it, 'taken from a morning print.' "[37]

With the exception of his spirited response to the Catholic laymen's support of his pre-election activities, Hughes refrained from any further public statements during the remainder of the year. "Whilst the battle was raging, and the little almighties that wield the Press here thought they were pelting & piercing" him, his correspondence with faithful friends acted as balm to the beleaguered prelate. Soon after the election, he sent a letter to Seward which attempted to make light of the opprobrium cast upon his episcopal head: "I was chafed & jealous when you *alone* were getting all the

---

[36] *New York Herald*, December 3, 1841. In addition, Pise would then assume the pastorate of St. Peter's Church. Cf. December 4, 1841.

[37] Kehoe, *Works of Hughes*, I, pp. 460–61.

abuse to which the exercise of the heart's benevolence entitles good
men, in this world of selfishness & corruption. But now that I am
classed with you in it, I am revenged and happy." Hughes believed
that there would eventually be "a reaction in my favor, and I shall
not value it if it should not prove equally strong in yours."[38] Seward's response was an attempt to ameliorate his friend's deep hurt.
He depicted both of them as suffering the common lot of enlightened individuals who were in advance of their times:

I have no concern for your ultimate vindication. It is your fortune as
well as mine that philanthropic conceptions for the improvement of
society come in conflict with existing interests founded in existing prejudices. I do not know what may have been your experience but although not yet old I have passed through such struggles, heretofore,
and distracting as they sometimes were I have seen the interests and
prejudices roll away together in a space so short that the result surprised
me.[39]

In addition to a pledge of renewed gubernatorial support in the
next legislative session, Seward lauded his friend and outlined in
bold strokes the larger task that Hughes still had before him: "You
have, my dear Sir, a high vocation here. One no less than that of
lifting the vast and influential emigrant Catholic population from
a condition of inferiority and exclusion, to equality and harmony
with all other sects and citizens. You are endowed with genius,
vigor, firmness, and appreciation of truth which seem to me guarantees of your success."[40] As soon as Hughes had written his reply
to the Catholic laity, he wrote a letter to Seward that expressed satisfaction with the content of the response. "I think I have covered the
whole ground and offered such a vindication as will have some
weight with the candid portion of the public." Although initially
he had intended to defend the governor's conduct on the school
question, the bishop had subsequently abandoned the idea for he
"feared that at this moment it might be unseasonable from *me*, and
perhaps injurious to yourself."[41]

Shortly after the November election, Hughes wrote a carefully
reasoned defense of the "Carroll Hall" venture to his lawyer friend

38 Hughes to Seward (New York, November 8, 1841), UR.
39 Seward to Hughes (Albany, November 10, 1841), UR.
40 Seward to Hughes (November 10, 1841), UR.
41 Hughes to Seward (New York, November 29, 1841), UR.

in Baltimore, William Read. Presenting the case from Hughes's point of view, the letter expressed neither compunction nor regret:

I know that if I did not go beyond my episcopal sphere, I went at least to the furthest verge of it. But the disease was desperate and required a desperate effort for its removal or mitigation. And if scurrility be punishment (and for me in sooth it is not) I have been well chastised. But all I intended has been accomplished just to the letter. The corrupt politicians have been taught a lesson which they will not soon forget. The Catholic body have been raised and united which never could have been done, if I had not thrown myself in the breach· The school question is beaten into the heads of public men whether they will or not. The authorities and the community at large, begin to acknowledge that there *are* such people as Catholics. A small school of infidel Catholics who preyed on the body, for their little offices. . . , has been extinguished forever—the Catholic body now united have shed them as alike a disgrace and a detriment—and have purified the passion of politics into something like reason, learning in the process, and perhaps for the first time, the propriety of shouting less and thinking more.[42]

This communication was not meant for Read's eyes alone. Even before the election, Archbishop Samuel Eccleston of Baltimore had forwarded to Hughes a copy of the *Baltimore Sun* that attacked and allegedly misrepresented the New York bishop's position on the school question. Eccleston had suggested that Hughes "furnish materials for a refutation or explanation. . . ."[43] Long accustomed to press criticism and busy with pre-election activities, Hughes never acted upon the archbishop's recommendation. Instead, he instructed Read to allow Eccleston to read the letter and then circulate it to Hughes's other friends in Baltimore.

Engaged in an extensive correspondence, lecturing and travelling, and performing his ordinary diocesan functions, Hughes watched a new year replace an old one as he awaited the opening of the new Legislature. All eyes were on the Legislature and all ears prepared to hear Seward's annual message. In one way or another, all the interested parties recognized that somehow the school controversy would be settled before the Legislature's spring adjournment. All the forces made ready for the last and crucial battle.

42 Hughes to William G. Read (New York, November 6, 1841), NYAA.
43 Samuel Eccleston to Hughes (Baltimore, November 1, 1841), NYAA.

⌣ X ⌣

Smooth Sailing in the Assembly

i

No sooner had the legislative session of 1842 begun than a clarion call alerting the Protestant community was sounded by the *New York Observer*. The paper saw signs on the political horizon that the Legislature was ready to accommodate the Catholics on the school question. The fact that many Democratic legislators seemed to be flocking to the Catholic standard gave credence to the *Observer*'s perception. Although "a great majority of the Protestant community" was solidly arrayed against the papist demand, the editor identified four groups who favored a change in the city's schools: the honestly committed; unscrupulous politicians who pandered popish votes; the great mass of Catholics; and Protestants "who have embraced the Oxford divinity [Pusey], and who differ from the Romanists more in name than in fact." Even though these groups constituted a distinct minority, continued Protestant *"inaction"* would cede the victory to the enemy by default. Protestants were asked to resist the destruction of the public schools "as citizens and Christians, as freemen and Protestants." And should the Catholics ever gain the day, the *Observer* forewarned that loyal Protestants would strive "to repeal a law imposed upon them against their wishes, and in defiance of their remonstrances."[1]

Even before the Legislature officially convened, the school question generated a flurry of behind-the-scenes excitement in the state capitol. The Democratic majority found itself in a predicament.

---

[1] *New York Observer*, February 5, 1842. Cf. January 8, 1842; *Christian Advocate and Journal* (New York), March 23, 1842.

Further ambiguity or procrastination on the school question almost certainly would provoke future Catholic retaliation at the polls. On the other hand, the overwhelming Democratic majority would bear full responsibility for the final legislative settlement of the problem. Greeley understood this dilemma and assured Seward that "Tammany must give up this *point* [the school question] or be used up by it."[2]

Certain that Seward's annual message would deal firmly with the school issue, the wary Democratic Assembly leadership carefully chose the membership of the Committee on Colleges, Academies, and Common Schools, which exercised prime responsibility for all educational matters in the state. As soon as the upstate Democrat, Levi Chatfield, was elected speaker, he announced his intention to appoint William Maclay as chairman of this committe. Since the New York assemblyman had supposedly been elected without pledge or commitment to any group, the presumption was that he would direct a thorough and objective inquiry into New York City's educational system. At first Maclay declined the chairmanship and urged the selection of the more experienced John Dix of Albany, a Democrat and former state superintendent of common schools. When Dix declined the office, Maclay was again offered the position, and this time he accepted. Two upstate Democrats and a city and upstate Whig completed the rest of the five-man committee.[3] The Senate counterpart of this committee was the equally important Committee on Literature, whose membership included two upstate Democrats and one upstate Whig.[4] Since the New York City senatorial delegation sustained the Public School Society's position, it was significant that the Democratic leadership preferred not to assign any of them to the committee.

As had been expected, Seward's message stressed the importance of solving New York's educational difficulties. He reminded the legislators that he had long considered educational improvement as his most important gubernatorial task. When he had first informed the Legislature about the thousands of neglected children in New York City who did not receive any education, he had not realized

2 Horace Greeley to Seward (New York, January 7, 1842), UR.

3 Horatio Seymour of Oneida County and Calvin Hulburd of St. Lawrence County were the other two Democratic members, while William Jones of New York and Emory Warren of Chautauqua County were the Whig representatives.

4 Henry Foster of Oneida County and John Hunter of Westchester County were Democrats, while Erastus Root of Delaware County was the single Whig representative.

the "magnitude of the evil" nor its causes. While less than nine thousand children throughout the rest of the state failed to receive a common school education, twenty thousand city children, primarily Catholic, were not instructed in the public schools. "What have been regarded as individual, occasional, and accidental prejudices, have proved to be opinions pervading a large mass, including at least one religious communion equally with all others entitled to civil tolerance. . . ."[5] The cause of this evil lay in the city's departure from the state system of education. Instead of the people having direct responsibility for their schools, New York City's system was monopolized by the privately chartered Public School Society. Although he acknowledged the efficiency and academic success of the Society schools, Seward labeled them a failure because they did not command the confidence of all the citizenry. In fact, argued the governor, no plan of education was defensible unless it conceded that "public instruction is one of the responsibilities of the government."

Seward's remedy for New York City's educational deficiencies was essentially Spencer's solution: extend the state system of common schools to the city, thereby vesting control of the schools in the hands of the people according to true republican principles. Nor would this proposal be an approval of sectarian education. Sectarianism was not an upstate issue and should not be an obstacle in the city. Seward believed that his plan "simply proposes, by enlightening equally the minds of all, to enable them to detect error wherever it may exist, and to reduce uncongenial masses into one intelligent, virtuous, harmonious and happy people." As he was soon to retire from public office, he cherished no fonder recollection "than that of having met such a question in the generous and confiding spirit of our institutions, and of having decided it upon the immutable principles on which they are based."[6]

Seward's new proposal indicates that he had overcome the ambiguity of his 1841 address and now steered closer to his original position. In 1840, he envisaged Catholic schools as being part of the common school system and entitled to common school funds. The following year he momentarily equivocated in declaring that "I have no pride of opinion concerning the manner in which the edu-

5 Baker, *Works of Seward*, II, p. 306.
6 Baker, *Works of Seward*, II, p. 309.

cation of those whom I have brought to your notice shall be secured." In 1842, Spencer's influence had left its mark, and Seward
embodied the principal features of his secretary's report. He advocated the extension of the state district-system of common schools
to the city while still permitting the Public School Society to retain
an important voice in New York education. In this way, Catholic
children could conscientiously attend the public schools while the
essential integrity of the city's present education system would remain secured. Seward reasoned that such a plan would silence
Catholic agitation and simultaneously preserve the essential usefulness of the Society. Furthermore, the extension of the state district system to the city would be an important step in the direction
of universal education—an ideal which always remained Seward's
principal concern. He realized that the Legislature would never
vote public funds for sectarian schools. A good politician, Seward
attempted to obviate Catholic objections without being branded a
supporter of sectarian education.[7]

Even before Seward's message, the Democratic *Evening Post*'s
Albany correspondent attributed partisan motives to the Whig governor. Although the reporter admitted that he could not vouch
for the accuracy of his statement, for he did not receive it firsthand,
he alleged that Seward consciously prepared a political dilemma for
the Democratically controlled Legislature. His scheme was to

come out on the Catholic school question more strongly than ever. There
are no Whigs among the Catholics, or none to speak of; and the party
which has the majority in the Legislature, will either be obliged to
follow [his] recommendations, or else they will drive their Catholic
friends over on [the governor's] side. [Seward] shall throw a firebrand
into their party which they cannot extinguish.[8]

There was some truth in this accusation. If Seward could accomplish his educational goal and at the same time embarrass the political opposition, so much the better. He was interested not only in
achieving universal education, but in practical political considerations as well, and at times the two interests converged. Seward did
not see any incompatibility between the two.

The Whig press accorded Seward's educational recommendation

---

7 Glyndon G. Van Deusen, *Thurlow Weed: Wizard of the Lobby* (Boston: Little,
Brown and Company, 1947), p. 360.
8 *New York Evening Post*, January 3, 1842.

a disdainful politeness. The *American* thought the message well written even though it emphatically disagreed with its educational sentiments. The *Commercial Advertiser* characterized the governor as "woefully misled" in his educational views and labeled his "courteous" attack on the Public School Society "as unjust as it is unkind."[9] Without questioning Seward's integrity, the *Observer* called his remarks a supremely "illogical argument." It denied that Seward really wished the district system brought to the city. Up to that time, there was no district "in which any number of men may organize a school in addition to the school already established, and draw money for its support." But under the governor's plan, any sectarian group could start a school which would be entitled to school funds. "And this must be the consequence if the Governor's plan is adopted." The *Observer* contended that Seward should not propose "to district the city" since it would not work well and would not mitigate Catholic complaints. Catholics would undoubtedly control certain districts, but in the majority of the districts, Catholics would be forced to attend schools in which they were the minority. Therefore, the editor suspected a political ruse wherein the politicians had joined forces with the papist hierarchy to subvert the public schools in order to gain Catholic votes. "Herod and Pilate may become friends, Whigs and Democrats may combine to destroy existing institutions, and deliver to the people such a system as is offered in the message before us, but we question whether the people of this State will ever consent to the decision."[10]

On the other side, the *Freeman's Journal* analyzed Seward's message as overcoming injustice with justice, exclusiveness with republicanism, and "sectarian bigotry" with "enlightened philanthropy." The governor's recommendation satisfied Catholics, for it was seen as a complete vindication of Hughes's unceasing efforts to prosecute the school question to its conclusion. But if a battle had been won, warned the editor, the war was far from over. "The enemy, though beaten at every point, has not yet capitulated." Catholics were urged to expedite the school matter energetically to a successful end by pressing it "on the immediate attention of the Legislature."[11]

9 *New York American*, January 5, 1842; *New York Commercial Advertiser*, January 6, 1842.

10 *New York Observer*, January 15, 1842. Cf. February 5, 1842.

11 *New York Freeman's Journal*, January 8, 1842.

Richard Blatchford, Seward's confidant in New York City, "like[d] that message right much. . . . it is the best you ever gave. . . . that school question is put irresistably and unanswerably." Greeley insisted that "the School Question *must* go right."[12] Hughes thought that the entire message was admirable, and he was "particularly pleased with the portion which I understood best, and in which I am most interested—the School Question." He thought that Seward's remarks helped to clarify the basic issues in the school contest and thus augured a brighter educational future for the state and the country. Hughes expressed anxiety over the increasingly successful non-sectarian movement in the public schools of the United States. He was aware that this movement extended beyond the confines of New York State and was deeply worried about its eventual acceptance:

America is trying a dangerous experiment in attempting as Mr. Spencer beautifully expressed it, a 'divorce of religion from literature.' It would not be well for the country, if that experiment should succeed. It will not, and the merit of giving it the first *check* will hereafter be traced to your views.[13]

Hughes congratulated Seward on his "firmness & consistency" throughout the whole school question "in circumstances well calculated to test the fortitude of your mind and the sincerity of your motives."[14] Since Seward had essentially incorporated Spencer's proposals in his message to the Legislature, Hughes sent another letter to the governor ten days later in which he presented an analysis of Spencer's postponed bill and his hopes for an educational bill that would be acceptable to the city's Catholics:

The spirit and principle of Mr. Spencer's Bill of last year embody the principles for which we contend. . . . The law should so [be] framed that any sufficient number of Citizens associating under its provisions should realise the blessings of education without having their religious prejudices whatever they may be, tampered with by any extraneous interference, or by any other authority except what might emanate from themselves. Now it seems to me that under the provisions of Mr. Spencer's Bill, this could be done. The object is to enlarge the field of knowledge—

12 Richard M. Blatchford to Seward (New York, January 6, 1842), UR; Horace Greeley to Seward (New York, January 7, 1842), UR.
13 Hughes to Seward (New York, January 10 and 20, 1842), UR.
14 Hughes to Seward (January 10, 1842), UR.

to spread abroad the benefits of education. This the state does. But the P.S. Society assumed to be the dispensers in addition of a certain amount of morality and religion—departments of education which the constitution in accordance with the law of nature and of God, left with parents & guardians, and of which they cannot be rightfully deprived. And yet these are important elements in the character of the future population of the city as well as of the state. Providence, I trust, with its own means of accomplishing salutary ends will do something for the poor children of N.Y. I am sometimes sick at contemplating their condition & prospects in life.[15]

ii

During January, 1842, Catholics were busy preparing another petition "for an alteration in the Public School System in the City of New York." Hughes notified Seward that this petition would soon arrive at Albany. When 12,476 "citizens" had signed the petition, a four-man delegation brought the document to William Maclay, who had offered to present it before the Assembly. On January 24, Maclay submitted the petition to the Assembly, which promptly referred it to the Committee on Colleges, Academies, and Common Schools, whose chairman was the "impartial" Maclay. The New York assemblyman informed his colleagues that no specific measure was contemplated "but such change as the Legislature in its wisdom should deem proper."[16] Ever on the alert, the Public School Society resolved to memorialize New York City's Common Council to take such measures to prevent passage of any school bill which would disrupt the present system of public education in the city. Nearly a month later, the Society finally delivered its memorial to the Board of Aldermen. In their appeal, the trustees urged the Common Council to ask the Legislature to suspend action on all pending educational legislation until a joint committee of the state and city officials investigated the whole school question. The Board of Aldermen re-

---

15 Hughes to Seward (New York, January 20, 1842), UR.

16 *Journal of the Assembly*, January 24, 1842, p. 142; *New York Freeman's Journal*, January 29, 1842; *New York Tribune*, January 27, 1842. The Catholic delegation included Tighe, Davey, Derry, and Gaffney. Although the petition had 12,476 signatures, the *New York Tribune* listed 12,151. Other petitions seeking an alteration in the city's school system were introduced to the Assembly on January 28 and January 31. *Journal of the Assembly*, January 28, 1842, p. 182, and January 31, 1842, p. 193.

ferred the trustees' request to its Committee on Laws and Applications to the Legislature for study and recommendation.[17] Once again, the protagonists were marshaling their forces for a final head-on clash.

Maclay's Committee on Colleges, Academies, and Common Schools required just three short weeks to report its findings to the Assembly. The committee left no doubt about what it considered to be the cause of the educational debate in New York City. Quoting statistics from the latest annual report of the superintendent of common schools (January 6, 1842), Maclay declared that whereas ninety-six per cent of all children between the ages of five and sixteen attended common schools throughout the state, New York City's attendance was less than sixty per cent. Even though the city's percentage was perceptibly lower than the rest of the state, this same city allocated more than three dollars and fifteen cents to instruct each pupil whereas the state average was less than one dollar and four cents per student. "In other words, the expense of instruction under the public school system in New York is more than three times the expense of instruction under the district school system." Maclay reiterated Seward's contention that the Public School Society had failed to gain the trust of a large number of the city's population.

The inescapable conclusion to be drawn, argued the committee, was "that the failure of the public schools to accomplish the objects contemplated by . . . [their] establishment, results, in a great degree, from a disinclination on the part of many parents to entrust these schools with the education of their children." By its own admission, the Society had been repeatedly obliged to defend its educational monopoly against discontented segments of the population. In addition to censuring the Society's private corporate character as essentially hostile to republican principles of government, the report accused the trustees of failing to discern the rapidly developing heterogeneity of the city population. New York City could no longer boast of a basically monolithic society. "Any system based upon the supposition that homogeneousness now exists, and all will therefore

[17] *PSS: Executive Committee,* January 24, 1842; *Proceedings of the Board of Aldermen,* February 21, 1842, p. 250; Memorial of the Trustees of the Public School Society to the Common Council of New York, *Document No. 75, Documents of the Board of Aldermen,* February 21, 1842, pp 577–83.

absolutely conform, or can be obliged to conform, assumes the end
to be attained, and overlooks the means of its accomplishment."[18]

And yet, these and all other considerations were quite beside the
point. The crucial question was whether the Society was successfully
expediting the universal education of the city's youngsters. Maclay's
committee concluded that it had "signally failed" in this task despite
repeatedly fruitless efforts to gain the confidence of the people. To
remedy this situation, the committee recommended "that the [state]
system [of common school education] shall, as far as it is practicable,
be extended to the city and county of New York."[19]

In accordance with these views, Maclay's committee submitted to
the Assembly "An act to extend to the city of New York the provisions of the general act in relation to common schools."[20] This bill
exhibited a remarkable similarity to the unsuccessful Spencer measure of the previous year. At each city election, qualified voters
would elect three commissioners and two inspectors of common
schools, whose compensation would be determined by the Common
Council. At the same election the voters would elect ward trustees,
who would bear immediate responsibility to "establish, maintain,
and regulate common schools" in their respective districts, subject
to the general regulation of the commissioners. For the purposes of
this act each ward would be considered a separate town with the
same powers, privileges, immunities, and advantages granted to
other towns in the state. The Common Council would collect a sum
of money equal to the state's appropriation of school moneys, although it would be permitted to raise additional funds that might be
needed to support the city's common schools. The commissioner
would distribute common school funds to each school in his ward
on a pro rata basis. Apportionment would be regulated by the average number of children between five and sixteen who actually attended the school. The schools of the Public School Society would

[18] Report of the Committee on Colleges, Academies, and Common Schools, on So
Much of the Governor's Message, as Relates to the Common Schools in the City of
New York, *Document No. 60, Documents of the Assembly*, February 14, 1842, pp. 5–6.
Cf. Annual Report of the Superintendent of Common Schools, *Document No. 12, Docu-
ments of the Assembly*, January 6, 1842, pp. 1–178; *Journal of the Assembly*, February
14, 1842, p. 317.

[19] *Document No. 60*, p. 8.

[20] *Journal of the Assembly*, February 14, 1842, p. 318. An extract of Maclay's bill is
found in the *New York Commercial Advertiser*, February 16, 1842.

remain intact under the general jurisdiction of the ward commissioners. Omission of any mention of sectarianism meant that Maclay subcribed to Spencer's principle of "absolute non-intervention," which prevailed throughout the state. On the other hand, contrary to the Spencer bill, school officials were to be salaried, and no provision was made for a board of education.

As soon as the bill was read, assemblyman Baker recommended that it be submitted to the electoral approval of the people of New York City before it was passed as state law. Maclay rejected this resolution on the ground that direct appeals to the people were legitimate only with regard to exceptional issues. He did not consider the school question as one of those rare occasions. Moreover, he wanted to make it clear to the Assembly that he was reflecting the true sentiment of his constituents on the school issue. Neither by petition nor through the press had the people requested that this measure be referred back to them. "During this and the last session" of the Legislature, Maclay had canvassed public opinion on this question and "he could say that he never heard an individual express a desire that it should be." The public had become convinced, declared Maclay, that the city school system contravened republican principles of government and did not successfully provide education for all the city's youngsters. The corrective to the situation was this bill, which would bring "children within the public schools, without infringing the conscientious right or opinions of any class of citizens." Apparently, the assemblyman had not looked very hard since it was obvious to all that public opinion concerning the alteration of New York City's school system was negative except for the Catholic attitude. In addition to Baker's resolution two other suggestions, including the "indefinite postponement of the whole subject," were decisively defeated and the bill was then referred to the committee of the whole house.[21]

The *Evening Post*'s Albany correspondent disliked the bill because it did not resolve the central dilemma of the school problem: the reconciliation of the exclusive monopoly of the Public School Society with the unlimited competition inherent in a republican government. "No law can be satisfactory which does not recognize the rights of the Public School Society, at the same time that it

[21] *New York Commercial Advertiser*, February 16, 1842. Cf. *Journal of the Assembly*, February 14, 1842, pp. 318, 323.

admits of the formation of rival associations." The reporter thought
that O'Sullivan's bill was still the "nearest approach to this that I
have seen. . . ."[22] The Society's staunchest supporter, the *Commercial
Advertiser*, reproached the sudden "change of front" by the Democratic party concerning the school question. The editor's scorpion
pen vented itself particularly upon Maclay's remarks about the city's
alleged hostility to the present school system. "Every man of intelligence in New York knows," declared the editor, that the assemblyman was in error and "greatly mistaken." The paper was convinced
that the Democratic majority intended to drive the bill through the
Assembly "without consideration or amendment."[23] Basically antagonistic to the Catholic position, the *Tribune* insisted that "Mr.
Maclay's bill does not reach the grievance which it undertakes to
cure." Under this bill, education would be placed under the control of local majorities which, in certain circumstances, meant Catholic majorities. "But," reasoned the *Tribune*, "the Catholic claim
must rest on Rights of Conscience and Equity—on the rights of
individuals and not masses—of minorities and not majorities."[24]

After the vendetta against Hughes, Bennett's *Herald* returned to
a more rational analysis of the issues. A superficial scrutiny was sufficient to convince any reasonable person that some alteration in the
present school system was absolutely essential. The religious bigots
notwithstanding, imminent action was vital. Maclay's bill seemed
to be a good remedy to improve the system. Therefore, urged Bennett, "by all means let us adopt this plan and give it a thorough and
impartial trial."[25] Extolling Maclay's report and bill for their "sound
republican and statesmanlike views," the *Freeman's Journal* hoped
that the Legislature would respond to the bill's challenge and give
Catholics a measure of justice at long last. It alerted the state legislators to be aware of Catholic opponents who were waiting at Albany, ready "to spring forward, seize upon and strangle the bill
which they knew was in preparation for releasing the cause of education from the narrow limits in which it has been so long held by
the hateful grasp of monopolizing bigots."[26] Greeley's *Tribune* felt

22 *New York Evening Post*, February 16, 1842.
23 *New York Commercial Advertiser*, February 16 and 17, 1842.
24 *New York Tribune*, March 15, 1842. Cf. *Christian Advocate and Journal* (New
York), March 9, 1842.
25 *New York Herald*, February 23, 1842.
26 *New York Freeman's Journal*, February 19, 1842.

that Catholic approval of the Maclay bill meant that Catholics preferred crumbs to nothing and warned that they considered this bill "a stepping-stone to something better."

Maclay's bill was not strictly a Democratic proposal. During the weeks following Seward's message to the Legislature, the governor, Weed, Hughes, and even Greeley conferred with Maclay on the legislative course of his bill. At one point ready to capitulate under heavy political and religious pressure, Maclay's resolve was strengthened by the politically suave and tough Weed. "I told him that so far as my political experience and observation went, men who, in the discharge of representative duties, acted upon their conviction, rarely suffered for it." However obnoxious Maclay's sponsorship of the school bill rendered him temporarily, the Whig boss assured the young Democrat that "his vindication would be sure and early."[27] After Maclay had drawn up the school bill, he consulted with Hughes before it was introduced into the Assembly. Apparently the bishop's reception of the bill was sufficiently reserved to elicit Seward's warning "that a new plan would be made odious and the odium of extortion fall upon you and the claimants." Instead, the governor counseled his friend to have two trusted representatives in Albany during the whole time that Maclay's bill was pending before the Legislature.[28] There is little doubt that Maclay and his Democratic colleagues; Seward, Weed and their Whig supporters; and Hughes and his Catholic followers were all using their influence to have the Maclay school bill become law.

In time, word leaked out concerning Maclay's consultation with Hughes, which helped neither the assemblyman nor the bishop. The *New York Standard* first broke the story that Maclay's school bill "was exhibited to *Bishop Hughes*, and approved by him, before it was introduced into the Assembly."[29] Sensing adverse reaction to a probable Catholic victory, Hughes quickly defended his action in a card sent to several papers. Choosing his words carefully, he denied that Maclay had "consulted me in relation to a single clause

[27] Weed, *Autobiography of Weed*, p. 502. Weed relates that Maclay's vindication came the same year, when he was elected to the United States House of Representatives.

[28] Seward to Hughes (Albany, February 7, 10, and 18, 1842), NYAA. In addition, the bishop sent three other letters to Seward, which were promptly destroyed by the governor upon the request of Hughes.

[29] *New York Standard*, cited in the *New York Commercial Advertiser*, March 29, 1842.

of it, nor is there to my knowledge a single clause in it framed to meet any wishes of mine on the subject. There is not a line or a syllable inserted in that bill or excluded from its provisions at my suggestion or by my agency." Hughes denied any responsibility for the initiation, "revision, alteration or amendment" of the bill. Although he lauded Maclay as a man of integrity and talent, he denied that the assemblyman had been "directly or indirectly under any guidance or influence of mine, in drawing up that bill. . . ."[30]

One of Seward's loyal supporters in the city wrote the governor that he thought that Hughes's explanation was "a notable evasion" and that the "Bishop is very silly to publish this card."[31] For all his protestation about integrity, Hughes never disavowed the charge that he had examined the bill before Maclay introduced it in the Assembly. This verbal equivocation did not go unnoticed. The *Commercial Advertiser* accused the bishop of denying everything but the real charge: "that the bill reported by Mr. Maclay had been *submitted* to Bishop Hughes, before it was brought into the Assembly and *approved* by him." Maclay was pictured as too clever a "political jesuit" to permit Hughes a hand in drafting or revising the bill. Instead, all this had been done before the assemblyman had submitted his bill "to the legate of the Holy See, for its approbation." Indeed, "Ignatius Loyola could not have been more devious than his devious successor," and the *Advertiser*, acidly predicted that "Mr. Maclay shall be a cardinal."[32] The *Observer* thundered its expected reaction in the same vein. Hughes's ambivalence was readily explained by the simple fact that he was a papist. But it was an abomination that a good Baptist like Maclay would dare "submit a bill to the consideration of a Romish Priest" because of "deference to the political influence of the Pope. . . ."[33] Although the *Evening Post* conceded Hughes's ambiguity, the Democratic daily, obviously trying to defend Maclay's action, maintained that "there was no more harm or impropriety" in showing the bill to the bishop "than in showing it to a trustee of the Public School Society."[34]

[30] *New York Herald*, April 2, 1842; *New York Commercial Advertiser*, April 2, 1842; *New York Evening Post*, April 2, 1842.

[31] Samuel Blatchford to Seward (New York, April 1, 1842), UR.

[32] *New York Commercial Advertiser*, April 2, 1842.

[33] *New York Observer*, April 9, 1842.

[34] *New York Evening Post*, April 2, 1842. Cf. Hassard, *Life of Hughes*, p. 249. Hassard maintains that Greeley, Weed, and Seward also conferred with Maclay in drawing up the bill. Greeley's position on the whole school question is at best equivocal since his newspaper expressed editorial hostility to the Maclay bill.

For nearly a month the Assembly took no action on the school bill. Finally, on March 12 Maclay convinced the chamber to make his bill a special order of business for March 16. But on that date debate floundered aimlessly, and there was danger that the bill might not pass this session of the Assembly. As a result, Maclay had the bill referred to a special committee consisting of one member from each senatorial district for a final examination. Two days later, this select committee brought in a slightly amended bill and "saw no reason why the same should not be passed into a law." The Assembly no doubt would have passed the Maclay bill the following day except that the lack of a quorum postponed the now predictable vote until the following Monday morning.[35]

All during this crucial period in March, the protagonists employed every means and maneuver to emerge the victors in the Assembly. Catholic agents remained in Albany, in close contact with their legislative supporters in both parties. In fact, it was charged that "the lobbies of both houses are besieged with Roman emissaries" seeking to destroy the city's public school system. Catholics answered by accusing the Public School Society's agent, William Rockwell, of once again attempting to influence various assemblymen to vote against the school bill. The *Freeman's Journal* reported that Rockwell "stood behind and was in immediate connection with Mr. B. F. Wells when the latter gentleman made the motion to postpone the subject indefinitely, and we have reason to believe that the words in which the motion was made, were dictated if not written out by Dr. Rockwell."[36] On March 7, the New York City Board of Aldermen's committee reported on the Society's memorial, which sought Common Council intervention at Albany. After sustaining the Society on all counts, the committee recommended the election, rather than the appointment, of the school commissioners for each ward whose duty was to distribute funds to the Society's schools "and such other schools as are now designated by the Common Council." The Common Council was urged to send a memorial to the Legislature that embodied the committee's report and recommendation. Unfortunately for the Society, the report was tabled, although it

[35] *Journal of the Assembly*, March 12, 1842, pp. 481–82; March 16, 1842, p. 521; March 18, 1842, pp. 538, 540–41; March 19, 1842, pp. 555–56; *New York Tribune*, March 18, 1842. The select committee consisted of Maclay, Ketchum, Davis, Cramer, Seymour, Harper, Stimson, and Warren.

[36] *New York Freeman's Journal*, February 19, 1842. Cf. *New York Commercial Advertiser*, February 18, 1842.

was printed for the use of Council members.[37] It is possible that the Council had begun to see the handwriting on the wall.

iii

The Public School Society's supporters had no intention of giving up without a fight. Just after the Maclay bill had been introduced in the middle of February, the *Commercial Advertiser* had questioned the authenticity of most of the signatures which appended the Catholic petition. Even if they were genuine, "where would the names of the remaining 35,000 voters of New York be found on this question, could they be collected?"[38] As events in the Assembly slowly began to augur passage of the bill, the Whig press closed ranks to collect the "remaining 35,000 voters of New York." Sufficient signatures were to be collected for a "call for the public meeting of those in favor of sustaining our public schools." Centers were established throughout the city where signed lists could readily be returned.[39] As the returns began to come in, the optimistic sponsors decided to hold a gigantic mass rally at City Hall Park on March 16 at five o'clock in the evening. The leaders of this rally trusted that such a tangible manifestation of public opinion would "roll up through the highlands of Albany, . . . shake the walls of the Capitol," forcing the Legislature to heed the majority's voice and reject the school bill in its entirety. One short week was required for this efficient organization to gather the signatures of about twenty thousand adults—"all writing their own names." Large placards announced the purpose of the rally and were posted at almost every city corner:

PUBLIC MEETING. The citizens of New York, in favor of sustaining the present PUBLIC SCHOOL SYSTEM of the city, which opens the doors of the Schools to ALL who choose to enter, and who are opposed to the passage

[37] *Proceedings of the Board of Aldermen*, March 7, 1842, p. 319; Report of the Committee on Laws and Applications to the Legislature on the Memorial of the Trustees of the Public School Society, in Relation to the Laws Now Before the Legislature, for the Extension of the Benefits of Common School Education, *Document No. 75, Documents of the Board of Aldermen*, March 7, 1842, pp. 567–76.

[38] *New York Commercial Advertiser*, February 17, 1842.

[39] *New York Commercial Advertiser*, March 8, 1842. Lists could be returned and blanks obtained at the offices of the *New York Commercial Advertiser*, the *New York Standard*, the *New York Journal of Commerce*, the Merchant's Exchange, the Mechanic's Exchange, and "various other public places."

of any law which shall destroy or injure these Schools, are requested to meet in the PARK, ON WEDNESDAY AFTERNOON, the 16th instant, at FIVE O'CLOCK, to express their sentiments and wishes on the subject.[40]

Bennett expressed reservations about the venture. His examination of the signatures revealed that the overwhelming number were Whigs while Democrats comprised not more than one in fifty. Therefore, argued the editor, the "call" could not be construed as representing Democratic opinion on the subject. He also objected to the phraseology of the "call." The rally was to unite all those opposed to the destruction of the public schools, and "this class embraces every sane man and woman in the city." The real demarcating principle separated those who wanted to reform the public schools from that class which advocated the preservation of an educational status quo. Bennett believed that the benefits of public school education could best be retained by incorporating the city system within the state system. Nevertheless, he intended to reserve judgment pending the outcome of the park rally. For good reason, he suspected possible trouble and counseled "everyone [to] keep perfectly cool."[41]

As early as three o'clock, small groups began to assemble in front of City Hall and around a large platform erected for the officers of the meeting. As five o'clock approached, the crowd was estimated at about five thousand persons. Although the majority of the spectators were Whigs, perhaps a thousand Democrats "of the most noisy and riotous class" were present. The *Herald* ominously reported that around and near the platform "a great many of the Catholic Irish," who "looked very black at the officers of the meeting . . . assembled, forming a solid phalanx of about 6 or 8, or perhaps even 10 deep."[42] At ten past five, the sponsors arrived on the platform and called the meeting to order. Mayor Robert Morris refused to preside at the meeting because his official position precluded officiating "at any public meeting of my fellow-citizens having in view subjects of legislation."[43] As a result Jacob Aims was chosen to chair the meet-

---

[40] *New York Herald*, March 17, 1842. Cf. *New York American*, March 14, 1842; *New York Commercial Advertiser*, March 15 and 16, 1842; *New York Tribune*, March 16, 1842.

[41] *New York Herald*, March 16, 1842. Cf. March 15, 1842.

[42] *New York Herald*, March 17, 1842. This picture of the park rally is a composite of all the newspaper accounts of the incident. Contrary to most accounts, the *Herald* maintained that the crowd did not exceed three thousand people.

[43] *New York Tribune*, March 17, 1842; *New York Herald*, March 17, 1842. Morris declined this invitation in a long letter to the rally's organizers. Although he praised

ing, and one vice-president from each ward and seven secretaries were selected as the meeting's officers. Amid cries of "cock-a-doodle-doo," "hats off," "down in front," "sit down, old square toes," the "call" of the meeting was ratified, and Thomas Fessenden proceeded to read a series of resolutions. As he rose, Fessenden appeared nervous, and his hand trembled a little. Unable to ignore this tremor, a "happy" Irishman in front of the platform shouted: "Be Jasus [*sic*], he's got the horrors! better take a drink, old boy! (Laughter)."[44]

In spite of this interruption, Fessenden read seventeen resolutions, which reiterated the essential position of the Public School Society on the school question. The city's school system was eulogized as an eminently successful one that would be seriously impaired by the introduction of the district system. The resolutions challenged the school figures used in Maclay's report and branded the assemblyman's statements and inferences as incorrect. The public schools were accessible to all the children of the community—rich and poor, native and immigrant, Protestant and Catholic. They were not sectarian schools but common schools wherein every child received "an education which will fit him, so far as elementary education is required, to discharge with credit not only the ordinary duties of life, but those which appertain to the highest civil offices in the country."

Despite the sharp tone of these resolutions, the Society's supporters realized that a certain amount of compromise was necessary. The Society would not oppose the election of public school commissioners in place of the present method of appointment. But the primary concession was embodied in the third resolution, wherein the Society admitted that it was but one of the educational agencies whose voluntary aid the Common Council had accepted

---

the Public School Society's excellent system of schools as superior to those in other parts of the state, he emphasized the "public evil" whereby a large portion of the citizenry did not attend any school. His solution to this problem suggested "that the Common Council by ordinance declare that any association of citizens may organize a school which shall receive a rateable proportion of the Common School moneys, provided such school conform to the rules and restrictions prescribed by the Common Council: among the restrictions it should be provided that no sectarianism or order of religion should be taught in them. . . . The present Societies and Schools would not be injured, and the children now not attending them, could be brought into a full participation of the benefits of a common school education."

44 *New York Herald*, March 17, 1842.

in the administration of common school education in New York City. The Council's designation of the Society did "not preclude any other institution from a like agency if the Common Council see fit to confer it; and no application has ever been denied by the Common Council, except in cases which demanded a recognition of religious peculiarities which would be wholly incompatible with the spirit of our political institutions." Finally, it was resolved that a twelve-man delegation, acquainted with the city's school system, hasten to Albany with the twenty thousand signatures and the resolutions and present them to the Assembly in an attempt to forestall passage of the Maclay bill.[45]

The editor of the *Commercial Advertiser*, William Stone, lauded the resolutions as "perspicuous" and "comprehensive" and seconded them. They were thereupon adopted, amid some shouts of disapproval. At this point, "one tall rawboned chap" close to the platform interrupted the proceedings by moving "that the Legislature be let alone—let them handle their own business alone—we've too many legislators here by a d—d sight." A roar of laughter shattered the staid assemblage, and a great deal of confusion ruffled the crowd. Sensing imminent trouble, the chairman wisely moved and had seconded the adjournment of the meeting—a scant half hour after it had begun. Chaos quickly descended upon the swiftly deserted platform. As officers and distinguished guests were hurrying from the area, "some dozen or twenty rowdies jumped upon the platform . . . determined to kick up a row." In its own inimitable style, the *Herald* painted a humorous picture of the pandemonium that followed. Censuring native roughs rather than Irish toughs, Bennett's reporter recorded the following scene:

The officers of the meeting then either fled precipitately or were driven off the platform, the chairs and tables were overturned; and one fellow caught up the pitcher of water and threw the contents of the pitcher indiscriminately over the retiring vice-presidents and secretaries, and the surrounding spectators about the platform. All the officers, we believe, managed to make their escape without any injury. Those of the crowd who rushed on to the platform and took possession of it, remained there a short time, shouting, laughing, yelling, and dancing about like half

45 *New York Herald*, March 17, 1842; *New York Tribune*, March 17, 1842. The following were appointed to the committee: Stephen Allen, Robert Cornell, Peter Cooper, Samuel Gilford, Edward Dayton, William Rockwell, George Depeyster, A. V. Williams, Lindley Murray, Andrew McGown, and Andrew Mickle.

crazy creatures; and finally they jumped off, and most of them rushed
through the Park and down Beekman street. After this a sort of half
Mormon, half Temperance preacher, mounted the platform and remained talking till the boys hooted him off. The crowd lingered about
till dark and then dispersed.[46]

The planners of the rally should have remembered that March 16
was the eve of St. Patrick's day!

Although the *Sun* and the *Freeman's Journal* generally substantiated this account, the Whig and nativist press questioned the
accuracy of the *Herald's* description and impugned it as one of
Bennett's usual "flights of fancy."[47] The *Observer* attributed any
disorder to the "Bishop's flock." Despite Catholic attempts to sabotage the rally, the meeting was organized, its purpose accomplished,
and an orderly adjournment effected. "Then, after the officers had
retired, the Bishop's parishioners displayed their spirit in their
favorite style, while the thousands of peaceable citizens retired to
their respective homes."[48] As one of the guests on the platform,
Stone assigned the "noises" and "opposition to the resolutions" to
a "dozen mischievous boys" and "some thirty or forty foreigners
who had planted themselves directly in front of the stage."[49] The
Sun refused to retract its report, while the *Herald* defended its
account and applauded its resolve never to suppress the truth at
the expense of "personal or party objects." Bennett believed that
such charges and insinuations were part of a concerted and sys-
tematic plot to weaken and, if possible, to destroy his independent
paper. This clique had failed to intimidate Bennett in the past,
and he was sure that it would be no more successful at the present
time.[50]

Since only about one out of every four signers of the "call" attended the park rally, it was anything but a success. If a mass demonstration to solidify legislative opposition to the school bill was what
the promoters wanted, this was certainly not it. Most of the Democratic and Catholic press dubbed the meeting a failure, and even the
Whig *American* pictured the small turnout as illustrating the
"difference between profession and practice." It took little effort for

46 *New York Herald*, March 17, 1842.
47 *New York Sun*, March 17, 1842; *New York Freeman's Journal*, March 19, 1842.
48 *New York Observer*, March 26, 1842.
49 *New York Commercial Advertiser*, March 26, 1842. Cf. March 17, 1842.
50 *New York Herald*, March 21, 1842.

people to sign their names on a piece of paper. But when the time came to test the constancy of their convictions, "not *one in ten* probably of the signers was on the ground."[51] Other Whig papers vainly attempted to excuse this poor showing. Thus, the *Commercial Advertiser* rationalized that the Society's supporters never expected a maximum attendance at so inopportune an hour as 5:00 P.M. Quality was more important than quantity, and the "meeting itself numbered 5,000 of our most respectable citizens." Such a defense convinced very few, and assemblymen like Paul Grout of New York City branded the park meeting as a "comparative failure."

iv

Even before the park fiasco, most astute political observers predicted the Assembly's passage of the Maclay bill. Substantial support from the Democratic majority precluded any possible Democratic-Whig coalition from upsetting the expected result.[52] According to its stated order of business, the Assembly reconsidered the Maclay bill on Monday, March 21—just five days after the park rally failure. No sooner had debate begun than a series of motions was introduced to shelve or at least forestall the bill. But this time, the bill's supporters defeated all attempts to postpone the measure or have it submitted to a city referendum. A Whig from New York City introduced an amendment "that no religious doctrine of sectarian character be in any manner taught or inculcated in any of the common or district schools in the city of New York." Maclay argued against this proposal on the ground that, since state school law did not include such a provision, the city should not be subjected to this additional obligation. Maclay's reasoning prevailed, and the amendment was rejected.

Finally, Maclay's bill was put to a vote, and the Assembly passed the measure by a vote of sixty-five to sixteen with forty-seven abstentions.[53] Analysis of the voting demonstrates that the bill enjoyed bi-partisan support since fifty-six Democrats and nine Whigs—just

---

51 *New York American*, March 17, 1842.

52 *New York Tribune*, March 15, 1842; *New York Observer*, March 19, 1842.

53 *Journal of the Assembly*, March 21, 1842, pp. 562–65. Although the vote is listed as sixty-four to sixteen, the next day Pentz, who had not voted, asked that his name be recorded in favor of the bill. As a result, the official vote stands at sixty-five to sixteen.

under one-third of the total Whig representation in the Assembly—supported the measure. The negative vote was also bi-partisan, with nine Democrats and seven Whigs against the bill. Two New York City Whigs voted against the bill and the remaining one did not cast a vote. The city's Democratic delegation gave almost unanimous support to the measure with only one abstaining from voting. By means of a political reversal, the Democrats, who for nearly two years had damned Seward for his school recommendation, now executed the first step in the alteration of the city school system and thus hoped to satisfy their loyal Catholic voters.

The press reacted rather predictably to the passage of the Maclay bill. Catholics praised it as a step in the right direction; the Democratic press accepted it as a *fait accompli* and graciously took credit for its passage; and Whig and nativist journals vehemently attacked it. The *Evening Post* hoped that maverick Catholic Democrats would now return to the fold, for the party had shown them "that the democracy [*sic*] are, in trying times, their friends." Together with the other papers throughout the state, the *Post* quoted assemblyman Grout's defense of the bill. He contended that the failure of the park rally "showed that the alleged feeling adverse to this bill, had been greatly exaggerated."[54] Even the *Albany Daily Advertiser* believed that the "comparative failure" of the park meeting was "one reason why this bill encountered so little opposition in the House."[55]

Concluding that the pope had been omnipotent in the New York Assembly, the *Commercial Advertiser* condemned the school bill as " 'conceived in sin' " and " 'brought forth in iniquity.' " The New York Democratic assemblymen had violated their pre-election pledge and betrayed their constituents for a handful of Catholic votes. The defeat of the sectarian amendment was perfectly clear to the editor: "Had the teaching of sectarianism been excluded, the ministers of Rome would not have been satisfied and their subjects might have yet witholden [*sic*] their votes from Tammany Hall. Hence, with rail-road rapidity, the bill has been hurried through the House, to meet the exigency of the coming charter [city] election."[56] The *Observer* expressed disgust with politicians since even those candidates "who were endorsed as safe on the school question"

54 *New York Evening Post*, March 22, 1842.

55 *Albany Daily Advertiser*, cited in the *New York Commercial Advertiser*, March 26, 1842.

56 *New York Commercial Advertiser*, March 24, 1842. Cf. March 23, 1842; *New York American*, March 24, 1842.

had betrayed their trust and "in the hour of trial have failed to do their duty."[57] The *Commercial Advertiser* carried a letter which fulminated against those base politicians who prostituted their principles for a political victory in the approaching municipal election. Although Maclay was the son of a Baptist minister and "must have drawn in with his mother's milk an abhorence [*sic*] of popery," the writer lamented that political expediency forced him "to yield principles which must be deeply imbedded in his heart."[58]

Hughes's Irish Protestant friend and supporter of the Catholic school position, Jacob Harvey, did not think that the Maclay bill would in practice alleviate Catholic complaints, especially in those wards where Catholics were a minority. As he analyzed the situation for Seward, the Assembly school bill would

give no satisfaction to either party—it will necessarily injure the Public Schools which are very popular with a great majority of Protestants, and as I said before, I doubt if the Catholics can get a majority of trustees in more than two wards. *My* original plan, I still believe to be the best, *situated as the poor children in this City are*, viz., to permit four or five of the present schools to be known as Catholic Schools among the parents of the children, having Catholic masters & Catholic books but still to be under the superintendence of the Trustees [of the Public School Society].[59]

Although he realized that there were some constitutional objections to this plan, Harvey felt the school question was too important to "permit any trifling objection to stand in the way" of a solution. The fact that Hughes was in favor of the bill surprised Harvey. But some of the bishop's close friends had informed Hughes that Catholics could never expect to get a stronger bill in their behalf. Catholics could not with "good grace seek for more favors than other Sects" and "must take their chance in those wards where they are in the minority!" In spite of this explanation of the political facts of life, Harvey opposed the end of the present public school system in New York City, especially "by a law which I do not think will *practically* benefit the Catholics."[60]

But the Maclay bill had not yet become law. The overwhelming Assembly vote did not fully test the strength of the opposition. This opposition was reserved for the more conservative Senate.

57 *New York Observer*, March 26, 1842.
58 *New York Commercial Advertiser*, March 24, 1842.
59 Jacob Harvey to Seward (New York, March 2, 1842), UR.
60 Jacob Harvey to Seward (New York, March 9, 1842), UR.

‿‿(XI)‿‿

The "Midnight Deed" of the Senate

i

If the Assembly had been regarded as a Catholic stronghold, the Senate was considered a bastion of opposition to any alteration of New York City's school system. The Democrats worked with only a slim two-vote majority, and both New York City Democratic senators, Isaac Varian and John Scott, were outspoken critics of the school bill. This was the considered consensus of opinion among the press and an inner circle of political savants. On the last day of March, the *Tribune*'s Albany correspondent wrote that "it is now settled that Mr. Maclay's School Bill is not to pass" the Senate "unless some decided change is effected." Since the New York delegation strongly opposed the measure, the *Tribune* predicted that upstate members would not pass it over the heads of their city colleagues. Tammany Hall had been unsuccessfully pressuring Varian to reconsider his position, and he was reported ready to "resign if his friends wished it, but must first vote against the bill."[1] Even Hughes expressed anxiety, in a letter he sent to Seward soon after the Maclay bill had passed the Assembly. He admitted the necessity of compromise on the school question. Although it was "not precisely the Bill we should like . . . , it goes so near to it that we shall be willing to give it a fair trial." Nevertheless, Hughes manifested some apprehension about Senate approval and indirectly suggested

1 *New York Tribune*, March 31, 1842. Cf. March 15 and 28, 1842; *New York Observer*, March 19, 1842. On the other hand, a few newspapers predicted Senate passage of the school bill: *New York Evening Post*, March 22, 1842; *New York Journal of Commerce*, cited in the *New York American*, March 24, 1842; *Albany Daily Advertiser*, cited in the *New York Commercial Advertiser*, March 26, 1842.

that Seward press Whig leaders to pocket enough Whig senatorial votes to ensure victory in the upper house.[2]

As soon as the Assembly had passed the Maclay bill, a clerk delivered it to the Senate for concurrence. After it was read, the Senate referred it to its Committee on Literature for study and recommendation.[3] In less than two weeks, on April 1, the Committee reported an amended school bill. Although the Democratic committee chairman, Henry Foster, conceded that the Assembly bill contained certain flaws, he felt that his committee's amendments removed these defects. Instead of authorizing eighty-six paid school officers, the Senate version would limit commissioners and inspectors only to necessary and reasonable expenses. To prevent the proliferation of new schools to the detriment of existing ones, no new school would be approved or erected unless the school officers were unanimous as to its necessity. A central board of education would be established to ensure uniformity and harmony in the city system. Most important of all, Spencer's principle of "absolute nonintervention" would be replaced by an explicit proscription of sectarian instruction in the city's public schools. Foster believed that these amendments would make the Maclay school bill palatable to the Senate.

Whig Senator Root maintained that the essential question was the preservation of the educational status quo in New York City. For his part, he was perfectly satisfied with the city's schools, and he advised "that it was always best to 'let well enough alone.' " In his opinion, the question to be decided was whether the Senate would consent to any alteration in New York City's school system. Once the Senate decided this fundamental question, the details of

[2] "Archbishop Hughes to Governor Seward on the School Question," *Records of the American Catholic Historical Society of Philadelphia*, XXIII (January, 1912), pp. 36–38. In a conference he had with Hughes, Greeley received the same impression that he forwarded to Weed:

I had a free conference with the Bishop last evening. He is calm, earnest and single-minded as ever. He says he feels the defects of the bill as deeply as any one but *he* is *in favor of taking whatever the adversary will give us*, and then looking for more. He says anything can be worse than to have Gov. Seward go out of office without the passage of *some* bill on this subject, and that any thing which can be done must be an advance and a modified triumph.

Horace Greeley to Thurlow Weed (New York, February 9, 1842), Weed Papers, University of Rochester.

[3] *Journal of the Senate*, March 22, 1842, p. 271; *Journal of the Assembly*, March 21, 1842, p. 565.

the bill could easily be worked out. On the other side, Foster suggested that the Senate first agree to the amendments and then cast a vote on the amended bill. Although Root reluctantly acceded to Foster's recommendation, the opposition managed to table the bill. During the next week, Foster, the Democratic manager of the school bill, could not get his colleagues to act upon it. Finally, on April 7, the Senate agreed to consider the measure in its afternoon session. However, the press of other legislative business forced a one-day delay in its deliberations. The Senate finally acted on April 8.[4]

ii

New York City prepared for its annual municipal election on April 12, with all the seats of the Common Council at stake. All parties conceded that the complexion of the new Council depended in large measure upon the fate of the school bill. Even before Maclay's bill had passed the Assembly, at a time when the Assembly seemed intent on ignoring the school question, the *Freeman's Journal* lamented that "according to appearances, nothing will be done until after the CHARTER [city] ELECTION. Then it will be debated . . . and it will be . . . defeated." In a new attempt to exercise political pressure, the Catholic leadership decided to repeat its independent action of the November election in order "to resist the oppression which it is attempted to force upon them [Catholics]." Past experience militated against an eleventh-hour organization of Catholic forces. Because the school question once again developed into the central issue of the campaign, Catholics were urged "to organize without loss of time, in the several wards and districts" in order

4 *Journal of the Senate*, April 1, 1842, p. 369; April 2, 1842, p. 385; April 6, 1842, p. 421; April 7, 1842, pp. 441–42. Cf. *New York Evening Post*, April 7, 1842; *New York Commercial Advertiser*, April 9, 1842. Before the Maclay bill had arrived in the Senate in January, Senator Dickinson had introduced a school bill modeled on Spencer's act of the previous session. This bill, together with a petition for an alteration of the city school system, was referred to the Committee on Literature, which refused to report it to the floor of the Senate. Seven times during March, Dickinson unsuccessfully tried to get his bill out of committee and on to the Senate floor. Apparently, while the battle was taking place in the Assembly, the upper chamber preferred not to act until a verdict had been reached there. *Journal of the Senate*, January 13, 1842, p. 47; January 25, 1842, p. 63; March 2, 1842, p. 192; March 9, 1842, p. 213; March 10, 1842, p. 222; March 11, 1842, p. 225; March 16, 1842, pp. 247–48; March 18, 1842, pp. 260–61; March 19, 1842, pp. 265–66. Cf. *New York Tribune*, January 17, 1842.

to demonstrate their unanimity and "hurl in the face of enemies of one party, and hypocrites of another, the thundering vote of indignant but honest men, who ask only what is right, and who will not submit tamely to what is wrong."[5]

When the Assembly approved the Maclay bill, the Catholic call for political regroupment was temporarily abandoned. But when it appeared possible that the Senate would reject even the amended school bill, Catholics quickly swung into political action. On April 7, forty-five Independent (Catholic) Democratic ward delegates convened at Carroll Hall to nominate their own candidates for city offices. A coalition of the Public School Society, "false Democrats," and recreant "Republicans" were accused of plotting the school bill's defeat. Varian and Scott were both denounced as supporters and pawns of "an odious corporate monopoly." As a result, these Catholic Independents "resolved to maintain no connection with men tainted with the aristocratic impurities of the Society, or willing to sustain the anti-Republican principles on which it is based." Having expressed these militant sentiments, the delegates proceeded to nominate Thomas O'Connor, the former "Carroll Hall" senatorial candidate, for mayor as well as nominees for the Common Council in the sixth, seventh, thirteenth, and fourteenth wards. The Democratic candidates in the other wards were endorsed as "safe" on the school question. Although Hughes did not attend this meeting—perhaps he had learned his lesson—his aggressive spirit certainly inspired the delegates' actions as well as the *Freeman's Journal*'s fighting call to action: "The contest cannot last—IF TRUE TO YOURSELVES, the cause in which you are engaged must be soon, and permanently triumphant! On then! Be United—and remember the words of last November—'NO FLINCHING!' "[6]

As Catholics resorted to direct political action, the nativist forces resurrected their pledge system. During the first week of April,

---

[5] *New York Freeman's Journal*, March 12, 1842.

[6] *New York Freeman's Journal*, April 9, 1842. Cf. *New York Tribune*, April 6, 1842. The Democratic candidates of the ninth and eleventh wards were not endorsed by the delegates, and the independent tickets in these wards had not yet been agreed upon. The candidates nominated at this meeting were the following:

Ward	Alderman	Assistant Alderman
Sixth	Shivers Parker	James Ryan
Seventh	Owen McCabe	Michael Hughes
Thirteenth	Edward Flanagan	J. Darcy
Fourteenth	Abraham Davis	

notices were read from several Methodist pulpits which invited their congregations to attend an important meeting. Small groups met initially at a number of Methodist churches and agreed to send delegates to a large meeting at Constitution Hall. On April 5, delegates assembled to prevent the choice of any candidate for the Common Council who supported a change in the city's school system.[7] Letters were addressed to each of the candidates for mayor, alderman, and assistant alderman that requested them to state explicitly whether they supported the present school system and opposed "any effort to divert the Public School moneys from their present channels."[8]

iii

Once again the Democratic party stood to lose votes to Catholic dissidents who meant business. Nativist dissatisfaction would cost the Democrats some votes that they could survive, but they could not afford to lose the large Catholic block, which was indispensable for any Democratic victory in New York City. There is little doubt that Tammany Hall conveyed its fears to the Democratic legislative leaders, who in turn made strenuous efforts to muster sufficient votes for the crucial test in the Senate. Since both Varian and Scott as well as the two New York City Whig senators, Gabriel Furman and Morris Franklin, were acknowledged opponents of the bill, Foster doubted that the Senate would pass a measure in opposition to the members whose district would be affected by it. In an attempt to ensure Democratic unanimity, Maclay arranged a meeting with Foster, Varian, and Scott to examine the possibility of a compromise solution. Varian remained adamant in his disapproval of the whole bill while Scott favored the election of school officers in June rather than at the city's annual municipal election in April. Maclay and

[7] *New York Evening Post*, April 5, 1842. The Methodist churches which held meetings were located on Forsyth Street, Mulberry Street, and Greene Street. The *Post* considered this action as part of a Whig plot to draw away Democratic votes at the coming election. The paper also emphasized that many members of these congregations strongly disapproved of the intrusion of politics into their churches. The *Post* also "heard" that a Dutch Reformed clergyman had refused to read the circular from his pulpit.

[8] *New York Tribune*, April 11, 1842; *New York Commercial Advertiser*, April 11, 1842.

Foster gladly conceded the point, and Scott was promised that this change would be incorporated into the amended version of the bill. Apparently, Scott was moving closer to the "orthodox" Democratic position.[9]

When the Senate reconvened for its Friday afternoon session on April 8, the legislators became engaged in a heated debate over the Maclay bill.[10] After a motion to adjourn was defeated, the Senate passed the amendments recommended by the Committee on Literature—including an additional amendment to hold the school elections in June rather than in April. Of the four New York City senators, only Scott supported the amendments. Franklin proposed that the bill should not be legislated until it was submitted to a city referendum. When this motion was rejected, the Senate ordered the amended version to be prepared for a third and final reading before a final vote was taken on the bill. Some time elapsed while the final draft was written. During this interval, Scott left the Senate chamber because, as it was later asserted, he was "much fatigued by the late sessions of previous nights." Scott later maintained that he, a Democratic opponent of the bill, and Senator Corning, a Whig supporter of the act, both agreed to retire from the Senate. In this manner, their " 'pairing off' would not alter the vote" in any way.

At about 9:30 P.M. the bill arrived in its final form, and Foster moved that it have its third reading. Furman protested the resolution because several senators who wished to vote on the question had already left the chamber for the night. But Furman's objection was overruled and the bill was promptly read. As further debate continued among various senators, Whig leaders quickly sent messengers to fetch their missing colleagues since the supporters of the Public School Society were determined to defeat the bill. Hopkins, Rhoades, and Root all hurriedly returned to their seats though Dixon thought the hour much too late. All during this period of frenzied activity and partisan maneuvering, Dickinson argued against the bill on the ground that it was deceptive and "did

9 Authority for this incident is Bourne, *History of Public School Society,* pp. 521–22.

10 The account that follows is a composite taken from the *Journal of the Senate,* April 8, 1842, pp. 456–67, and certain newspaper accounts: *New York Sun,* April 11, 1842; *New York Evening Post,* April 11, 1842; *New York Tribune,* April 11, 1842; and the *New York Commercial Advertiser,* April 11, 1842.

not give the petitioners any relief." Other Whigs, particularly Furman, vigorously criticized the bill and vainly tried to show the superiority of the existing educational system. But this last minute oratory convinced no one. This was to be a strict party vote.

The votes had been carefully counted beforehand, a successful parliamentary procedure had reduced the Whig contingent, and Scott had conveniently retired for the night because he was "much fatigued." At ten forty-five, the president pro tem of the Senate called upon the weary legislators to put the amended Maclay school bill to a test. As soon as the votes were tallied, the significance of Scott's absence became immediately apparent. The Senate passed the school bill by a vote of thirteen to twelve.[11] A straight party vote, all the Whigs voted against the measure while only the New York Democrat Varian did not support it. If Scott had been present, a tie vote would have defeated the bill. In fact, seven senators—four Whigs and three Democrats—were absent for this decisive vote. If the four Whigs together with Scott would have voted against the bill and the three Democrats supported it, the school bill would have been defeated seventeen to fifteen.

As soon as the official vote was announced Furman gave notice that he intended to move for a reconsideration of this vote the next morning before a full Senate. To forestall this latest Whig maneuver, Foster countered "that said vote be now reconsidered." Whig senators quickly replied that Foster's motion was nothing more than a ruse "to choke off all opportunity fairly to review this question." For nearly an hour the argument raged over the propriety of reconsidering the vote before adjournment. As the hour neared midnight, the president pro tem called for a vote, and Furman's motion for reconsideration was predictably defeated by a vote of thirteen to eleven with only Varian's abstention altering the previous vote. The next morning, April 9, a clerk delivered the amended Maclay bill to the Assembly for its approval. O'Sullivan's motion that the Assembly "concur with the Senate in their amendments to the said bill" was overwhelmingly endorsed by a vote of eighty to twenty-one. As soon as the Senate was informed of this

---

11 The senators who voted on this bill were the following: for the affirmative—Bartlit, Bockee, Clark, Denniston, Ely, Faulkner, Foster, Hunter, Paige, Ruger, Sherwood, Strong, and Varney—13; for the negative—Dickinson, Franklin, Furman, Hard, Hopkins, Hunt, Nicholas, Peck, Rhoades, Root, Varian, and Works—12.

confirmatory action, the new legislation was quickly brought to the governor for his signature. A relieved Seward signed the school bill the same day—just three days before New York City's local election.[12]

In its amended form the new school law required that each city ward elect two commissioners, two inspectors, and five trustees of common schools each June. The commissioners would constitute a board of education, which would meet at least once every three months. These unsalaried school officers would have the same powers and duties as their counterparts throughout the rest of the state and would be recompensed only for reasonable expenses. For the purpose of this law, each ward would be considered as a separate town with the same powers and privileges granted to other towns in the state. When the school officers of a particular ward collectively approved the need for an additional school, they could then proceed to organize, erect, and staff the new institution. The city supervisors would be responsible for collecting an annual sum of money equal to the city's share of common school funds for the fiscal year. They were further empowered to raise an additional sum of one-twentieth of one per cent of the value of real and personal property, if necessary, for the operation of the city's common schools. The respective ward commissioners would then distribute these funds to each ward school on a pro rata basis. Distribution of funds would be determined according to the average number of children over four and under sixteen who had actually attended a particular school during the preceding year. All resident city children between these ages could attend any of the city's common schools without the imposition of any rate-bills or other forms of tuition.

The schools of the Public School Society as well as other specified schools would be incorporated within this system. These schools would be subject to the general jurisdiction of the ward commissioners but would be operated by their respective trustees, managers, or directors. Especially significant was the absence of Spencer's principle of "absolute non-intervention" with regard to religious instruction. Section fourteen of the law denied public funds to any school "in which any religious sectarian doctrine or tenet shall be taught, inculcated or practiced. . . ." School officers were authorized to en-

---

12 *Journal of the Assembly*, April 9, 1842, pp. 887–88, 920; *Journal of the Senate*, April 9, 1842, p. 477.

force this important provision by periodic inspections of the schools in their respective wards.[13] Thus the school bill passed into law.

The Whig press did not easily forget the "much fatigued" Scott. Certain that his fateful departure from the Senate chamber would evoke sharp criticism, the senator sent an explanation of his action to the *New York Standard*. Dated April 8, 1842, and with the time listed as "11 P.M.," the letter reiterated his contention that he had "paired off" with Corning "as our both remaining would not alter the vote. I state this to explain to you why my name will not appear on the final vote."[14] Although the Democratic press wisely remained silent, the Whig opposition censured Scott's explanation as fraudulent and excoriated Corning for betraying his word. The Whig press denied that Scott had "paired off" with Corning since the latter had already "paired off" with Senator Platt, a Whig opponent of the school bill—an allegation never refuted by Corning. On the contrary, Corning tacitly acknowledged, and Platt openly asserted, that they had agreed to "pair off" on all political questions. Nevertheless, Corning resorted to a rather dubious distinction. Although he substantiated Platt's contention, he did not view the school bill as a political question and thus thought himself free to "pair off" with Scott on an educational question. This rationale convinced no one, and Platt publicly rebuked Corning for betraying their agreement and then justifying it with a verbal distortion:

He [Corning] with much apparent pleasure and kindness yielded to my proposition, saying he would vote upon no question of a political character in which my feelings were enlisted. At this period the school question produced more feeling than any other subject of legislation, and my sentiments had upon all occasions been freely avowed when sought upon that point. I therefore concluded that this question was the one above all others upon which Mr. Corning would feel bound to withhold his vote. I cannot, however, say that that question was particularly designated; but the term, 'political questions,' I supposed embraced all questions upon which a party division could be had, and the school question in particular. . . . I understand Mr. Corning justifies himself as pairing off with Judge Scott upon the plea that he did not

13 An Act to Extend to the City and County of New York the Provisions of the General Act in Relation to Common Schools, *Laws of New York*, 65 Session, 1842, chapter 150, April 11, 1842, pp. 184–89; *Document No. 86, Documents of the Board of Aldermen*, April 18, 1842, pp. 691–98. Concerning a superintendent, see footnote 19.
14 *New York Standard*, cited in the *New York Commercial Advertiser*, April 22, 1842.

consider the school question a political question, and therefore there was nothing contained in his agreement with me that rendered it inconsistent to pair off with the Judge. Upon this plea I think he has been quite unfortunate in the bill he has selected for his protection, for the fact cannot be disguised that it was as much the creation of political consideration as any other subject of legislation.[15]

After printing Platt's telling analysis, the *Commercial Advertiser* thought it best that Scott and Corning "should remain dumb."

Nor did this seem to be the complete story. Whig correspondents who were present in the Senate chamber that eventful night accused Scott of prizing his Senate seat more than his personal integrity and political independence. Since a preliminary canvass of the important vote indicated a tie, these reporters asserted that the Democratic chieftains made strenuous efforts "to induce Senator Scott to *dodge*" the roll call. For half an hour before the Senate voted on the bill, a Democratic boss, John Van Buren, allegedly succeeded in detaining Scott in an anteroom during the call of the crucial vote. Thus, the senator possibly was not at home resting from "much fatigue" but was in a Senate antechamber conversing with a Democratic politico. With due allowance for the partisan overtones of these reports, some kind of a political agreement undoubtedly had been arranged between Scott and Corning. Certainly, Corning's official silence and lack of self-vindication strongly indicated that the Whig senator had entered into a political deal.[16]

Scott and Corning were attacked for their cowardly action—"skulking," as it was called—and the Whig and nativist press condemned the new school law with crusading vengeance. The *American* christened the law as "an act to encourage sectarian feuds at elections, and to seduce Protestants into the church of Rome." The paper pitied the intrusion of politics into education and predicted that papists would regard the sectarian proscription clause as "*a dead letter*."[17] "Treachery to the People" and "The Pope Triumphant" were the headlines which blazed across the pages of the *Commercial Advertiser* as it damned all the alleged enemies of the

15 *New York Commercial Advertiser*, May 31, 1842.

16 *New York Tribune*, April 11, 12, and 26, 1842; *New York Journal of Commerce*, cited in the *New York Observer*, April 16, 1842; *New York Commercial Advertiser*, April 22, May 5, and May 31, 1842; *Albany Daily Advertiser*, cited in the *New York Commercial Advertiser*, May 5, 1842.

17 *New York American*, April 11 and 12, 1842.

public schools. In an article entitled "Triumph of the Roman Catholics," the *Observer* lamented the fact that the public school system, "the glory and defence of the city," had at last entered its final hour. As past civilizations had lost their once vaunted glory and grandeur, so now the same fate awaited New York City. "*Sic transit gloria urbis.*" The weekly labeled Protestant indifference as responsible for the Catholic triumph. But all was not lost; Protestant retrenchment could repeal this "odious law" at the next session of the Legislature.[18] The *Tribune* focused its criticism on the high financial cost of the new school law. The formerly gratuitous services of the Public School Society's trustees would now be performed by one hundred and fifty-five school officers who would either be salaried or on expense accounts: "*One hundred and fifty-five* persons to be paid by the Public for services now better performed *without cost.*"[19]

The Episcopalian organ, *The Churchman*, thought that the proscription of sectarian instruction only aggravated the evil which the Legislature had attempted to eliminate. Since religion could never really be removed from the public schools, *The Churchman* saw only two possible alternatives: "either define a system of religious education, and give it the sanction and authority of law, or . . . throw the whole matter wide open for the various religious denominations, Christian and Infidel, Protestant and Romanist, to manage in their own way." Rejecting both alternatives, however, the Legislature had proceeded to enact a law which satisfied only those who were ready to evade its provisions. But if the law were faithfully executed, the Episcopalian weekly suggested, it would be more properly entitled

---

[18] *New York Observer*, April 16, 1842. Cf. *New York Commercial Advertiser*, April 11, 1842; *New York Evangelist*, April 28, 1842.

[19] *New York Tribune*, April 11 and 12, 1842. This newspaper listed the following new school officials:

1 additional commissioner of common schools in each ward	17
2 inspectors for each ward	34
5 trustees for each ward	85
1 clerk for the Board of Education	1
1 clerk for the commissioners of each ward	17
1 deputy superintendent of schools	1
Total	155

Although the law did not mention a superintendent of schools, "an act of May 26, 1841, legislating for the state as a whole with the exception of the city, but now made applicable locally by incorporation in the act of April 9, 1842, provided for a county superintendent of common schools appointive by the Board of Supervisors." Bluhm, "Board of Education," p. 481.

"An Act for the more effective exclusion of religion, and for the better establishment and propagation of Atheism."[20]

Although the *Freeman's Journal* supported the bill, its approval was not enthusiastic. Catholics rejoiced that the Public School Society's educational monopoly had been broken and the schools finally returned to the direct control of the people. But the unwarranted Senate amendments to the original Maclay bill thwarted the extension of complete justice to Catholics. The passage of time, prophesied the editor, would necessitate further reform and liberality and ultimately vindicate the Catholic school position.[21] On the other hand, Bennett's *Herald* lauded the new law as best calculated to meet the objections of the Public School Society's supporters as well as "the reasonable demands" of Catholics. The Democratic press generally reiterated Bennett's analysis. Passed by a Democratic Legislature, the law's proscription of sectarian instruction rendered its provisions inoffensive to all groups—or so thought the *Evening Post*. Whig cries of "popish schools" were just so much political propaganda for the forthcoming municipal election. Now that the school bill was law, the *Sun* urged a reconciliation between all classes, sects, and parties which would restore peace to the city so that "millions would grow up to bless them."[22]

New York City was not quite ready for this utopian era of harmony and tranquillity. One last surge of hatred would unloose itself and be crowned by an infamous election riot.

iv

As in the November, 1841, election, the school issue became the crucial matter in New York City's annual election in April. One of Seward's Catholic Whig supporters stated this position very succinctly in a letter to the governor: "the School Question is the all important subject of debate in our city, the discussion of which I am satisfied will decide the approaching Spring Election."[23] Greeley

---

20 *The Churchman* (New York), cited in the *New York Freeman's Journal*, April 16, 1842.

21 *New York Freeman's Journal*, April 16, 1842.

22 *New York Herald*, April 11, 1842; *New York Evening Post*, April 11, 1842; *New York Sun*, April 11, 1842.

23 David Nagle to Seward (New York, March 9, 1842), UR.

thought that the Whigs would carry the city "if my friend Bishop Hughes's School bill don't [*sic*] pass. . . ." On the other hand, he felt that "the chance is the other way" if the Maclay bill became law.[24] Most knowledgeable persons understood the close relationship of the passage of the school bill with New York City's election returns. In their denunciation of the new law, the Whig and nativist press charged that the unanimous Democratic support of the bill was a surrender to Catholic political pressure. "The great object was to conciliate Bishop Hughes and his voters, and that at once and before the Charter [city] Election." The *Commercial Advertiser* charged that the Catholic entry in the November election loomed large at Tammany Hall, and the latest Independent Catholic nominations forced city Democrats to capitulate to Hughes by unanimously supporting the school bill.

Certainly, Catholic maneuvers immediately following passage of the amended Maclay bill seemed to lend credence to these charges. On April 11, one day before the city election, the Independent Catholics withdrew all their nominees and announced that "the regular democratic candidates will be supported." That the passage of the school bill was the direct cause of this decision was strongly implied by Thomas O'Connor's resignation from the mayoralty race. He informed the delegates that the "contingency on which your nomination of me, and my consenting to stand as a candidate for the office of Mayor of the city of New York, has now ceased to be possible."[25] Most city Democrats were once again united in their traditional struggle against the Whigs. The party had done its legislative "duty" and now received its political reward. Tammany Hall could not forget that the two or three thousand Democrat votes which the Catholic leadership controlled meant the difference between the party's success or defeat at the polls. Such proceedings did not the escape the watchful eye of the *Observer*: "If there are any who doubt that Romanism is the source of this measure, let them understand that the Bishop's party was in the field, with their charter [city] officers nominated for the election. . . . But *immediately after the passage of the bill*," concluded the weekly, "their nomina-

[24] Horace Greeley to Oriah Bowe (Albany, March 30, 1842), Greeley Papers, New York Public Library.
[25] *New York Evening Post*, April 11, 1842.

tions were withdrawn as they had nothing more to gain by separate organization."[26]

Rather than revive their independent ticket, nativists decided to throw their support to the Whig candidates. On April 5, delegates at Constitution Hall had voted to send inquiries to all nominees concerning their position on the school question. Even though the school bill had since become law, on election eve the Whig press published the replies, which were grouped into "satisfactory" and "unsatisfactory" responses. Of the twelve wards that responded, twenty-three out of twenty-four Whigs were endorsed while only two Democratic candidates were considered safe enough. Because Mayor Morris encouraged the establishment of schools beyond the control of the Public School Society, he was not endorsed while the Whig Phoenix's response was labeled "satisfactory" because he favored an educational status quo in the city.[27]

Both major political parties employed eleventh-hour tactics to garner additional electoral support. On the same day that the amended Maclay school bill was passed, a committee of Whigs pledged their party to campaign for the "immediate and vigorous . . . repeal of this law." Since all Whigs were unanimous in this action, the committee felt that the election of any Democrat to the Common Council would jeopardize this endeavor. The *Tribune*, the *Commercial Advertiser*, and the *American* each published these resolutions in an attempt to sway votes to the Whig cause.[28] The Democrats, on the other hand, distributed a circular, on election eve, to all Catholic homes in the eleventh ward warning that a Democratic Common Council was essential to preserve the hard-earned but still precarious school law:

To the Friends of Civil and Religious Liberty. Fellow Citizens: the triumph is complete! The iron hand of Oppression, which has so long borne us down, is about to be staid [*sic*], and that even-handed Justice, which we have a right to expect from that Party with whom we have

[26] *New York Observer*, April 16, 1842. Cf. *New York American*, April 12, 1842; *New York Commercial Advertiser*, April 12, 1842.

[27] *New York Commercial Advertiser*, April 11, 1842; *New York Tribune*, April 11, 1842; *New York Evening Post*, April 11 and 12, 1842. No replies were recorded for wards six, nine, eleven, twelve, and thirteen.

[28] *New York Tribune*, April 11, 1842; *New York Commercial Advertiser*, April 11, 1842; *New York American*, April 11, 1842.

long and honestly acted, is about to be awarded to the Catholics and
their Posterity of this city. We have not asked for a portion of the Public
School money as a favor from the Corporation [New York City govern-
ment] or State; we claim it, and shall continue to, as one of the dearest
rights guaranteed to us and our children by the free Constitution of
our adopted country.

We are happy, however, to have it in our power to state to you that
the bill which has been for some time pending before the Legislature,
has passed.

We hail the event as a Glorious New Era in the history of our Religion
in this Country, and call with confidence upon our friends to support
the Democratic Republican Charter [city] Ticket, headed by Abraham
Hatfield for Alderman, *who has given every satisfaction that he will
support our Cause*, if elected to the Common Council.

Every Catholic cannot but see the necessity of keeping a Democratic
majority in the Common Council, and thus avoid the power of our bitter
and ancient enemy, the Orange men, who have taken upon themselves
the name of Whig in this country. If they should again succeed to power
in this city and state the law giving us our part of the School Money will
most assuredly be repealed·

Irishmen! Look well to it!

                                              Many Catholics.[29]

Just as in the state election of the previous November, so now in
this city election, both political parties ran scared right down to the
wire.

With the Catholic independents once again back in the Democratic fold and a Whig-nativist coalition pledged to repeal the school
law, New Yorkers went to the polls on Tuesday, April 12. Although
the Democrat Morris was re-elected as mayor by nearly two thousand
votes, control of the Common Council passed from Democratic to
Whig control by one vote. Both the Board of Aldermen and the
Board of Assistant Aldermen now comprised nine Whigs and eight
Democrats. Official results in several contested wards sustained this
slim Whig majority.[30] Both parties claimed victory, since the Whigs
wrested control of the Common Council while the Democrats retained the mayoralty and eight of the seventeen Council seats. Newspaper appraisals and election-night disturbances indicate that the
Whigs did not win the election so much as internal Democratic

29 *New York Tribune*, April 18, 1842.
30 *New York Tribune*, April 13 and 20, 1842; *New York Herald*, April 14, 1842;
New York Sun, April 14, 1842; *New York American*, April 29, 1842.

strife lost it. Both the *Evening Post* and the *Tribune* believed that this dissension caused several Democratic defeats in a few closely contested wards. Greeley candidly attributed the Whig gains "to quarrels among the . . . [Democrats] which mother Tam failed for once to silence."[31]

Although most voting districts throughout the city reported no unusual election disturbances, this was not the case in the predominantly Catholic sixth ward where an uneasy morning calm slowly gave way to a late afternoon and evening storm.[32] Since the Democrats had decided to support the Catholic school position, party leaders ignored nativist Democratic sensibilities, which precipitated a deep rift between rival factions and their respective ward choices. Several minor and isolated scuffles during the early afternoon hours portended serious trouble ahead. At about 4:00 P.M. ominous signs developed as the rivals began to group their forces for a show of strength. The anti-Catholic partisans, collectively called the Spartan Band, included nativists and Irish Protestants (Orangemen) while the Irish-Catholic faction was known as the Faugh-o-Ballagh. A large mob of Spartans began to search for their Catholic counterparts. They met on Centre Street, and a sharp clash ensued in front of the city prison. Catholics fared the worst in this first encounter and tactically withdrew for reinforcements and additional weapons.

As 6:00 P.M. approached, the combatants returned to the scene. After a "fight . . . bloody and horrible in the extreme," Catholics regained control of Centre Street. At this point Morris arrived with the police in an attempt to restore order. The *Herald* later accused the police of vicious brutality in their treatment of Irish-Catholic participants. By this time the streets were crowded with partisans, cliques, and the curious, and ten thousand people were estimated to have inundated the area. But the brawl was far from over. Abandoning Centre Street, several Spartan mobs roamed the immediate

---

[31] *New York Tribune*, cited in the *New York Evening Post*, April 13, 1842; Allan Nevins and Milton H. Thomas (eds.), *The Diary of George Templeton Strong, 1835–1875* (New York: Macmillan Company, 1952), I, p. 177.

[32] The account of the riot is a composite taken from the following, often contradictory, sources: *New York American*, April 13 and 16, 1842; *New York Commercial Advertiser*, April 13, 1842; *New York Evening Post*, April 13, 1842; *New York Herald*, April 13, 1842; *New York Tribune*, April 13, 1842; *New York Freeman's Journal*, April 16, 1842; Frederick W. Seward, *Autobiography of Seward*, p. 598; Nevins and Thomas, *Diary of Strong*, I, pp. 177–78.

vicinity, indiscriminately attacked unsuspecting Catholics, and even invaded private homes "and drove out the occupants of several of them." Frightened Catholics fled in all directions, and some took refuge in the Sixth Ward Hotel. At about 8:00 P.M., however, some Spartans broke into the hotel, violently ejected the refugees, shattered the furniture of the first two floors, "and gutted the place as completely, as if there had been a fire there." Since the hotel also served as a polling center, the election inspectors barely escaped "the brickbats and other missiles" hurled through the windows.

Now the riot began to reach its ugly climax. Near the hour of nine, the Spartans, "flushed with victory" and "lost to all sense of humanity," moved "hooting and yelling" through the dark streets in the direction of Hughes's house since "in some way they considered [him] at the bottom of all the excitement." When they arrived at the episcopal residence, which was located at the rear of St. Patrick's Cathedral, the rioters pelted the building with stones and assorted debris. The doors were knocked down, the windows smashed, and most of the furniture damaged or destroyed. Fortunately, Hughes and the cathedral staff were not at home, though "the aged and respectable Bishop Dubois" lay confined to a sick bed in a back room on the ground floor. With mob violence replacing individual decency and social responsibility, the Spartans did not even spare "the much alarmed and distressed" Dubois and smashed all the windows of the bishop's room. Had not the mayor and his harried police force arrived on the scene when they did, Dubois would have been in danger of physical violence and the cathedral and the episcopal house probably put to the torch.

As soon as word spread that Hughes's residence was under attack, incensed Catholics rushed to the scene and the rescue. Fearing the swelling of this major riot into even greater dimension, several Catholic clergymen, recently arrived on the scene, successfully persuaded their parishioners to permit the city authorities to handle the situation. Nevertheless, many Irish women formed a cordon around the cathedral to keep the " 'sinners' off" with prayer and "valor." Morris finally called out the militia to protect St. Patrick's "as [additional] violence was apprehended." Rumors spread that St. Peter's Catholic Church on Barclay Street was under attack, and Morris promptly ordered "one regiment of horse and a company of another regiment" alerted for immediate deployment. This impending action proved to be unnecessary, and as midnight approached, both the participants and the crowd began to disperse with the authorities in full control of the situation. To be on the safe side, however, the police continued to patrol the area for several hours afterward.

Every responsible citizen and the entire city press denounced the riot and especially the "unmanly" attack on Hughes's residence. On the same day that Seward sent a letter of regret to the bishop for the "outrages committed against you and the church over which you preside," Harvey wrote a letter to Seward which expressed shame at the assault against the bishop's residence: "What a glorious comment, on our 'civil and religious liberty' is the attack on Bishop Hughes' house!"[33] Nevertheless, some of the Whig press attributed the riots in the "bloody sixth" to the "passage of the late public school act, which has greatly exasperated our citizens—not only our native citizens, but those of our adopted countrymen who are Protestants."[34]

Even Seward ascribed the disorder to general dissatisfaction with the new school law. However, he felt that outbreaks of violence would have the effect of accelerating Hughes's vindication on the school question. "When it comes you will enjoy the respect and gratitude not as now of one denomination or class immediately interested but of all classes and of the American People."[35] The *Freeman's Journal* rejected this explanation and charged that it was the "no-popery" crusade fanned by the unscrupulous "Puritan Press" which provoked "a profligate gang of rioters to violence."[36] Even Harvey supposed that "some of the defenders of the Protestant cause, had read the attacks on the Bishop contained in the Commercial, American, Express, etc. of monday [April 11] and tuesday [April 12]."[37] Hughes discounted the seriousness of the affair since he did not think the riot was "the work of a mob strictly speaking, but of some routed fragment of a fighting party." However, in a letter to Seward the bishop did express some consolation that the riot "has been universally condemned."[38]

33 Jacob Harvey to Seward (New York, April 14, 1842), UR.
34 *New York Standard*, cited in the *New York Commercial Advertiser*, April 13, 1842.
35 Seward to Hughes (Albany, April 14, 1842), UR.
36 *New York Freeman's Journal*, April 16, 1842.
37 Jacob Harvey to Seward (New York, April 14, 1842), UR.
38 Hughes to Seward (New York, May 5, 1842), UR.

The *Tribune* made a plea for all parties to end further religious
bitterness in New York. "If this Spirit be not checked," warned the
editor, the city would become "the sport and prey of fiendish mobs—
of men fighting and slaying each other on account of Religion, while
none of them possess any worth having."[39] The bitter controversy
and subsequent riot had caused serious social and religious dislo-
cation in the community, and constituted a grave threat to the
educational system of the city. But Greeley's dictum was easier
stated than practiced. The riot had passed, but the religious wounds
were deep and would long remain.

39 *New York Tribune*, April 18, 1842.

∽(XII)∼

The End Is the Beginning

i

"In order to understand the American people one must understand their belief in education." And in order to understand this American commitment to education, it is necessary to understand the integral relationship between education and the political life of the nation. For American education has long been affected by numerous political coalitions that have insisted upon specific educational directions within different historical frameworks.

The New York school question was a case in point, for it was essentially a political issue. Since a political body was competent to grant or deny relief, the political complexion of New York was crucial to any solution of the educational question. No sooner did immigrants step from their dirty and crowded ships than the Democratic party accepted them with open arms. The Whigs, on the other hand, early exhibited a marked antagonism to foreigners as aliens, as Catholics, and as members of a lower social and economic class. George Templeton Strong represented this negative Whig feeling when he characterized immigrants as "Wretched, filthy, bestial-looking Italians and Irish, and creations that looked as if they had risen from the lazarettos of Naples . . . ; in short, the very scum and dregs of human nature. . . . A dirty Irishman is bad enough, but he's nothing comparable to a nasty French or Italian loafer."[1]

Yet it was a Whig governor who precipitated the school dispute by urging state support for Catholic schools. Although he received some upstate Whig support, New York City Whigs never endorsed

[1] Nevins and Thomas, *Diary of Strong*, I, p. 94. Cf. Francis J. Grund, *Aristocracy in America* (New York: Harper Torchbooks, 1959), pp. 107–8.

245

his measure, and led the vanguard of opposition during the entire dispute. Almost naturally, Seward became closely associated with the Whig-inclined Catholic bishop of New York, and this episcopal-gubernatorial coalition never faltered during the three-year struggle. Instead of condemning outright any school legislation favorable to Catholics, the Democrats at first skirted the issue since they considered Whig opposition strong enough to prevent its passage. The Democratic party had a chance to solidify and perhaps even to increase its Catholic support at the November, 1841, election, but the party preferred to remain ambiguous on the school question. Thereupon, Hughes swung into political action and organized the "Carroll Hall" ticket while the nativists retaliated with the Union ticket.

Even though the Catholics ran against three opposition parties, they emerged as an important balance of power not only within the Democratic party but also in New York City politics. Since the Democratic party could not afford subsequent Catholic defection, it was forced to sponsor legislation which would remedy, at least in part, Catholic educational complaints. Thus, Democratic assemblymen joined forces with Seward Whigs and supporters of Hughes and easily engineered the Maclay school bill through the Assembly. Tammany Hall then arranged a political deal between Scott and Corning so that the amended school bill was able to squeak through the Senate. Passage of the school bill quickly returned the Catholic Irish to the Democratic fold, in time for New York City's municipal election. The Whig-nativist alliance elicited the wrath of Seward and partly influenced his decision to withdraw temporarily from public life. But his position on the school question was not forgotten by his enemies. Not only did it cost him Whig support in the early 1840's, but it also played a role in his being denied the Republican presidential nomination two decades later in 1860.[2] Hughes wisely

2 Alexander McClure, *Recollections of Half a Century* (Salem, Mass.: Salem Press Company, 1902), pp. 216–18. McClure declares that "Seward's attitude on the school question when Governor of New York . . . made his election [and thus his nomination] impossible in 1860." The Know-Nothing Party still exerted considerable influence and held the balance of power in both Indiana and Pennsylvania, which were key states in any Republican victory. Know-Nothings would not vote for any man who was sympathetic to the Catholic Church and friendly to Catholic immigrants. Therefore, McClure asserts, the Republican convention at Chicago passed over Seward and nominated Abraham Lincoln. Cf. Edward E. Hale, Jr., *William H. Seward* (Philadelphia: George W. Jacobs and Company, 1910), p. 148; Bruce Catton, *The Coming Fury* (Garden City, New York: Doubleday and Company, 1961), pp. 58–59; Carl Wittke, *We Who Built America*, revised edition (Cleveland: The Press of Western Reserve University, 1964), p. 155.

remained aloof from further partisan political involvements though he could never live down his reputation as a political manipulator. In his reminiscences, which he wrote toward the end of his life, he still smarted because all his efforts to blunt this reputation had failed—even though he concluded unconvincingly that "I have long since ceased to trouble myself about this erroneous impression."[3] It is clear that, in successive stages, it was an upstate Whig-Roman Catholic-Democratic coalition that passed the New York school bill in 1842. Nativist pressure and city Whig political power were insufficient to block the coalition even though the Catholics never achieved their primary goal. Only because the Catholic claim was endorsed by the majority political fusion—whether out of conviction or from political expediency—did Catholics receive even "partial redress." But neither side achieved a complete victory in the controversy—a result not uncommon in the delicate interplay of educational and political forces in American society.

ii

And so the school question had come to a close. Or had it? Hughes remained convinced of the justice in the Catholic position. New York City's public schools were religiously unacceptable to Catholics, and therefore he sought public subsidization of Catholic schools. To this end he used all his powers of persuasion. He represented a united Catholic front; he petitioned the Common Council for relief; and he debated his opponents before this municipal body. After the first Catholic legislative ventures met with a temporizing postponement, Hughes played a bold hand and organized an independent political ticket to emphasize Catholic unanimity and determination. But when the State Legislature finally passed the amended Maclay bill in 1842, Catholics were really no better off than they had been in 1840. Hughes had sought public funds for Catholic schools, and he received instead public schools allegedly devoid of sectarianism.

True, the Public School Society's monopoly had been broken, and astute observers began to count the death knell of this once powerful organization. It was now obvious that the Society's days were numbered. With "melancholy forebodings of the future," the trustees issued their thirty-seventh Annual Report in May, 1842. They

---

3 Browne, "Memoir," p. 152.

reiterated their belief that the new school legislation would subject public education to the blighting influence of partisan politics and sectarian animosity. The educational superiority of the Society's schools was "overthrown" and the "glory of their system . . . dimmed, they fear, forever." The report acknowledged that the death blow had been struck and that it was just a matter of time before the Society closed its doors. Nevertheless, the trustees would continue their work until the new and "impractical" system finally "impaired" and "destroyed" the educational glory that was New York.[4] Eleven years of parallel existence with New York City's district school system under the Board of Education had convinced both groups that such an overlapping situation was not feasible. And so in 1853, after forty-eight years of educational service, the Public School Society delivered its final dirge, surrendered its independent trust to city authorities, and turned its schools over to the district school system, where they became an indistinguishable part of the educational system of New York City.[5] In this connection, contemporary accounts bitterly acknowledged the "triumph of the Roman Catholics."

But if Hughes had succeeded, it was a pyrrhic victory. His episcopal colleague in Philadelphia, Francis Kenrick, thought that Hughes had been "fairly worsted" in the school dispute. When the Common Council had initially denied the Catholic application for school funds, Bishop John England of Charleston wrote that he quite expected such a decision. Catholics could expect this unfair

4 *Thirty-Seventh Annual Report of the Trustees of the Public School Society of New York* (New York: Mahlon Day and Company, 1842), pp. 5–6.

5 *Dissolution of the Public School Society of New York, Being the Report of the Committee Appointed to Make the Necessary Arrangements for Terminating Its Existence, in Conformity with the Act of June 4, 1853.* (New York: Commercial Advertiser Book and Job Printing Office, 1853). Despite the hostility of the Protestant majority, therefore, the Society was forced to abdicate its former educational mandate to a publicly supported and publicly controlled system of common schools. "When Governor Seward proposed to subsidize the Catholic schools of New York City," concludes Rush Welter, "the state legislature responded by depriving the Protestant Public School Society of its subsidy and by barring state aid to religious education." Rush Welter, *Popular Education and Democratic Thought in America* (New York: Columbia University Press, 1962), p. 106. As an educational midpoint in New York City between public support of sectarian education and an increasingly secular publicly controlled public school system, the Society served as a reservoir of opposition to the use of public funds for denominational education. Despite the strong and humanly understandable arguments of Hughes and other Catholic Churchmen, the Society embodied the persistent opposition of the American majority to any public subsidization of religious education.

treatment to continue because of the mounting prejudice against them among their fellow Americans:

We write deliberately when we state that, probably, there is not a town or city council in the United States that would not have decided in the same way. . . . We do not think it likely that a public body can be found in the United States which does not, without its own consciousness or suspicion, think and act under the influence of great prejudice against Catholics, their claims, their rights, their principles, their religion, and their politics. . . . It is, therefore, that we said that the Catholic cannot expect justice from any public body in this country, because every such body is more or less under the influence of that prejudice which we have so imperfectly described.[6]

Although Hughes realized that the new school law did not grant the "positive benefit" which Catholics had sought, he thought that it provided "the triumph of a principle" and vindicated both Seward's and his efforts. In a letter to Seward, he expressed deep gratitude for the governor's efforts in achieving a measure of educational justice for New York Catholics. "With all its imperfections," Hughes believed that the act would "be of considerable service to the diffusion of knowledge in this city among that class who stand most in need of it, and who have been hitherto most neglected."[7] When he penned his reminiscences in 1858, he continued this line of reasoning. He characterized the new law as a "partial redress" and still gloried that it doomed the Public School Society's "wicked monopoly which claimed to take charge of the minds and hearts of Catholic children." Even though the district school system was "very different indeed, from what I would have recommended," nevertheless Hughes described it as "an immense improvement on the one which it replaced."[8]

Years after the dispute, there was still confusion in the public mind, both Catholic and non-Catholic, concerning its outcome. When the Catholics of New Orleans were preparing in 1851 to seek public funds for their schools, Archbishop Anthony Blanc communicated with Hughes for clarification as to the success of New York Catholics in their quest for public aid:

I am anxious to know from yourself, how far you succeeded in the attempt you made in New York some years ago. Some have been under the

6 *United States Catholic Miscellany*, XX, No. 34, 1841.
7 Hughes to Seward (New York, May 5, 1842), UR.
8 Browne, "Memoir," pp. 151–52.

impression that you obtained such a proportion of funds as you desired; others say you were not altogether unsuccessful, though you did not obtain all you desired, without being able to say exactly what was the nature of the benefit you derived from the contest.[9]

In his reply, Hughes summarized the issues and encouraged Blanc to make the fight for public support even though the request would no doubt be rejected:

Our school contest has resulted in a very great amelioration. Before it began the whole common school education in the city was in the hands of a close corporation composed of bigots. Now it is open, and Catholics have the power to be and to appoint their own school commissioners, according to their numbers in different wards in the city, but still under general laws which I think unjust and inexpedient. I took good care never to express myself satisfied with the change, altho' it was much for the better. We, as Catholics, have not, nor do I desire that we should have, any right or authority to expend public money in support of public education, at least when all will be convinced that for the benefit of the country, a change is desirable.

I will say to you, that my great object was to establish this question on the right basis, in however small a district. I did not succeed, but at least I did something in the right direction towards success. Time, I trust will do the rest. . . .

Fight against it [public education] by all means in the name of God and the United States. You may, probably will be defeated. . . . The very defeat of the question will be a gain.[10]

Even some New Yorkers evidenced confusion over the outcome of the controversy. In 1849, an upstater wrote Seward that the school question was not properly understood, "for there is an impression in certain quarters that the latter [Catholics] have privileges & advantages under the existing laws which are not enjoyed by the citizens generally."[11] Seward's explanation was less colored and much more matter-of-fact than Hughes's analysis. As a privately controlled, though publicly supported, Protestant educational corporation, the Public School Society operated the city's schools "in such a way as to raise conscientious objections by the Catholics against the instruction given in the schools." As a result of this situation, "Cath-

---

9 Anthony Blanc to Hughes (New Orleans, December 16, 1851), NYAA.

10 Hughes to Anthony Blanc (New York, January 3, 1852), NYAA.

11 H. V. R. Schermerhorn to Seward (Walnut Grove [near Geneva], January 17, 1849), UR.

olics refused to send their children to the public schools and thus one-fourth or one-fifth of the children of New York were left to grow up without education." Since Seward regarded education as essential to the success of republican government, he offered his initial suggestion to subsidize Catholic schools, which was later amended to replace the Society with the state district system of schools:

What was recommended was to let the Catholics support schools of their own and receive their own share of the public monies. What was *done* was to divide the city into school districts and let the schools be organized and conducted by trustees and a Board of Education elected by the People—without reference to religion. This is the new system. It is the same that always existed in the rural parts of the state. It immediately brought in the Catholic children. The abuse was a religious close monopoly of education with the public funds. The reform consists in having abolished the monopoly.[12]

It is evident that the bishop and the former governor did not view the outcome in the same light. For Seward, New York's solution was an end; for Hughes, it was a midpoint. Since the district school system was an immense improvement over the Society and since the present number of Catholic schools was insufficient to provide an "exclusively Catholic training" for all the children of the diocese, Hughes felt "obliged to tolerate the attendance of our poor children at these schools until we should, with time and the blessing of Almighty God, be enabled to erect schools of our own for their exclusively Catholic training."[13]

None of the protagonists in the controversy advocated religious indifferentism or secularism in the schools. Instead, the majority of Protestants advocated a nondenominational Christianity as the only compromise between "infidelity" and denominational instruction. In his *Public Schools and Moral Education*, Neil McCluskey convincingly argues that this "principle turned out to be only a compromise, for the 'medium' between sectarianism and atheism became in practice a form of sectarianism which did not long satisfy even the more liberal religious groups."[14] It certainly did not satisfy Hughes.

---

12 Seward to H. V. R. Schermerhorn (Auburn, February 20, 1849), UR. This brief correspondence between Seward and Schermerhorn was discovered in 1961 at Old Museum Village at Smith's Cove, Monroe, New York, as the museum was preparing a Civil War exhibit. Cf. *New York Times*, September 23, 1961.

13 Browne, "Memoir," p. 152.

14 McCluskey, *Public Schools*, p. 98.

Despite an impulsive and single-minded personality that often made him insensitive to the Protestant pulse of nineteenth-century America, Hughes realized that there was no such thing as nonsectarian Christianity or undenominational religion. When nondenominationalism was taught, sectarianism was taught, regardless of the brand or the label.

The Bible was a case in point. Both Catholics and Protestants accepted the Bible as the word of God. But at this point a line of demarcation appeared. Protestants read several versions and believed in private interpretation while Catholics insisted upon an authorized version of the Bible approved by the authority of the Church. For Protestants, Bible reading in the public schools without note or comment was a religious, or at least a moral, act; for Catholics, this type of Scripture reading signified Protestant sectarianism. Yet even before the passage of the school bill, the new state superintendent of common schools, Samuel Young, judged the "New Testament as in all respects a suitable book to be daily read in our Common Schools, and I earnestly and cordially recommend its general introduction for this purpose."[15] Under New York City's first superintendent of schools, William Stone, staunch opponent of the Catholic school position and editor of the *Commercial Advertiser,* and his successor, Meredith Reese, public school Bible-reading became firmly entrenched. In opposition to Catholic objections, the Board of Education ruled in 1844 "that the Bible without note or comment, at the opening of the schools is not inculcating or practising any religious or sectarian doctrine or tenet of any particular Christian or other religious sect."[16]

Since Hughes believed that religion could never effectively be excluded from the public schools and regarded religious neutrality as an illusion, his first attempt was to de-Protestantize the public schools. He failed because the nondenominationalism which he denounced as sectarianism was the compromise that Protestants believed successfully avoided sectarianism and atheism. Once it became apparent that he would not be successful in this task, he led a

15 *New York Observer,* March 12, 1842. Cf. *New York Freeman's Journal,* March 12, 1842. John C. Spencer had resigned his state position in October, 1841, in order to serve as secretary of war in President Tyler's cabinet. Cf. John C. Spencer to Thurlow Weed (Albany, October 5, 1841), UR; *New York Tribune,* December 23, 1841; *Journal of the Senate,* January 5, 1842, p. 30.

16 "Bible in the Schools," *Report to the Board of Education of the City of New York,* November, 1844, p. 12, cited in Fell, "Hughes," p. 93.

concerted effort to acquire public funds for his Catholic schools as an alternative. Even though the district system was a vast improvement over the Public School Society, Hughes did not accept it as the answer to the Catholic educational dilemma. In evaluating the advantages of the new school law to Catholics, the *Freeman's Journal* emphasized Hughes's position that "we have to consider more the evils from which it relieves us, than the positive benefits which it confers."[17] But this negative victory was not the Catholic answer. Although Hughes permitted Catholic children to attend public schools, he viewed this situation as only a temporary measure. For nondenominationalism was solidly entrenched in the public schools, and Bible reading without note or comment was the order of the day. As late as 1862, Hughes informed an Irish audience in Cork that American public schools were still teaching religiously offensive material to Catholic children "by stealth. . . . We know and see the effect of the teaching at such schools. The children become irreverent and profane towards their parents. . . ."[18]

As time went on, however, and a decreasing emphasis was given to religious instruction in the public schools, Hughes transferred his main volleys from an attack "on the sectarian bias of the public schools" to an emphasis on public school godlessness. Although he had accused the Society's schools of being dens of infidelity, emphasis upon "Godless education" in secularist public schools became the bishop's major theme in later years. He characterized the common school as a "dragon . . . devouring the hope of the country as well as religion." Scarcely able to control his contempt, Hughes denounced public education as equivalent to "Socialism, Red Republicanism, Universalism, Infidelity, Deism, Atheism, and Pantheism—anything, everything, except religionism and patriotism."[19] Although this choice of epithets was unique to Hughes, he was not alone in pursuing this line of attack. His friend and former secretary, Bishop James Roosevelt Bayley of Newark, deplored the alleged practical results of a common school education:

Experience has since shown that the new system . . . is one which, as excluding all religious instruction, is most fatal to the morals and religious principles of our children, and that our only resource is to

17 *New York Freeman's Journal*, April 30, May 14, 1842. Nevertheless, these two issues offer an interesting defense of the new school law.
18 Kehoe, *Works of Hughes*, II, p. 774. Cf. Meiring, "Councils of Baltimore," p. 141.
19 Hughes to Anthony Blanc (New York, January 3, 1852), NYAA.

establish schools of our own, where sound religious instruction shall
be imparted at the same time with secular instruction. If we needed any
evidence upon the matter it would be found in the conduct and behavior of those of our children who are educated under the Christian
Brothers, when contrasted with those who are exposed to the pernicious
influences of a public school.[20]

In a harsh attack on public education, a committee at the First
Plenary Council of Baltimore in 1852 diagnosed its disease as the
"exclusion of all religion therefrom, in other words, its Godlessness."[21] Thus, the public schools simply could not win. If they inculcated religious values, they were labeled as sectarian; if they
excluded religion, they were branded as secularistic or atheistic.[22]

Such colored descriptions by Hughes, Bayley, the First Plenary
Council, and other Catholic ecclesiastics painted an extreme version
of what eventuated as a common American-Catholic attitude toward
public education. This severe censure also convinced many Protestants that the Catholic Church was a dangerous enemy pledged
to destroy the American public school system. Certainly, Hughes
stands out as a major figure who helped to inculcate this unfortunate
attitude in many generations of American Protestants.[23] Furthermore, his complaints about sectarian public schools made him as
responsible as Horace Mann for the eventual secularization of public education. If Mann's non-sectarian compromise "set in motion
a process which has resulted in the legal secularization of most
modern public school education," then the New York bishop's logic

20 Maguire, *Irish in America*, p. 435.

21 Meiring, "Councils of Baltimore," p. 140.

22 Meiring, "Councils of Baltimore," p. 136: "This transference from the attack on
the sectarian bias of the public schools to the emphasis on godlessness is the most
perplexing change in the history of parochial education." This crucial question
still awaits serious study.

23 During the rest of the nineteenth century, Protestants and nativists intermit-
tently "discovered" Catholic plots to subvert the country by undermining the public
schools. And who began this war on public education? The name of the Catholic
culprit registered very clearly in the minds of many Americans. In 1876, Daniel Ullmann was sure that he knew the answer. Why none other than John Hughes of New
York. "The great Archbishop, with his clear grasp of mind, saw that, inside the
schoolhouses, would be the battleground." *Amendment to the Constitution of the
United States, Non-Sectarian and Universal Education, Veteran Association, Order
of United Americans, Annual Dinner, New York, February 22, 1876, Remarks of
Daniel Ullmann, LL.D.* (New York: Baker and Godwin, 1876), p. 9. After more than
three decades, the New York bishop still retained his reputation for initiating a
Catholic conspiracy to destroy the public school system of the United States.

necessarily made him an unwitting ally in this secularization process.[24]

Although the *Freeman's Journal* waged continuous warfare against the public schools, especially during the 1850's, Hughes deliberately avoided all further public controversy over the school question. He had made up his mind that further agitation for public aid for Catholic schools was hopeless—notwithstanding the optimism exhibited in his reminiscences. Instead, he abandoned the public schools and decided to concentrate his efforts on building and developing his own parochial school system. Hughes publicized this decision in an article he wrote in December, 1849, for the *Freeman's Journal*: "How are we to provide for the Catholic education of our children? I answer: Not by agitating the questions of the constitutionality, legality or expediency of State schools. Let us leave these points to be settled by the politicians. . . . Let us leave the public schools to themselves."[25] Certainly the time was right at midcentury. Just the previous year Pope Pius IX had urged all bishops to establish Catholic schools, while in 1850 New York was raised to an archdiocese and Hughes elevated to archbishop. All during the 1840's, Hughes had grappled with many important problems connected with the establishment of a parochial school system: financial support, control of school property, teaching personnel, and the publication of suitable textbooks for Catholic schools.[26] Now the new archbishop could synthesize all of these factors into a carefully formulated policy; and in his Circular Letter of 1850, Hughes enunciated the classic formula for the erection of Catholic schools that has guided Catholic educational policy to the present time:

It may not be out of place to urge upon you the necessity of providing for the primary education of your children, in connection with the principles of our holy religion. I think the time is almost come when it will be necessary to build the school-house first, and the church afterwards. Our fellow-citizens have adopted a system of general education which I fear will result in consequences, to a great extent, the reverse of those which are anticipated. They have attempted to divorce religion, under the plea of excluding the sectarianism from elementary educa-

---

24 McCluskey, *Public Schools*, p. 97.

25 *New York Freeman's Journal*, December 15, 1849.

26 A detailed account of Hughes's handling of these problems is found in Austin Flynn, "The School Controversy in New York, 1840–1842, And Its Effect on the Formulation of Catholic Elementary School Policy" (unpublished Ph.D. thesis, Notre Dame, University of Notre Dame, 1962), pp. 123–64.

tion and literature. There are some who seem to apprehend great mischief to the State, if the children in our public schools should have an opportunity of learning the first elements of the Christian doctrine in connection with their daily lessons. Happily they require of us only to contribute our portion of the expense necessary for the support of this system. This, as good citizens, we are bound to do; especially as we are not compelled to send our children to such schools, to receive the doubtful equivalent which is to be given for the taxes collected. I hope that the friends of education may not be disappointed in their expectations of benefits from this system, whilst for myself, I may be allowed to say that I do not regard it as suited to a Christian land, whether Catholic or Protestant, however admirably it might be adapted to the social condition of an enlightened paganism.[27]

Hughes lost no time in promulgating this dictum and had it immediately codified into diocesan legislation: "Let parochial schools be established and maintained everywhere; the days have come, and the place, in which the school is more necessary than the church." Before the archbishop appointed a new pastor for a church, he charged him to "proceed upon the principle that, in this age and country, the school is before the church."[28] Eminently a man of action, Hughes caused this policy to have effective results. By 1854, the number of Catholic schools had increased to twenty-eight and had instructed 10,061 pupils. Three years later the number of Catholic-school students climbed to 12,938, and by 1862, two years before his death, Hughes could boast that 15,000 Catholic youngsters were receiving a Catholic education in his diocese. To staff his expanding school system, he invited various religious teaching orders to implement their educational commitment in New York. The Religious of the Sacred Heart, the Jesuits, the Christian Brothers, the Sisters of Mercy, the Ursulines, the Sisters of Notre Dame, and the Sisters of the Good Shepherd all accepted Hughes's call.[29]

During the early 1850's, Catholics in many different states strug-

27 Kehoe, *Works of Hughes*, II, p. 715.

28 John J. Considine, *The History of Canonical Legislation in the Diocese and Province of New York, 1842–1861* (Washington, D. C.: Catholic University of America, 1935), pp. 18–19.

29 These school figures include all levels of Catholic education, primary through college. Cf. Browne, "Memoir," p. 153; *New York Herald*, January 22, 1857, and October 1, 1862; *New York Observer*, February 2, 1854; Connors, *Church-State Relationships*, p. 46.

gled to obtain public funds for their schools.[30] When all of these efforts proved fruitless, as Hughes no doubt knew they would, an increasing number of bishops concluded that the only alternative was to develop their own systems of education. Hughes's efforts in New York impressed other bishops, and they looked to his experience to help them in their own attempts to establish diocesan parochial school systems. Before long, school building programs were under way in the Catholic dioceses of Baltimore, Pittsburgh, Chicago, Cincinnati, Boston, and Philadelphia. Under Hughes's initial impetus and later educational legacy after his death in 1864, the collective body of Catholic bishops gradually promulgated progressively more stringent regulations concerning the establishment and organization of parochial schools. In a period of less than forty years—a period which witnessed the Know-Nothing excess, the Civil War and Reconstruction efforts, and the rapid transformation of American society—a separate system of Catholic schools began to emerge and develop parallel to the generally established public school system.

The First Plenary Council of Baltimore (1852) urged the bishops "to see that schools are established in connection with the churches of their dioceses" while the Second Provincial Council (1866), stressing the religious indifferentism of the increasingly secularistic public schools, repeated this admonition and pressed "Pastors to apply their efforts in accord with their resources to construct Parochial Schools, wherever it can be done."[31] Finally, in 1884, the Third Plenary Council removed all options from both clergy and laity. Bishops and priests were no longer urged, but rather required, to build parochial schools; and laymen were no longer admonished to send their children to Catholic schools, but were bound to do so unless a bishop granted an exception for a serious cause. "Having carefully investigated all these [educational] matters," the council solemnly decreed that "Near each church, where it does not exist, a parochial school is to be erected within two years from the promulgation of this Council, and it is to be maintained in perpetuum, unless the Bishop, on account of grave difficulties, judges that a

30 Flynn, "School Controversy," pp. 193–226. These states included New York, Michigan, Pennsylvania, Ohio, Massachusetts, Iowa, Alabama, and Virginia. Catholic tactics varied widely in the different states.

31 Meiring, "Councils of Baltimore," pp. 145, 185.

postponement may be allowed."[32] In less than sixty years, the American Catholic hierarchy's idealism of 1829, its insistence in 1840 that "we are always better pleased to have a separate system of education for our children," and its constant admonitions in 1852 and 1866 to establish parochial schools were finally translated into official Catholic policy and legislation in 1884.

The school controversy in New York had convinced Hughes that Catholic educational needs could only be met by establishing a system of diocesan parochial schools. When other bishops failed in their quest for public school funds, they began to follow Hughes's lead in developing parochial schools. The American hierarchy finally legislated parochial schools for the entire American Catholic Church in 1884—nearly half a century after Hughes had decided to chart this educational course. Although frequently blustery, rash, and reckless, Hughes played a major role in planting the parochial school idea that blossomed into the legislation of 1884. "After 1840, when attempts to gain public support for New York parochial schools failed" declares McCluskey, "Catholic interest and energy began to be expended almost exclusively on Catholic parochial and private schools, leaving the public schools as a semi-Protestant domain."[33] As a result, many Catholic authors have honored Hughes as the father of Catholic education in America. If this be so, then it is paradoxical that the father of American Catholic education should also have acted as a catalyst in the eventual secularization of American public education.

---

[32] Meiring, "Councils of Baltimore," pp. 231, 301–2.

[33] Neil McCluskey, "A Changing Pattern," in Daniel Callahan (ed.), *Federal Aid and Catholic Schools* (Baltimore: Helicon Press, Inc., 1964), p. 31.

Bibliography

PRIMARY SOURCES

MANUSCRIPTS

Gulian C. Verplanck Papers (MSS in the New York Historical Society).
Horace Greeley Papers (MSS in the New York Public Library).
James Gordon Bennett Papers (MSS in the New York Public Library).
John C. Spencer Papers (MSS in the New York Historical Society).
John Hughes Papers (MSS in the Archives of the Archdiocese of New York, St. Joseph's Seminary, Yonkers, New York).
Minutes of the Free (Public) School Society of the City of New York, 1805–1853 (MSS in the New York Historical Society).
Parke Godwin Papers (MSS in the New York Public Library).
Thurlow Weed Papers (MSS in the New York Historical Society).
Thurlow Weed Papers (MSS in the Rush Rhees Library, University of Rochester).
William Henry Seward Papers (MSS in the New York Historical Society).
William Henry Seward Papers (MSS in the Rush Rhees Library, University of Rochester).

PUBLIC DOCUMENTS

Annual Reports of the Public School Society, 1824–1853.
Bills of the Senate and Assembly of the State of New York.
Concilia Provincilia, Baltimori Habita ab Anno 1829, usque ad Annum 1840. Baltimore: John Murphy, 1842.
Documents of the Assembly of the State of New York.
Documents of the Board of Aldermen of the City of New York.
Documents of the Senate of the State of New York.
Finegan, Thomas E. (ed.). *Judicial Decisions of the State Superintendent of Common Schools from 1822 to 1913.* Albany: University of the State of New York, 1914.
Journal and Documents of the Board of Assistants of the City of New York.
Journal of the Assembly of the State of New York.
Journal of the Senate of the State of New York.
Laws of the State of New York.
Lincoln, Charles Z. (ed.). *Messages from the Governors of the State of New York.* 11 vols. Albany: State of New York, 1909.

Manual of the Corporation of the City of New York. New York, 1854.
Proceedings of the Board of Aldermen of the City of New York.

WRITINGS OF PUBLIC FIGURES

"Archbishop Hughes to Governor Seward on the School Question," *Records of the American Catholic Historical Society of Philadelphia,* XXIII (January, 1912), 36–38.

Baker, George E. (ed.). *The Works of William H. Seward.* 3 vols. New York: J.S. Redfield, 1853.

Brownson, Henry F. (ed). *The Works of Orestes A. Brownson.* 20 vols. Detroit: Thorndike Nourse, 1882–87.

Kehoe, Lawrence (ed.). *Complete Works of the Most Rev. John Hughes, D.D.* 2 vols., sec. ed. New York: American News Company, 1865.

"Letter of Archbishop Hughes on the School Question, 1841," *Researches of the American Catholic Historical Society of Philadelphia,* XXII (1905), 262–64.

Mann, Horace. "Fifth Annual Report of the Secretary of the Board of Education," *Common School Journal,* IV (1842), 321–81.

Mann, Mary Peabody, and George C. Mann. *Life and Works of Horace Mann.* 5 vols. Boston: Lee and Shepard, 1891.

McElrone, Hugh P. (ed.). *The Works of the Right Reverend John England.* 2 vols. Baltimore: Baltimore Publishing Company, 1884.

Ryan, Alvan S. (ed.). *The Brownson Reader.* New York: P. J. Kennedy and Sons, 1955.

DIARIES, REMINISCENCES, AUTOBIOGRAPHIES

Beardsley, Levi. *Reminiscences.* New York: Charles Vinten, 1852.

Francis, John W. *Old New York; or Reminiscences of the Past Sixty Years.* New York: Charles Roe, 1858.

Greeley, Horace. *Recollections of a Busy Life.* New York: J.B. Ford and Company, 1868.

Haswell, Charles Haynes. *Reminiscences of an Octogenarian of the City of New York, 1816–1860.* New York: Harper and Brothers, 1896.

Hubbard, Nathaniel T. *Autobiography with Personal Reminiscences of New York City from 1798–1875.* New York: John F. Trow and Son, 1875.

McClure, Alexander K. *Recollections of Half a Century.* Salem, Massachusetts: Salem Press Company, 1902.

Nevins, Allan, and Milton H. Thomas (eds.). *The Diary of George Templeton Strong, 1835–1875.* 4 vols. New York: Macmillan Company, 1952.

Nichols, Thomas L. *Forty Years of American Life.* 2 vols. London: John Maxwell and Company, 1864.

Seward, Frederick W. (ed.). *Autobiography of William H. Seward from 1831 to 1834 With a Memoir of His Life and Selections from His Letters from 1831 to 1846.* New York: D. Appleton and Company, 1877.

Thébaud, Augustus J. *Forty Years in the United States of America, 1839–1885.* New York: United States Catholic Historical Society, 1904.

Thorburn, Grant. *Fifty Years' Reminiscenses of New York.* New York: Daniel Fanshaw, 1845.

Tuckerman, Bayard (ed.). *The Diary of Philip Hone, 1828–1851.* 2 vols. New York: Dodd, Mead and Company, 1889.

Weed, Harriet A. (ed.). *Autobiography of Thurlow Weed.* Boston: Houghton, Mifflin and Company, 1883.

PAMPHLETS

Amendments to the Constitution of the United States, Non-Sectarian and Universal Education, Veteran Association, Order of the United Americans, Annual Dinner, New York, February 22, 1876, Remarks of Daniel Ullmann, LL.D. New York: Baker and Godwin, 1876.

By-laws of the Trustees of the Public School Society, of New York, as Revised and Adopted, November, 1829. New York: Mahlon Day, 1829.

By-laws of the Trustees of the Public School Society, of New York, as Revised and Adopted, January, 1833. New York: Mahlon Day, 1833.

By-laws of the Trustees of the Public School Society, of New York, as Revised and Adopted, January, 1833, and November, 1836. New York: Mahlon Day, 1836.

By-laws of the Trustees of the Public School Society, of New York, as Revised and Adopted, February, 1841. New York: Mahlon Day, 1841.

Dissolution of the Public School Society of New York, Being the Report of the Committee Appointed to Make the Necessary Arrangements for Terminating its Existence, in Conformity With the Act of June 4, 1853. New York: Commercial Advertiser Book and Job Printing Office, 1853.

Reasons of the Trustees of the Public School Society, for Their Remonstrances Against the Petition of the Roman Catholic Benevolent Society, to be Admitted to a Common Participation of the School Fund. New York: Mahlon Day, 1831.

Report of the Committee on the Propriety of Studying the Bible in the Institutions of a Christian Country, Presented to the Literary Convention at New York, October, 1831. New York: Joshua Leavitt, 1832.

NEWSPAPERS

The Churchman (New York)
The Log Cabin
New York American
New York Catholic Register
New York Christian Advocate and Journal
New York Christian Intelligencer
New York Commercial Advertiser
New York Evangelist
New York Evening Post
New York Freeman's Journal
New York Herald
New York Journal of Commerce

New York Observer
New York Sun
New York Times
New York Tribune
New York Truth Teller

TEXTBOOKS

Hale, Salma. *History of the United States.* Cooperstown, New York, 1842.
Malte-Brun, Conrad. *A System of Universal Geography.* 8 vols. Philadelphia and Boston, 1827–32.
Murray, Lindley. *The English Reader.* Bridgeport, 1830.
———. *Introduction to the English Reader.* Philadelpha, 1847.
———. *Sequel to the English Reader.* New York, 1845.
New York Reader, Number 3. New York, 1819–40.
Putnam, Samuel. *Sequel to the Analytical Reader.* New York, 1824.

SECONDARY SOURCES

BOOKS

Adams, William F. *Ireland and Irish Emigration to the New World from 1815 to the Famine.* New Haven: Yale University, 1932.
Alexander, D.S. *A Political Study of the State of New York.* 4 vols. New York: H. Holt and Company, 1906–9.
Andrews, Rena M. *Archbishop Hughes and the Civil War.* Chicago: University of Chicago, 1935.
Asbury, Herbert. *The Gangs of New York.* New York: Alfred A. Knopf, 1929.
Baker, George E. *The Life of William H. Seward.* New York: J.S. Redfield, 1855.
Bancroft, Frederic. *The Life of William Seward.* 2 vols. New York: Harper and Brothers, 1900.
Bennett, William Harper. *Catholic Footsteps in Old New York.* New York: Schwartz, Kirwin and Fauss, 1909.
———. *Handbook to Catholic Historical New York City.* New York: Schwartz, Kirwin and Fauss, 1927.
Benson, Lee. *The Concept of Jacksonian Democracy.* New York: Atheneum, 1964.
Berrian, William. *An Historical Sketch of Trinity Church, New York.* New York: Stanford and Swords, 1847.
Billington, Ray Allen. *The Protestant Crusade, 1800–1860.* New York: Macmillan Company, 1938.
Bluhm, Solomon. "Genesis and Establishment of New York City's Board of Education, 1840–1855." Unpublished Ph.D. thesis, New York, New York University, 1951.
Boese, Thomas. *Public Education in the City of New York.* New York: Harper and Brothers, 1869.
Booth, Mary L. *History of the City of New York.* New York: R.C. Clark, 1866.

Bourne, William O. *History of the Public School Society of the City of New York.* New York: Wm. Wood and Company, 1870.

Brann, H.A. *Most Reverend John Hughes.* New York: Dodd, Mead and Company, 1892.

Brodhead, John R. *History of the State of New York.* 2 vols. New York: Harper and Brothers, 1871.

Brown, Samuel Windsor. *The Secularization of American Education.* New York: Teachers College, Columbia University, 1912.

Burns, James A. *The Catholic School System in the United States.* New York: Benziger Brothers, 1908.

——. *The Growth and Development of the Catholic School System in the United States.* New York: Benziger Brothers, 1912.

Burns, James A., and Bernard J. Kohlbrenner. *A History of Catholic Education in the United States.* New York: Benziger Brothers, 1937.

Butts, R. Freeman, and Lawrence A. Cremin. *A History of Education in American Culture.* New York: H. Holt and Company, 1953.

Byrne, Stephen. *Irish Emigration to the United States.* New York: Catholic Publication Society, 1873.

Callahan, Daniel (ed.). *Federal Aid and Catholic Schools.* Baltimore: Helicon, 1964.

Carlson, Oliver. *The Man Who Made News.* New York: Duell, Sloan and Pearce, 1942.

Catton, Bruce. *The Coming Fury.* Garden City, New York: Doubleday and Company, 1961.

Chickering, Jesse. *Immigration into the United States.* Boston: Charles C. Little and James Brown, 1848.

Clarke, Richard H. *Lives of the Deceased Bishops of the Catholic Church in the United States.* 3 vols. New York: Richard H. Clarke, 1888.

Confrey, Burton. *Secularism in American Education—Its History.* Washington, D.C.: Catholic University of America, 1931.

Connors, Edward M. *Church-State Relationships in Education in the State of New York.* Washington, D.C.: Catholic University of America, 1951.

Considine, John J. *The History of Canonical Legislation in the Diocese and Province of New York, 1842–1861.* Washington, D.C.: Catholic University of America, 1935.

Cremin, Lawrence A. *The American Common School: An Historic Conception.* New York: Teachers College, Columbia University, 1951.

Cubberly, Ellwood P. *Public Education in the United States.* Boston: Houghton, Mifflin Company, 1919.

Culver, Raymond B. *Horace Mann and Religion in the Massachusetts Public Schools.* New Haven: Yale University, 1929.

Curran, Francis X. *The Church and the Schools.* Chicago: Loyola University, 1954.

Dayton, Abram C. *Last Days of Knickerbocker Life in New York.* New York: G.P. Putnam's Sons, 1897.

Diffley, Jerome Edward. "Catholic Reaction to American Public Education, 1792–1852." Unpublished Ph.D. thesis, Notre Dame, Indiana, University of Notre Dame, 1959.

Dix, Morgan. *A History of the Parish of Trinity Church in the City of New York.* 4 vols. New York: G.P. Putnam's Sons, 1906.

Draper, Andrew Sloan. *Origin and Development of the Common School System of the State of New York.* Syracuse, New York: C.W. Bordeen, 1903.

Dunn, William Kailer. *What Happened to Religious Education?* Baltimore: Johns Hopkins University, 1958.

Dushkin, Alexander M. *Jewish Education in New York City.* New York: Bureau of Jewish Education, 1918.

Duvall, Sylvanus Milne. *The Methodist Episcopal Church and Education up to 1869.* New York: Teachers College, Columbia University, 1928.

Ellis, John Tracy. *American Catholicism.* Chicago: University of Chicago, 1956.

—— (ed.). *Documents of American Catholic History.* Milwaukee: Bruce Publishing Company, 1956.

——. *A Guide to American Catholic History.* Milwaukee: Bruce Publishing Company, 1959.

Ernst, Robert. *Immigrant Life in New York City, 1825–1863.* New York: Columbia University, 1949.

Farley, John. *The Life of John Cardinal McCloskey.* New York: Longmans, Green and Company, 1918.

Fell, Marie Leonore. "Bishop Hughes and the Common School Controversy." Unpublished Master's thesis, Washington, D.C., Catholic University of America, 1936.

——. *The Foundations of Nativism in American Textbooks, 1783–1860.* Washington, D.C.: Catholic University of America, 1941.

Finegan, Thomas E. *The Establishment and Development of the School System of the State of New York.* Syracuse, New York: C. W. Bardeen, 1913.

Fish, Carl Russell. *The Rise of the Common Man.* New York: Macmillan Company, 1927.

Fitch, Charles E. *The Public School.* Albany, New York: J. B. Lyon Company, 1904.

Flick, Alexander C. (ed.). *History of the State of New York.* 10 vols. New York: Columbia University, 1933–37.

Flynn, Austin. "The School Controversy in New York, 1840–1842, and its Effect on the Formulation of Catholic Elementary School Policy." Unpublished Ph.D. thesis, Notre Dame, Indiana, University of Notre Dame, 1962.

Fox, Dixon R. *The Decline of Aristocracy in the Politics of New York.* New York: Longmans, Green and Company, 1919.

Fox, Louis H. *New York Newspapers, 1820–1850: A Bibliography.* Chicago: University of Chicago, 1928.

Gabel, Richard J. *Public Funds for Church and Private Schools.* Washington, D.C.: Catholic University of America, 1937.

Gerard, James W. *The Impress of Nationalities upon the City of New York.* New York: Columbia Spectator Publishing Company, 1883.

Gibbons, James. *A Retrospect of Fifty Years.* 2 vols. Baltimore: John Murphy Company, 1916.

Gibson, Florence E. *The Attitudes of the New York Irish toward State and National Affairs, 1848–1892.* New York: Columbia University, 1951.

Goebel, Edmund J. *A Study of Catholic Secondary Education During the Colonial Period up to the First Plenary Council of Batlimore, 1852.* Washington, D.C.: Catholic University of America, 1936.

Greene, Evarts B. *Religion and the State.* New York: New York University, 1941.

Grinstein, Hyman B. *The Rise of the Jewish Community of New York, 1654–1860.* Philadelphia: Jewish Publication Society of America, 1945.

Grund, Francis J. *Aristocracy in America.* New York: Harper Torchbooks, 1959.

Guilday, Peter. *A History of the Councils of Baltimore (1791–1884).* New York: Macmillan Company, 1932.

―――― (ed.). *The National Pastorals of the American Hierarchy (1792–1919).* Westminster, Maryland: Newman Press, 1954.

Hale, Jr., Edward E. *William H. Seward.* Philadelphia: George W. Jacobs and Company, 1910.

Hale, William H. *Horace Greeley, Voice of the People.* New York: Harper and Brothers, 1949.

Hall, Arthur Jackson. *Religious Education in the Public Schools of the State of and City of New York.* Chicago: University of Chicago, 1914.

Hansen, Marcus Lee. *The Immigrant in American History.* Cambridge, Massachusetts: Harvard University, 1948.

Hassard, John R.S. *Life of the Most Reverend John Hughes, D.D.* New York: D. Appleton and Company, 1866.

Hobson, Elsie Garland. *Educational Legislation and Administration in the State of New York from 1777 to 1850.* Chicago: University of Chicago, 1918.

Ingersoll, D.D. *The Life of Horace Greeley.* Chicago: Union Publishing Company, 1873.

Jackson, Sidney L. *America's Struggle for Free Schools.* Washington, D.C.: American Council on Public Affairs, 1941.

Jensen, H.E. *American Religious Journalism to 1845: Its Role in the Organization of American Christianity.* Chicago: University of Chicago, 1927.

Johnson, A.W., and F.H. Yost. *Separation of Church and State in the United States.* Minncapolis: University of Minnesota, 1948.

Johnson, Willis F., and Ray B. Smith. *Political and Governmental History of the State of New York.* 6 vols. Syracuse, New York: Syracuse University Press, 1922.

Kaiser, M. Laurina. *The Development of the Concept and Function of the Catholic Elementary School in the American Parish.* Washington, D.C.: Catholic University of America, 1955.

Lamb, Martha J. *History of the City of New York.* 2 vols. New York: A.S. Bernes, 1877–1880.

Lord, Robert H., John E. Sexton, and Edward T. Harrington. *History of the Archdiocese of Boston.* 3 vols. New York: Sheed and Ward, 1944.

Lothrop, Thornton K. *William Henry Seward.* Boston and New York: Houghton, Mifflin and Company, 1896.

McCluskey, Neil Gerard. *Catholic Viewpoint on Education.* Revised edition. Garden City, New York: Image Books, 1962.

―――― . *Public Schools and Moral Education.* New York: Columbia University, 1958.

Maguire, John Francis. *The Irish in America*. 4th edition. New York: D. and J. Sadlier and Company, 1887.

Mahoney, Charles J. *The Relation of the State to Religious Education in Early New York, 1633–1825*. Washington, D.C.: Catholic University of America, 1941.

Maynard, Theodore. *Orestes Brownson, Yankee, Radical, Catholic*. New York: Macmillan Company, 1943.

Meiring, Bernard Julius. "Educational Aspects of the Legislation of the Councils of Baltimore, 1829–1884." Unpublished Ph.D. thesis, Berkeley, University of California, 1963.

Myers, Gustavus (edited and revised by Henry M. Christman). *History of Bigotry in the United States*. New York: Capricorn Books, 1960.

———. *The History of Tammany Hall*. New York: Boni and Liveright, 1917.

Nevins, Allan. *The Evening Post, A Century of Journalism*. New York: Boni and Liveright, 1922.

Nolan, Hugh J. *The Most Reverend Francis Patrick Kenrick, Third Bishop of Philadelphia, 1830–1851*. Philadelphia: American Catholic Historical Society of Philadelphia, 1948.

O'Brien, Frank M. *The Story of the Sun, New York: 1833–1928*. New York: D. Appleton and Company, 1928.

O'Brien, Mary Agnes. *History and Development of Catholic Secondary Education in the Archdiocese of New York*. New York: Columbia University, 1949.

O'Connell, Geoffrey. *Naturalism in American Education*. New York: Benziger Brothers, 1936.

O'Donnell, John Hugh. *The Catholic Hierarchy of the United States, 1790–1922*. Washington, D.C.: Catholic University of America, 1922.

Palmer, A. Emerson, *The New York Public School*. New York: Edwin C. Hill Company, 1908.

Power, Francis J. *Religious Liberty and the Police Power of the State*. Washington, D. C.: Catholic University of America, 1948.

Randall, S.S. *History of the Common School System of the State of New York*. New York: Ivison, Blakeman, Taylor and Company, 1871.

Reisner, Edward H. *The Evolution of the Common School*. New York: Macmillan Company, 1930.

Ryan, Mary Perkins. *Are Parochial Schools the Answer?* New York: Holt, Rinehart and Winston, 1963.

Schlesinger, Arthur Meier. *Political and Social History of the United States, 1829–1925*. New York: Macmillan Company, 1926.

Schlesinger, Arthur Meier, Jr. *Orestes A. Brownson: A Pilgrim's Progress*. Boston: Little, Brown and Company, 1939.

Scisco, Louis Dow. *Political Nativism in New York State*. New York: Columbia University, 1901.

Seitz, Don Carlos. *Horace Greeley*. Indianapolis: Bobbs-Merrill, 1926.

Sharp, John K. *History of the Diocese of Brooklyn, 1853–1953*. 2 vols. New York: Fordham University, 1954.

Shaughnessy, Gerald. *Has the Immigrant Kept the Faith?* New York: Macmillan Company, 1925.

Shea, John G. *History of the Catholic Church in the United States.* 4 vols. New York: John G. Shea, 1886–92.

Smith, Gregory Bernard. "The Public School Controversy of 1840." Unpublished Master's thesis, New York, Columbia University, 1936.

Smith, John Talbot. *The Catholic Church in New York.* 2 vols. New York: Hall and Locke Company, 1908.

Smith, Sherman M. *The Relation of the State to Religious Education in Massachusetts.* Syracuse, New York: University of Syracuse, 1926.

Soper, Wayne W. *Development of State Support of Education in New York State.* Albany, New York: University of the State of New York, 1933.

Still, Bayrd. *Mirror for Gotham.* New York: New York University Press, 1956.

Sweet, William Warren. *The Story of Religion in America.* New York: Harper and Brothers, 1950.

Tyler, Alice Felt. *Freedom's Ferment.* New York: Harper and Row, 1962.

Van Deusen, Glyndon G. *Horace Greeley, Nineteenth-Century Crusader.* Philadelphia: University of Pennsylvania, 1953.

——. *Thurlow Weed: Wizard of the Lobby.* Boston: Little, Brown and Company, 1947.

Van Kleeck, Edwin R. "The Development of Free Common Schools in New York State." Unpublished Ph.D. thesis, New Haven, Yale University, 1937.

Voight, John T. "The Secularization of Elementary School Education in the City of New York." Unpublished Master's thesis, Washington, D.C., Catholic University of America, 1937.

Welter, Rush. *Popular Education and Democratic Thought in America.* New York: Columbia University, 1962.

Whalen, Mary Rose Gertrude. *Some Aspects of the Influence of Orestes A. Brownson on His Contemporaries.* Notre Dame, Indiana: University of Notre Dame, 1933.

Wilson, J.G. (ed.). *Memorial History of the City of New York.* 4 vols. New York: New York History Company, 1892–93.

Wish, Harvey. *Society and Thought in America.* 2nd edition, 2 vols. New York: D. McKay Co., 1962.

Wittke, Carl. *The Irish in America.* Baton Rouge, Louisiana: Louisiana State University, 1956.

——. *We Who Built America.* New York: Prentice Hall, Inc., 1945.

——. *We Who Built America.* Revised edition. Cleveland: The Press of Case Western Reserve University, 1964.

Yeager, M. Hildegarde. *The Life of James Roosevelt Bayley, First Bishop of Newark and Eighth Archbishop of Baltimore, 1814–1877.* Washington, D.C.: Catholic University of America, 1947.

ARTICLES

Browne, Henry J. "Archbishop Hughes and Western Civilization," *Catholic Historical Review*, XXXVI (October, 1950), 257–85.

——. "The Archdiocese of New York a Century Ago: A Memoir of Archbishop Hughes 1838–1858," *Historical Records and Studies*, XXXIX–XL (1952), 132–90.

——. "Public Support of Catholic Education in New York, 1825–1842: Some New Aspects," *Historical Records and Studies*, XLI (1953), 14–41.

Bushnell, Horace. "Christianity and Common Schools," *Common School Journal of Connecticut*, II (January 15, 1840), 102–3.

Carthy, Mary Peter. "Old St. Patrick's," *Historical Records and Studies*, XXIII (1947), 1–109.

Desmond, H.J. "A Century of Irish Immigration," *American Catholic Quarterly Review*, XXV (1900), 518–30.

Fitzpatrick, Edward A. "The American Hierarchy and Education," *Catholic School Journal*, 51 (April, 1951), 107–11.

Foik, Paul J. "Pioneer Efforts in Catholic Journalism in the United States (1809–1840)," *Catholic Historical Review*, I (1915), 258–70.

——. "The Truth Teller," *Mid-America*, XII (1929), 37–56.

French, William M. "Horace Mann and New York State Education," *New York State Education*, 24 (April, 1937), 536–37; 569–76.

Guilday, Peter. "Gaetano Bedini: An Episode in the Life of Archbishop John Hughes," *Historical Records and Studies*, XXIII (1933), 87–170.

Hald, Henry M. "The Catholic School Debate of 1840," *Catholic World*, 136 (1932), 38–44.

Hodge, Charles. "The Education Question," *Princeton Review*, XXVI (1854), 504–44.

Klinkhamer, M. Carolyn. "Historical Reasons for Inception of Parochial School System," *Catholic Educational Review*, LII (1954), 73–94.

Lucey, Michael Henry. "Administration of the Parish Schools," *Catholic World*, 94 (October, 1911), 59–72.

——. "Attempted Settlements of the School Question," *Catholic World*, 93 (September, 1911), 729–41.

——. "Efforts to Regain State Support for Catholic Schools," *Catholic World*, 93 (August, 1911), 596–609.

——. "The Founding of New York's First Parish School," *Catholic World*, 93 (June, 1911), 361–70.

——. "The New York Constitutional Convention on State Aid to Church Schools," *Catholic World*, 92 (March, 1911), 789–95.

——. "State Support of Parish Schools," *Catholic World*, 93 (July, 1911), 498–509.

McAvoy, Thomas T. (trans. and ed.). "Bishop Bruté's Report to Rome in 1836," *Catholic Historical Review*, XXIX (1943), 177–233.

——. "The Formation of the Catholic Minority in the United States, 1820–1860," *Review of Politics*, 10 (1948), 13–34.

McCadden, Joseph J. "Bishop Hughes Versus the Public School Society of New York," *Catholic Historical Review*, L (1964), 188–207.

Pratt, John W. "Governor Seward and the New York City School Controversy, 1840–1842," *New York History*, XLII (1961), 351–64.

——. "Religious Conflict in the Development of the New York Public School System," *History of Education Quarterly*, V (1965), 110–20.

Reilly, M. Patricia Ann. "The Administration of Parish Schools in the Archdiocese of New York, 1800–1900," *Historical Records and Studies,* XLIV (1956), 45–83.

Rossi, Peter H., and Alice S. Rossi. "Background and Consequences of Parochial School Education," *Harvard Educational Review,* XXVII (1957), 168–99.

Ryan, Leo Raymond. "Old St. Peter's," *Historical Records and Studies,* XV (1935), 1–282.

Van Deusen, Glyndon G. "Seward and the School Question Reconsidered," *Journal of American History,* LII (1965), 313–19.

Index

"Absolute non-intervention," 213, 227

"Address of the Roman Catholics to Their Fellow Citizens of the City and State of New York," 57, 58–59, 60

Aims, Jacob, 219, 220

Albany, New York, 217, 218

Albany Daily Advertiser: labels City Hall rally a failure, 224

Aldermen, Board of: agrees to hearing, 73; denies second Catholic petition, 97, 98; praises schools of Public School Society, 97; faults Catholic schools, 97, 98; rejects use of public funds for sectarian schools, 98; tables memorial to Legislature, 217, 218

American Protestant Union, 166, 184, 185, 186

American Society for the Diffusion of Useful Education, 14, 15

Are Parochial Schools the Answer? x. *See* Ryan, Mary Perkins

Arts and Sciences and Schools, Committee on (Board of Assistant Aldermen): receives first Catholic petition, 32; rejects first Catholic petition, 44, 45–48, 49

Assistant Aldermen, Board of, 32

Atheism, 251. *See* Deism; Infidelity

Babylon, Scarlet Lady of. *See* Catholicism, Roman

Baldwin, Elbridge G., 167, 185n, 188n

Baltimore, First Plenary Council of: condemns public school godless-

ness, 254; urges establishment of parochial schools, 257, 258

Baltimore, First Provincial Council of: view of education, 6

Baltimore, Fourth Provincial Council of: meeting of, 1; view of education, 4; criticizes public education, 5–7; urges establishment of parochial schools, 6, 7

Baltimore, Second Plenary Council of: urges establishment of parochial schools, 257, 258

Baltimore, Third Plenary Council of: establishes national policy of parochial schools, xi, 257, 258

Baltimore Sun, 203

Barnard, Henry, viii, 1, 19

Bayley, James Roosevelt, 253, 254

Bennett, James Gordon: editor of *New York Herald*, 72; supports part of Catholic claim, 72, 73; lampoons educational dispute, 158, 159; attacks Hughes's political actions, 181; charges conspiracy between Hughes and Seward, 181; personal vendetta against Hughes, 197–99, 200; urges establishment of independent American Catholic Church, 199, 200, 201; studied for Catholic priesthood, 197; branded dangerous by Hughes, 201; defends accuracy of *Herald*'s reporting, 222. *See New York Herald*

Bethel Baptist Church: controversy over, 36, 56, 137

Bible: King James Version unacceptable to Catholics, 5, 6; King James

Version defended, 64; view of Hughes, 77; view of Ketchum, 83–84; view of Sedgwick, 81; differences over, 252

Billington, Ray, 11, 12, 100, 103, 104. *See The Protestant Crusade, 1800–1860*

Blanc, Anthony, 74, 249, 250

Blatchford, Richard, 156, 158, 168, 209

Bluhm, Solomon, 153

Bond, Thomas, 75, 86, 87

Bradford, Nathaniel G., 167, 185*n*, 188*n*, 189

Bradish, Luther, 159

Brady, James T., 183, 184

Brooklyn, New York, 147

Browne, Henry J., 100

Brownlee, William: suspects Catholicism in America, vii; involved in Maria Monk affair, 86; responds to Hughes's educational position, 158, 160, 161–64, 165; writes public letters to Hughes, 164, 165

Brownson, Orestes, 11

Burns, James A., 53, 100

Canada, 161

Carman, Richard, 167, 188*n*

Carroll, Charles, 116

Catholicism, Roman: Protestant fear of, vii; increasing militancy of, vii; immigrant nature of, 110; political maneuvering of, 217

Central Executive Committee on Common Schools, 126

Channing, William, 183

Chatfield, Levi, 205

Chemung, County of, 121

Chenery, Cyrus, 167, 188*n*

Christ, Jesus, 111

Christian Brothers, 256

Churchman, The (New York): generally supports Catholic position, 64, 65, 66*n*; favors Catholic argument at "great debate," 94, 95; op-

poses Hughes's political actions, 179; believes Maclay law fosters atheism, 236, 237

Church-State Relationships in Education in the State of New York, 112. *See* Connors, Edward M.

City Hall Park, 218

City Hall rally, 218, 219, 220, 221, 222, 223

Clay, Henry, 169, 183

Coger, Jr., John, 167, 188*n*

Colleges, Academies, and Common Schools, Committee on (State Assembly): O'Sullivan bill referred to, 150; membership of, 205; receives Catholic petition, 210; report of, 210, 211; proposes educational legislation, 212, 213

Commissioners of School Money, 39

Common Council of Brooklyn, New York, 147

Common Council of New York City: distributes school funds, 31, 37; receives Catholic petition, 112; attacked by Hughes, 125; opposes passage of Spencer bill, 147; election of, 240, 241. *See* Board of Aldermen; Board of Assistant Aldermen

Common schools. *See* Public schools

Connors, Edward M., 112. *See Church-State Relationships in Education in the State of New York*

Conscience: of Catholics, 55, 56, 77, 101; of Protestants, 100

Constitution Hall, 230, 239

Cortez, Fernando, 105, 106. *See* School books

Cousin, Victor, 14

Cranmer, Thomas, 106, 108, 118

Cremin, Lawrence, viii. *See The Transformation of the School*

Daly, Charles P., 183

Daly, Timothy, 172, 189*n*

Davezac, Auguste, 169, 172, 188*n*

Davy, Tighe, 172, 189n
Deism, 55. *See* Atheism; Infidelity
Delaware, County of, 121
Democratic Party (in New York State); equivocates on Seward's educational proposal, 13, 14; intrudes in Catholic educational efforts, 43; refuses to support Catholic position, 169, 170, 174, 175, 176, 177, 179, 180, 182, 183, 184; rejects Catholic endorsement, 174, 176; attacks Catholic election ticket, 183, 184; victorious in November, 1841, election, 188, 189; decides to give partial support to Catholic position, 204, 205, 211, 212, 213, 217, 223, 224; chooses membership of legislative committees, 205; supports Maclay bill in Assembly, 223, 224; supports amended Maclay bill in Senate, 230, 231, 232, 233; aranges a political deal, 230, 231, 232, 234, 235; role in New York City election of April, 1842, 238, 239, 240, 241; internal division in, 240, 241; role in school dispute, 245, 246, 247; welcomes immigrants into, 243
Denman, William, 41, 42
De Tocqueville, Alexis, 143
Detroit, Michigan, 193
Discord among Catholics, 41, 42–43, 44
District schools: view of Spencer, 135, 136; view of *New York Commercial Advertiser*, 143; view of letter-writer to *New York Evening Post*, 143
Dix, John, 205
Dubois, John: president of Mount St. Mary's College, 8n; third bishop of New York, 8n; petitions Rome for coadjutor, 8; suffers paralytic stroke, 9, 10; difficulties with Hughes, 9, 10, 11; objects to school books in public schools, 112; attacked by Bennett, 199; residence attacked in riot, 242
Dutch Reformed Church, Remonstrance of, 35, 36

East Broome Street Baptist Church, Remonstrance of, 34
Eaton, J. H., 8
Eccleston, Samuel: archbishop of Baltimore, 9; Hughes seeks advice of, 9; offers aid to Hughes, 203
Educational legislation (New York State); law of 1813, 36, 37, 45, 46, 56, 79; law of 1824, 31, 36, 37, 45, 46, 56, 58, 61, 77, 79, 89, 137; law of 1842, 212, 213, 227, 233, 234
Elections (New York State): of Seward, 13; of Seward's re-election, 119–21, 122; New York City (April, 1841), 128, 129, 130; November, 1841, 166–97; New York City (April, 1842), 228, 237–44
England, John, 248, 249
English Reader, 117. *See* Murray, Lindley; School books
Erin Conservative Association, 122
Eucharist, 162

Faugh-o-Ballagh, 241
Fell, Leonore, 104n, 105. *See* School books
Fenwick, Benedict, 9
Fessenden, Thomas, 220
Field, David D., 169, 185, 188n, 189
Foreign Conspiracy Against the Liberties of the United States, vii. *See* Morse, Samuel F. B.
Foster, Henry, 227, 228
Franklin, Morris, 168, 177, 185, 230, 231, 232n

Gabel, Richard J., 112. *See Public Funds for Church and Private Schools*
Gerard, James W., 167, 188n
Glasier, George G., 169, 185, 188n, 189

Good Shepherd, Sisters of the, 256
Gottsberger, John, 172, 184, 189
Graham, Jr., Charles M., 167, 185*n*, 188*n*
"Great Debate," 103–18, 119
Greeley, Horace: helps elect Seward, 13; evaluates Seward's re-election, 122; admits Whig defeat in November, 1841, election, 190; argues for a solution of school question, 209; view on New York City election (April, 1842), 237, 238; urges end of religious bitterness, 244
Greene, County of, 121
Gregory XVI, Pope, 163
Grout, Paul, 169, 172, 188*n*, 223, 224

Hale, Salma, 117. *See History of the United States*; School books
Hamilton, John C., 167, 188*n*
Harrison, William Henry, 169
Harvey, Jacob: friend of Seward, 27; foresees Catholic political union, 170, 171; unfavorable reaction to Maclay law, 225; denounces election riot, 243
Hawks, Wright, 137
History of the United States. See Hale, Salma; School books
Hogan, Robert, 115, 148*n*
Hone, Philip, 120
Hughes, John: view of religion in America, vii, viii; leader in parochial school movement, x; seeks aid in Europe, 1–12; travels in Europe, 8, 29, 113; returns from Europe, 7, 8, 51, 52; born in Ireland, 8; emigrates to United States, 8; studies for priesthood, 8; ministry in Philadelphia, 8; coadjutor bishop of New York, 8; difficulties with Dubois, 9, 10, 11; seeks advice of Eccleston, 9; seeks advice of Rome, 9, 10; supplies energetic episcopal leadership to New York, 11; Brownson's view of, 11; personality of, 11, 12; Billington's view of, 11, 12; lacks understanding of Protestant tenor of United States, 12; establishes St. John's College (later called Fordham), 12; scores non-Catholic "petitions" for school funds, 33, 34; attacks decision of Board of Assistant Aldermen, 50; renews Catholic drive for public funds, 52; organizes bi-weekly meetings of Catholics, 53, 54; attacks schools of Public School Society, 54, 55–56, 57; calls public schools sectarian and deistic, 54, 55; believes Catholics victims of double taxation, 55, 56; declares Catholics denied religious liberty and freedom of conscience, 55, 56, 77; interpretation of 1813 and 1824 school laws, 56; calls Public School Society a private monopoly, 56, 57, 78; responsible for *Address of Roman Catholics. . .* , 57; denies possibility of religious neutrality in public schools, 59, 60, 252; sends copy of *Address* to Seward, 66, 67; responsible for second Catholic petition to Common Council, 67, 68, 69; corresponds with Blanc, 74; speaks at "great debate," 76, 77, 78, 85, 89–92, 93; impressed with Sedgwick, 81, 82; responds to Ketchum, 85, 92, 93, 125; attacks public school books, 103, 105–11; unco-operative with Public School Society expurgation efforts, 115, 116; denies Catholic interference in Seward's re-election, 121; abhors Catholic desertion of Seward at polls, 122, 123; attacks *New York Truth Teller*, 122; attacks decision of Board of Aldermen, 100, 125, 160; praises Spencer's report, 141; disagrees with Seward over strategy, 141, 142; attacks Common Council, 155; responds to Ketchum's educational position, 158, 159, 160;

rejects nondenominationalism, 160, 252; organizes Catholic political ticket, 171, 172, 173; consults with Weed, 171; attacked by press, 178; 179–80, 181, 182, 196, 197, 216; justifies his political action, 181, 182, 193, 194–95, 196, 202, 203; his political action defended, 182, 183, 192, 193; attacks New York City press, 195; personally insulted by Bennett, 197, 198, 199, 200; brands Bennett dangerous, 201; praised by Seward, 202; commends Seward's fourth annual message, 209, 210; urged by Seward to accept Maclay bill, 215; denies responsibility for Maclay bill, 215, 216; praises Maclay, 216; seeks passage of Maclay bill, 226, 227; discounts election riot, 243; close relationship with Seward, 246; view of Maclay law, 249, 250, 251, 253; analyzes school dispute for Blanc, 250; calls public schools offensive to Catholics, 253; accuses public schools of godlessness, 253, 254; arouses fears among Protestants, 254; unwittingly helps secularism in public education, 254, 255, 258; abandons public education, 255; elevated to archbishop, 255; states classic formula for parochial schools, 255, 256; urges establishment of parochial school system, 255, 256; spearheads parochial school movement, 256, 257, 258; "father" of Catholic education in America, 258

Hume, David, 108. *See* School books
Huss, John, 106, 115, 116. *See* School books

Immigrants (Irish-Catholic): Seward friend of, 16–18; demand equality of citizenship, 57, 58; Americanization program for, 84
Infidelity, 58. *See* Atheism; Deism
Ireland, 8, 18, 125n, 253

Irish Heart, An, 114n

Jesuits (Society of Jesus), 256
Jews, 151
Jews of New York, Petition of the, 33
Jones, David R. F., 169, 172, 185, 186, 188n
Jones, William, 167, 185n, 188n, 189

Kennedy, William Bean, 4. *See The Shaping of Protestant Education*
Kenrick, Francis, 248
Kent, William, 156, 157n
Ketchum, Hiram: lawyer for Public School Society, 75; abusive tactics of, 78; opposes public funds for sectarian schools, 82; insults Hughes, 82; view of education, 82, 83, 84; favors public school nondenominationalism, 83, 140; takes issue with Sedgwick, 83; admits Public School Society is a private corporation, 84; ridiculed by Hughes, 92, 93, 125; travels to Albany, 136; denounces Spencer's report, 137, 138–39, 140, 145, 156, 158; rejects principle of "absolute non-intervention," 139, 140; nominated for judgeship, 155, 156; loses nomination for judgeship, 156, 157
Kohlbrenner, Bernard, 100

Latin America, 161
Laws and Applications to the Legislature, Committee on (Board of Aldermen), 211
Lefevere, Peter Paul, 193
Leopoldine Society, 52, 53
Lessons for Schools, taken from the Holy Scriptures, in the Words of the Text, without Note or Comment, 109, 110, 113, 117. *See* School books
Levins, Thomas, 200
Lewis, Samuel, viii, 1, 3
Literature, Committee on (state Senate): Spencer report referred to,

137; submits bill to Senate, 145, 146; membership of, 205; reports amended Maclay bill to Senate, 227

Log Cabin, The, 122

Lord, Jr., Daniel, 168, 177, 185

Luther, Martin, 106, 107, 108, 118. *See* School books

Lyttleton, George, 105. *See* School books

Maclay, William B.: nominated for state Assembly by Democrats, 169; nominated for state Assembly by Catholic ticket, 172; supports Democratic disclaimer, 176; nominated for state Assembly on Union ticket, 185; chairman of Assembly educational committee, 205; presents Catholic petition to Assembly, 210; presents report of his committee, 211, 212; offers educational bill to Assembly, 212, 213; rejects public referendum in New York City, 213; confers with Hughes, 215, 216; his meeting with Hughes attacked, 215, 216; opposes religious amendment to his bill, 223; attacked in press, 225

McCluskey, Neil, 251, 258

McKeon, James, 96, 137

McMurray, William, 169, 172, 188*n*

Malte-Brun, Conrad, 113, 117. *See A System of Universal Geography;* School books

Mann, Horace, viii, 1, 2, 3, 104, 254

Mercy, Sisters of, 256

Methodist Episcopal Church, Remonstrances of the, 34, 70, 71, 72

Mills, Caleb, viii, 1

Minturn, Robert B., 136, 137

Monk, Maria, 86, 160, 162, 163

Morris, Robert, 219, 239, 240, 241, 242

Morse, Samuel F. B.: fears Catholicism in the United States, vii; author, vii; president of American Protestant Union, 166; co-organizer of Union ticket, 184, 185, 186. *See Foreign Conspiracy Against the Liberties of the United States*

Mott, Samuel F., 136

Mount, Richard E., 167, 188*n*

Murray, Lindley (textbook writer), 106, 113, 117, 118. *See* School books

Murray, Lindley (trustee of Public School Society), 113

Nagle, David, 173, 174

New York American: disagrees with Seward's proposals, 208; bemoans poor attendance at City Hall rally, 222, 223; attacks Maclay law, 235; publishes Whig resolutions, 239

New York Catholic Register: supports Seward's proposals, 41, 42; Hughes receives copies of, 51

New York Christian Advocate and Journal: denies infidelity in public schools, 64; defends King James Bible in public schools, 64; warns of Catholic political maneuvering, 128; urges personal pledges from candidates, 166, 167; attacks Hughes's political tactics, 178

New York Commercial Advertiser: attitude toward Seward's third annual message, 124; attacks Spencer's report, 142, 143; rejects Democratic disclaimer, 174, 175; urges Irish-Catholics to abandon Democratic Party, 175; defends Whig candidates, 177, 178; attacks Catholic ticket, 179; attacks Union ticket, 186; attacks Seward's fourth annual message, 208; denounces Maclay bill and Democrats, 214; scores Hughes-Maclay conference, 216; urges petition against Maclay bill, 218; defends City Hall rally, 223; condemns Maclay bill and law, 224, 225, 235, 236; charges Catholic political pressure, 238; publishes Whig resolutions, 239

New York, County of, 126

New York Evangelist: attacks Catholic political ticket, 178

New York Evening Post: reports rejection of Catholic petition, 49, 50; denounces political posters as Whig trick, 129, 130; attacks Spencer's report, 130, 131; view of O'Sullivan bill, 154; attacks Seward's withdrawal of nomination to Ketchum, 157; fears Whig "no popery" crusade, 170; denounces Catholic political ticket, 176, 177; attacks Whig candidates, 177; attacks Hughes as politician, 180; emphasizes Catholic political freedom, 180; scores Hughes's card, 182; admits Catholic political strength, 190; attributes political motives to Seward, 207; defends Maclay-Hughes conference, 216; urges Irish-Catholics to return to Democratic Party, 224; praises Maclay law, 237; evaluates New York City April, 1842, election, 241

New York Freeman's Journal: publishes Power's views on education, 29, 30; responds to *The Churchman*, 65, 66; approves of Hughes's treatment of Ketchum, 92, 93; lauds Hughes's efforts at "great debate," 94; attacks Board of Aldermen's rejection of Catholic petition, 99, 100; urges Catholics to remain constant, 101; decries Pentz's defeat, 130; praises Spencer's report, 143, 144; prophesies demise of Public School Society, 144; disappointed at Senate postponement, 154; attacks other New York papers, 154, 155; sees relationship between deficient public schools and vice, 165; defends Hughes's political action, 182; warns of future Catholic political action, 191, 192; praises Seward's fourth annual message, 208; supports Maclay bill, 214; warns of

political maneuvering of Public School Society, 217; labels City Hall rally failure, 222; fears defeat of Maclay bill, 228; urges Catholic political regroupment, 229; unenthusiastic over amended Maclay law, 237; relates election riot to anti-Catholicism, 243; evaluation of Maclay law, 253; continues attack on public schools, 255

New York Herald: admits Quaker influence in public schools, 72, 117; view on anti-Catholic school books in public schools, 72, 117; reports Brownlee's speech against Catholic position, 160, 161–64, 165; attacks Hughes's political actions, 181; rejects Hughes's card, 182; warns of election riots, 186, 187; believes November, 1841, election solves school dispute, 190; warns of future Catholic political organization, 192; denounces Hughes's influence, 193; denounces Hughes's social and political philosophy, 196; engages in personal vendetta against Hughes, 197, 198, 199, 200; urges establishment of independent American Catholic Church, 199, 200, 201; praises Power and Pise, 199, 200, 201; supports Maclay bill, 214; reports on City Hall rally, 219, 220, 221, 222; praises Maclay law, 237; charges police brutality, 241

New York Journal of Commerce: publishes anti-Catholic letter, 147, 148; reports Democrats reject Catholic school position, 169; co-organizes Union ticket, 184, 185, 186; acknowledges Hughes's political influence, 189, 190

New York Observer: favors rejection of Catholic petition by Board of Assistant Aldermen, 49; denies all Catholic charges, 63, 64; warns of new Catholic petition, 67; praises Hughes's efforts at "great debate,"

94; extolls Ketchum's speech, 94; praises Board of Aldermen's rejection of Catholic petition, 99; warns of new Catholic maneuvers, 101, 102; view on Seward's re-election, 120; comments on Seward's third annual message, 124; suspects Catholic political action, 127, 128, 154; attacks Hughes and Catholic ticket, 178; condemns Hughes's social and political philosophy, 196, 197; warns of possible Catholic educational victory, 204; rejects Seward's fourth annual message, 208; attacks Maclay-Hughes conference, 216; accuses Catholics of disorder at City Hall rally, 222; expresses disgust with politicians, 224, 225; condemns Maclay law, 236; charges Catholic political pressure, 238, 239

New York Reader, 105, 117. *See* School books

New York Standard: attacks Maclay-Hughes conference, 215

New York Sun: view on funds for Catholic schools, 73; praises Spencer's report, 143; attacks Hughes's political maneuvering, 179, 180; warns of election riots, 186, 187; analyzes political choices in November, 1841, election, 187; labels City Hall rally failure, 222; urges return of peace to New York, 237

New York Sunday Times: defends Hughes's political action, 182, 183

New York Tribune: asks for reason in educational dispute, 154; cautions Whigs on educational position, 166, 167, 168; taunts Democrats over Pentz, 169; rejects Democratic disclaimer, 174, 175; attacks Pentz's educational posture, 176; attacks Union ticket, 186; believes Maclay bill not the solution, 214, 215; condemns high cost of

Maclay law, 236; publishes Whig resolutions, 239; evaluates April, 1842, New York City election, 241; urges end of religious bitterness, 244

New York Truth Teller: attacks Seward's educational proposal, 41, 42; attacked by Hughes, 122

Nondenominationalism. *See* Public schools

Non-sectarianism. *See* Public schools

North Dutch Church, 160, 164, 165

Notre Dame, Sisters of, 256

Nott, Eliphalet, 20, 25

O'Connor, Joseph, 126, 127

O'Connor, Thomas, 172, 189, 229

O'Sullivan, John L.: introduces school bill in Assembly, 150, 151–52, 153; nominated on Democratic Assembly ticket, 169; nominated on Catholic political ticket, 172; clarifies his educational position, 176; urges Assembly approval of Maclay bill, 232

Otsego, County of, 121

"Pairing off": Scott-Corning, 231, 234, 235; Corning-Platt, 234, 235

Papism. *See* Catholicism, Roman

Paulding, John, 76

Penn, William, 105, 106. *See* School books

Pentz, Daniel: praised by Catholics, 126, 129; re-election of, 128; defeated for Common Council, 130; nominated on Democratic Assembly ticket, 169; nominated on Catholic political ticket, 172; clarifies his educational position, 176; attacked by *New York Tribune*, 176

Philadelphia, Mercantile Library of, 193

Pierce, John D., 1

Pise, Constantine Charles: present at "great debate," 86; sends letter to Verplanck, 126, 127; praised by Bennett, 200, 201; responds to Bennett, 200, 201

Pius IX, Pope, 255

Political Nativism in New York State. *See* Scisco, Louis Dow

Political posters, 129, 218, 219, 239, 240

Popery. *See* Catholicism, Roman

Power, John: co-vicar general, 29; view of education, 29, 30; organizes Catholics to seek public school funds, 29; present at church councils, 29; travels to Albany, 31, 40; seriously ill, 44; addresses Catholic meeting, 51, 52; accuses public schools of sectarianism, 63; present at "great debate," 86; view of public school books, 113, 114, 115, 116; addresses a second meeting of Catholics, 125; praised by Bennett, 199, 200, 201; responds to Bennett, 200, 201

Pratt, John W., 22*n*, 25, 120

Presbyterian of the West: attacks Catholic political ticket, 179

Princeton Review, 118. *See* School books

Public funds for Catholic schools: arguments against, 34, 35, 36, 37, 38, 39, 44, 45–48, 49, 60, 61; arguments in favor of, 41, 42, 50, 55, 56, 59

Public Funds for Church and Private Schools, 112. *See* Gabel, Richard J.

Public school funds: petitions for, 31, 32, 33, 67, 68, 69; remonstrances against, 34, 35, 36, 37, 38, 39, 69, 70, 71, 72

Public schools: purpose of, 1; non-denominationalism in, ix, 2, 3, 4, 37, 58, 83, 104, 133, 134, 135, 136, 139, 140, 142, 160, 251; Catholic dis-

satisfaction with, ix, 5, 30, 41, 42, 58, 59, 95, 104; religious neutrality in, 59, 60, 62, 63, 252; no advocacy of secularism in, 134, 251

Public Schools and Moral Education, 251. *See* McCluskey, Neil

Public School Society of New York: originally known as Free School Society, 19; organization of, 19, 20; remonstrates against Catholic petition, 36, 37–38, 39; highly esteemed in community, 40, 41; attacked by Hughes, 54, 55, 56, 57; schools accused of being sectarian and deistic, 54, 55; accused of being a private monopoly, 56, 57, 151; reply to *Address of Catholics. . . ,* 60, 61, 62; answers charges against, 61, 62, 63, 89, 90, 91; remonstrates against second Catholic petition, 69, 70; participates in "great debate," 79–84; responds to Hughes's arguments, 90, 91; attempts to expurgate school books, 112–18; opposes Catholic petition to state Legislature, 128; praised by Brooklyn educators, 147; questionable tactics of, 148; *New York Freeman's Journal* predicts demise of, 144; praised by New York City Commissioners of Education, 165; attacked by Seward, 206; urges defeat of educational legislation, 210, 211; attacked by Maclay committee, 212, 213; maneuvers against Maclay bill, 217; presents position at City Hall rally, 220, 221; schools included in new school law, 233, 234; dissolution of, 247, 248

Purcell, John, 116

Purdy, Elijah, 75, 86, 169, 185, 188*n*, 189

Putnam, County of, 121

Putnam, Samuel, 106, 117. *See* School books

Quaker influence in public schools,
  68, 69, 70, 71, 72
Quakers, 151

Read, William, 197, 203
Reese, David, 87, 88, 89
Reese, Meredith, 252
Reformed Presbyterian Church, Re-
  monstrance of, 35, 36
Religious liberty, 55, 56
Religious *tabula rasa*, 55
Riot: in election, 237, 241, 242, 243
Rockwell, William, 148, 217
Romanism. *See* Catholicism, Roman
Rome, Church of. *See* Catholicism,
  Roman
Ryan, Mary Perkins, x. *See Are Pa-
  rochial Schools the Answer?*

Sacred Heart, Religious of the, 256
St. James' Church, 53, 54
St. John, Horace, 167, 185n, 188n
St. John's College (later called Ford-
  ham), 12, 51
St. Patrick's Cathedral, 242
St. Peter's Church, 31, 32, 43, 242
Sanford, Edward, 169, 185, 188n,
  189
Schneller, Joseph, 30, 43
School books in public schools: anti-
  Catholic in tone, 103; Protestant
  orientation of, 103; view of
  Hughes, 92, 103, 105–11; historical
  and religious volumes, 105–8, 109;
  "sectarian" and "infidel" volumes,
  109–10, 111; Lyttleton, George,
  105; Penn, William, 105, 106; Cortez, Fernando, 105, 106; *New York
  Reader*, 105, 117; *Sequel to the
  Analytical Reader*, 106, 117; Huss,
  John, 106, 117; Putnam, Samuel,
  106, 117; Murray, Lindley, 106,
  107–8, 109, 113, 117, 118; *Sequel
  to the English Reader*, 106, 107–8,
  109, 113, 117, 118; Luther Martin,
  106, 107, 108, 113, 118; Cranmer,
  Thomas, 106, 108, 118; Hume,

David, 108; *Lessons for Schools,
  taken from the Holy Scriptures, in
  the Words of the Text, without
  Note or Comment*, 109, 110, 113,
  117; Christ, Jesus, 111; expurgation efforts of Public School
  Society, 112–18; view of Varela,
  113, 116; Malte-Brun, Conrad, 113,
  117; *A System of Universal Geography*, 113, 117; view of Power, 30,
  113, 114, 115; *An Irish Heart*,
  114n; negotiations of Public School
  Society with Hughes, 115, 116;
  English Reader, 117; Hale, Salma,
  117; *History of the United States*,
  117; view of *Princeton Review*,
  118; view of Brownlee, 161
Scisco, Louis Dow, 100. *See Political
  Nativism in New York State*
Scotch Presbyterian Church, Petition
  of, 33
Scott, John: votes against postponement of Spencer bill, 150; initially
  opposed to Maclay bill, 226; denounced by Catholics, 229; favors
  election of school officers in June,
  230, 231; absent from Senate chamber, 231, 232, 235; "pairing off"
  with Corning, 231; political dealing of, 246
Sedgwick, Theodore: lawyer for Public School Society at "great debate,"
  75; summarizes educational legislation of New York State, 79, 80;
  claims no anti-Catholic sentiments
  on his part, 80; role of government
  in education, 80, 81; urges a common Bible, 81; praised by Hughes,
  81, 82; view of education, 80; at
  issue with Ketchum over Bible, 83
Sequel to the Analytical Reader, 106,
  117. *See* School books
Sequel to the English Reader, 106,
  107–8, 109, 113, 117, 118. *See*
  School books
Seward, Frederick, 27, 157
Seward, William: friend of Weed, 13;

elected governor of New York, 13; in correspondence over education, 13, 14, 15; first annual message of, 15, 16; educational and social thought of, 16, 17, 18, 19; friend of Irish immigrants, 17, 18; "higher law" doctrine of, 17; trip to Ireland, 18; delivers Sunday School address, 19; in communication with Barnard, 19; investigates New York City education, 19, 20, 21; seeks advice of Weed and Nott, 20; second annual message of, 20, 21, 22; proposes public funds for Catholic schools, 21; motivation for proposal, 22–27; hypersensitive to criticism, 26, 27; interested in universal education, 26; speaks to Hibernian Society of Albany, 43; receives copy of *Address of Roman Catholics. . . ,* 66, 67; re-election of, 119–21, 122; friend of Hughes, 121; third annual message of, 123, 124; seeks educational compromise, 123, 124; discusses strategy with Hughes, 141, 142; withdraws Ketchum nomination, 155, 156, 157, 158; aware of Catholic political ticket, 170, 171; accused of conspiracy with Hughes, 181; analyzes Whig defeat in November, 1841, election, 191; praises Hughes, 202; fourth annual message of, 205, 206, 207, 208, 209, 210; press reaction to fourth annual message of, 207, 208; praised by Hughes, 209, 210; urges Hughes to accept Maclay bill, 215; signs amended Maclay law, 233; analyzes election riot, 243; close relationship with Hughes, 246; denied presidential nomination in 1860, 246; analyzes school dispute, 250, 251

Shaping of Protestant Education, The, 4. See Kennedy, William Bean

Sixth Ward Hotel, 242

Spartan Band, 241, 242

Spencer, John C.: secretary of state and state superintendent of schools, 127; studies Catholic petition, 128; attacked in *New York Evening Post,* 130; answers attack, 131; report of, 130, 131–35, 136, 150, 153; essentially supports Catholic position, 136; advocates principle of "absolute non-intervention," 134, 135; praised by Hughes, 141; attacked by *New York Commercial Advertiser and New York Sun,* 142, 143; praised by *New York Freeman's Journal,* 143, 144

Spring, Gardiner, 87, 88, 89

Stevens, Linus W., 167, 185*n*, 188*n*

Stevens, Samuel, 155

Stone, William, 221, 222, 252

Stowe, Calvin, viii, 1

Strong, George Templeton, 245

Sunday Schools, 4, 19

Swackhamer, Conrad, 169, 172, 188*n*

Sweeney, Hugh, 51, 96

System of Universal Geography, A, 113, 117. See Malte-Brun, Conrad; School books

Tammany Hall, 143, 183, 224, 230, 246

Teachers in public schools: Catholic, 61, 70; Quaker, 70

Tioga, County of, 121

Townsend, Solomon, 169, 172, 185, 186, 188*n*

Transformation of the School, The, viii. See Cremin, Lawrence

Tucker, Joseph, 167, 185*n*, 188*n*, 189

Tyler, John, 121, 169

Unitarians, 151

Ursulines, 256

Van Buren, John, 235

Van Buren, Martin, 120

Van Der Lyn, Henry, 13, 14, 15

Varela, Felix: co-vicar general, 29;
editor of *New York Catholic Register*, 41; defends Seward's educational proposal, 41, 42; cites Catholic dissatisfaction with public
schools, 41, 42; criticizes public
school books, 113, 116
Varian, Isaac, 169, 185, 188, 226, 229,
230, 232
Verplanck, Gulian: state senator
from New York County, 126;
friendly to Catholic position, 126;
submits Catholic petition to state
Senate, 127, 128; urges passage of
Spencer bill, 148, 149; refuses re-
nomination, 167, 168

Walsh, Michael, 172, 189n
Wardner, George, 25
Washington Hall, 192
Webster, Daniel, 169, 183
Weed, Thurlow: called "The Dictator," 13; supports Seward for
governor, 13; Seward seeks advice
of, 20; approves Seward's educational proposal, 25; opposes Ketchum's nomination for judgeship,
156; defends Seward's withdrawal
of Ketchum nomination, 157, 158;
consults with Hughes, 171; shocked
at Whig defeat in November, 1841,
election, 191; encourages Maclay,
215
Weir, George, 169, 172, 188n
Wells, B. F., 217
Whig Party (in New York State):
mixes politics and education, 43;
cool to Seward's re-election bid,
119–21, 122; tainted with nativism,
120, 121, 245; Irish-Catholic fear
of, 121; opposes Catholic position,
167, 168, 174, 175, 176, 177, 186;
division in national party, 168,
169, 191; loses November, 1841,
election, 188, 189, 190, 191; helps
pass Maclay bill in Assembly, 223,
224; unanimous Senate opposition
to amended Maclay bill, 226, 231,
232, 233; New York City election
of April, 1842, 237, 238, 239, 240,
241; role in school dispute, 245,
246, 247
Wiley, Calvin, viii, 1
Wittke, Carl, 103

Young, Samuel, 252

This book was set in eleven-point Baskerville. It was composed, printed, and bound by Heritage Printers, Inc., Charlotte, North Carolina. The paper is Warren's Olde Style, manufactured by S. D. Warren Company, Boston. The design is by Mary Thomas.